T0383216

Innovation and Sustainability in Governments and Companies: A Perspective to the New Realities

RIVER PUBLISHERS SERIES IN MULTI BUSINESS MODEL INNOVATION, TECHNOLOGIES AND SUSTAINABLE BUSINESS

Series Editors:

Peter Lindgren
Aarhus University, Denmark

Annabeth Aagaard
Aarhus University, Denmark

The River Publishers Series in Multi Business Model Innovation, Technologies and Sustainable Business includes the theory and use of multi business model innovation, technologies and sustainability involving typologies, ontologies, innovation methods and tools for multi business models, and sustainable business and sustainable innovation. The series cover cross technology business modeling, cross functional business models, network based business modeling, Green Business Models, Social Business Models, Global Business Models, Multi Business Model Innovation, interdisciplinary business model innovation. Strategic Business Model Innovation, Business Model Innovation Leadership and Management, technologies and software for supporting multi business modeling, Multi business modeling and strategic multi business modeling in different physical, digital and virtual worlds and sensing business models. Furthermore the series includes sustainable business models, sustainable & social innovation, CSR & sustainability in businesses and social entrepreneurship.

Key topics of the book series include:

- Multi business models
- Network based business models
- Open and closed business models
- Multi Business Model eco systems
- Global Business Models
- Multi Business model Innovation Leadership and Management
- Multi Business Model innovation models, methods and tools
- Sensing Multi Business Models
- Sustainable business models
- Sustainability & CSR in businesses
- Sustainable & social innovation
- Social entrepreneurship and -intrapreneurship

For a list of other books in this series, visit www.riverpublishers.com

Innovation and Sustainability in Governments and Companies: A Perspective to the New Realities

Editors

Ernesto Leon-Castro
Instituto Tecnologico de Sonora, Mexico

Manoj Sahni
Pandit Deendayal Energy University, India

Fabio Blanco-Mesa
Universidad Pedagógica y Tecnológica de Colombia, Colombia

Victor Alfaro-Garcia
Universidad Michoacana de San Nicolas de Hidalgo, Mexico

Jose Merigo
University of Technology Sydney, Australia

River Publishers

Routledge
Taylor & Francis Group

NEW YORK AND LONDON

Published 2023 by River Publishers
River Publishers
Alsbjergvej 10, 9260 Gistrup, Denmark
www.riverpublishers.com

Distributed exclusively by Routledge
605 Third Avenue, New York, NY 10017, USA
4 Park Square, Milton Park, Abingdon, Oxon OX14 4RN

Innovation and Sustainability in Governments and Companies: A Perspective to the New Realities / by Ernesto Leon-Castro, Manoj Sahni, Fabio Blanco-Mesa, Victor Alfaro-Garcia, Jose Merigo.

Routledge is an imprint of the Taylor & Francis Group, an informa business

ISBN 978-87-7022-844-2 (hardback)
ISBN 978-87-7004-046-4 (paperback)
ISBN 978-10-0380-749-0 (online)
ISBN 978-10-3262-396-2 (master ebook)

Contents

Preface

The book "Innovation and Sustainability in Governments and Companies: A Perspective to the New Realities" is created from a selection of works exhibited at the V International Conference on Innovation and Sustainability (ICONIS). The main objective is to present a series of applied research in different sectors, governments, and countries under a current approach, considering the new realities of the markets. Among the topics addressed are competitiveness, industry Industry 4.0, tourism, quality of remote work, the effect of covid COVID in different sectors, and financial analysis, among others. Finally, it is intended that this book serves as a basis for researchers, students, and the general public to identify the way they can use to approach the different types of studies and applied methodologies and, in turn, allow them to solve problems and concerns within their various areas, of application.

Editors:

Ernesto Leon-Castro
Instituto Tecnologico de Sonora, Mexico

Manoj Sahni
Pandit Deendayal Energy University, India

Fabio Blanco-Mesa
Universidad Pedagógica y Tecnológica de Colombia, Colombia

Victor Alfaro-Garcia
Universidad Michoacana de San Nicolas de Hidalgo, Mexico

Jose Merigo
University of Technology Sydney, Australia

List of Figures

List of Tables

List of Contributors

Alicia, María, *Universidad La Salle Bajío, Mexico*

Alvarez, Pavel A., *Universidad Autónoma de Occidente, Unidad Regional Culiacan, Mexico*

Álvarez-García, José, *Universidad de Extremadura*

Araceli Lira Chávez, *Facultad de Contaduría y Ciencias Administrativas de la, Universidad Michoacana de San Nicolás de Hidalgo, Mexico*

Arenas, Laura, *Universidad de Barcelona, España*

Ávila-Carreón, Fernando, *Department of Basic Sciences, Instituto Tecnologico de Morelia, Mexico*

Bernal, Maria, *Universidad Autónoma de Occidente, Unidad Regional Culiacan, Mexico*

Blanco-Mesa, Fabio, *Universidad Pedagogica y Tecnologica de Colombia, Colombia*

Callejas-Cuervo, Beatriz, *Universidad Pedagógica y Tecnológica de Colombia, Colombia*

Camargo, Nancy, *Universidad Pedagógica y Tecnológica de Colombia, Colombia*

Castro-Páez, Héctor Adrian, *Universidad Pedagogica y Tecnologica de Colombia, Colombia*

Cervera, Claudia Malcón, *Department of Business Intelligence, Business School, UPAEP University, Mexico*

Cruz-Aké, Salvador, *Instituto Politecnico Nacional, Mexico*

Daniela Alejandra Niño Amézquita, *Universidad Pedagógica y Tecnológica de Colombia, Colombia*

Diana María Dueñas Quintero, *Universidad Pedagógica y Tecnológica de Colombia, Colombia*

Edith Sarai Duran-Tovar, *Universidad Michoacana de San Nicolás de Hidalgo, Facultad de Contaduría y Ciencias Administrativas, Mexico*

Fernando Castelló-Sirvent, *ESIC Business & Marketing School, Spain*

Flores-Romero, Martha Beatriz, *Faculty of Accounting and Management, Universidad Michoacan de San Nicolas de Hidalgo*

Franco-Bravo, *Universidad La Salle Bajío, Mexico*

Gerardo Gabriel Alfaro-Calderón, *Universidad Michoacana de San Nicolás de Hidalgo, Facultad de Contaduría y Ciencias Administrativas, Mexico*

Gil-Lafuente, Ana M., *Universidad de Barcelona, España*

Hernández, Juan Gabriel López, *Universidad Autónoma de Baja California, Mexico*

Hernández, Juliana Cortés, *Universidad Pedagogica y Tecnologica de Colombia, Colombia*

Hernández, Roberto Carlos Valdés, *Universidad Autónoma de Baja California, Mexico*

Irazú, Azeneth, *Universidad La Salle Bajío, Mexico*

José Álvarez-García, *Departamento de Economía Financiera y Contabilidad, Facultad de Empresa, Finanzas y Turismo, Universidad de Extremadura, Spain*

Leon-Castro, Ernesto, *Unidad Navojoa, Instituto Tecnologico de Sonora, Mexico*

María de la Cruz Del Río-Rama, *Departamento de Organización de Empresas y Marketing, Facultad de Ciencias Empresariales y Turismo, Universidad de Vigo, Spain*

Martha Beatriz Flores-Romero, *División de Ingeniería en Gestión Empresarial, Tecnológico Nacional de México, Instituto Tecnológico Superior de Huichapan, Mexico*

Mendoza, Berenice, *Faculty of Accounting and Administrative Sciences, Michoacan University of San Nicolás de Hidalgo, Mexico*

Mercado, Karla Janette López, *Facultad de Ciencias Administrativas y Sociales, Universidad Autónoma de Baja California, Mexico*

Miriam Edith Pérez-Romero, *Facultad de Contaduría y Ciencias Administrativas, Universidad Michoacana de San Nicolás de Hidalgo, Mexico; División de Ingeniería en Gestión Empresarial, Tecnológico Nacional de México, Instituto Tecnológico Superior de Huichapan, Mexico*

Montaudon Tomas, Cynthia M., *Department of Business Intelligence, Business School, UPAEP University, Mexico*

Moreno, José Manuel Valencia, *Facultad de Ciencias Administrativas y Sociales, Universidad Autónoma de Baja California, Mexico*

Muñoz, Manuel, *Management Department, Universidad de Sonora, Mexico*

Nuñez-Maldonado, Abraham, *Faculty of Accounting and Management, Universidad Michoacan de San Nicolas de Hidalgo*

Paez, Mónica Claudia Casas, *Universidad Autónoma de Baja California, Mexico*

Pinto López, Ingrid Nineth, *Department of Business Intelligence, Business School, UPAEP University, Mexico*

Priscila Ortega Gómez, *Facultad de Contaduría y Ciencias Administrativas de la, Universidad Michoacana de San Nicolás de Hidalgo, Mexico*

Rodríguez-Moreno, Diana Cristina, *Universidad Pedagógica y Tecnológica de Colombia*

Romero, Miriam Edith Pérez, *Faculty of Accounting and Management, Universidad Michoacan de San Nicolas de Hidalgo*

Valdez, Cuitláhuac, *Universidad Autónoma de Occidente, Unidad Regional Culiacan, Mexico*

Vanessa Roger-Monzó, *ESIC Business & Marketing School, Spain*

Vega, José Luis Arcos, *Universidad Autónoma de Baja California, Mexico*

Victoria, Olivia Denisse Mejia, *Facultad de Ciencias Administrativas y Sociales, Universidad Autónoma de Baja California, Mexico*

Villanueva, Adelaida Figueroa, *Universidad Autónoma de Baja California, Mexico*

Wesman, Ricardo Ching, *Universidad Autónoma de Baja California, Mexico*

Yáñez Moneda, Alicia L., *Department of Business Intelligence, Business School, UPAEP University, Mexico*

Zavala-Berbena, *Universidad La Salle Bajío, Mexico*

Zoe Tamar Infante Jiménez, *Facultad de Contaduría y Ciencias Administrativas de la, Universidad Michoacana de San Nicolás de Hidalgo, Mexico*

List of Abbreviations

BRICS	Brazil, Russia, India, China, and South Africa
CBA	Cost–benefit analysis
CFE	Comisión federal de electricidad
DI	Dupont identity
ECLAC	Economic commission for Latin America
ELECTRE	ELimination Et Choix Traduisant la REalité
EVA	Economic value added
FANP	Fuzzy analytical network process
FAO	Food and agriculture organization
GCI	Global competitiveness index
GDP	Gross domestic product
ICT	Information and communication technologies
INEGI	National institute of statistics, geography and informatics
IRR	Internal rate of return
KMO	Kaiser−Meyer−Olkin
MCDM	Multicriteria decision-making
MSE	Mexican stock exchange
NPV	Net present value
OECD	Organization for economic cooperation and development
OMG	Object management group
PCSE	Panel corrected standard errors
PML	Process modeling language
PP	Payback period
PPP	Public−private partnership
PQI	Price and Quotation Index
RE	Renewable energy
RGDP	Real GDP
ROA	Return on assets
ROE	Return on capital
ROS	Return on sales

SDG	Sustainable development goals
SME	Small- and medium-sized enterprise
SOI	Sustainability-oriented innovation
SPEM	Software process engineering metamodel
SPI	Software process improvement
TFP	Total factor productivity
TOPSIS	Technique for order of preference by similarity to ideal solution
TSE	Tehran Stock Exchange
UNFCCC	United nations framework convention on climate change

1

Analysis of the Competitiveness of the Magical Towns of Mexico as Tourist Destinations

Miriam Edith Pérez-Romero[1,2], Martha Beatriz Flores-Romero[2], José Álvarez-García[3], and María de la Cruz Del Río-Rama[4]

[1]Facultad de Contaduría y Ciencias Administrativas, Universidad Michoacana de San Nicolás de Hidalgo, Mexico
[2]División de Ingeniería en Gestión Empresarial, Tecnológico Nacional de México, Instituto Tecnológico Superior de Huichapan, Mexico
[3]Departamento de Economía Financiera y Contabilidad, Facultad de Empresa, Finanzas y Turismo, Universidad de Extremadura, Spain
[4]Departamento de Organización de Empresas y Marketing, Facultad de Ciencias Empresariales y Turismo, Universidad de Vigo, Spain

Abstract

In their quest to be a catalyst for local tourism in Mexico, Magical Towns compete with highly competitive national and international tourist destinations. It is vital to study and comprehend the competitiveness of these tourist locations in order to create solutions to face competition and affect economic development. This research work aims to determine the tourism competitiveness of the Magical Towns of Mexico from the resources inherited, created, and supported. The methodology used was the exploratory factor analysis. The extracted factors' factorial scores were used to create a competitiveness index, and, finally, the result was translated into a scale of 0 – 100 to make it easier to read. Todos Santos (62.89) is the most competitive Magical Town, while Bustamante is the least competitive (11.53). Expanding cultural resources, tourism infrastructure, events, additional tourism services, and accessibility are some of the ways these locations can improve their competitiveness.

Keywords: Destination competitiveness, tourism competitiveness index, magical towns, exploratory factor analysis.

1.1 Introduction

Magical Towns is a tourism promotion program aimed at quaint and unique places in Mexico (Flores et al., 2021a); it acts directly on those towns that have preserved, valued, and defended their historical, cultural, and natural heritage (Secretary of Tourism-SECTUR, 2018), seeking to take advantage of the patrimonial wealth of Mexican communities (López, 2018). Having characteristics conducive to tourism, the towns with the designation Magical Town are considered an option to diversify inland tourism (Núñez & Ettinger, 2020; Shaadi et al., 2018). During the 20 years of validity of the Magical Towns program, a total of 132 appointments have been granted; however, these destinations face a growing number of competitors, both national and international, a situation that requires effectively managing their available resources and capacities.

Understanding the importance and value of tourism in the global economy has allowed tourism to contribute to the competitiveness of a region and allows managers to consider the steps they can take to ensure advantages over other regions (García & Siles, 2015). In the same vein, given the diversity of tourist destinations and increasingly demanding customers, it becomes a necessity to develop competitive destinations capable of satisfying demand in a sustainable way, as well as increasing market share in balance with effective exploitation (Saavedra, 2012; Avila, 2011). Market trends in tourism make it necessary to propose processes of renewal of destinations and increase their competitiveness (Vera & Baños, 2010). In this way, to gain a favorable position in the market, tourism competitiveness is the key (Leung & Baloglu, 2013).

The competitiveness of a destination has considerable implications for the entire tourism industry, which makes it an objective of great interest for public and private tourism agents (Sánchez, 2012). It is then that the measurement of competitiveness is a primary need (Gandara et al., 2013) which importance and usefulness lie in being a tool for the classification of tourist destinations and the formulation of policies (Mendola & Volo, 2017; Amaya et al., 2017). Strategies are needed to boost the competitiveness of the tourism sector (Armenski et al., 2017) and enhance our own capacities to achieve sustainable development over time (Granados et al., 2016). Competitiveness is a challenge that tourist destinations currently face to preserve their position in the market (Pérez et al., 2021).

In Mexico, the development of tourist destinations is limited as there are no conditions of competitiveness; particularly, in the Magical Towns, their competitiveness is unknown and it is through the study, analysis, and understanding of tourism competitiveness that the establishment of suitable strategies to achieve economic development is facilitated. This research work aims to determine the tourism competitiveness of the Magical Towns of Mexico from the resources inherited, created, and supported. The structure of this chapter is as follows: Section 1.2 shows the theoretical foundation that guides this research; Section 1.3 presents the methodology, where the steps of the exploratory factor analysis are described; Section 1.4 points out the main results regarding the tourism competitiveness of the Magical Towns of Mexico; finally, Section 1.5 takes up the main findings.

1.2 Preliminaries

This section addresses the theoretical−conceptual foundations that have been seen as relevant and necessary in this research. First, the theory of tourism competitiveness is examined and then the Magical Towns of Mexico are discussed.

1.2.1 Tourism competitiveness

Competitiveness has been present in tourism research since 1990 (Ritchie & Crouch, 2003). Tourism competitiveness is defined as a destination's ability to create, integrate, and deliver tourism experiences, including value-added goods and services that tourists consider important (Wei-Chiang, 2009); multiple factors intervene in this concept, although it is only in a few where the greatest options of success or failure reside (Alonso, 2010). The concept has evolved from focusing on tourism attractiveness to strategically developing the tourism industry in a more holistic way (Kim, 2012).

To determine and explain the competitiveness of destinations, authors such as Poon (1993), Crouch & Ritchie (1999), Hassan (2000), Kim (2001), Health (2003), Ritchie & Crouch (2003), Dwyer & Kim (2003), Acerenza (2009), Wei-Chiang (2009), Alonso (2010), and Jiménez & Aquino (2012) have proposed models, which among their variables include the environment, destination management, comparative advantage, competitive advantage, tourism infrastructure, key resources and attractions, demand, price, and cost of tourism, location or the destination, environment, and security, mainly.

In addition, the causes and effects of destination competitiveness have recently been described by Flores et al. (2021b), finding among these causes are environmental commitment, inherited resources, resources created, general infrastructure, quality of service, accessibility, hospitality, destination management; and among the effects on sustainable development, tourism demand, customer satisfaction, tourism spending, profitability, prosperity, and the arrival of tourists, mainly.

1.2.2 Magical Towns

The Magical Towns offers a complementary and diversified tourist offer toward the market (Center for Social Studies and Public Opinion, 2017). A Magical Town is a town that has symbolic attributes, legends, history, transcendent facts, and ordinariness, which mean a great opportunity for tourist use (SECTUR, 2001). The localities that are attached to the Magical Towns program have, through this denomination, a category that identifies them as diversifying elements of the country's tourist offer (Shaadi et al., 2018). A town called Magical Town must have different architectural, historical, or contemporary elements, emblematic buildings, festivals, and traditions, artisan production, traditional cuisine, and a tourist destination of support in a radius of influence no greater than 1 hour away (García & Guerrero, 2014).

The Magical Towns program raises the possibility of benefiting small towns in addition to providing them with the opportunity to recover their cultural, festive, gastronomic, natural, artistic, historical heritage, and even the capacity of proposal and management of some local groups, although it also contemplates towns with a great tourist trajectory (López, 2018). According to the Organization for Economic Cooperation and Development (OECD, 2012), Magical Towns is one of the most successful tourism programs, because it has managed to boost the growth of rural communities and towns, in addition to generating the conservation of natural landscapes and local cultural traditions.

During the 20 years of the Magical Towns program, a total of 132 appointments have been granted, of which 26 (20%) are distributed in the northern region, 85 (64%) in the central region, and 21 (16%) in the southern region of Mexico. Figure 1.1 shows the number of Magical Towns for each state of Mexico. The states of Puebla and the State of Mexico have the highest

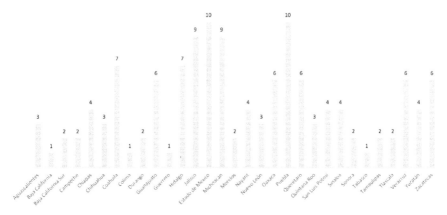

Figure 1.1 Number of Magical Towns by state.
Source: Own elaboration based on information available in DataTur Comprehensive Tourism Analysis.

number of appointments, each with 10; on the contrary, the states of Baja California, Colima, Guerrero, and Tabasco have only one appointment each. It is worth mentioning that Mexico City does not appear in the graph as it does not have any appointment.

Magical Towns can be considered as an alternative or non-mass form of tourism in Mexico, because as described by López and Palomino (2008), this type of tourism presents a new trend whose objective is to provide shared experiences in a unique environment, as well as participate in the cultural expressions of rural, indigenous, and urban communities. Likewise, it has been identified that among the 132 Magical Towns, the following tourist typologies are covered: sun and beach tourism, nature tourism or eco-tourism, adventure tourism, rural tourism, cultural tourism, religious tourism, gastronomic tourism, and geotourism.

In October 2016, derived from the results of the tourist statistics of the 2014 economic census by the National Institute of Statistics, Geography and Informatics (INEGI), SECTUR prepared for the first time a section for Magical Towns. The following statistics correspond to the 82 different Magical Towns designated until 2013:

- They concentrate 7.8% of the total economic units with tourist activities (38,693 units). The highest concentration is in the retail trade, with a total of 17,673 units; Also noteworthy is the sector of temporary

accommodation services and food and beverage preparation, which groups 16,103 units.
- The Magical Towns of San Cristóbal de las Casas, Taxco, Comitán de Domínguez, Lagos de Moreno, Cholula, Dolores Hidalgo, and Pátzcuaro concentrate 40.9% of the economic units, that is, about 15,829 units.
- They registered a gross tourist census value added of 10,292 million pesos, which represents 2.4% of the total tourism nationwide.
- The share of retail trade in the gross tourism census value added was 58.5% while the temporary accommodation services and food and beverage preparation sector participated with 24.2%, so that these two sectors account for 82.7% of the total in Magical Towns.
- The Magical Town of Metepec was the one that presented the greatest contribution to the gross tourist census value added with 14.8%, followed by San Cristóbal de las Casas with 8.4%, Comitán de Domínguez with 6.7%, and Cholula with 4.7%.
- 117,972 occupations are generated, which is equivalent to 4.3% of the total tourists. The two sectors that generate the highest volumes of tourist occupancy are temporary accommodation and food and beverage preparation services, as well as retail trade, with a total of 49,273 and 49,030 people employed respectively in 2013.
- The Magical Towns of San Cristóbal de las Casas, Comitán de Domínguez, Metepec, Taxco, Cholula, Lagos de Moreno, Pátzcuaro, Valladolid, Dolores Hidalgo, Valle de Bravo, Tecate, and Coatepec are the ones that generate just over half (51.6%) of the total jobs in these destinations.
- The gross formation of tourist fixed capital (FBKFT) amounted to 642.3 million pesos, which is equivalent to 1.8% nationally, being the two sectors with the highest volume of FBKFT retail trade with 414.7 million pesos and temporary accommodation services and food and beverage preparation with 132.8 million pesos.

1.3 Methodology

The focus of this research is quantitative since it is based on the measurement of the characteristics of social phenomena (Bernal, 2010) − in this case, tourism competitiveness. With respect to the design of the research, it is descriptive since it is inferred that the Magical Towns as tourist destinations have a series of characteristics that make them an objective of study; it is also transversal because data will be obtained from the population at a particular time.

The universe of study is the 132 existing localities in Mexico that have the designation of Magical Town from 2001, when the program began, to 2020. The study data have been taken at the municipal level because in several cases, this is the last level of disaggregation of the information provided by INEGI, in addition to the fact that the tourist promotion of the Magical Towns can consider tourist attractions that are nearby. Based on the above, it is important to note that an appointment was granted to San Martín de las Pirámides and Teotihuacán; however, these localities are located in different municipalities, both in the State of Mexico, which is why data from both municipalities have been included and a total of 133 individuals are under study. The information was taken from the year 2020.

To evaluate tourism competitiveness, inherited resources, resources created, and support resources were established as dimensions of this variable. In turn, sub-dimensions and indicators were defined for each of them, proposing a total of 7 sub-dimensions and 37 indicators. To obtain the information corresponding to each indicator, secondary sources such as the National Statistical Directory of Economic Units, the Cultural Information System of Mexico, and the Ministry of Tourism, mainly, were used. With the information obtained, a database was generated in Excel.

An exploratory factor analysis was then carried out as developed by Guillermo and García (2010, 2015) to evaluate the municipal competitiveness index in the municipalities of Puebla and in municipalities of metropolitan areas of the different states of the Mexican Republic, in addition to Navarro and Zamora (2013) who examined the municipal competitiveness of tourism in Michoacán.

Factor analysis is a multivariate technique that aims to simplify the multiple and complex relationships that may exist between a set of observed $X_1, X_2, \ldots, X_p$ variables. Specifically, it is a question of finding a set of $k < p$ factors not directly observable $F_1, F_2, \ldots, F_k$ that sufficiently explain the observed variables losing the minimum of information, so that they are easily interpretable (principle of interpretability) and that they are the least possible, that is, small k (principle of parsimony) (Pérez, 2004). In this case, the exploratory factor analysis allowed to analyze the indicators of each sub-dimension and dimension that makes up the variable of tourism competitiveness.

It began with the typification of the indicators, a step that sought that all the indicators had a similar contribution to the determination of the proximities, and, in turn, there are no variables that, due to the fact of being very dispersed, contribute more to the calculation of the distances (Pérez, 2004). This was achieved with a transformation of the standard normal distribution with zero mean and variance one through the following equation (Zamora & Cruz, 2020):

$$Z_{ij} = \frac{(Y_{ij} - Y_j)}{S_j},$$

where Y_{ij} is the variable j of individual i, Y_j is the arithmetic mean of variable j, and S_j is the standard deviation of variable j.

Immediately, the contrasts prior to the extraction of factors were applied; this was with the intention of analyzing the relevance of applying the factor analysis. The correlation matrix, its determinant, the Bartlett sphericity test, and the Kaiser−Meyer−Olkin (KMO) statistic were used. Subsequently, the optimal number of factors was determined, for which the criteria of scree test and eigenvalue were used. Factors were then extracted using the main components method. The next step was the rotation of factors to identify the structure of association between variables and factors; for this, the varimax method was used. The rotation effect is to redistribute the variance to obtain a pattern of factors or components with greater meaning (Kendall & W. R., 1990). The varimax redistribution method focuses on simplifying the vectors of the columns of factors (components) as much as possible; maximum simplification is achieved by reaching values such as +1 (positive association) or −1 (negative association) and other charges close to 0 (absence of association) (Santos et al., 2003). Their scores were immediately obtained through the regression method.

To construct the competitiveness index of the Magical Towns, the factorial scores of the extracted factors were used, that is, values that were multiplied by the standardized variables. These results were transformed into a scale from 0 to 100 in order to facilitate their interpretation (OECD & JRC, 2008), based on the following formula:

$$I_{ij} = \left(\frac{IN_{IJ} - \min_j (X_i)}{\max_j (X_i) - \min_j (X_i)} \right) \times 100,$$

where I_{ij} represents the value of indicator i on the scale from 0 to 100 for observation j, IN_{IJ} is the value of indicator i for observation j, $\min_j (X_i)$ represents the lowest indicator of observation j, and $\max_j (X_i)$ is the largest indicator of observation *j*. Finally, each factor was multiplied by the proportion it explains, thus obtaining a weighted average. Exploratory factor analysis was performed in the R Studio software.

1.4 Results

The exploratory factor analysis eliminated 20 of the 37 indicators initially considered, leaving 17 indicators that are distributed in the 7 sub-dimensions and these in turn in the 3 dimensions proposed: inherited resources, resources created, and support resources. When applying the contrast tests, the following results were found: the determinant presented a value close to 0 (2.813277E-09); indicators are positively correlated (see Figure 1.2); Bartlett's sphericity test resulted in a *p* value = 0; the KMO test gave an MSAg (measure of sufficiency or adequacy) of 0.86 (interpreted as meritorious according to Hair et al., 2009) and MSAj values were higher than 0.5 in all cases (see Figure 1.3).

Three factors to be extracted from the eigenvalues and the scree test were defined. Figure 1.4 exemplifies the result of the eigenvalues, and in the same figure, the result of applying the function "fa.parallel" of R Studio is observed, which suggests three factors.

The three factors were extracted and the loads were rotated. Figure 1.5 presents the results obtained. The three factors together explain 77% of the variance, the commonality of each of the variables is greater than 60%, each factor is composed of a number greater than three variables, the average square root of the residuals is 0.06, and the principles of interpretability and parsimony are met (Pérez, 2004).

The first factor explains 33% of the variance and is made up of eight indicators: BAB (infrastructure of restaurants and bars), BAC (travel agencies), BBA (recreational activities), BBB (sports activities), BBD (cinemas), BCA (medical services), BCB (gas stations), and BCC (banking/financial services); see Table 1.1.

The second factor explains 23% of the variance and together with the first factor accumulate 56% of the variance; it is made up of five indicators: AAE (beach offer), BAD (tour operators), BAE (car rental), BAH (tourist transport), and BCE (botanical gardens and zoos); see Table 1.2.

The third factor explains 21% of the variance and together with the two previous factors accumulates 77% of variance; it is made up of four indicators: ABF (museums), BAA (hotel infrastructure), BAF (rental of buses, trailers, etc.), and CAC (ground transport services) (see Table 1.3).

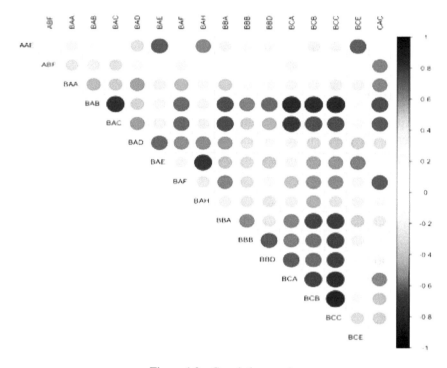

Figure 1.2   Correlation graph.

Source: Own elaboration.

```
Kaiser-Meyer-Olkin factor adequacy
Call: KMO(r = r_rff)
Overall MSA =  0.86
MSA for each item =
 AAE  ABF  BAA  BAB  BAC  BAD  BAE  BAF  BAH  BBA
0.70 0.84 0.87 0.92 0.92 0.91 0.80 0.85 0.79 0.90
 BBB  BBD  BCA  BCB  BCC  BCE  CAC
0.88 0.88 0.90 0.87 0.85 0.67 0.87
```

Figure 1.3   KMO test results.

Source: Own elaboration.

The Tourism Competitiveness Index of the Magical Towns of Mexico is presented in the annexes section; it is mentioned below the Magical Towns

```
[1] 9.13527977 2.29916281 1.57178410 0.91472130
[5] 0.59642123 0.53745379 0.39688983 0.36095963
[9] 0.25830408 0.23708417 0.18182090 0.14920108
[13] 0.11413481 0.09053740 0.07692469 0.04742643
[17] 0.03189398
Parallel analysis suggests that the number of factors = 3  and the number of components = 3
```

Figure 1.4   Eigenvalues and result of the function "fa.parallel."

Source: Own elaboration.

```
Principal Components Analysis
Call: principal(r = r_rff, nfactors = 3, residuals = TRUE, rotate = "varimax",
   method = "Bartlett")
Standardized loadings (pattern matrix) based upon correlation matrix
      RC1   RC2   RC3   h2    u2  com
AAE 0.15  0.86 -0.01 0.77 0.233 1.1
ABF 0.07 -0.06  0.81 0.67 0.335 1.0
BAA 0.13  0.43  0.69 0.68 0.317 1.8
BAB 0.80  0.14  0.51 0.92 0.077 1.8
BAC 0.67  0.17  0.59 0.82 0.180 2.1
BAD 0.23  0.65  0.51 0.74 0.260 2.2
BAE 0.33  0.86  0.08 0.85 0.151 1.3
BAF 0.43  0.27  0.64 0.67 0.333 2.2
BAH 0.30  0.71  0.21 0.63 0.370 1.5
BBA 0.66  0.40  0.31 0.69 0.308 2.1
BBB 0.78  0.32  0.01 0.71 0.285 1.3
BBD 0.80  0.22  0.08 0.69 0.308 1.2
BCA 0.84  0.05  0.36 0.84 0.155 1.4
BCB 0.83  0.30  0.25 0.85 0.153 1.5
BCC 0.89  0.32  0.21 0.94 0.062 1.4
BCE 0.17  0.81  0.02 0.68 0.321 1.1
CAC 0.37 -0.02  0.85 0.85 0.146 1.4

                         RC1  RC2  RC3
SS loadings             5.62 3.87 3.52
Proportion Var          0.33 0.23 0.21
Cumulative Var          0.33 0.56 0.77
Proportion Explained    0.43 0.30 0.27
Cumulative Proportion   0.43 0.73 1.00

Mean item complexity =  1.5
Test of the hypothesis that 3 components are sufficient.

The root mean square of the residuals (RMSR) is  0.06
```

Figure 1.5   Loads of rotated factors.

Source: Own elaboration.

that come under the top 10, which is presented in Table 1.4. The most competitive Magical Town, with an index of 62,892, is Todos Santos, located in the municipality of La Paz, Baja California Sur; specifically, it has the

Table 1.1   Factor loads of the first factor.

Abbreviation	Dimension	Sub-dimension	Indicator	Factorial load
BCC	Resources created	Complementary services to tourism	Banking /financial services	0.889
BCA	Resources created	Complementary services to tourism	Medical services	0.845
BCB	Resources created	Complementary services to tourism	Gas stations	0.832
BAB	Resources created	Touristic infrastructure	Infrastructure of restaurants and bars	0.802
BBD	Resources created	Events	Cinemas	0.798
BBB	Resources created	Events	Sport activities	0.783
BAC	Resources created	Touristic infrastructure	Travel agencies	0.665
BBA	Resources created	Events	Recreational activities	0.658

Source: Own elaboration.

Table 1.2   Factor loads of the second factor.

Abbreviation	Dimension	Sub-dimension	Indicator	Factorial load
AAE	Legacy resources	Natural resources	Beach offer	0.863
BAE	Resources created	Touristic infrastructure	Car rental	0.855
BCE	Resources created	Complementary services to tourism	Botanical gardens and zoos	0.806
BAH	Resources created	Touristic infrastructure	Tourist transport	0.706
BAD	Resources created	Touristic infrastructure	Tour operators	0.651

Source: Own elaboration.

first position in the second factor with a value of 100.00. It also has the third position in the first factor with a value of 68,358. With respect to the second factor, Todos Santos stands out from the rest of the Magical Towns by having the largest beach offer and the largest number of establishments for car rental. With respect to the first factor, it stands out by having the largest offer of

Table 1.3 Factor loads of the third factor.

Abbreviation	Dimension	Sub-dimension	Indicator	Factorial load
CAC	Support resources	Destination accessibility	Ground transport services	0.848
ABF	Legacy resources	Cultural resources	Museums	0.810
BAA	Resources created	Touristic infrastructure	Hotel infrastructure	0.694
BAF	Resources created	Touristic infrastructure	Rental of buses, trailers, etc.	0.636

Source: Own elaboration.

Table 1.4 Top 10 of the Magical Towns of Mexico in the Tourism Competitiveness Index.

Magical Town	Factor 1	Factor 2	Factor 3	Competitiveness Index	Position
Todos Santos	68.358	100.000	12.956	62.892	1
Tlaquepaque	95.791	0.000	30.541	49.436	2
Sayulita	48.379	68.955	23.602	47.862	3
Metepec	100.000	0.016	0.000	43.005	4
Isla Aguada	57.850	28.744	10.848	36.428	5
San Cristóbal de las Casas	1.887	13.912	100.000	31.985	6
Cholula	58.191	11.263	2.557	29.091	7
Orizaba	51.417	6.198	18.714	29.022	8
Guadalupe	45.926	5.761	19.700	26.796	9
Tulum	3.683	63.167	20.562	26.086	10

Source: Own elaboration.

medical service and cinemas; it is the second town with the largest offer of gas stations, sports activities, restaurants, and bars; and it is the third town with the largest offer of travel agencies, banking, and financial services.

On the other hand, the least competitive Magical Town with a score of 11,526 is Bustamante, located in the municipality of Bustamante, Nuevo León. Bustamante scored 9100 in the first factor, 15,482 in the second factor, and, finally, 10,995 in the third factor. Regarding the indicators analyzed, the Magical Town of Bustamante has only 2 museums, 2 medical services, 1 gas station, 2 banking/financial services, 21 restaurants and/or cafes, and 8 hotels.

1.5 Conclusions

With the results obtained in the development of this research, it can be affirmed that the inherited resources, the resources created, and the support resources are factors that determine the level of tourism competitiveness of the Magical Towns of Mexico. Through these factors, the competitiveness of the Magical Towns was measured, generating a Tourism Competitiveness Index (ICT) for the 132 Magical Towns of Mexico. Once the tourist competitiveness of the Magical Towns has been analyzed, the results obtained allow comparing the most outstanding indicators and those that are susceptible to improvement depending on each competitiveness factor.

The results achieved in the current research work contribute directly to the vision that has been proposed by the national strategy of Magical Towns, which seeks to position Mexico as a competitive and avant-garde tourism power, which achieves equitable, fair, and balanced development between communities and regions, through the sustainable use of cultural and natural heritage. With the exception of natural resources, the rest of the indicators of each competitiveness factor can be created by human beings, and it is recommended to identify the resources that are needed in each destination, as well as the quality of those already existing to immediately integrate into the development plans of each town actions aimed at having all the indicators mentioned in the previous paragraph both in quality and in sufficient quantity to meet the needs and expectations of the tourists who visit the Magical Town.

One of the constraints noted was that the analytic data were collected at municipal level; while this is understandable, it would have been fascinating to have data from a specific locality, as this is thought to have an impact on the outcome. The COVID-19 pandemic is also seen as a limitation, since it changed the pace of tourism dynamics and will make it difficult to subsequently compare the index obtained in this work.

As future lines of research for Magical Towns, the following are visualized: to evaluate the satisfaction of the residents since the designation of Magical Town was granted to the place; to evaluate the perception and satisfaction of the tourist about tourist services and in general about the Magical Town to analyze the use of ICTs by the different tourist services and by the Magical Town in general, as tools for the promotion and tourism marketing of the place; to evaluate the quality of the service provided by the various establishments directly involved in the tourist activity; to assess the economic impact that Magical Towns had during and after the pandemic. Finally, it is considered feasible to carry out this same study in various periods of time, with the aim of studying the evolution of each Magical Town on tourism competitiveness.

References

Acerenza, M. (2009). *Competitividad de los destinos turísticos*. México: Trillas. (In Spanish)

Alonso, V. H. (2010). Factores críticos de éxito y evaluación de la competitividad de destinos turísticos. *Estudios y Perspectivas en Turismo, 19,* 201 - 220. (In Spanish)

Amaya, C. M., Sosa, A. P., Moncada, P. (2017) Determinantes de competitividad turística en destinos de sol y playa mexicanos. En *Región y sociedad, 68,* 279-315. (In Spanish)

Armenski, T., Dwyer, K., Pavlukovic, V. (2017). Destination competitiveness: public and private sector toruism mangemente in Serbia. En *Journal of travel research,* 1-15.

Ávila, R. M. (2011). *Turismo cultural en México*. México: Trillas. (In Spanish)

Bernal, C. (2010). *Metodología de la investigación*. Colombia: Pearson Educación. (In Spanish)

Centro de estudios sociales y de opinión pública. (2017). *Programa de pueblos mágicos: valorización turística de la cultura, documento de trabajo núm. 249.* http://www5.diputados.gob.mx/index.php/esl/Centros-de-Estudio/CESOP/Novedades/Documento-de-trabajo.-Programa-de-Pueblos-Magicos-valorizacion-turistica-de-la-cultura (In Spanish)

Crouch, G., Ritchie, J. R. (1999). Tourism, competitiveness and societal prosperity. En *Journal of Business Research, 44 (3),* 137 – 152.

Dywer, L., Kim, C. (2003). Destination competitiveness: a models and determinants. *Current Issues in Tourism, 6 (5),* 369-414.

Flores-Romero, M. B., Pérez-Romero, M. E., Álvarez-García, J., Del Río-Rama, M. d. l. C. (2021a). Bibliometric mapping of research on Magic Towns of Mexico. *Land, 10 (852),* 1-24.

Flores-Romero, M. B., Pérez-Romero, M. E., Álvarez-García, J., Del Río-Rama, M. d. l. C. (2021b). Fuzzy techniques applied to the analysis of the causes and effects of Tourism Competitives. *Mathematics, 9 (777),* 1-16. DOI: 10.3390/math9070777

Gandara, J. M., Chim-Miki, A. F., Domareski, T. C., Biz, A. A. (2013) La competitividad turística de Foz Do Iguacu según los determinantes del Integrative Model de Dwyer & Kim: Analizando la estrategia de construcción del futuro. En *Cuadernos de Turismo, 31,* 105 – 128. (In Spanish)

García, D.; Guerrero, H. (2014). El programa Pueblos Mágicos: análisis de los resultados de una consulta local ciudadana. El caso de Cuitzeo, Michoacán, México. *Economía y Sociedad, 18,* 71-94. (In Spanish)

García, A., Siles, D. (2015). Como mejorar la competitividad turística de un destino: análisis del mediterráneo español y recomendaciones a los gestores de los destinos. En *Revista de Análisis Turístico, 19,* 1-11. (In Spanish)

Granados, H., Girlado, O., Acevedo, N. (2016). Promoción de la competitividad y el desarrollo territorial en los municipios del valle de Aburrá. En *Semestre Económico, 19,* 93-116. (In Spanish)

Guillermo, S. B. et al. (2010). *Índice de competitividad para el municipio de Puebla.* México: Universidad Autónoma de Puebla. (In Spanish)

Guillermo, S. B., García, I. G. (2015). Índice de competitividad municipal 2013: Metodología para su construcción basada en Análisis Factorial y su aplicación en municipios urbanos de México. En *Revista de Métodos Cuantitativos para la economía y la empresa, 20,* 112-153. (In Spanish)

Hassan, S. (2000). Determinants of Market Competitiveness in an Environmentally Sustainable Tourism Industry. En *Journal of Travel Research, 38 (3),* 239 – 245.

Heath, E. (2003). Towards a model to enhance destination competitiveness: a Southern African perspective. En *Journal of hospitality and tourism management, 10 (2).*

Jiménez, P., Aquino, F. K. (2012) Propuesta de un modelo de competitividad de destinos turísticos. *Estudios y perspectivas en turismo, 21,* 977 – 995. (In Spanish)

Kendall, M., W. R., B. (1990). *Dictionary of Statistical Term.* Edinburgh, United Kigndom: Oliver and Boyd.

Kim, N. (2012). *Tourism destination competitiveness, globalization and strategic development from a development economics perspective.* Tesis doctoral. Universidad de Illinois en Urbana – Champaign. Illinois, Estados Unidos.

Leung, S. Y., Baloglu, S. (2013). Tourism competitiveness of Asia Pacific Destinations. *Tourism Analysis, 18,* 371-384.

López, L. (2018). Las territorialidades del turismo: el caso de los Pueblos Mágicos en México. *Atelie Geográfico, 12 (1),* 6-24. (In Spanish)

López, G., Palomino, B. (2008). Políticas públicas y ecoturismo en comunidades indígenas de México. En *Teoría y Praxis, 5,* 33-50. (In Spanish)

Mendola, D., Volo, S. (2017). Building composite indicators in tourism studies: measurements and applications in tourism destination competitiveness. En *Tourism Management, 59,* 541-553. (In Spanish)

Navarro, J. C. L., Zamora, A. I. (2013). *Competitividad Municipal del Turismo en Michoacán.* México: Editorial Morevalladolid S. de R. L. de C. V.Núñez, G., Ettinger, C. (2020). La transformación de un territorio cultural. El desarrollo de los pueblos mágicos en México: Pátzcuaro como caso de estudio. *Revista Urbano, 41,* 40-57. (In Spanish)

OECD (2012). *Tourism trends and policies.* Available online: https://www.oe cd-ilibrary.org/industry-and-services/oecd-tourism-trends-and-policies-2 012_tour-2012-en (access on 07/04/2021).

OECD & JRC (2008). *Handbook on constructing composite indicators: methodology and user guide.* Recuperado de: https://www.oecd.org/sdd /42495745.pdf

Pérez, C. (2004). *Técnicas de análisis multivariante de datos. Aplicaciones con SPSS.* España: Pearson Prentice Hall. (In Spanish)

Pérez-Romero, M. E., Flores-Romero, M. B., Alfaro-García, V. G. (2021). Tourism and destination competitiveness: an exploratory analysis applying the forgotten effects theory. *Journal of Intelligent & Fuzzy Systems, 40,* 1795-1804. DOI: 10.3233/JIFS-189186

Poon, A. (1993). *Tourism, technology and competitive strategies.* Reino Unido: CAB International

Ritchie, J. R. B., Crouch, G. I. (2003). *The competitive destination: a sustainable tourism perspective.* CABI Publishing.

Shaadi Rodríguez, R. M. A., Shaadi Rodríguez, L. del S., Pulido-Fernández, J. I., Rodríguez Herrera, I. M. (2018). Magic peoples programme – its localities in phase of involvement. *Anatolia, 30 (2),* 189–199.

Saavedra, M. (2012) Una propuesta para la determinación de la competitividad en la pyme latinoamericana. En *Pensamiento y gestión, 33,* 93 – 124. (In Spanish)

Sánchez, M. (2012). Análisis cuantitativo del impacto económico de la competitividad en destinos turísticos internacionales. En *Revista de Economía Mundial, 32,* 103-125. (In Spanish)

Santos, J., Muñoz, A., Juez, P., y Cortiñas, P. (2003). *Diseño de encuestas para estudios de mercado.* España: Centro de Estudios Ramón Areces. (In Spanish)

SECTUR (2001). *Reglas de operación Pueblos Mágicos.* Available online: http://www.sectur.gob.mx/wp-content/uploads/2018/10/Memoria-Docum ental-Pueblos-M%E2%80%A0gicos-Incorporaci%C2%A2n-y-Permane necia.pdf(accesson07/04/2021).(InSpanish)

Secretaría de Turismo (2016). *Estadística turística derivada de los censos económicos 2014. Pueblos Mágicos.* https://www.datatur.sectur.gob.mx/ Comite%20de%20Estadisticas%20del%20Sector%20Turismo/CENSOS _ECONOMICOS_2014_PM.pdf (In Spanish)

Vera, J. F., Baños, C. J. (2010). Renovación y re-estructuración de los destinos turísticos consolidados del litoral: las prácticas recreativas en la evolución del espacio turístico. *Boletín de la Asociación de Geógrafos Españoles, 53,* 329-353. (In Spanish)

Wei-Chiang, H. (2009). Global competitiveness measurement for the tourism sector. *Current Issues in Tourism, 12 (2),* 105-132.

Zamora, A. I., Cruz, G. (2020). Competitividad del sistema turístico de las ciudades mexicanas patrimonio mundial. En *Revista de El Colegio de San Luis, X (21),* 5 – 30. (In Spanish)

ANNEXES

Annex 1   Tourism Competitiveness Index of the Magical Towns of México (complete table).

Magical Town	Factor 1	Factor 2	Factor 3	Competitiveness Index	Position
Todos Santos	68.358	100.000	12.956	62.892	1
Tlaquepaque	95.791	0.000	30.541	49.436	2
Sayulita	48.379	68.955	23.602	47.862	3
Metepec	100.000	0.016	0.000	43.005	4
Isla Aguada	57.850	28.744	10.848	36.428	5
San Cristóbal de las Casas	1.887	13.912	100.000	31.985	6
Cholula	58.191	11.263	2.557	29.091	7
Orizaba	51.417	6.198	18.714	29.022	8
Guadalupe	45.926	5.761	19.700	26.796	9
Tulum	3.683	63.167	20.562	26.086	10
Valle de Bravo	43.339	17.946	5.575	25.525	11
Atlixco	39.270	7.073	17.348	23.692	12
Comitán de Domínguez	26.055	7.038	37.824	23.528	13

Annex 1   (Continued.)

Magical Town	Factor 1	Factor 2	Factor 3	Competitiveness Index	Position
Compostela	20.196	25.809	23.978	22.901	14
Lagos de Moreno	34.747	10.910	15.726	22.461	15
Isla Mujeres	5.842	56.837	5.685	21.098	16
Mexcaltitán	25.012	21.097	11.267	20.126	17
Tecate	28.930	11.294	13.918	19.586	18
Valladolid	27.322	11.328	16.178	19.515	19
Ajijic	31.023	14.070	6.344	19.274	20
Jerez de García Salinas	25.355	11.173	17.422	18.958	21
Palenque	10.787	16.147	34.470	18.789	22
Pátzcuaro	20.742	13.251	21.414	18.676	23
Mineral del Pozo	22.667	12.927	18.438	18.603	24
Salvatierra	25.570	12.834	13.385	18.459	25
Dolores Hidalgo	22.110	10.714	20.002	18.122	26
Tepotzotlán	25.758	11.582	12.478	17.919	27
Santiago	26.471	15.809	6.568	17.899	28
Loreto	3.275	39.262	16.124	17.540	29
Taxco	19.492	14.579	16.495	17.209	30
Tequisquiapan	17.136	18.183	16.242	17.209	31
Huauchinango	22.008	14.592	12.108	17.111	32
Coatepec	16.587	19.413	14.921	16.985	33
Linares	24.409	14.444	7.960	16.978	34
Mazunte	0.000	50.189	7.113	16.977	35
Tacámbaro	23.388	12.413	11.273	16.824	36
Zacatlán de las manzanas	19.952	12.055	16.721	16.710	37
Tequila	14.968	20.328	15.372	16.685	38
Huamantla	19.610	12.831	15.203	16.386	39
Papantla	16.277	18.260	13.984	16.253	40
Sombrerete	19.991	14.269	12.306	16.199	41
Calvillo	22.001	13.050	10.263	16.147	42
Melchor Múzquiz	21.827	13.073	10.051	16.021	43
Jiquilpan	20.585	14.006	9.855	15.714	44
El Rosarito	12.437	26.731	8.483	15.658	45
Xicotepec	16.366	13.741	16.210	15.536	46
Yuriria	20.461	13.047	10.223	15.472	47
Teotihuacán	13.136	21.124	12.552	15.375	48
Bacalar	8.333	25.848	13.694	15.035	49
Chiapa de Corzo	9.714	20.466	17.070	14.926	50
Chignahuapan	14.800	17.173	12.412	14.867	51

Annex 1 (Continued.)

Magical Town	Factor 1	Factor 2	Factor 3	Competitiveness Index	Position
Cuetzalan del Progreso	8.997	21.231	16.251	14.626	52
Nochistlán	19.148	15.096	6.639	14.555	53
Bernal	11.692	13.690	20.037	14.545	54
El Fuerte	16.802	14.239	11.207	14.522	55
Jalpa	14.499	14.949	14.073	14.519	56
Santa Clara del Cobre	17.282	14.869	9.063	14.339	57
Parras de la Fuente	14.675	15.615	12.096	14.261	58
Huichapan	16.948	14.449	9.052	14.066	59
Tlatlauquitepec	16.714	15.106	8.540	14.025	60
Sisal	13.762	21.442	6.194	14.023	61
Jalpan de Serra	7.790	18.563	18.526	13.921	62
Creel	9.760	18.802	14.824	13.840	63
Paracho	16.471	14.823	8.335	13.780	64
Magdalena de Kino	13.955	13.949	13.294	13.775	65
Comonfort	15.854	13.670	10.488	13.750	66
Mapimí	13.710	15.330	11.538	13.610	67
Ixtapan de la Sal	14.555	15.506	9.538	13.486	68
Cadereyta	14.292	13.869	11.750	13.479	69
Mazamitla	10.896	18.459	11.865	13.427	70
Cuitzeo	14.400	13.827	11.429	13.426	71
Amealco de Bonfil	14.701	14.073	10.453	13.366	72
Tepoztlán	5.279	16.430	22.756	13.343	73
Arteaga	13.701	14.688	11.189	13.319	74
Mocorito	14.893	15.227	8.581	13.289	75
Xilitla	5.376	21.864	16.115	13.222	76
Santa María del Río	14.357	15.783	8.566	13.221	77
Malinalco	11.945	15.580	12.487	13.182	78
Zimapán	15.349	15.139	7.447	13.153	79
Zempoala	12.775	14.871	11.648	13.099	80
Real de Asientos	14.999	15.725	7.095	13.083	81
Mascota	12.892	14.668	11.576	13.070	82
Nombre de Dios	13.522	15.647	9.295	13.018	83
Comala	7.559	21.034	12.564	12.953	84
Tlaxco	11.732	16.707	10.674	12.939	85
Tapijulapa	12.585	14.720	11.343	12.890	86
Coscomatepec	13.372	14.475	9.913	12.769	87
Pinos	12.250	15.082	11.010	12.765	88
Xico	10.170	14.893	14.347	12.715	89
Izamal	12.405	15.241	10.304	12.689	90

Annex 1 (Continued.)

Magical Town	Factor 1	Factor 2	Factor 3	Competitiveness Index	Position
Villa del Carbón	13.455	15.503	7.738	12.526	91
Real del Monte	7.791	14.923	17.353	12.512	92
Santa Catarina Juquila	9.366	16.862	12.656	12.503	93
Tula	13.577	15.493	7.463	12.501	94
Tlayacapan	10.377	15.199	12.875	12.498	95
San Martín de las Pirámides	11.084	16.772	9.712	12.420	96
Tapalpa	12.551	16.280	7.918	12.419	97
Aculco	13.688	15.561	6.852	12.404	98
Huautla de Jiménez	12.620	15.804	8.148	12.368	99
Talpa de Allende	9.882	16.500	11.677	12.352	100
San Pablo Villa de Mitla	9.360	16.344	12.340	12.260	101
Huasca de Ocampo	10.998	17.494	8.360	12.234	102
Tetela de Ocampo	10.485	14.254	12.623	12.193	103
Palizada	12.545	15.955	7.376	12.172	104
San José de Gracia	12.666	15.899	7.181	12.155	105
Tonatico	11.867	16.286	7.954	12.136	106
Cosalá	11.658	15.500	9.148	12.133	107
El Oro	12.113	15.216	8.696	12.121	108
Tecozautla	10.754	15.840	10.028	12.084	109
Angangueo	12.178	16.232	7.262	12.067	110
Alamos	11.083	15.841	9.415	12.060	111
San Sebastián del Oeste	10.783	16.281	9.235	12.014	112
Jala	11.366	15.234	9.411	11.999	113
San Pedro y San Pablo Teposcolula	11.995	15.839	7.654	11.976	114
Viesca	11.567	15.616	8.493	11.952	115
Teul González Ortega	11.173	15.432	9.322	11.951	116
Tlalpujahua	9.549	15.339	11.949	11.934	117
Maní	12.416	15.967	6.559	11.900	118
Mier	11.009	15.665	9.056	11.878	119
Cuatro Ciénegas	8.851	15.033	13.159	11.869	120
Aquismón	11.826	16.085	6.978	11.795	121
San Joaquín	10.590	15.497	9.537	11.778	122
Mineral del Chico	11.190	16.574	7.380	11.777	123
Pahuatlán	11.504	15.890	7.576	11.759	124

Annex 1   (Continued.)

Magical Town	Factor 1	Factor 2	Factor 3	Competitiveness Index	Position
Capulálpam de Méndez	11.477	16.364	7.015	11.738	125
Real de Catorce	8.886	16.638	10.634	11.684	126
Tzintzuntzan	9.566	15.322	10.968	11.671	127
Casas Grandes	10.675	15.734	8.730	11.668	128
Zozocolco	11.503	16.140	6.832	11.633	129
Guerrero	11.605	16.156	6.621	11.625	130
Batopilas	11.257	16.323	6.979	11.621	131
Candela	11.283	16.212	6.778	11.545	132
Bustamante	9.100	15.482	10.995	11.526	133

Source: Own elaboration.

2

Economic Performance of Organic Berries in Mexico

Priscila Ortega Gómez, Zoe Tamar Infante Jiménez, and Araceli Lira Chávez

Facultad de Contaduría y Ciencias Administrativas de la,
Universidad Michoacana de San Nicolás de Hidalgo, Mexico

Abstract

This study identifies and analyzes the determining factors in the economic performance of Mexico's organic berries at the subnational level from 2013 to 2020. The panel data method was used by creating three unbalanced models. According to the results, the economic performance of organic berries depends mainly on increasing the number of cultivated hectares, obtaining higher yields, and improving domestic prices as well as the average rural price. The conclusion is that improving the economic performance of Mexico's organic berries entails an increased production. However, this depends on the international demand, which currently has been increasing, while the yield per hectare is mainly a function of the technology and techniques used. On the other hand, rural and domestic prices are largely determined by international prices.

Keywords: Economic performance, berries, Mexico.

2.1 Introduction

Organic agriculture represents a sustainable alternative to customary agriculture. It can contribute to reduce hunger, poverty, and rural inequality. It preserves the cultural diversity of natural resources since it uses soils that are not degraded or contaminated, and it generates healthy and better quality food. It also helps to generate jobs because of a higher production and use of labor. Organic agriculture holds an average increased production of 20% more than customary farms. In addition, it has increased biodiversity, improved water quality, and generated greater profitability as well as greater nutritional value in its products (Häring et al., 2001; UN, 2020; Organic Research Centres Alliances, 2009; Seufert & Ramankutty, 2017).

Sustainable consumption behaviors have generated greater demand for organic products based on a growing awareness of the environment lately. A sustainable consumption behavior occurs when a consumer adopts two positive attitudes: the consumer shows greater involvement and responsibility so that the needs of future generations are not put at risk, and the consumer becomes aware of sustainability and the environment by minimizing the use of natural resources, toxic materials, and waste emissions. This is all related to the meaning of organic agriculture. It is defined as a production system that maximizes orchard resources focusing on increasing soil fertility and biological activity, and it maximizes the use of non-renewable resources by avoiding synthetic fertilizers and pesticides for the protection of natural resources and human health (Aceleanu, 2016; FAO, 2020; Salgado-Beltrán & Beltrán-Morales, 2011; Veracruz & Hernández, 2016).

According to FiBL & IFOAM-ORGANICS INTERNATIONAL (2021), currently, only 1.5% of agricultural land is organic; however, mainly in recent years, there has been a substantial increase in organic agricultural land in many countries. In 2019, 187 countries registered 72.3 million hectares of organic farmland. The countries with the largest areas of organic farmland were Australia (35.7 million hectares), Argentina (3.7 million hectares), and Spain (2.4 million hectares). All registered organic area was more than 72 million hectares. It represents a growth of over 2 million compared to the previous year. These lands were managed by 3.1 million producers in 2019 with an increasing trend since 2018, when almost 2.8 million producers were registered, India, Uganda, and Ethiopia being the most important holders.

This change in consumer preferences has played a crucial role in increasing organic production as the demand for organic products has grown substantially. Sales exceeded 106 billion euros in 2019. The United States was by far the main market with 44.7 billion euros, followed by Germany with 11.9 billion, France with 11.3 billion, and China with 8.5 billion. Also, other European and American countries remained within the top 10 of the largest organic food markets such as Italy, Canada, Switzerland, UK,

Sweden, and Spain, which together add up to 16.9 billion euros. As for the highest per capita consumption worldwide, it was registered by Denmark and Switzerland with 344 and 338 euros, respectively, in 2019. These countries continue to show an increasing trend considering that they registered a per capita consumption of 312 euros each in 2018. Given these circumstances, there are greater opportunities for producers and companies not only in their countries of origin, but also to expand their markets internationally by exporting their products to other countries (FiBL & IFOAM-ORGANICS INTERNATIONAL, 2021; FAO, Committee on Agriculture, 1999; Gomiero, 2018).

Organic agricultural exports regularly sell for 20% more than customary products. Even so, the profitability of organic production can be highly unsteady due to vulnerability to pests, climate changes, etc., among other factors. In addition, little research has been done to assess long-term market prices although the study is relevant as the profitability of organic agriculture contributes to local food security, food safety, and household income encouragement (FAO, 2019b).

Mexico has managed to increase its presence in the production and marketing of organic food worldwide, especially in the production of fruits, vegetables, and coffee. The organic fruit sector in particular has registered a remarkable growth in recent years (SIAP, 2021), which is attributed to the growing global demand for this type of food.

The production of berries in Mexico has experienced a remarkable increase in recent years, and it concentrates in eight Mexican states: Baja California, Baja California Sur, Michoacán, Jalisco, Querétaro, Tlaxcala, Guanajuato, and Puebla. However, the production of the latter four states is still very incipient and/or inconsistent. The group of fruits known as berries is also called fine fruits, *frutillas*, or forest fruits because they are small and intensely colored. This includes strawberries, blueberries, blackberries, and raspberries (FIRA, 2016).

The production and exports of Mexican organic berries hold economic, ecological, and social importance as these products satisfy a growing international demand. So, this research seeks to identify and analyze the main factors that influence the economic performance of these foods.

This paper is structured as follows. Section 3.1 is the introduction, and Section 3.2 corresponds to a literature review, which is mainly based on the theories of economic growth. Subsequently, Section 3.3 describes the model and data used. Finally, the results and conclusions obtained are presented.

2.2 Theoretical and Conceptual Framework

2.2.1 Economic performance and agricultural sector

When we talk about economic performance, we know that such definition is framed within the theories of economic growth and the various factors that can explain it. Therefore, there are several definitions of economic growth. Some of these definitions relate to this research. Enriquez (2016) and Chetthamrongcha (2020) defined economic growth as the increase, rise, or quantitative expansion of income and the value of final goods and services produced in the economic system during a certain period. This is measured and reflected through the growth rate of a country's gross domestic product (GDP).

From Antoine de Montchrétien's (1575–1621) point view, economic growth is related to an increase of wealth that can be obtained through territorial extension and gold possessions, understanding the cultivated surface as "territorial extension." Francois Quesnay (1758), in Tableau Economique, mentioned that agriculture is the productive activity that generates net products in a circular flow of income and expenditure. In contrast, John Maynard Keynes (1883–1946) argued that economic growth is influenced by the level of investment, the level of savings, and the possibilities of opening new investments. Supporting this perspective, Michal Kalecki (1899–1970) supported the relationship between investment and economic growth.

Examining the effects of exports on economic growth through the export-led growth hypothesis, we found a causal relationship with better performance in growth than in import substitution policies (Balassa, 1978). Thirlwall (1979) established a relationship between economic growth and trade balance based on the restricted growth model of the balance of payments (Holland et al., 2004).

According to a study by Meador and O'Brien (2019), the agricultural sector is a factor for economic growth in the case of Rwanda; this country has experienced significant economic growth as a result of that sector's expansion. In another study, Chetthamrongcha (2020) deduced that some macroeconomic indicators are important to the agricultural sector such as the interest rate, agricultural land, the unemployment rate, agricultural exports, crude oil prices, inflation, government expenditure, trade openness, and the exchange rate.

Also, Chowdhury (2020) found a positive relationship between economic growth and government consumption expenditure, fertility rate, inflation rate, and agricultural sector growth, and a negative relationship between economic growth and population growth. On the other hand, Kumar (2019) revealed a positive and significant relationship between economic growth and foreign direct investment in the agricultural sector.

According to Onegina et al. (2020), the basis of economic growth is increasing labor productivity in agriculture and reducing the time needed for food production. Hofman (2017), on the other hand, concluded that a negative contribution of the total factor productivity (TFP) reflects a long-term economic growth in countries and sectors, even if there is investment in the last 20 years.

Badibanga and Ulimwengu (2020) showed that additional agricultural investment coupled with improved agricultural input productivity will accelerate the country's pace toward achieving growth and poverty reduction goals. In the same vein, Phiri et al. (2020) found a significant impact in both the short run and long run of agricultural production on economic growth, with unit effect coefficients of 0.428 and 0.342, respectively. The effects tend to be high because more than two-thirds of the rural population depends on agriculture, which has been a catalyst for food security.

According to the Economic Commission for Latin America (ECLAC), the factors of economic growth in Latin American structuralism are the balance between imports and exports, meaning productivity and tariff protection to obtain distributive equity (Enriquez, 2016).

Regarding the organic sector, Milosevic (2020) obtained that competitiveness and production capacity of organic producers in Serbia should be strengthened through the tax system. This will contribute to the sustainable and long-term growth of this activity and consequently to the economic growth and development of the country.

2.2.2 Performance of organic farming

Numerous studies have tried to estimate performance of organic agriculture in comparison to conventional farming finding different results. For example, a study in India found that organic farming activities were very favorable for improving degraded lands. These findings may favor the implementation of policies to manage organic agricultural production in India (Yadava & Komaraiah, 2021).

Another study, also in India, investigated small-scale tea producers in Assam; it was found that the annual income obtained from 1 hectare of small-scale organic tea cultivation is higher than the income from conventional production. However, it was identified that organic yields are lower than conventional yields by 10%, and this in turn generates a decrease in income. However, organic tea cultivation is considered to be an economically viable alternative for small-scale producers over a time span of 10 years, as long as producers obtain a high and stable yield after transitioning from conventional to organic (Deka & Goswami, 2021).

In another study conducted in Lebanon, it was found that organic agriculture, even though beneficial, is increasingly costly mainly due to the high production costs incurred by producers as well as the inefficient organization of the organic value chain (Aoun et al., 2022).

In Bangladesh, a study was carried out to examine the historical development of organic agriculture as well as its current status. It detected the bottlenecks in the growth of this activity. Unlike the previous study, it was found that input prices are lower than in conventional agriculture and similar productivity was identified. In addition to this, price premiums make organic production as a whole beneficial and suitable for smallholder farmers in Bangladesh. Farmers achieved lower production costs through reduced use of external chemical inputs, higher prices, and thus higher profits, which translated into benefits from organic farming (Ferdous et al., 2021).

Just like Deka and Goswami (2021) and Ferdous et al. (2021), Durham and Mizik (2021) found that, in economic terms, production costs can be reported to be lower in organic agriculture than in conventional agriculture, in addition to the existence of higher prices in organic markets; however, lower yields were detected in organic farms, mainly in fruit production, vegetables, and the livestock sector. Even so, it can be pointed out that organic systems outperform conventional systems, since organic agriculture can generate important benefits in environmental terms for local communities.

For organic agriculture to be considered as contributing to sustainable agricultural development, it needs to be economically viable for farmers, i.e., the income obtained must be at least as high as that of conventional agriculture (Meemken & Qaim, 2018).

2.2.3 Land, prices, and yields

Several investigations have been mainly oriented to contrast yields between organic and conventional agriculture. In some cases, it was shown that yields in organic production were higher than yields in conventional production, although in other cases, they were considerably lower. In this sense, the average yield of organic agriculture is lower due to the higher costs it incurs, which leads to higher average prices. As a result, consumers sometimes end up paying a higher price given the lower yields of organic products that do not necessarily convert into higher dividends for producers (Meemken & Qaim, 2018).

In contrast to organic agricultural production, some authors consider that the low yields it generates lead to the use of a greater amount of land, which generates greater deforestation and a loss of biodiversity. This contrasts with the supposed environmental benefits of organic agriculture. Ecological, social, and economic benefits are very important for sustainable food security. However, these benefits are achieved through good agricultural production practices in specific organic commodity crops. In such crops, yields are almost equal to those of conventional crops; however, this does not apply to all organic products at present (Seufert et al., 2012).

A study conducted in Punjab, Pakistan revealed that in terms of agricultural production, the yield of conventional producers was 11% higher than that of organic producers. However, consumers maintained their preference for organic products (Aslam et al., 2020). This implies a change in preferences and consumption habits, as long as income is sufficient.

According to Croeder and Reganold (2015), organic production is in a profit range between 22% and 35%, which is more profitable than conventional production. Despite this, as mentioned above, yields of organic products are lower and therefore farmers receive higher prices as long as their products are certified. The additional to the average price of organic production is around 30%; these incentives make it more attractive than conventional production (Crowder & Reganold, 2015).

Agriculture today should be focused on caring for the environment and mitigating climate change. The problem is that inputs are insufficient to raise yields of organic crops in all countries that are dedicated to producing sustainably, leading to the impossibility of meeting the global demand for this type of food (Timsina, 2018).

To improve agricultural sustainability, it is essential to guarantee yields, mitigate environmental impacts, and reduce climate change. Organic agriculture is sustainable as long as yields increase, orienting production toward better distribution and consumption habits and with adequate agroecological management (Brzozowski & Mazourek, 2018).

Organic agriculture is economically sustainable depending on the geographical location where it is grown and the types of crops; the benefits obtained come mainly from the price premium of these crops. This implies the need for further studies in various locations, products, and situations (Aoun et al., 2022).

When producers decide to adopt organic agriculture, their main incentive is higher prices than conventional agricultural products. At the same time, the aim is to maintain food security, which also allows them to increase exports in the face of higher production and increased domestic demand due to the increase in population and income (Ferdous et al., 2021).

Badley et al. (2007) state that the yields of organic agriculture in advanced countries are in the order of 92.2% compared to the dividends of traditional farming. On the other hand, yields range from 180.2% in the case of developing countries, which could change world production in a short time.

In less developed countries, smallholder farmers have low education standards and limited access to agricultural training. This implies that more land area is required to produce the same amount of agricultural goods in these countries, given the yields in developed countries (Meemken & Qaim, 2018).

A study in Germany revealed that larger plots reduce agricultural costs, including labor. Thus, producing organically with the same plot sizes and distances between plots is cheaper and therefore generates higher dividends. This led to the conclusion that increasing the size of plots generates economies of scale, reduces unproductive times, and improves the utilization of agricultural activities (Heinrichs et al., 2021).

The best alternative to conventional agriculture is organic agriculture, since it generates healthy products with minimal environmental impact. However, the debate still prevails as to which of the two systems is more profitable for producers in each sector. Likewise, the challenge for organic agriculture is to be more economically feasible so that it can be considered fully sustainable considering the three dimensions: environmental, social, and economic.

According to this theoretical and empirical review, we can conclude that the main variables contributing to economic growth are yield, prices, cultivated area, agricultural land, income, and demand. Thus, the methodology used, considering these factors that influence economic growth, or in other words, the economic performance of organic berries in Mexico, is presented below.

2.3 Methodology

The model proposed for the present study was selected based on the previous section, mainly detecting the same most recent studies (most of them from 2018−2022 in databases such as Elsevier, Google Scholar, X-MOL, etc.);

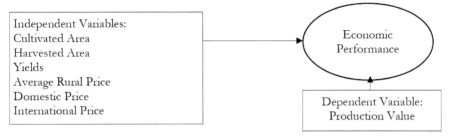

Figure 2.1 Model of economic performance variables for Mexico's organic berries.
Source: Author's design based on empirical and theoretical evidence.

thus, it collected information from the empirical evidence through interviews with 20 organic berry producers from the Los Reyes, Michoacán, and Ziracuaretiro regions during 2019 and 2020.

Based on the above, the proposed model is composed of the variables: cultivated area, harvested area, yields, average rural price, domestic price, and international price as independent variables; and the value of production as a dependent variable.

The data on some variables – dependent variable such as Production Value and independent variables such as Cultivated Area, Harvested Area, Yields, and Average Rural Price – were obtained from SIACON (Agri-food information system for consultation). This is an electronic tool designed to generate dynamic reports on annual statistics of the agricultural, livestock, and fishery subsectors. The information can be consulted at state and municipal levels. It has information on all national crops by cycle, water modality, and with annual data for the 1980–2018 series.

The data for the National Price variable were retrieved from the SNIIM (National Information and Market Integration System). This is a service of the Ministry of Economy that provides information on the behavior of wholesale prices of agricultural, livestock, and fishery products traded in national and international markets.

The data for the International Price variable were obtained from the Food and Agriculture Organization of the United Nations (FAO) – FAOSTAT. This database on food and agriculture provides freely accessible data for more than 245 countries and 35 regions since 1961.

Once the data were obtained, the statistical software R version 4.0.0 was used, and three unbalanced panel data models were constructed to identify the

Table 2.1   Definition of variables and data sources.

Variable	Description	Source
Production value (thousands of pesos)	It is the monetary value, expressed in national currency (pesos), of the production volume obtained at the end of the production cycle	Agri-food information system for consultation (SIACON)
Cultivated area (Ha)	It is the agricultural area in which the seed of any crop is deposited after soil preparation	Agri-food information system for consultation (SIACON)
Harvested Area (Ha)	This is the area from which the production was obtained	Agri-food information system for consultation (SIACON)
Yields (Ton/Ha)	Result of dividing the programmed production by the programmed area to be harvested	Agri-food information system for consultation (SIACON)
Average rural price ($/Ton)	Price paid to the producer for first-hand sales, whether at the plot, farm, and/or production zone level	Agri-food information system for consultation (SIACON)
Domestic price (Kilogram)	Average domestic wholesale price	National Information and Market Integration System (SNIIM)
International price (Ton/USD)	Average international wholesale price	Food and Agriculture Organization of the United Nations (FAO)

Source: Authors' design.

relationship between the independent variables and the dependent variable from 2013 to 2020, with a total of 95, 90, and 90 observations, respectively.

The period selected corresponds to the information available. The data for variables National Price and International Price were based on data from customary berries because there is no information at national level on these variables for organic berries.

Panel data is a special type of pooled data in which the same cross-sectional unit (a household, a company, or a state) is analyzed over time, i.e., the dimensions of space and time are found in panel data.

A balanced panel is one in which each subject − a company, individuals, etc. − has the same number of observations. The panel is unbalanced if there are different numbers of observations. There are short panels and long panels. A short panel is one in which the number of subjects is more than the number of periods. In a long panel, T is greater than N (Gujarati & Porter, 2010).

The panel data model for this research is given by formula (2.1):

$$
\begin{aligned}
\text{Valordelaproduccion}_{it} \quad\quad &(2.1)\\
= \alpha + \beta_1 \text{Superficiesembrada}_{it} &+ \beta_2 \text{Superficiecosechada}_{it}\\
+ \beta_3 \text{Rendimiento}_{it} &+ \beta_4 \text{Preciomediorural}_{it}\\
+ \beta_5 \text{Precionacional}_{it} &+ \beta_6 \text{Preciointernacional}_{it} + \varepsilon
\end{aligned}
$$

$$
i = 1, \ldots, N
$$
$$
t = 1, \ldots, T,
$$

where α is the constant, β represents vector $q \times 1$ of the parameters to be estimated, i is the ith subject, t is the period of the variables, and ε is the error.

Panel data regression can be estimated through several different models: pooled regression, fixed effects, and random effects, among others. In the pooled regression model, the observations on different individuals are simply grouped in a single regression without foreseeing individual differences that could generate different coefficients; it does not take into account their cross-sectional and time-series nature. In the fixed effects model, the observations are pooled, but each variable is expressed as a deviation from its mean value for each time-steady feature of individuals, and then an ordinary least squares regression is estimated on the mean-corrected values.

As for the random effects model, we assume that the values of individual differences are the values of the intercept, but we recognize that individuals in the sample are from a random draw; so the individual differences are random rather than fixed (Gujarati & Porter, 2009; Hill et al., 2011).

The following steps were carried out in the R software to determine the panel and model of best adjustment and explanation:

1. The pooled data model was calculated by applying logarithms to the variables, except for the Yields variable because it is a percentage.
2. Robust Newey–West estimators were used because of the exposure to heteroscedasticity and serial correlation errors.
3. Then, the Within Group fixed effects model was estimated.
4. Robust Newey–West estimators were used for the fixed effects model.
5. The fixed effects model allows us to calculate the Alphas for all units and find out if they are significant. Therefore, Alphas and significance were calculated for each state.

6. To choose between the two models (pooled and fixed effects) the *F*-test was used. If the *P*-value is less than 5%, the fixed effects model is the best choice.

The following section presents the models and results for each of the data panels.

2.4 Results

Three models were used to meet the goal of this research. The first without the Domestic Price variable, the second without the state of Baja California Sur, and the third without the International Price variable and without the state of Baja California Sur; this was due to the availability of information.

For the first panel (without the Domestic Price variable), the significant variables obtained through the pooled regression model were Logarithm of Cultivated Hectares with a *P*-value of 0.001 and a significance level of 1%, and the Yields variable with a *P*-value of 0.083 and a significance level of 10%. The model was exposed to heteroscedasticity and serial correlation errors; therefore, robust Newey−West estimators were used. So, variable Logarithm Cultivated Ha obtained the same results, a *P*-value of 0.0001 and a significance level of 1%, whereas the Yields variable showed a *P*-value of 0.074 and a significance level of 10%.

Next, the fixed effects model was constructed, and the same significant variables were obtained − Logarithm Cultivated Ha and Yields. The Logarithm Cultivated Ha variable obtained a *P*-value of 0.0001 and was significant at 1%. The Yields variable had a *P*-value of 0.035 and was significant at 5%. Subsequently, the *F*-test was performed to compare the Betas of the fixed effects model with the Betas of the pooled regression model and verify if they were different or not. The result was a *P*-value greater than 5%; therefore, the pooled regression model was chosen. The variables that influence the pooled regression model for the first panel are Logarithm Cultivated Ha and Yields (see Table 2.2).

As for the second model (without the state of Baja California Sur), the only significant variable obtained through the pooled regression model was the Logarithm of Average Rural Price, with a *P*-value of 0.042 and a significance level of 5%. When applying the Newey−West robust estimators, the significant variables obtained were Yields and Logarithm of Average Rural Price. The Yields variable showed a *P*-value of 0.041 and a significance level of 5%, whereas Logarithm of Average Rural Price had a *P*-value of 0.031 and

Table 2.2 Pooled regression model for the production value equation.

Variable	Coefficient	Standard error	T-value	P-value
Constant	0.897	11.985	0.128	0.900
Log (Cultivated Ha)	1.222	0.279	5.811	0.0001***
Log (Harvested Ha)	−0.089	0.194	−0.946	0.362
Yields	0.007	0.004	1.949	0.074*
Log (ARP)	0.175	0.214	0.848	0.413
Log (IntPrice)	0.386	1.592	0.432	0.673

Signif. codes: *$P < 0.1$; **$P < 0.05$; ***$P < 0.01$.
Source: Author's design based on data obtained in the statistical software R, version 4.0.0.

Table 2.3 Pooled regression model for the production value equation.

Variable	Coefficient	Standard error	T-value	P-value
Constant	2.592	14.491	0.323	0.755
Log (Cultivated Ha)	−0.576	2.945	−0.393	0.705
Log (Harvested Ha)	1.486	2.980	0.985	0.354
Yields	0.004	0.002	2.441	0.041**
Log (ARP)	0.809	0.333	2.630	0.031**
Log (DomPrice)	−0.644	0.414	−1.657	0.137
Log (IntPrice)	0.194	1.232	0.424	0.683

Signif. codes: *$P < 0.1$; **$P < 0.05$; ***$P < 0.01$.
Source: Author's design based on data obtained in the statistical software R, version 4.0.0.

was significant at 5%. Afterwards, the fixed effects model was calculated, and variable Logarithm of Average Rural Price was obtained as significant at 1% with a P-value of 0.001. After calculating the F-test, a P-value greater than 5% was obtained; so the pooled regression model was chosen (see Table 2.3).

Finally, in the third model (without the state of Baja California Sur and without International Price), variables Yields, Logarithm of Domestic Price, and the Constant were obtained as significant through a pooled regression. Yields had a P-value of 0.088 and were significant at 10%; Logarithm of Domestic Price had a P-value of 0.009 and was significant at 1%, whereas the Constant showed a P-value of 0.032, and it was significant at 5%. When applying the Newey−West robust estimators, the significant variables were Yields at 1%, Logarithm of Domestic Price at 5%, and the Constant at 10%. Based on the fixed effects model, the Logarithm Harvested Ha variable was significant at 10% with a P-value of 0.076; Logarithm of Average Rural

Price was significant at 5% with a *P*-value of 0.016; and Domestic Price was significant at 5% with a *P*-value of 0.019. The *F*-test resulted in a *P*-value greater than 5%; so the pooled regression model was chosen (see Table 2.4).

Table 2.4   Pooled regression model for the production value equation.

Variable	Coefficient	Standard error	*T*-value	*P*-value
Constant	12.057	4.959	2.039	0.065*
Log (Cultivated Ha)	−1.331	2.968	−0.933	0.370
Log (Harvested Ha)	2.433	2.982	1.668	0.122
Yields	0.004	0.002	3.079	0.010***
Log (ARP)	0.352	0.236	1.167	0.266
Log (DomPrice)	−0.961	0.304	−3.049	0.011**

Signif. codes: $*P < 0.1$; $**P < 0.05$; $***P < 0.01$.

Source: Author's design based on data obtained in the statistical software R, version 4.0.0.

According to the results obtained from the three models, it is understood that the best adjustment was the pooled regression model. This is because the p-values obtained were greater than 5% after running the F-test. The third model had the highest number of significant variables. Here, the state of Baja California Sur and the International Price variable were not added.

According to the results obtained, the growth of organic berry production in Mexico depends largely on increasing the cultivated hectares. This should be a response to the increased global demand to obtain higher profits. There is a strict control in each production process to reduce losses and waste, as well as to improve domestic prices and the average rural price. These prices depend on international prices, which were not significant because we considered the prices of customary berries due to a lack of information for organic berries. However, international prices remain important for this research, given the incidence they have on domestic and rural prices. It is well known that international prices are taken as reference to stipulate the latter.

2.5 Conclusions

This study analyzes the performance of organic berries in Mexico at the subnational level from 2013 to 2020 using a panel data tool. According to the literature reviewed, the agriculture sector is of vital importance for economic growth. There is greater awareness for consuming safe food, which has led to a growing demand for organic products such as organic berries.

Thus, it is important to determine the main variables that affect the performance of organic berries in Mexico. For this study, we considered Production Value, Cultivated Area, Harvested Area, Yields, Average Rural Price, Domestic Price, and International Price.

According to the results obtained from the three constructed models, the first panel (without Domestic Price) obtained a positive relationship through the pooled regression model with a significance level of 1% for the Logarithm of Harvested Hectares and a positive relationship with a significance level of 10% for the Yields variable. The production value was taken as the dependent variable, and the independent variables were Logarithm of Cultivated Hectares, Logarithm of Harvested Hectares, Yields, Logarithm of Average Rural Price, and Logarithm of International Price. Regarding Harvested Ha, the Production Value increases positively 1.22 for each harvested hectare. Therefore, for each extra harvested hectare, the production value would increase in 3393.96 pesos. The production value increases positively by 0.007 for each unit of yields. Therefore, the production value increases by 1007.02 pesos for each extra unit of yields.

The second panel, (without the state of Baja California Sur) obtained a positive relationship through the pooled regression model with a significance level of 5% for Yields and Logarithm of Average Rural Price. The production value was taken as the dependent variable, and the independent variables were Logarithm of Cultivated Hectares, Logarithm of Harvested Hectares, Yields, Logarithm of Average Rural Price, Logarithm of Domestic Price, and Logarithm of International Price. The production value increases positively by 0.004 for each unit of yields. So, the production value will increase by 1004.00 pesos for each extra unit of yields. In the case of the Average Rural Price variable, the production value increases 0.809 for each unit. So, for each extra unit of average rural price, the production value increases by 2245.66 pesos.

The third panel (without the state of Baja California Sur and without the International Price variable) obtained a positive relationship with a significance level of 1% for Yields, and a significance level of 10% for the Constant, as opposed to a negative relationship with the Logarithm of Domestic Price, which showed a significance level of 5%. On the other hand, for each unit of yields, the production value increases positively by 0.004. So, the value of production will increase by 1004.00 pesos for each extra unit of yields. The Logarithm of Domestic Price is reduced negatively by −0.96. So, the production value will decrease by 2614.30 pesos for each additional unit of Domestic Price.

According to the above, we can conclude that the economic performance and, therefore, the growth of organic berry production in Mexico depends largely on increasing the cultivated hectares, obtaining higher yields, as well as improving domestic prices and the average rural price. Such growth in performance could contribute to the sustainability of this activity in its three dimensions: economic, social, and environmental.

The lack of official information limits the depth of the research. The SIAP (Agri-food and Fisheries Information Service), which is the agency responsible for collecting information and feeding the SIACON, should collect information on other variables related to organic agricultural products and determine the phenomena that positively or negatively affect the sector's production value. In this research, these factors are not observed due to the limited access.

The main limitations of the study were the availability of data and information to include more variables, since even though organic agriculture has been practiced for a long time in Mexico, it had been on a small scale. It was not until 1999 that official information on organic agriculture began to be registered and published in the SIAP in Mexico.

For future lines of research, we suggest a comparative study between organic and conventional berries to determine the type of production with the best economic performance.

References

Aceleanu, M. I. (2016). Sustainability and competitiveness of Romanian farms through organic agriculture. *Sustainability (Switzerland)*, 8(3).

Aoun, M., Abebe, G. K., & Traboulsi, A. (2022). *Renewable Agriculture and Food Systems Performance of organic farming in developing countries: a case of organic tomato value chain in Lebanon.* https://doi.org/10.1017/S1 742170521000478

Aslam, W., Shahzad Noor, R., Ullah, S., & Chen, H. (2020). Comparative economic analysis of crop yield under organic and conventional farming systems in Punjab, Pakistan. *Asian J Agric & Biol*, 8(2), 113–118. https: //doi.org/10.35495/ajab.2020.02.093

Badibanga, T., & Ulimwengu, J. (2020). Optimal investment for agricultural growth and poverty reduction in the democratic republic of congo a two-sector economic growth model. *Applied Economics*, *52*(2), 135–155. https://doi.org/10.1080/00036846.2019.1630709

Badgley, C., Moghtader, J., Quintero, E., Zakem, E., Chappell, M. J., Avilés-Vázquez, K., Samulon, A., & Perfecto, I. (2007). Organic agriculture and the global food supply. *Renewable Agriculture and Food Systems*, *22*(2), 86–108. https://doi.org/10.1017/S1742170507001640

Balassa, B. (1978). Exports and economic growth. *Journal of Development Economics*, *5*, 181–189.

Brzozowski, L., & Mazourek, M. (n.d.). *sustainability A Sustainable Agricultural Future Relies on the Transition to Organic Agroecological Pest Management*. https://doi.org/10.3390/su10062023

Chetthamrongchai, P., Somjai, S., & Chankoson, T. (2020). The contribution of macroeconomic factors in determining the economic growth, export and the agricultural output in agri-based asean economies. *Entrepreneurship and Sustainability Issues*, *7*(3), 2043–2059. https://doi.org/10.9770/jesi.2020.7.3(40)

Chowdhury, I. (2020). Extended exogenous growth model: Application and investigation the long-term growth determinants of Bangladesh. *Asian Economic and Financial Review*, *10*(1), 35–53. https://doi.org/10.18488/journal.aefr.2020.101.35.53

Crowder, D. W., & Reganold, J. P. (2015). Financial competitiveness of organic agriculture on a global scale. *Proceedings of the National Academy of Sciences of the United States of America*, *112*(24), 7611–7616. https://doi.org/10.1073/PNAS.1423674112/SUPPL_FILE/PNAS.1423674112.SD01.XLS

Deka, N., & Goswami, K. (2021). Economic sustainability of organic cultivation of Assam tea produced by small-scale growers. *Sustainable Production and Consumption*, *26*, 111–125. https://doi.org/10.1016/J.SPC.2020.09.020

Durham, T. C., & Mizik, T. (2021). *Comparative Economics of Conventional, Organic, and Alternative Agricultural Production Systems*. https://doi.org/10.3390/economies

Enríquez, I. (2016). Las teorías del crecimiento económico: notas críticas para incursionar en un debate inconcluso. *Revista Latinoamericana de Desarrollo Económico*, 73–126. https://doi.org/10.35319/lajed.20162564

FAO. (2020). *FAO*. Concepto Agricultura Orgánica. http://www.fao.org/3/ad818s/ad818s03.htm

Ferdous, Z., Zulfiqar, F., Datta, A., Hasan, A. K., & Sarker, A. (2021). Potential and challenges of organic agriculture in Bangladesh: a review.

Journal of Crop Improvement, *35*(3), 403–426. https://doi.org/10.1080/15
427528.2020.1824951

FiBL &IFOAM-ORGANICS INTERNATIONAL. (2021). The World of
Organic Agriculture. Statistics and Emerging Trends 2021. Research
Institute of Organic Agriculture (FiBL), Frick, and IFOAM – Organics
International, Bonn. https://shop.fibl.org/CHen/mwdownloads/downl
oad/link/id/1294/?ref=1

FIRA. (2016). *Panorama agroalimentario berries 2016*. https://www.gob.mx
/cms/uploads/attachment/file/200633/Panorama_Agroalimentario_Berries
_2016.pdf

Gujarati, D.; Porter, D. (2009). *Econometría* (Quinta edi). McGraw-Hill.

Häring, A., Dabbert, S., Offermann, F., & Nieberg, H. (2001). Benefits
of Organic Farming for society. *European Conference–Organic Food
and Farming-Towards Partnership and Action in Europe, Copenhagen,
Denmark*, *10*(11.05), 2001.

Heinrichs, J., Kuhn, T., Pahmeyer, C., & Britz, W. (2021). Economic effects
of plot sizes and farm-plot distances in organic and conventional farming
systems: A farm-level analysis for Germany. *Agricultural Systems*, *187*,
102992. https://doi.org/10.1016/J.AGSY.2020.102992

Hill, C.; Griffiths, W.; Lim, G. (2011). *Principles of econometrics* (Fourth
Edi). Wiley.

Hofman, A., Mas, M., Aravena, C., & De Guevara, J. (2017). Crecimiento
económico y productividad en Latinoamérica. El proyecto LA-KLEMS. In
Trimestre Económico (Vol. 84, Issue 334). https://doi.org/10.20430/ete.v
84i334.302

Holland, M., Vilela Vieira, F., & Canuto, O. (2004). Economic Growth
and the Balance-of-Payments Constraint in Latin America. *Investigación
Económica*, *63*(247), 45–74.

Kumar, M., & Gopalsamy, S. (2019). Agricultural sector FDI and economic
growth in saarc countries. *International Journal of Recent Technology and
Engineering*, *8*(2 Special Issue 10), 116–121. https://doi.org/10.35940/ijr
te.B1019.0982S1019

Meador, J., & O'Brien, D. (2019). Placing Rwanda's agriculture boom: trust,
women empowerment and policy impact in maize agricultural cooperatives. *Food Security*, *11*(4), 869–880. https://doi.org/10.1007/s12571-019-
00944-9

Meemken, E.-M., & Qaim, M. (2018). *Organic Agriculture, Food Security,
and the Environment*. https://doi.org/10.1146/annurev-resource

Milošević, G., Kulić, M., Durić, Z., & Durić, O. (2020). The taxation of agriculture in the republic of serbia as a factor of development of organic agriculture. *Sustainability (Switzerland)*, *12*(8). https://doi.org/10.3390/SU12083261

Onegina, V., Megits, N., Antoshchenkova, V., & Boblovskiy, O. (2020). Outcome of capital investment on labor productivity in agriculture sector of Ukraine. *Journal of Eastern European and Central Asian Research*, *7*(1), 12–26. https://doi.org/10.15549/jeecar.v7i1.355

UN. (2020). *UN*. Sustainable Development Goals.https://www.un.org/sustainabledevelopment/es/objetivos-de-desarrollo-sostenible/

Organic Research Centres Alliances. (2009). *Organic Research Centres Alliances*. Influencing Food Enviroments for Healty Diets. http://www.fao.org/organicag/oa-portal/en/?no_cache=1

Phiri, J., Malec, K., Majune, S., Appiah-Kubi, S., Maitah, M., Maitah, K., Gebeltová, Z., & Abdullahi, K. (2020). Agriculture as a determinant of Zambian economic sustainability. *Sustainability (Switzerland)*, *12*(11), 1–14. https://doi.org/10.3390/su12114559

Salgado-Beltrán, L., & Beltrán-Morales, L. F. (2011). *Factors that influence sustainable consumption of organic products in the Northwest Mexico*. *27*(3), 265–279. www.universidadyciencia.ujat.mx

Seufert, V., & Ramankutty, N. (2017). Many shades of gray—the context-dependent performance of organic agriculture. *Science Advances*, *3*(3).

Seufert, V., Ramankutty, N., & Foley, J. A. (2012). Comparing the yields of organic and conventional agriculture. *Nature*, *485*(7397), 229–232. https://doi.org/10.1038/NATURE11069

SIAP (2021). Servicio de Información Agroalimentaria y Pesquera. Anuario estadístico de la producción agrícola. https://nube.siap.gob.mx/cierreagricola/

Timsina, J. (2018). Can Organic Sources of Nutrients Increase Crop Yields to Meet Global Food Demand? *Agronomy*, *8*, 214. https://doi.org/10.3390/agronomy810021

Veracruz, E. De, & Hernández, D. S. (2016). *La certificación orgánica de la agricultura como estrategia de combate a la pobrezaáobrezestudio en la región Totonaca*. 5.

Yadava, A. K., & Komaraiah, J. B. (2021). Benchmarking the performance of organic farming in India. *Journal of Public Affairs*, *21*(2). https://doi.org/10.1002/PA.2208

3

Social Conformation as a Difficulty in Improving Wages in Mexico

Berenice Mendoza[1], Salvador Cruz-Aké[2], and Fernando Ávila-Carreón[3]

[1]Faculty of Accounting and Administrative Sciences, Michoacan University of San Nicolás de Hidalgo, Mexico
[2]Instituto Politecnico Nacional, Mexico
[3]Department of Basic Sciences, Instituto Tecnologico de Morelia, Mexico

Abstract

To observe the complexities of achieving a better salary scheme based on the educational level of the individual, the social composition of human capital is studied, which we can basically consider as a family structure made up of marital status, number of hours dedicated to work, to study, number of members as well as the type of home in which they live. A database from the National Institute of Statistics and Geography of Mexico was used, in which data mining, regressions and statistics were carried out to determine the salary effect on human capital.

Keywords: Wages, human capital, social structure

3.1 Introduction

Human capital is the knowledge possessed by each individual. As he increases his knowledge, his potential will grow. On the basis of all human capital are attitudes; in them, you can see the behavior of people and how all behavior can be modified (Velázquez Valadez, 2004). Theodore Schultz in 1960 argued: I propose to treat education as an investor in man and to treat its consequences as a form of capital. As education becomes part of the

43

person who receives it, I will refer to it as human capital. Since it becomes an integral part of a person, it cannot be bought, sold or treated as property in our institutions. However, it is a form of capital if it provides a productive service of value to the economy (Schultz, 1960).

Human capital can be understood within the current economy as an engine of organizational development, taking it as the main advantage in companies to develop in their environments (Tinoco & Soler, 2011).

The concept of human capital has been studied since the middle of the last century, it is therefore a recent study. Various authors have taken this concept and studied it from different angles (Schultz, 1961; Becker, 1962; Benhabib & Spiegel, 1994; Psacharopoulos, 1995). One of the aspects studied by various researchers is the direct relationship of human capital with the formation of developed economies and its role as a trigger for economic development, to this study are added international organizations that closely investigate its role within each country (OCDE, 2007; Kido Cruz & Kido Cruz, 2015; Ministerio de Educación Cultura y Deporte, 2015; UNESCO 2009).

In 2007, the OCDE said that:

The ability of individuals and countries to benefit from this new knowledge economy depends largely on their human capital, which is defined by educational level, skills, aptitudes, and qualifications. Consequently, governments are becoming more and more concerned with raising levels of human capital. One of the most important ways they can do this is through education and training, which are now considered highly relevant factors in stimulating economic growth. (OCDE, 2007)

The study of human capital has taken new directions such as the role of public policies in the educational process, acquisition of skills, accessibility to new technologies and even the relationship between wages and gender (Ehrenberg & Smith, 2012; Machin, 2014; Refrigeri & Aleandri, 2014; Rustiadi, 2015; Koch et al., 2015; Calderon 2015; Rahayu et al., 2015; Miciuła, 2016; Lee & Lee, 2016; Perri, 2016; Mason et al., 2016).

Human capital becomes more relevant for those countries in which their economies are still developing, which is why many authors have carried out various studies to understand how environments, the segmentation of social classes, and cultural differences affect the development of the economy of a country, in particular, we have Latin American authors, of course, Mexico has also been developing research around this concept, in particular from its profitability (Herrero, 2000; Salas, 2002; Morduchowicz, 2004; López & Almagro, 2005; Kido Cruz & Kido Cruz, 2015; Lächler, 1999; Angulo et al., 2000; López-Acevedo et al., 2005).

The topic that we have been dealing with in this introduction is already included in a theory, the "human capital theory."

The human capital theory explains why there is an increase in education spending. Thus, countries have observed economic growth if they invested in education and that is directly related to the economic growth of the national product (Salas, 2002). This is an optimistic theory, since it contemplates the idea that education is a tool that will help the individual to have a higher income, and the society to prosper, and over time, eradicate poverty (Vandenberghe, 1999).

The objective of this research is to study human capital through the analysis of the salaries of household heads in Mexico, using the 2016 National Household Income and Expenditure Survey (ENIGH), in particular, to analyze the social conformation (family structure made up of marital status, number of hours dedicated to work, study, work, number of members as well as the type of household in which they live) as a difficulty to improve wages in Mexico.

Our analysis is based on a survey, the ENIGH 2016. The ENIGH is the National Survey of Household Income and Expenditure of the National Institute of Statistics and Geography of Mexico, in which every two years data from the same population mix are analyzed, such as expenditures, income, occupation, and social characteristics of households selected. The ENIGH has been applied as such since 1992, although its history dates back to 1956 carried out by the General Directorate of Statistics (DGE).

The topics covered by the survey are diverse (household income, household current expenditure, financial perceptions, and household characteristics, among others), this analysis is based on the educational level of the heads of the household considering their salary perceptions of their home and social behaviors such as family structure, number of hours dedicated to work, study and number of family members.

Although we have a mega database with thousands of data with dozens of indicators, it was necessary to choose the ones we required, based on the population information and household concentration, we used data mining. With this tool we chose to analyze salaries in Mexico, taking into consideration some of the 31 states, exclusively male and female heads of families with their educational level. Data mining takes large sets of information and observes similar behaviors that can resemble a certain pattern, mining itself is widely used for various topics, in particular, there are several in which they analyze the gender gap in different countries with this tool (Hirsch & Schnabel, 2012; Hajian et al., 2014; Petreski et al., 2014; Ghaljahi et al., 2018; Lauwo, 2018).

When we want to consider the salaries of an individual in relation to their educational level, the Mincer Equation is considered in the first instance, but we were interested in going a little further and seeing other factors that could affect the salary of a person, so at this equation, we added some indicators that gave us a much higher level of explanation than education itself.

The methodology used for this work is first to take some indicators that interest us in the megabase using data mining, then considering the Mincer equation in which it defines the salary of an individual based on their work experience and their educational level, added different indicators to this equation and we analyzed it with regressions. Other additional information that interested us, after data mining, statistics were carried out to give an overview of what happened.

At the end of this analysis, we observed complications in getting more salary in those who have a greater number of household members, those who are of course with less education, and in general the disadvantage towards women in terms of the number of hours dedicated to work, study and cleaning the home.

3.2 Preliminaries

The Mincer equation in his representation talks about the relationship between work experience and education on wages, we can see it as follows:

$$\ln Y = \beta_0 + \beta_1 s + \beta_2 t + \beta_3 t^2 + \varepsilon,$$

where $Y :=$ wage; $s :=$ schooling; $t :=$ years of labour experience.

Several authors with different techniques and diverse data sets have studied the Mincer equation (Psacharopoulos, 1994; Gary S. Becker, Kevin M. Murphy, 1994; Cabañete, 1997; Psacharopoulos, 1995; Cabañete, 1997; Lopez-Acevedo, 2001; Falgueras, 2008; Morduchowicz, 2004; Seoane & Álvarez, 2010; Austria and Venegas-Martínez 2011; Humphreys, 2012; Heckman et al., 2013; Kredler, 2014; Francine & Lawrence, 2016).

3.3 Results and Discussion

3.3.1 Analysis of the Mincer equation with elements of social conformation for Mexico

Taking the 1974 Mincer equation as a reference, we are going to analyze the income of the head of household, which is both related to education, sex, work experience, type of household, total household members and minors, using the base of ENIGH 2018 data. The econometric analysis was performed using EViews-10, we made the regression with the next equation:

$$\text{lnsal} = c(1) + c(2) * \text{household edu} + c(3) * \text{laboral exp} + c(4) *$$
$$\text{laboral\_exp}^2 + c(5) * \text{home class} + c(6) * \text{tot int} + c(7) * \text{menores},$$

where lnsal := natural logarithm of salaries of the heads of family; househol_edu :=schooling of the head of the family; laboral exp := work experience of the head of the family; laboral exp^2 := work experience of the head of the family squared; home class := kind of home class of the heads

Table 3.1 Regression model of human capital performance with social conformation for female heads of household in Mexico.

Dependent Variable: LN_SALARY
Method: Least Squares (Gauss-Newton / Marquardt steps)
Sample: 1 20476
Included observations: 20475
LN_SALARY=C(1)+C(2)*HOUSEHOL_EDU+C(3)*LABORAL_EXP+C(4)
   *LABORAL_EXP_2+C(5)*HOME_CLASS+C(6)*TOT_INTEG+C(7)
   *MENORES

	Coefficient	Std. Error	t-Statistic	Prob.
C(1)	8.576403	0.033267	257.807	0
C(2)	0.169231	0.002485	68.10406	0
C(3)	0.010348	0.001102	9.387585	0
C(4)	-0.000102	1.30E-05	-7.864222	0
C(5)	0.155411	0.008681	17.90239	0
C(6)	0.259433	0.004638	55.94178	0
C(7)	-0.28546	0.007673	-37.20544	0

R-squared	0.411723	Mean dependent var	10.6503
Adjusted R-s	0.41155	S.D. dependent var	0.915425
S.E. of regres	0.702227	Akaike info criterion	2.131222
Sum squarec	10093.24	Schwarz criterion	2.133933
Log likelihoc	-21811.39	Hannan-Quinn criter.	2.132108
F-statistic	2387.519	Durbin-Watson stat	1.6268
Prob(F-statis	0		

Note: Own elaboration based on ENIGH 2018.

of family; tot integ := number of the integrants of the house; menores := number of minors in the house.

The regression obtained is shown in Table 3.1

As we could observe in the previous regression, the largest component that explains the salary is total household members, followed by education, the type of household explained in third place, we can observe that the minors explain it in a negative term. From this regression, it is understood that having minors in a household can influence a salary decrease.

3.3.2 Familiar structure analysis for Mexico with data mining

3.3.2.1 Hours dedicated to home and health in Mexico City and Michoacán

Regarding the marital situation, in Michoacán and Mexico City, both men and women live as a couple or are married, mostly the latter, regardless of the academic degree (Figure 3.1).

In the case of Mexico City, you can see two peaks in singles when they have the first degrees, and when they are at the professional level. Married people are among the first degrees of study and professionalism, and there are also those who live with their partner or in a free union. In the last degrees of study (master's and doctorate), the indicator that stands out slightly from the others is when they are married (Figure 3.2).

For Michoacán, singles also have low education and professional degrees; married are those who have few studies and those who have a professional; those who live with their partner or in common union have a basic education. We observe that those who have more studies (master's and doctorate) will be the single indicator that is observed the most.

In relation to the number of hours that people work in CDMX, it is almost the same number of hours dedicated to any level of studies, but they work a little more than they. The hours dedicated to studying decrease as people have more studies, that is, at the primary, secondary, and high school levels, they dedicate more time to study than at those at higher levels (30 average hours against 25 average), and in general, they dedicate a couple of hours more than they do the study (Figures 3.3 and 3.4).

In CDMX, the time dedicated in hours to care, women are above men, around 30 hours of almost any social level, however, those who have fewer hours dedicated to care are those who have a doctorate, while they spend an average of 20 hours, dedicating fewer hours the more they have studied. At all levels of education, women spend more time doing housework than they do.

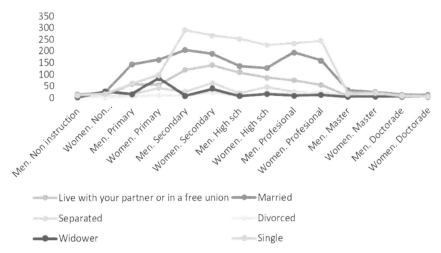

Figure 3.1 Marital situation with degree of study in CDMX 2016. Source: Own elaboration based on ENIGH 2016.

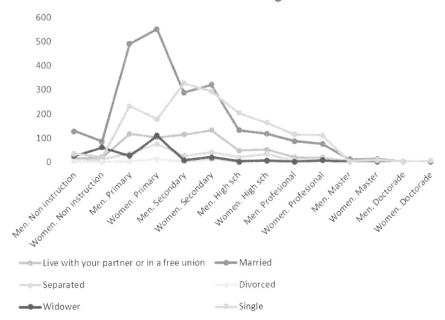

Figure 3.2 Marital situation with degree of study in Michoacán 2016. Source: Own elaboration based on ENIGH 2016.

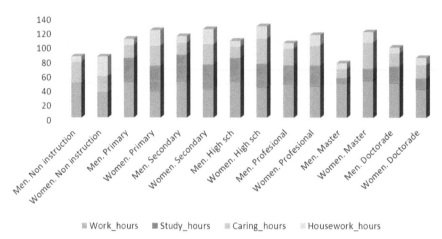

Figure 3.3 Hours of work, study, care and housework in CDMX 2016. Source: Own elaboration based on ENIGH 2016.

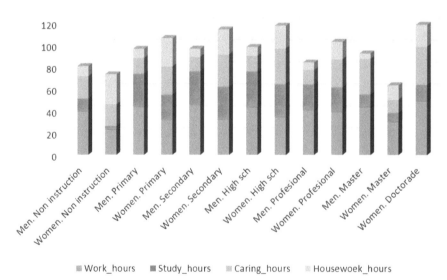

Figure 3.4 Hours of work, study, care, and housework in Michoacán 2016. Source: Own elaboration based on ENIGH 2016.

HOME CLASS

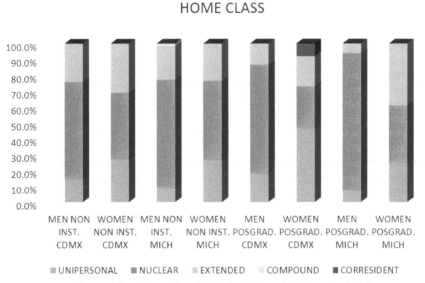

Figure 3.5 Home Class in Mexico City and Michoacán, 2016.
Source: Own elaboration based on ENIGH 2016.

In CDMX, the men who spend more time at home are those with a technical or normal career.

They do more study hours than they do in Michoacán. In caring hours, they spend an average of 30 hours caring for another person (children, the elderly, the sick, or the disabled) a week, while they spend an average of 13 hours in the state of Michoacán. In general, women spend an average of 25 hours doing housework against men who spend an average of 7 hours a week doing work.

3.3.3 Home Class

Within the household class, we find five classifications: single person, nuclear, co-resident, extended, and compound. A one-person household will be one in which the household will consist of a single person who is the head of the household; the nuclear home is formed with only one group (primary family member); in the extended one, the household is made up of the primary group plus other family groups or relatives; the compound has people from a nuclear or extended household with people who are not related to the head of the household; co-residents are households where the people who live in it are not related to the head of the family.

Table 3.2   Household members by educational level in Mexico.

Number of household members	
Formal education of the head of the household	Average
Non instruction	3
Preschool	4
Incomplete primary	4
Complete primary	4
Incomplete secondary	4
Complete secondary	4
Incomplete high school	4
Complete high school	4
Incomplete professional	3
Complete professional	3
Postgraduate	3

Note: Own elaboration based on ENIGH 2016.

If we now analyze the type of home in Mexico City and Michoacán, it is analyzed according to Table 3.2 and Figure 3.5 that most men tend to live more in nuclear homes and that the more studies they have, they tend to live in homes of this type. On the other hand, females, if they have less education, tend to live in nuclear homes, but the more education they have, they live in another type of home, such as a one-person home in the case of CDMX, or extended, as in the case of Michoacán.

As indicated in Table 3.2, the more studies there are, the lower the number of household members.

3.4 Conclusions

In order to calculate the human capital in the Mincer equation, this study first analyzed the information with data mining, later the regression was carried out by considering some other elements, such as the number of household members, minors, and type of household.

In this regression it is observed that the greatest influence on wages is the total number of household members, so we will consider that if this number is higher it will make it more difficult for wages, since the expenses will be more within the family. In second place is education, which in this sense we can take as human capital, being that if it develops it could positively contribute to a wage increase, not being the case if it does not have it. From this regression, the total number of minors is considered as a difficulty for a better salary.

If we consider the study by gender, the greatest difficulty in achieving a higher salary is in general the number of household members, in the indicators we analyze, but for them, it has a greater negative influence on the salary than for men. In addition, women are badly influenced by the number of hours dedicated to housework, the hours dedicated to caring for children and the elderly, since regardless of their educational level, in general, they dedicate the same number of hours, compared to men, who spend more time studying than they do.

Men can dedicate more time to work than women, so this is also reflected in women's wages.

Within the type of home that we analyze, we can observe that the higher-grade women have to live alone, but men, in general, regardless of their school grade, live in nuclear homes, that is, father, mother, and children. The more studies in general people have fewer members in their families. Marital status occurs mostly in people with less education, this is more notable in states not in the capital of the country.

We conclude that social conformation is presented as a difficulty to improve wages, within which having minors, the total number of members of a family, and the type of household directly influence wages, being they more affected than they.

References

Angulo, H., Rojas, M., & Velázquez, I. (2000). Rentabilidad de la inversión en capital humano en México Rentabilidad de la inversión en capital humano en México. *Economía Mexicana. Nueva Época*, *IX* (January 2000), 113–142.

Austria, M. A., & Venegas-Martínez, F. (2011). Rendimientos Privados de la Educación Superior en México en 2006. *El Trimestre Económico*, *LXXVIII*(2), 441–468. http://www.eltrimestreeconomico.com.mx/index.php/te/article/view/39/41

Becker, G. S. (1962). investment in Human Capital : A Theorytical Analysis. In *The Journal of Political Economy* (Vol. 70, Issue 5, pp. 9–49). https://doi.org/10.1086/258724

Benhabib, J., & Spiegel, M. (1994). The role of human capital in economic development. Evidence from aggregate cross-country data. *Journal of Monetary Economics*, *144*, 117–143. https://doi.org/10.1016/0304-3932(94)90047-7

Cabañete, A. (1997). La demanda de Educación Superior en el Sistema Público Catalán. Un modelo estructural de previsión de la demanda universitaria pública presencial en Cataluña. *Universitat Politécnica de Catalunya. Departament D'Organització D'Empreses.*

Calderon Sergio. (2015). Tendencias Globales en Capital Humano 2015. oderando en el nuevo mundo del trabajo. *Deloitte University Press*, 28–72. https://doi.org/www.tendencia@yeyee.com

Ehrenberg, R. G., & Smith, R. S. (2012). Modern Labor Economics Theory and Public Policy - Eleventh Edition. In *Journal of Chemical Information and Modeling* (Vol. 11). Prentice Hall. https://doi.org/10.1017/CBO97811 07415324.004

Falgueras, I. (2008). La teoría del capital humano: orígenes y evolución. *Temas Actuales de Economía, 2*, 17–48.

Francine, D., & Lawrence, M. (2016). The Gender Wage Gap: Extent, Trends, and Explanations. *IZA Discussion Papers, Institute for the Study of Labor (IZA), 9656*. https://www.econstor.eu/bitstream/10419/130341/1/dp9656. pdf

Gary S. Becker, Kevin M. Murphy, R. T. (1994). Economic Growth 1. *Human Capital: A Theoretical and Empirical Analysis with Special Reference to Education (3rd Edition), January*, 323–350. http://www.nber.org/chapter s/c11239

Ghaljahi, M., Rahdar, S., Almasi, S. Z., Ahmadi, S., & Igwegbe, C. A. (2018). Survey dataset on the externalizing self-esteem and gender effects on self-esteem subscales of students in Zabol University of Medical Sciences, Iran. *Data in Brief, 21*, 407–413. https://doi.org/10.1016/j.dib.2018.10.019

Hajian, S., Domingo-Ferrer, J., & Farràs, O. (2014). Generalization-based privacy preservation and discrimination prevention in data publishing and mining. In *Data Mining and Knowledge Discovery* (Vol. 28, Issues 5–6). https://doi.org/10.1007/s10618-014-0346-1

Heckman, J. J., Lochner, L. J., & Todd, P. E. (2013). Fifty Years of Mincer Earnings Regressions. *Journal of Chemical Information and Modeling, 53*(9), 1689–1699. https://doi.org/10.1017/CBO9781107415324.004

Herrero, P. P. (2000). Economía de la Educación: Una Disciplina Pedagógica en Pleno Desarrollo. *Ediciones Universidad de Salamanca, 12*, 143–158.

Hirsch, B., & Schnabel, C. (2012). Women Move Differently: Job Separations and Gender. *Journal of Labor Research, 33*(4), 417–442. https://doi.org/ 10.1007/s12122-012-9141-1

Humphreys, J. (2012). An alternative to the Mincer model of education The basic Mincer model. *University of Queensland, 1954*, 1–14.

Kido Cruz, A., & Kido Cruz, M. T. (2015). Modelos teóricos del capital humano y señalización: un estudio para México. *Contaduría y Administración*, *60*(4), 723–734. https://doi.org/10.1016/j.cya.2014.06.001

Koch, A., Nafziger, J., & Nielsen, H. S. (2015). Behavioral economics of education. *Journal of Economic Behavior and Organization*, *115*, 3–17. https://doi.org/10.1016/j.jebo.2014.09.005

Kredler, M. (2014). Vintage human capital and learning curves. *Journal of Economic Dynamics and Control*, *40*, 154–178. https://doi.org/10.1016/j.jedc.2014.01.003

Lächler, U. (1999). Education and Earnings Inequality in Mexico. *The World Bank, Policy Research Working Paper Series: 1949, 1999, July 1998*. http://search.proquest.com/docview/56203232?accountid=17248

Lauwo, S. (2018). Challenging Masculinity in CSR Disclosures: Silencing of Women's Voices in Tanzania's Mining Industry. *Journal of Business Ethics*, *149*(3), 689–706. https://doi.org/10.1007/s10551-016-3047-4

Lee, J.-W., & Lee, H. (2016). Human capital in the long run. *Journal of Development Economics*, *122*, 147–169. https://doi.org/10.1016/j.jdeveco.2016.05.006

Lopez-Acevedo, G. (2001). Evolution of Earnings and Rates of Returns to Education in Mexico. *The World Bank, Policy Research Working Paper 2691, October*.

López-Acevedo, G., Tinajero, M., & Rubio, M. (2005). Mexico: Human Capital Effects On Wages And Productivity. *World Bank Policy Research Working Paper*, *3791*. http://siteresources.worldbank.org/EXTLACREGT OPPOVANA/Resources/SkoufiasProgresaanditsimpactonhumancapitala ndthewelfareofhh.pdf

López, S. L., & Almagro, a C. (2005). Economía de la educación: capital humano y rendimiento educativo. *Análisis Económico*, 79–106. http://www.analisiseconomico.com.mx/pdf/3604.pdf

Machin, S. (2014). Developments in economics of education research. *Labour Economics*, *30*, 13–19. https://doi.org/10.1016/j.labeco.2014.06.003

Mason, A., Lee, R., & Jiang, J. X. (2016). Demographic dividends, human capital, and saving. *Journal of the Economics of Ageing*, *7*, 106–122. https://doi.org/10.1016/j.jeoa.2016.02.004

Miciula, I. (2016). The Measurement of Human Capital Methods. *Folia Oeconomica Stetinensia*, *16*(1). https://doi.org/10.1515/foli-2016-0003

Ministerio de Educación Cultura y Deporte. (2015). *Panorama de la Educación. Indicadores de la OCDE 2015.* http://www.mecd.gob.es/dctm/ine e/internacional/panorama-de-la-educacion-2015.-informe-espanol.pdf?d ocumentId=0901e72b81ee9fa3

Morduchowicz, A. (2004). *Discusiones de economia de la educación.* http: //unesdoc.unesco.org/images/0015/001507/150777so.pdf

OCDE. (2007). *Capital humano: Cómo moldea tu vida lo que sabes. Resumen en español.* 1–7. http://www.oecd.org/insights/38435951.pdf

Perri, T. (2016). Online education, signaling, and human capital. *Information Economics and Policy, 36,* 69–74. https://doi.org/10.1016/j.infoecopol.2 016.06.001

Petreski, M., Blazevski, N. M., & Petreski, B. (2014). Gender Wage Gap when Women are Highly Inactive: Evidence from Repeated Imputations with Macedonian Data. *Journal of Labor Research, 35*(4), 393–411. https: //doi.org/10.1007/s12122-014-9189-1

Psacharopoulos, G. (1994). Returns to investment in education: A global update. *World Development, 22*(9), 1325–1343. https://doi.org/10.101 6/0305-750X(94)90007-8

Psacharopoulos, G. (1995). The Profitability of Investment in Education: Concepts and Methods. *Human Capital Develpment and Operations Policy. HCO. Working Papers,* 1–22. https://doi.org/10.1017/CBO978110741 5324.004

Rahayu, D., Ismail, M., Santoso, D. B., & Pratomo, D. S. (2015). Do Natural Resources and Human Capital Matter to Regional Income Convergence? (A Case Study at Regencies/Municipalities of Kalimantan Area – Indonesia). *Procedia - Social and Behavioral Sciences, 211,* 1112–1116. https: //doi.org/10.1016/j.sbspro.2015.11.148

Refrigeri, L., & Aleandri, G. (2014). The Economics of Education as Educational Science. *Procedia - Social and Behavioral Sciences, 116,* 2059–2063. https://doi.org/10.1016/j.sbspro.2014.01.519

Rustiadi, S. (2015). Creating Better Education System, Building Stronger Human Capital: A Creative Industries Perspective. *Procedia - Social and Behavioral Sciences, 169*(August 2014), 378–386. https://doi.org/10.101 6/j.sbspro.2015.01.323

Salas, M. (2002). Cuatro décadas en economía de la educación. *Revista de Educación, 328,* 427–449. http://www.educacionyfp.gob.es/dam/jcr: 399c556a-58ea-467e-861d-f27e6fa96f1d/re3282310861-pdf.pdf

Schultz, T. W. (1960). Capital Formation by Education. *Journal of Political Economy, 68*(6), 571–583. https://doi.org/10.1086/258393

Schultz, T. W. (1961). *Investment in Human Capital* (p. 17). The American Economic Review.

Seoane, M. J. F., & Álvarez, M. T. (2010). Las ecuaciones de Mincer y las tasas de rendimiento de la educación en Galicia. *Asociación de Economía de La Educación, Chapter 14 in Investigaciones de Economía de La Educación, Vol. 5*, 285–304.

Tinoco, C., & Soler, S. (2011). Aspectos generales del concepto "capital humano." *Revista Criterio Libre*, *9*(14), 203–226.

Unesco. (2009). Indicadores de la educación Especificaciones técnicas. *UNESCO Institute for Statistics*, 10. http://www.uis.unesco.org/Library/Documents/eiguide09-es.pdf

Vandenberghe, V. (1999). Economics of education. The need to go beyond human capital theory and production-function analysis. *Educational Studies*, *25*(2), 129–143. https://doi.org/10.1080/03055699997864

Velázquez Valadez, G. (2004). Las organizaciones y el capital humano. *Liderazgo Del Tercer Milenio Opciones Para Aumentar La Productividad*, 82–88. http://www.mundosigloxxi.ciecas.ipn.mx/pdf/v03/09/05.pdf

4

Household Conditions for Remote Work in the Quaternary Sector in Mexico

Ingrid Nineth Pinto López, Cynthia M. Montaudon Tomas, Alicia L. Yáñez Moneda, and Claudia Malcón Cervera

Department of Business Intelligence, Business School, UPAEP University, Mexico

Abstract

The conditions of homes for remote work employees in the quaternary sector have had during the period of confinement imposed by the COVID-19 pandemic in Mexico are analyzed. A scale is developed, validated, and applied to 1026 workers in the quaternary sector in 27 states of the Mexican Republic. The results allow for analyzing the emotional, financial, space, privacy, and furniture conditions in which people are carrying out remote work, as well as areas of opportunity to prevent effects on health and work productivity.

Keywords: Remote work, COVID-19, quaternary sector, Mexico

4.1 Introduction

The declaration of a state of emergency caused by the global health crisis derived from COVID-19 forced the adoption of a series of extraordinary and urgent measures to preserve the health of the population and the continuity of business activities (Ruíz, 2021).

The disrupting nature of confinement measures meant that a significant proportion of workers had to adapt to remote work and migrate their professional activities from the office to the home. The challenge of remote work from home implied that they faced diverse and, in some cases, adverse situations such as adapting the home to carry out professional activities, time and task management, and the unprecedented fusion of work and family life (Montaudon et al., 2021).

In Mexico, the declaration of phase three due to the COVID-19 pandemic reduced the mobility of people and implied the suspension of face-to-face activities in companies, government organizations, and those considered non-essential. Therefore, most organizations saw the need to migrate to remote work. The challenges were enormous because migration to telework for many organizations seemed distant, and employees very abruptly faced the need to use technological platforms as a means of contact, communication, and coordination with their work teams (Guarded, 2021).

This chapter aims to analyze the conditions for remote work in the homes of workers in the quaternary sector in Mexico. The study analyzes two dimensions, household conditions and effects on employment and income. The data collection was carried out between 5 and 8 months after employees moved their professional activities home, allowing a period of adaptation to the new normal. To carry out the analysis, 1,026 surveys were applied to workers in the quaternary sector. The results allow for evaluating under what conditions the employees worked during this period, as well as identifying areas of opportunity for a modality that, at least partially, will be maintained in the future.

4.2 Background

4.2.1 Research in the field of remote work

Research on the topic of remote work shows a growing trend in recent years. A bibliometric analysis carried out with information from the SCOPUS data repository from 1971 to 2022 shows that 1,945 scientific documents have been published, of which 32.65% are open access. It stands out that 44.98% have been published from 2020 to 2022, during the COVID-19 pandemic (ELSEVIER, 2021). The annual distribution of the publications is shown in Figure 4.1.

As shown in Figure 4.1, from 1970 to 2019, an average of 21.83 publications were published per year, having some peaks in 2012 with 60 publications, 2016 with 62, and 2019 with 71 publications. Although a growing trend is observed in these years, the period from 2020 to 2022 shows an unusual growth that goes up to 619 publications in 2021, with an average of publications per year of 291.66 in this last period.

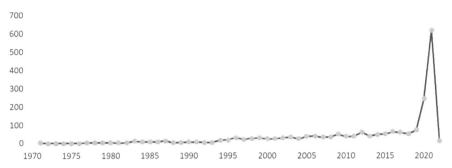

Figure 4.1 Annual distributions of the publications.

Source: Elaborated by the authors with data from Scopus obtained on December 13, 2021.

The publications are classified mainly into articles (61.49%), conference papers (24.42%), book chapters (5.14%), and reviews (5.03%); some of the publications exceed a thousand citations.

Publications on remote work are mainly made in the areas of social sciences (35.27%), computer science (28.33%), business, management, and accounting (25.19%), engineering (20.77%), medicine (12.03%), and psychology (9.25%). The countries that have published the most publications are the United States (28.89%), the United Kingdom (6.17%), Japan (5.60%), Canada (5.55%), Australia (4.99%), and Germany (4.78%). A large number of organizations are involved in research, mainly universities, from which the following stand out: Tampere University (0.77%), Radboud University (0.77%), Rensselaer Polytechnic Institute (0.77%), Lally School of Management (0.77%), The University of Sydney (0.72%), University of Melbourne (0.72%), and Georgia Institute of Technology (0.66%).

4.2.2 Remote work

Work has changed significantly in recent years, and it was as a result of the COVID-19 pandemic that a new classification of workers was created (Montaudon et al., 2021; World Economic Forum, 2020), represented in three categories:

a) Essential workers, whose jobs are linked to maintaining safety, health, and well-being. It includes frontline workers whose jobs were not suspended due to the pandemic.

b) Displaced workers whose jobs have been suspended or limited due to sanitary conditions.

c) Remote workers, referring to employees who work outside the company's facilities; those who can work remotely and keep their jobs when migrating to work from home because they have the basic conditions of internet access.

Remote work is recognized as a flexible form of work (Olivier, 2020); the International Labor Organization (ILO, 2020) defines it as *"the use of information and communication technologies to work outside the employer's facilities"*.

Remote work, under normal conditions, entails several benefits for workers, organizations, and society in general (Pérez & Gálvez, 2009). Regarding workers, some advantages are that the work is done without a specific location or time, and people can work at any time and place (Montaudon-Tomas et al., 2021). It allows for a better balance between work, family, and personal life, increases flexibility and productivity, and reduces commuting times (Osio, 2010). As for organizations, they become more agile, flexible, and competitive, in addition to reducing some fixed costs such as light, electricity, heating, and physical spaces, among others (Buffer, 2019). Remote work also contributes to the environment by reducing traffic congestion, improving housing conditions, and avoiding overcrowding in cities. In terms of equality, remote work allows the insertion of people with some disabilities into the labor world, among others (Osio, 2010; Buffer, 2019).

The health crisis derived from the COVID-19 pandemic and the forced migration to remote work significantly reduced the advantages of this type of flexible work which was not favorable for everyone because the potential of remote work varies substantially due to the infrastructure available to support online activities (Montaudon-Tomas et al., 2021).

In Mexico, around 72% of workers worked remotely after the confinement measures (Statista, 2020).

4.2.3 Quaternary sector

The economic sectors are the division of the economic activity of a state or territory and are classified as primary, secondary, tertiary, quaternary, and quinary (Kenessey, 1987).

Due to the growing importance of information, the existence of a newer economy sector is considered, the quaternary, which complements the three traditional sectors, primary, secondary, and tertiary (Sueli, 2015). The quaternary sector groups activities related to the intangible value of information, encompassing the management and distribution of said information.

Particularly, the quaternary sector groups economic activities based on knowledge, which are impossible to mechanize, such as the generation and exchange of information, innovation, technology, consulting, education, research and development, and financial planning, among other services or intellectual activities (Rosenberg, 2020).

In general, the quaternary sector includes all activities related to the development and research of new information and communication technologies that are applied to all sectors of the economy and lead in scientific-technological research that is directed towards the reduction of costs, taking advantage of markets, the production of innovative ideas, and new production and manufacturing methods, among others (Sueli, 2015).

4.3 Methodology

4.3.1 Investigation process

The collection of primary data that support this investigation was carried out in the months of August to November 2020, between 5 and 8 months after the confinement measures, and especially isolation at home were enforced by the authorities of the Health Secretariat in Mexico and abided by the 32 states of the Mexican Republic. It is important to mention that, when the data was collected, the workers were used to remote work as they had been carrying it out for a few months.

4.3.2 Research design

The research is quantitative with a non-experimental cross-sectional descriptive design. It is non-experimental with a descriptive scope (Hernández-Sampieri et al., 2108) since its purpose is to analyze the conditions of homes for remote work in employees of the quaternary sector in Mexico from a set of variables and estimate its occurrence. It is cross-sectional because data collection was carried out in a single period of time in a representative sample of the population (Ibidem). The sampling technique is non-probabilistic through the design of a scale sent by electronic means.

4.3.3 Scale and sample

The variables analyzed in this research correspond to a subset of data from a scale developed for a much larger study that assesses the conditions and effects of remote work in different dimensions of professional and personal life in workers who, derived from the health emergency, moved their professional activities to a telework modality (Montaudon-Tomas et al., 2021). The designed scale is made up of several dimensions, namely: effects on employment, income, and spending; conditions in homes; access to technology and digital skills; time and task management; job performance; workplace health and wellness; family relationships, and; the future of remote work.

The dimensions of working from home conditions and effects on employment and income are analyzed in this study, considering only workers from the quaternary sector. Thirty-two variables are analyzed, including classification data, dichotomous questions, multiple-choice questions, and questions on a 7-point Likert scale.

4.3.4 Validación

The sample for the complete study was collected in Mexico between August and November 2020; it consists of 1026 observations with 32 variables.

The validation of the scale was carried out with Cronbach's alpha (Quero, 2010), yielding a result of 0.9235, which shows that it is highly reliable. According to George & Mallery (2003), values above 0.9 have excellent weighting. The software used to perform the calculation is STATA (see Table 4.1).

4.4 Results and Analysis

The classification data shows that the average age of the participants is 45.29 years old with a range of 18–79 years old. 56.68% correspond to the female gender, 42.93% to the male gender, and 0.39% prefer not to specify. Regarding marital status, 55.12% are married, 31.32% single, 1.66% widowed, 6.93% divorced, and 4.98% common-law union.

The participants are located in 27 of the 32 states of the Mexican Republic, and the participation percentage in each state is shown in Figure 4.2. 53.66% of the participants are located in the central region, 25.56% in the northeast region, 15.51% in the western region, 3.22% in the southeast, and 2.05% in the northwest region.

A Likert scale of 7 assigned values is used, as observed in Table 4.2. The results of the indicators formulated on a Likert scale are presented in Table 4.3. The mean, standard deviation, and level of agreement or disagreement are included for each item. For the level of disagreement, the values from 1 to 3 are grouped, and for the level of agreement, the values from 5 to 7

Table 4.1 Cronbach's alpha results.

Item	Indicator	Code	Cronbach's alpha
1	Age	Age	0.9237
2	Gender	Gender	0.9241
3	Marital status	Status	0.9243
4	Place of residence	State	0.9243
5	Sector in which they are employed	Sector	0.9242
6	Square meters of the house	House_mts	0.9238
7	You have an adequate space to carry out work from home	Space_house	0.9223
8	Number of people in your household who work and/or study from home during the pandemic	Workhome_total	0.9240
9	You feel like you have more digital distractions than when you were in the office	Distraction	0.9222
10	Sometimes the noise from the house or the noise from the environment is annoying or affects your work performance	Noise	0.9215
11	The furniture you have at home is ergonomic or is prepared to work several hours at a computer	Furniture	0.9229
12	You consider that you can organize yourself well by working from home	Organization_home	0.9220
13	Since working from home, you feel that you work more	Works_more	0.9234
14	You have had to do work even on weekends	Works_weekend	0.9226
15	You feel more tired working from home	Tiredness	0.9213
16	You feel distracted more often than at the office	More_distraction	0.9214
17	You have had a harder time staying motivated	Motivation	0.9212
18	You feel more stressed working from home	More_stressed	0.9207
19	Has had to attend to family matters during work hours	Family_issues	0.9226
20	Even working from home, you have been able to create a separation between time for work and time for family	Separation_time	0.9224
21	You consider that some members of your family have invaded your workspace	Invasion	0.9214
22	Certain expenses have increased at home since the family nucleus works and/or studies from home	More_expenses	0.9226

Table 4.1   Continued.

Item	Indicator	Code	Cronbach's alpha
23	Even after the pandemic ends, you would like to continue working from home	Continue	0.9226
24	You have to help the children in their school activities	Help_children	0.9241
25	Does working from home feel like you lack privacy?	Privacy	0.9216
26	Do you have a room where you can close the door to avoid distractions during video conferencing?	Closed_room	0.9229
27	Do you use a screen or place yourself in a background that prevents other participants in video conferences from seeing your home?	Screen	0.9238
28	What happened to your job during the pandemic?	Employment	0.9240
29	What happened to your income during the pandemic?	Income	0.9237
30	What happened to your benefits during the pandemic?	Benefits	0.9239
31	You have had to turn to someone else's support to help you with your children	Support_children	0.9240
32	How many members of your family share the internet?	Internet_share	0.9238

Table 4.2   Likert scale values.

Value	Interpretation
7	Completely in agreement
6	In agreement
5	Partially in agreement
4	Neither in agreement nor disagreement
3	Partially in disagreement
2	In disagreement
1	Completely in disagreement

are grouped; the value 4 is considered neutral. Table 4.4 groups the indicators formulated as dichotomous questions.

4.4.1 Conditions in the home analysis

The number of people who cohabit in one house is on average 3.42, of which on average 2.57 people work and/or study. If the other members of the family

Table 4.3 Results for each indicator.

Indicator	Mean	Standard deviation	Level of agreement (%)		
			Disagreement (1–3)	Neutral (4)	Agreement (5–7)
You have an adequate space to carry out work from home	5.42	1.79	16.39	10.14	73.46
You feel like you have more digital distractions than when you were in the office	3.92	2.26	43.55	11.62	44.82
Sometimes the noise from the house or the noise from the environment is annoying or affects your work performance	4.45	2.18	34.63	11.80	53.56
The furniture you have at home is ergonomic or is prepared to work several hours at a computer	3.46	2.27	55.02	9.65	35.31
You consider that you can organize yourself well by working from home	5.41	1.68	13.17	14.43	72.39
Since working from home, you feel that you work more	6.18	1.47	6.15	6.63	87.12
You have had to do work even on weekends	5.94	1.69	10.25	6.05	83.69
You feel more tired working from home	5.13	2.06	22.14	9.85	68.00
You feel distracted more often than at the office	3.92	2.26	43.45	13.76	42.77
You have had a harder time staying motivated	4.27	2.20	36.29	12.87	50.82
You feel more stressed working from home	4.18	2.28	38.90	14.56	46.53
Has had to attend to family matters during work hours	4.32	2.28	36.48	10.63	52.88

Table 4.3   Continued.

Indicator	Mean	Standard deviation	Level of agreement (%)		
			Disagreement (1–3)	Neutral (4)	Agreement (5–7)
Even working from home, you have been able to create a separation between time for work and time for family	4.67	2.09	28.00	16.19	55.80
You consider that some members of your family have invaded your workspace	2.87	2.15	63.18	11.91	24.90
Certain expenses have increased at home since the family nucleus works and/or studies from home	4.89	2.20	26.10	11.14	62.75
Even after the pandemic ends, you would like to continue working from home	4.41	2.24	31.31	16.97	51.70

Table 4.4   Dichotomous questions.

Indicator	Yes (%)	No (%)
Do you have children?	65.2	34.8
Does working from home feel like you lack privacy?	44.49	55.51
Do you have a room where you can close the door to avoid distractions during video conferencing?	72.59	27.41
Do you use a screen or place yourself in a background that prevents other participants in video conferences from seeing your home?	50.15	49.85

who live in the same home are also considered, such as young children or older adults, on average, 3.27 people per household share the internet.

Regarding the size of the homes, the average is 165.51 square meters in a range of 50 to 1600 square meters.

65.5% of the participants have children, of which 50.67% study in private institutions, 31.63 in public institutions, and 17.69 in public and private institutions; the average number of children is 1.34. 13.29% of the participants stated that they had resorted to the support of someone to help them with their children. 52.88% claim to attend to family matters during work hours.

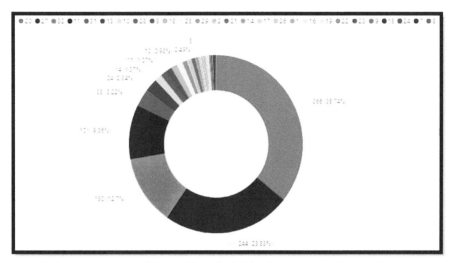

Figure 4.2 Distribution by state.

Source: Developed by the authors. Abbreviations: 1. Aguascalientes, 2. Baja California, 5. Chiapas, 7. Coahuila de Zaragoza, 8. Colima, 9. Durango, 10. Estado de México, 11. Estado de México, 13. Hidalgo, 14. Jalisco, 15. Michoacán de Ocampo, 16. Morelos, 17. Nayarit, 18. Nuevo León, 19. Oaxaca, 20. Puebla, 21. Querétaro, 22. Quintana Roo, 23. San Luis Potosí, 24. Sinaloa, 25. Sonora, 26. Tabasco, 27. Tamaulipas, 28. Tlaxcala, 29. Veracruz de la Llave, 31. Zacatecas, 32. Ciudad de México CDMX.

Among the positive things, most participants stated that they have an adequate space to carry out work from home, including a room where they can close the door to avoid distractions during videoconferences. They can organize themselves well, and even working from home, they have been able to create a separation between time for work and time for family. Even after the pandemic and confinement measures end, they would like to continue working from home.

Among the negative things is that most of the participants state that the noise from the house or the noise from the environment affects their work performance; that the furniture they work with at home is inadequate; that they work longer, even on weekends; feel more tired; are more frequently distracted; it is difficult for them to stay motivated; they lack privacy, and use a screen or are placed in a background that prevents other participants in the videoconferences from seeing their home.

4.4.2 Analysis of the effects on employment and income

Regarding employment, 30.15% of the participants state that their employment remained the same with a few hours from home, 63.02% stated that they moved entirely to remote work, 2.24% lost their job, and 4.59% did not answer the question.

Regarding income, 72.68% of the participants stated that it remained the same, 3.12% said it increased, 21.17% stated that their income decreased, 1.76% lost their income, and 1.27% did not answer the question. Regarding benefits, 73.12% stated that they remained the same, 18.48% said they were reduced, 1.37% stated they increased, 4.2% lost them, and 2.83% did not answer the question. 62.75% of the participants state that their expenses have increased since they work at home.

4.5 Conclusion

There are both pros and cons to this study. The pros of the study are it stands out that most of the participants state that they have an adequate space to carry out work from home; a room where they can close the door to avoid distractions; they can organize themselves well; they have managed, even working from home, to create a separation between time for work and time for family; and most would like to continue working from home.

However, the cons of the study are that, for most of the participants, the noise from the house or the environment affects their work performance; the furniture they work with is inadequate; they work longer, even on weekends; feel more tired; are more frequently distracted; it is difficult for them to stay motivated; they use screens or backgrounds to prevent their home from being seen.

It is relevant to acknowledge that employees in the quaternary sector had the best conditions to adapt to remote work even before the pandemic and a general background in the use of information and communication technologies. Nevertheless, other sectors such as the primary, secondary and tertiary, were not in a favorable position regarding digital skills. Therefore, it will be essential to analyze the future of jobs in this sector and the new ways of working because there is a widening gap regarding jobs in the quaternary sector.

In Mexico, remote work increased with the arrival of the COVID-19 pandemic, but until then, it had not been regulated. It was until January 2020 that the reforms to the legislation were done, specifically to article 311 of the Federal Labor Law in the areas of teleworking and home office, which specified the responsibilities of both employees and employers (STPS, 2020) concerning remote work. Regulations have supported remote work and provided the basis for organizations to continue promoting more flexible work arrangements, so that remote and hybrid working conditions can be maintained in the long run.

References

Buffer. (2019). State of Remote Work. https://buffer.com/state-of-remote-wo rk-2019

George, D., Mallery, P. (2003). *SPSS for Windows step by step: A Simple Guide and Reference.* 4a. ed. Boston: Ayllyn and Bacon.

Guardado, S. C. (2021). COVID-19 en México: Reflexión del teletrabajo en tiempo de pandemia. UNAM. https://virtual.cuautitlan.unam.mx/rudics/?p =3269

ELSEVIER. (2021). Scopus. https://www.elsevier.com/es-mx/solutions/sco pus

Foro Económico Mundial. (2020). The Future of Jobs Report 2020. World Economic Forum, Geneva, Switzerland. https://www.weforum.org/report s/the-future-of-jobsreport-2020

Hernández-Sampieri, R., Mendoza-Torres, C. P. (2018). *Metodología de la Investigación.* McGrawHill

Kennesey, Z. (1987). The primary, secondary, tertiary, and quaternary sectors of economy. Obtenido de: https://onlinelibrary.wiley.com/doi/10.1111/j. 1475-4991.1987.tb00680.x

KPMG. (2021). Teletrabajo en México: retos para su implementación. https: //home.kpmg/mx/es/home/tendencias/2021/04/teletrabajo-en-mexico-reto s-para-su-implementacion.html

Montaudon, C. M., Pinto, I. N., Olivera, E., Amsler, A. (2021*). Estado del tra- bajo remoto en México durante la pandemia de COVID-19.* Observatorio de Competitividad y Nuevas Formas de Trabajo, UPAEP Universidad.

Montaudon-Tomas, C. M., Pinto-López, I. N., Yáñez-Moneda, A. L., Amsler, A. (2021). The Effects of Remote Work on Family Relationships. Chapter in Future of Work, Work-Family Satisfaction, and Employee Well-Being in the Fourth Industrial Revolution. IGI Global.

Olivier, R. (2020). Llega la era del trabajo flexible. *Capital Humano,* 356, 105-111.

Organización Internacional del Trabajo OIT. (2020). El teletrabajo durante la pandemia de COVID-19 y después de ella.

Osio, L. (2010). El teletrabajo: Una opción en la era digital. *Observatorio Laboral Revista Venezolana,* 3(5), 93-109.

Quero, M. (2010). Confiabilidad y coeficiente Alpha de Cronbach. *Telos,* 12(2), 248-252.

Rosenberg, M. (2020). The 5 Sectors of the Economy. Obtenido de: https://www.thoughtco.com/sectors-of-the-economy-1435795

Statista. (2020). Porcentaje de empleados que trabajaron en casa durante el confinamiento en México en junio de 2020. Obtenido de: https://es.statist a.com/estadisticas/1147384/porcentaje-empleados-home-office-mexico/

Sueli, A. (2015). Mercadotecnia, servicios y usuarios de información: Sector cuaternario y las bibliotecas. UNAM. https://www.redalyc.org/jatsRepo/2 85/28543667002/movil/index.html

Secretaría del Trabajo y Previsión Social STPS. (2020). Entra en vigor reforma que regula el teletrabajo en México. https://www.gob.mx/stps/ prensa/entra-en-vigor-reforma-que-regula-el-teletrabajo-en-mexico

5

Organizational Management Systems: An Analysis in Higher Education

Azeneth Irazú, Franco-Bravo, María Alicia Zavala-Berbena

Universidad La Salle Bajío, Mexico

Abstract

Organizational management systems have contributed to the processes of Higher Education Institutions (HEI), to the extent they are considered to be organizational entities applying the principles and procedures of management for the continuous improvement of their substantive processes. The purpose of this chapter consists of assessing the status of the art of scientific production over the management systems in the HEI by providing a description of their evolution in the two most recent decades, the analysis of the concurrence of keywords of the texts, the assessment of the content and the categorization of the subject area of their study courses. All of this allowed the characterization and assertion of its development as an emergent construct to become visible within the field of knowledge. The methodology developed as a bibliometric analysis of the journals of the Web of Science from 2000 to 2021, instrumented using the Vos Viewer software, considering the following descriptors: "Management System" AND "Higher Education" NOT "Learning." Resulting from this search, 136 articles were found, which explained the growth of the amount of literature within the time frame specified. Then, a network analysis was carried out using the keywords of the texts, which brought a set of conceptual structures over the management systems in the HEIs. Also, a content analysis of the journals was performed, which generated a categorization based on its subject matter relationship. The results highlighted a growing tendency of the scientific literature of the area and the targeting of greater interest and relevance, which may be considered as a reflection of the initiatives of the institutions for testing organizational management models and providing follow-up to the immediate and future impacts of their practical implementation. The findings are highly relevant for researchers interested in exploring new approaches to organizational management systems and developing future research allowing to move forward in the understanding of the educational phenomenon.

Keywords: Organizational management systems, universities, Mexico

5.1 Introduction

The literature regarding organizational management systems in higher education has greatly increased showing its relevance over organizational practices causing different effects in their substantive functions. In the case of higher education institutions (HEIs), management entails two substantial action fields: the one defined as an educational entity, and the one that is doing it as an organizational entity.

As educational bodies, the HEIs comply with substantive teaching, research, and extension functions, which are supported by procedure functions, among which process management are included and which are carried out to achieve their mission. Regarding the organizational field, management has a greater connotation in terms of the principles of administration and control, subject to the strategic framework.

This implies that a management system is a tool for harnessing and lining up the finer elements of organizational actions and resources toward attaining the maximum goals (Kaplan & Norton, 2007). With that in mind, organizational management is offered as a polysemantic concept addressing different fields of organizational action. Even though it concludes the internal action of resources and participants, to a functional strategic level (Hofer & Shendel, 1978), the orientation regarding the results may be variable, which may be materialized in the structuring of value chains in order to achieve competitive advantages (Porter, 1985, 1990). Additionally, the HEIs are oriented toward intangible issues, such as management of knowledge (Nonaka & Takeuchi, 1999) or toward the essential needs of the organization (Prahalad & Hamel, 1990). It is thus confirmed that the intention of organizational management is to direct all performance efforts toward organizing the goals set out by the organizations.

This organic and business vision used to operate the management systems has reached the educational institutions, conceived also as value units that shall provide outflows to address specific expectations and demands of the environment in which they are inserted. It is possible that, because of that, they are adopting models regarding organizational management, initially designed for the productive sector, for the sake of improving their internal operation, which includes issues such as financial, processes, structural, and contributors. In this vein, management systems may be built-in for this sector to achieve improvements in education, linkage, and other services. However, the intangibility and successive effects are characteristic of a service such as education, enabling more complex understanding and structuring of management systems, which are linked to both, internal issues (processes, capacities, and resources), as well as external issues (product, market, and environment), material and immaterial. From this, it follows the necessity that they may be studied from different disciplinary fields, broadening the theoretical and methodological perspectives from which they are addressed.

The intention of literature regarding management systems in HEIs is to provide consistency and systematization, perspectives, and approaches addressed by scholars in the field. For that, a revision of the scientific literature in the Web of Science (WOS) from 2000 to 2021, in order to achieve state-of-the-art scientific production regarding the management systems in HEIs through the description of its evolution in the last two decades, the analysis of concurrency of keywords of texts, content analysis, and categorization of subject areas of study.

5.2 Method

In order to achieve the goal, variables such as central theoretical construction were considered over management systems and their field of application: higher education institutions. With this in mind, the keywords, and logical operators "management system*" AND "higher education*" NOT "learning," were entered into the database of the Web of Science (WOS). The search was filtered by the following specialty fields: "Education", "Educational Research" or "Business" or "Public Administration" or "Management", limiting the search to "articles," "articles subject to revision," or "early access." The search was directed to all the fields of the publication and the term "learning" was excluded in order to refine the results of the topics related to the administrative and organizational field of management systems; rather than, the pedagogical or didactic order. Under this scheme, the acquisition of 136 scientific texts within WOS was produced during the period from 2000 to 2021.

The survey was intended to respond to two research questions:

a) What is the tendency of scientific production regarding the management systems within HEIs? For that, the Vos Viewer Software was used in order to get indicators based on the keywords and co-occurrences.
b) Which are the contextual or thematic fields being addressed by the surveys of management systems within the HEIs? Over which the analysis of the content of analysis was generated, in order to later on relating them by affinity and identifying converging subjects in literature.

5.3 Results

5.3.1 Trending of scientific production on management systems in HEIs

According to the issue dates and the classification by research area, the literature regarding management systems of HEIs has increased in the last five years, being more abundant in the areas of education and educational research (see Figure 5.1). The above may be considered to be a reflection that higher education institutions were becoming interested in experimenting with organizational management models allowing to provide follow-up to their substantive functions through organizational displays explaining the achievement of their goals (García, 2016), directing toward promoting their permanence in a highly competed and challenging context (Escorcia y Barros, 2020).

Second, it has been found that the business and economics area has had considerable growth. The management systems, surveyed from these areas, resume on the importance of economic management of the company, including the financial and optimization obstacles of processes and resources to reach their goals efficiently. This sustains a double complexion in managing the HEIs; that is linked to the substantive services that an educational agency shall provide, but also, that encasing it as an entity sowing challenges of any organizational entity.

However, despite the fact there is an increase in the volume of the relevant literature, scientific production is still a little scarce if it is considered that the greatest production framework (2015 to 2020) barely reaches an average of 16.4 of the yearly publications.

Regarding the works reported within this period, Table 5.1 shows the authors and publications of greater relevance, considering the number of mentions acquired.

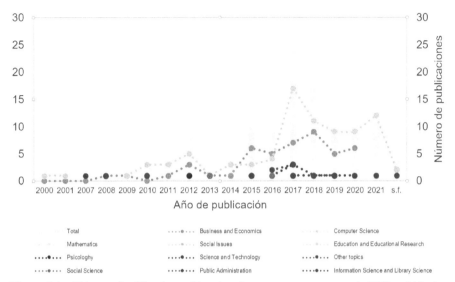

Figure 5.1 Volume of publications addressing the management systems in HEIs, within the period between 2000 and 2021.

Note: Own compilation based on data from the Web of Science research on September 1, 2021.

The articles of authors with the greatest impact in the area are directed toward the analysis and implementation of management systems of the performance of college workers (Decramer, Smolders, & Vanderstraeten, 2013); meanwhile, some other works are outlined, which show a critical position of scholars related to the means and resources to measure their work and scenarios behind the said procedures (Kallio, Kallio, Tienari, & Hyvönen, 2016; Martin-Sardesai, & Guthrie, 2018). Also, there are some articles with topics specialized in the management of knowledge and components, such as its creation, consolidation, distribution, and combination, which are explained by the specific functions of the higher education institutions (Sein-Echaluce, Abadía-Valle, Bueno-García, & Fidalgo-Blanco, 2017).

Aside from the works largely quoted, the analysis of the bibliometric networks generated from the keywords used was carried out.

Figure 5.2 shows the network diagram including a color scale mapping the prevalence of the subject of study over the management systems in the latest decades.

Figure 5.2 shows how thematic cores related to the keywords "higher education," "performance," "management," "implementation," "model," and

Table 5.1   The most quoted works in the literature on the management systems in the HEIs reported in the period between 2000 and 2021.

Authors	Name of publication	Year	Count of mentions
Decramer, A; Smolders, C; Vanderstraeten, A	Employee performance management culture and system features in higher education: relationship with employee performance management satisfaction	2013	155
Decramer, A; Smolders, C; Vanderstraeten, A; Christiaens, J	The Impact of Institutional Pressures on Employee Performance Management Systems in Higher Education in the Low Countries	2012	84
Kallio, KM; Kallio, TJ; Tienari, J; Hyvonen, T	Ethos at stake: Performance management and academic work in universities	2016	82
Decramer, A; Smolders, C; Vanderstraeten, A; Christiaens, J; Desmidt, S	External pressures affecting the adoption of employee performance management in higher education institutions	2012	68
Bauwens, R; Audenaert, M; Huisman, J; Decramer, A	Performance management fairness and burnout: implications for organizational citizenship behaviors	2019	61
Manatos, MJ; Sarrico, CS; Rosa, MJ	The integration of quality management in higher education institutions: a systematic literature review	2017	55
Hamid, S; Ijab, MT; Sulaiman, H; Anwar, RM; Norman, AA	Social media for environmental sustainability awareness in higher education	2017	54
Sein-Echaluce, ML; Abadia-Valle, AR; Bueno-Garcia, C; Fidalgo-Blanco, A	Interaction of Knowledge Spirals to Create Ontologies for An Institutional Repository of Educational Innovation Best Practices	2017	51
Martin-Sardesai, A; Guthrie, J	Human capital loss in an academic performance measurement system Human capital loss in an academic performance measurement system	2018	44
Stensaker, B; Norgard, JD	Innovation and isomorphism: A case study of university identity struggle 1969–1999	2001	38
Poli, M; Pardini, S; Passarelli, I; Citti, I; Cornolti, D; Picano, E	The 4A's improvement approach: a case study based on UNI EN ISO 9001:2008	2015	37

Table 5.1 Continued.

Authors	Name of publication	Year	Count of mentions
Thunnissen, M; Van Arensbergen, P	A multi-dimensional approach to talent An empirical analysis of the definition of talent in Dutch academia	2015	36
Wang, M; Morley, MJ; Cooke, FL; Xu, JP; Bian, HM	Scholars, strategists, or stakeholders? Competing rationalities and impact of performance evaluation for academic managers in Chinese universities	2018	33

Note: Own compilation as of the data acquired from the Web of Science with a search date on September 1, 2021.

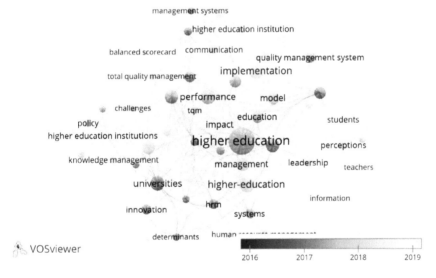

Figure 5.2 Network diagram of co-occurrences by keywords in the literature regarding management systems in HEIs.
Note: Vos Viewer with data from the Web of Science researched on September 1, 2021.

"impact" are highlighted. This confirms the tendency of this type of institution to be adopted regarding the quality references from guidelines over the management systems, as well as the interest to find out of experiences regarding the implementation and their entailing effects. Peripherally, the cores related to "innovation", "knowledge management", "challenges" and

Table 5.2   Clusters composed of keywords of literature regarding the management systems in HEIs.

Cluster 1 (13 items)	Cluster 2 (12 items)	Cluster 3 (10 items)
Communication	Balance scorecard	Government
Higher education institutions	Business	Higher education
Implementation	Higher education institutions	Higher-education
Improvement	Impact	HRM
ISO 9001	Knowledge management	Human Resource-management
Management systems	Organization performance	Human resource-management
Model	Performance management	Information
Organizations	Policy	Service
Performance	Public management	Systems
Quality management systems	Strategic management	Work
Social media	Total quality management	
Sustainable development	Universities	
TQM		
Cluster 4	Cluster 5	Cluster 6
(8 items)	(8 items)	(5 items)
Academics	Accreditation	Culture
Accountability	Leadership	Determinants
Challenges	Organization-climate	Governance
Educations	Perceptions	Innovation
management	Quality	Sustainability
Managerialism	Quality management	
quality assurance	Students	
University	Teachers	

Note: Own compilation from clusters comprised by Vos Viewer and from texts from the Web of Science with research dated September 1, 2021.

"policy" are shown, which refer to variables linked to the globalized context, contended and changing, while framing the performance of HEIs in recent years.

The network analysis by keywords showed a total of 56 items composed of six clusters entailing intrinsic similarities, which are shown in Table 5.2. The relevance of these pooling consists of revealing potential current research regarding the management systems in HEIs.

Cluster 1 nests the term "management system" around the terms related to quality management and referents, such as ISO 9001, where even the word "model" is present. This provides a clear indication that management systems are processed from a guided or modeled perspective, traditionally labeled as ISO 9001 or quality improvement systems.

On the other hand, the keywords in cluster 2 comprise a set, which seems to relate to a strategic level of HEIs, regarding terms related to the organizational performance and to measurement indicators, including issues concerning the strategic handling of the organization.

Cluster 3 groups terms regarding the staff and partners, work, and governance systems, related to intangible structures of design of work, information, and labor.

Cluster 4 differentiates terms, such as "management," related to issues relevant to management and accountability, that is to say, issues of a more administrative nature within the organizations, also seemingly linked to the term "quality," but now at the "assurance" stage.

Cluster 5 shows terms referring to the actors of HEIs ("students" and "teachers"), and this relates to the term "perceptions" and with aspects related to the organizational and leadership atmosphere.

Finally, cluster 6 relates the term "governance" to the words, such as "culture," "innovation," and "sustainability," also connected to the term "determinants."

Based on the above, one would assume that there is clear research currently nested in management systems toward adopting quality referents such as ISO 9001. Also, there is a clearly marked orientation from studies reflecting the interest in understanding the perspective of central actors of the educational process: teachers and students. On the other hand, the occurrence of an agenda in the governance of HEIs, related to innovation and sustainability issues; as well as the implicit mandate showing its organizational efficiency, through measurement systems of performance and organizational output indicators.

5.3.2 Analysis of the scientific production by contextual or thematic fields

This analysis was generated from the revision of the content of articles and based on the treatment and context under which the management systems were studied. Scientific texts were grouped by affinity, and 14 categories were identified, which were prioritized from higher to lower according to the number of publications recorded. Table 5.3 shows the categories achieved and their descriptions.

Table 5.3 Prioritization of literature on management systems in HEIs, identified in the analysis of contents.

Category	Number of articles published	Category description
Implementation of management systems under generic references	24	Models, mechanisms, implementation experiences, and practices in the adoption of references that are adopted from the business field
Management of substantive processes	19	Actions, interventions, improvements, or practices that occur in central processes of HEIs such as education, research, services to industry, and others
Context, institutional agendas, and government policies	13	Impact of pressures and external forces in the context of HEIs on management systems and organizational practices
Personal performance	12	Performance evaluation systems for academic or administrative personnel of HEIs, including connections with compensation or promotion systems
Assessment, accreditation, and certification of the quality in educational institutions	11	Models, mechanisms, implementation experiences, and practices in the adoption of quality references concerning education
University governance	11	Aspects related to accountability, commitment, communication, decision-making, and formal mechanisms that provide direction to HEIs
System planning	10	Mechanisms for the design, coordination, integration of actions and resources to achieve the organizational objectives of HEIs
Attention to stakeholders	8	Needs, expectations, or perceptions of those affected by the organizational action of HEIs.
Infrastructure and support	8	Provisioning and support systems for the performance of substantive processes
Personal management	7	Processes related to human resources management or intellectual capital management.
Organizational performance evaluation	5	Organizational management results, at the strategic or operational level
Knowledge management	4	Transfer or sharing of organizational knowledge for essential HEI functions or administrative improvement

	Table 5.3	Continued.
Category	Number of articles published	Category description
Working environment	2	Physical, security, psychological or social conditions that affect the disposition of actors involved in organizational processes or in the production of HEI services
Risk and contingencies	2	Systems for identification, measurement, treatment, and control of uncertain and adverse situations in HEIs

Note: Own compilation from texts coming from the Web of Science with a search date on September 1, 2021.

5.3.3 Implementation of management systems under generic referents

When referring to generic referents, it refers to a management scope that has been dominated by the business world. The norms and standards emerging from this type of organization have introduced meaningful barriers for their extrapolation to the educational context. The scientific literature regarding this line of investigation, underlines surveys highlighting the importance of intangible elements related to the participation and the commitment of actors and adopters of management systems, as well as the consideration of factors boosting or inhibiting the implementation of these systems.

The fact that the studies performed over the results stand out over the results obtained as a result of adopting the management systems, performing comparisons between related organizations to test the impacts of this kind of referents. Table 5.4 shows the most representative authors of these categories and the aspects addressed in their works.

5.3.4 Management of substantive processes

Substantive processes refer to the essential activities of HEIs, this refers to the processes related to teaching, research, and extension, representing the existence of higher education institutions. According to the literature relevant in Table 5.5, one can notice that the works of research produced online refer to the curricular processes of supply and demand of educational programs, the management of performance of students and teachers, the use of information technologies, and communication as part of the educational process. Also, teaching is also explored in the management of university

Table 5.4   Implementation of management systems under generic referents: summary of state-of-the-art.

Author(s)	Issues
Africano, Rodrigues y Santos, 2019	Comparison between Angolan universities
	Level of implementation of the quality system (IOS 9001)
	Improvements achieved through implementation
Basir, Davies, Douglas y Douglas, 2017	Comparative studies between two Malaysian universities
	Contribution of academic culture to system maintenance
Ben-Zvi-Assaraf y Ayal, 2010	Influence of curricular content related to environmental issues on students' abilities
Da Silva, Oliveira, Mantoan y Dos Santos, 2020	Integrated systems for the use of shared research spaces (laboratories)
	Effects on resource efficiency
	Case study
Duarte, Ramos-Pires y Goncalves, 2014	Case study
	Implications for school dropout
Fernandez-Cruz, Rodriguez-Mantilla y Diaz, 2020	Impact on school climate
Jain y Pant, 2010	Modeling for the implementation of an ISO 14001 system based on contextual analysis (IER-FODA)
Kargyte, 2015	Quality management models
	Comparison between specific and generic quality benchmarks
Kasperaviciute-Cerniauskiene y Serafinas, 2018	Perception of system users
	Diffusion of innovation, adoption of ISO 9001 systems
	Compatibility and adaptability as advantages
	Cost and duration as a negative effect
Martinez-Gil y Hernandez-Moreno, 2019	Case study
	Proposal for strengthening the teaching process
Medina, Cruz, Castro, y Cruz, 2017	Study of 26-degree programs at four universities
	Maturity level in the formalization of degree processes
Michael y Elser, 2019	Personal waste management to contribute to the implementation of environmental management systems
	Costs derived from the programs
Mohamed, Ghani y Basir, 2016	Factors affecting the implementation of management systems
Navarro, 2012[1](a)	Management systems
Navarro, 2012[2](a)	Management systems
Navarro, 2012[3](a)	Management systems
Navarro, 2012[4](a)	Management systems
Pehlivan y Cicek, 2021	Fuzzy axiomatic design
	Quality management system design
	Knowledge-based model for identification of gaps in QMS compliance level

Table 5.4 Continued.

Author(s)	Issues
Perez y Warden, 2011	Inter-university comparison of the implementation of intellectual capital frameworks among universities
Poli et ál, 2015	Study from 2008 to 2012
	Audit and evaluation as tools for continuous improvement
	Impact on institutional performance indicators
Saltos, Garces, Cruz, y Garces, 2017	Study of 26-degree programs at four universities
	Maturity level in the formalization of degree processes
Santana, Moreira, Roberto y Azambuja, 2010	Institutional and neoinstitutional theories
	Complex and changing contexts
Simonova y Fomenko, 2017	Integrated perspective from consumer groups, norms, and standards
	Evolution and development of its elements from the different quality models
Yalcin, 2012	Communication problems faced by teachers

Note: Own compilation from data acquired from the Web of Science with the date of search on September 1, 2021.
(a) The four records belong to the chapters in the book, but in the Web of Science, also are shown under the classification of articles.

extension and continuous education. This necessity is set as of certain social processes which may have become more complex for practical implementation, which is essential for HEIs to comply with their function of promoting the development of their participating communities.

5.3.5 Context, institutional agendas, and government policies

This category shows the different contextual forces delineating the institutional governance and ending up defining, to a large extent, the internal processes existing in HEIs. As noted in Table 5.6, the scientific production highlights the critical and reflexive surveys of researchers and scholars regarding the contextual forces and pressures oriented toward adopting management practices. Special mention shall be given to the fact that government educational institutions, whose management systems have been revised from the conception of a steering service, condition which is subordinated to adopting administrative practices within the framework of government administration.

Also, the adoption of specific agendas of evaluation, accreditation, and certification is shown as a subject of a growing study of interest among researchers, since it reveals implications for the operating context of management, and therefore, an intrinsic transformation of their systems. Also,

Table 5.5   Management of substantial processes of HEIs: summary of state-of-the-art.

Author(s)	Issues
Acevedo, Acosta, Nazco y Rodriguez, 2020	Student assessment
Benson y Whitworth, 2014	Pedagogy and management of online courses
Berkova, Boruvkova y Lizalova, 2018	Motivations in students for the selection of educational offerings
Bezerra y Tavares 2015	Educational offerings oriented toward social responsibility
Ferede, et ál, s.f.	Use of ICTs in the educational process
Giovanelli, Rotondo y Marino, 2017	Student performance management based on the use of ICTs
Gonzalez-Aportela, Batista-Mainegra, y Fernandez-Larrea, 2020	Management of the university extension process
Jorgensen et ál, 2018	Technology use by teachers
Kultur y Yazici, 2014	Adoption of technology for course management
Li, 2018	Graduate education outcomes
Lopez, 2021	Curricular elements on sustainable development
Robinson, 2017	Technology-based educational process
Romanova et ál, 2019	Implementation of courses based on continuing education
Sein-Echaluce, Abadia-Valle, Bueno-Garcia y Fidalgo-Blanco, 2017	Educational innovation is based on knowledge spirals
Shelton, 2017	Technology use by teachers
Sytnyk y Zinovieva, 2021	Technology-based educational process
Vargas y Heyes, 2016	Design of the educational offer with a focus on sustainability
Voce, 2015	Use of technology in the educational process
Whitworth y Benson 2014	Pedagogy and management of online courses

Note: Own compilation based on information from the Web of Science research on September 1, 2021.

there seems to be a side substantiating sustainable development as a strategy to be considered in the management of HEIs.

Another relevant issue in the context of HEIs is internationalization, which is shown as a growing tendency among HEIs toward finding better international classifications and more attractive programs for the potential demand of students.

5.3.6 Personal performance

The themes framed within this category are oriented toward the study of the variables attached to performance, conducts, and dispositions of institutional actors (scholars, administrative staff, and students) and the outputs

Table 5.6 Context, institutional agendas, and government policies: summary of the state-of-the-art.

Author(s)	Issues
Adeyemo, 2019	Use of Quality Management System (QMS) and education system quality objectives in an integrated agenda and its implications for operational systems Philippines case
Becker, De Campos y Da Silva, 2017	Integration of sustainability, from institutional plans to curricula
Bin Rais et ál, 2021	Functioning of a QMS from a global perspective in the twenty-first century
Chen y Zhang, 2018	Relationship between the internationalization of higher education and the subsequent study trend of foreign students
Dal Molin, Turri y Agasisti, 2017	Introduction of government reforms (New Public Management) for institutional performance management
Fuchs et ál, 2020	Strategic management in support of green marketing strategies
Hoffman et ál, 2013	Critique of management trends focused on strategic internationalization policy in the Finnish system Ethics related to ICT-based networks
Kim, 2021	Influence of changes in laws and educational content
Martin-Sardesai, Irvine, Tooley y Guthrie, 2017	Government research evaluations, academic freedom
Santos, 2020	Adoption of modern public administration practices (New Public Management)
Stensaker y Norgard, 2001	External pressures and the struggle for organizational identity
Stigger, 2018	Impact of internationalization and massification on institutional changes
Wigmore-Alvarez, Ruiz-Lozano y Fernandez-Fernandez, 2020	Integration of social responsibility: influence from the size and geographic location of the institution

Note: Own compilation based on the information from the Web of Science researched on September 1, 2021.

of organizational behavior. As noted in Table 5.7, there is a timely interest to find out the perception that the staff of HEIs keeps over performance systems. Also, the personal evaluation systems are revised in terms of the effects leading to the organizational life of HEIs. Also, surveys regarding the institutions and their actors are incised by contextual forces and internal pressures.

Table 5.7   Staff performance: summary of the state-of-the-art.

Author(s)	Issues
Angiola, Bianchi y Damato, 2018	Performance management systems, performance indicators
Bauwens, Audenaert, Huisman y Decramer, 2019	Equity in performance management, burnout and organizational citizenship
Decramer et ál, 2012	Institutional pressure
Decramer, Smolders y Vanderstraeten, 2013	Satisfaction with performance management systems
Decramer, Smolders, Vaderstraeten y Christiaens, 2012	Impact of the social and political-institutional environment
Gonzalez-Sanchez, Gutierrez-Lopez, y Palanca, s.f.	Performance systems that drive knowledge transfer
Kallio, Kallio, Tienari y Hyvonen, 2016	Perception of the academics
Khan y Christensen, 2021	Perception about compensation systems
Lim, 2021	Use of bibliometric technologies to evaluate performance in academic functions
Martin-Sardesai y Guthrie, 2018	Perceptions of human capital on research performance systems
	Staff performance evaluation, organizational performance (specific function-research)
Osipova, Kolodeznaya y Shevtsov, 2018	Labor productivity of educators and student expulsion
Susanj, Jakopec y Doric, 2020	Job roles, performance management, and strategic approach

Note: Own compilation based on information from the Web of Science searched on September 1, 2021

5.3.7 Assessment, accreditation, and certification of the quality in educational institutions

The adoption of referents in order to assess, accredit and certify the quality of educational institutions is projected as a guideline, toward which the management system shall be oriented. As shown in Table 5.8, the organizational management systems have impacted in HEIs through conceptual and methodological models to promote the quality of their processes. An important block of these surveys focuses on the study of accreditation and institutional certification devices, the function complied within the institutional processes, and critical factors of success. A critical research line that questions the viability of performance measurements adopting the HEIs and which are presumed as frameworks for assessing educational quality. Also,

Table 5.8 Assessment, accreditation, and certification of the quality of education: summary of the state-of-the-art.

Author(s)	Issues
Brennan y Shah, 2000	Quality management, intrinsic value systems, and extrinsic values (provided by society and economy) and their impact on life in the academic profession
Collado y Garaycochea, 2020	Comparative analysis of experience in countries with more mature quality models
Diaz y Mediano, 2015	Approaches to total quality programs
Diez, Iraurgi y Villa, 2018	The permanence of quality certification increases the perception of educational quality
Golowko, Kopia, Geldmacher y Forster-Pastor, 2017	Evaluations and responses of the institutions on their results. Institutions generate unique and different quality systems, with little internal and external transparency
Manatos, Sarrico y Rosa, 2017	Systematic literature review on quality management
Mgaiwa, s.f.	Leadership initiatives to ensure educational quality
Pandi, Paranitharan y Jeyathilagar, 2018	Critical success factors in the implementation of quality models, from a teacher's perspective
Sarbu, Ilie, Enache y Dumitriu, 2009	Stakeholder feedback and client satisfaction as a condition for "real quality" in higher education
Yeung, 2018	Quality indicators from the accreditation and certification referents
Zeledon-Ruiz y Araya-Vargas, 2019	Experiences in the process of program accreditation: an axis for the achievement of quality and innovation

Note: Own compilation based on information from the Web of Science searched on September 1, 2021.

the existence of surveys addressing the factors that enable the implementation of these systems, and the specificities of certain educational environments so they may be adopted.

5.3.8 University governance

This category shows the studies related to the university governance models conceived as an exercise to perform institutional functions that imply government structures, management, and leadership processes to make decisions (see Table 5.9). The works of this section show a position of leadership and governance, as articulating bodies of the management systems, both, as actors, as part of the functions, activities, and flows of communication, and information. Within the framework, there is a focus on the actors, their functions, and collegiate bodies. Also, issues of conflict between the different strategic actors are addressed, and between them the set of these and the institutional policies.

Table 5.9   University governance: summary of the state-of-the-art.

Author(s)	Issues
Balyer, 2011	Implications for academic freedom
Bashmakov, 2018	Decision-making on project authorization
Blackmore y Sawers, 2015	Gender-sensitive leadership in vice chancellor positions
Costa, Tonolli y De Oliveira, 2016	Process approach, based on Business Process Management (BPM) for maintenance management
Debski, Cieciora, Pietrzak y Bolkunow, 2020	Differences in organizational culture between public and private HEIs for the adoption of management systems
Drach y Lytvynova, 2020	Research governance characteristics: accountability, trust and control, efficiency and quality; transparency in decision-making; flexibility in organizational structures
Hamid et ál, 2017	Use of social networks to promote commitment to sustainability and communication
Longhurst, 2009	Roles of the university dean
	University governance models
Sergeeva et ál, 2021	Communication management in the university education system
Stensaker, Hovdhaugen y Maassen, 2019	Work of collegiate bodies assisting with the formal structures of the HEIs for the adoption of management systems
Tapanila, Siivonen, y Filander, 2020	Implications for academic work: decrease in decision-making and control

Note: Own compilation based on information from the Web of Science searched on September 1, 2021.

5.4 Conclusions

Upon reviewing the literature on management systems in HEIs, it is noticeable that there is an increase in publications in the last lustrum that, while it is moderate, it reflects the interest of said institutions to experience models of organizational management hand in hand with the study of educational phenomenon and management of knowledge, which goes beyond the field of administration and business to transform into a complex construct with its own and specific characteristics to the nature and functions of HEIs.

The analysis of concurrences of the keywords of the texts selected, along with their contents, is revealing the fields of interest which have been addressed within 1) the paradigms of management systems of HEIs under generic referents; 2) the management of substantive processes of HEIs (teaching, research, and extension); 3) the contextual forces limiting the institutional governance; 4) the performance of the institutional actors (scholars, administrative, and students); 5) the processes of assessment, accreditation, and certification of quality of HEIs, and; 6) the university governance as a factor of success to achieve institutional goals.

It is unquestionable that the organizational management system has extended the processes of HEIs favoring the achievement of their mission and goals as organizational bodies; however, their arrival is still early in this field and the need to overcome the positivist vision that considers the organizations as a linear and predictable mechanical process to have an access to emerging paradigms, unexpected and complex, is noted, in order to result in new management models in the educational field with more innovational and interactive proposals among their components and environments.

References

Acevedo, INR; Acosta, AM; Nazco, MA; Rodriguez, NR (2020). The Integral Evaluation of the Undergraduate Students, Expression of Quality in their Formation: Notes and Reflections. Revista conrado, 16(74), 54-63.

Adeyemo, KS (2019). Predictors of the Use of Quality Management System (Qms) Processes for the Asean Agenda. Higher education policy in the Philippines and Asean integration: demands and challenges, 60-75. 10.1163/9789004411326_004

Africano, N; Rodrigues, AS; Santos, G (2019). The Main Benefits of the Implementation of the Quality Management System in Higher Education Institutions in Angola. Quality innovation prosperity-kvalita inovacia prosperita, 23(3), 122-136. 10.12776/QIP.V23I3.1292

Angiola, N; Bianchi, P; Damato, L (2018). Performance Management in Public Universities: Overcoming Bureaucracy. International journal of productivity and performance management, 67(4), 736-753. 10.1108/IJPPM-01-2017-0018

Balyer, A (2011). Academic Freedom: Perceptions of Academics in Turkey. Egitim ve bilim-education and science, 36(162), 138-148.

Bashmakov, DV (2018). Authorizing Decisions in Projects of Network Interaction in Higher Education. Upravlenets-the manager, 9(4), 102-107. 10.29141/2218-5003-2018-9-4-11

Basir, SA; Davies, J; Douglas, J; Douglas, A (2017). The Influence of Academic Culture on Quality Management System Iso 9001 Maintenance within Malaysian Universities. Journal of higher education policy and management, 39(3), 320-340. 10.1080/1360080X.2017.1298199

Bauwens, R; Audenaert, M; Huisman, J; Decramer, A (2019). Performance Management Fairness and Burnout: Implications for Organizational Citizenship Behaviors. Studies in higher education, 44(3), 584-598. 10.1080/03075079.2017.1389878

Becker, DV; de Campos, SAP; da Silva, TN (2017). A Brazilian University Facing Challenge of Education for Sustainable Development. Handbook of theory and practice of sustainable development in higher education, vol 2, 233-244. 10.1007/978-3-319-47889-0_17

Benson, AD; Whitworth, A (2014). Research on Course Management Systems in Higher Education Preface. Research on course management systems in higher education, VII-X.

Ben-Zvi-Assaraf, O; Ayal, N (2010). Harnessing the Environmental Professional Expertise of Engineering Students-The Course: Environmental Management Systems in the Industry. Journal of science education and technology, 19(6), 532-545. 10.1007/s10956-010-9219-6

Berkova, K; Boruvkova, J; Lizalova, L (2018). Motivation of Students of Economic and Technical Study Programmes as A Tool of Competitiveness of Universities and Colleges: Empirical Study. Journal on efficiency and responsibility in education and science, 11(4), 72-77. 10.7160/eriesj.2018.110401

Bezerra, MJS; Tavares, MCB (2015). Organizational Social Responsibility: Adding Value to the Production Engineer's Training Process - The Case of Uezo Junior Consulting of the Estate University of the West Zone. Sistemas & gestao, 10(2), 324-335. 10.7177/sg.2015.v10.n2.a9

Bin Rais, RN; Rashid, M; Zakria, M; Hussain, S; Qadir, J; Imran, MA (2021). Employing Industrial Quality Management Systems for Quality Assurance in Outcome-Based Engineering Education: A Review. Education sciences, 11(2), -. 10.3390/educsci11020045

Blackmore, J; Sawers, N (2015). Executive Power and Scaled-Up Gender Subtexts in Australian Entrepreneurial Universities. Gender and education, 27(3), 320-337. 10.1080/09540253.2015.1027670

Brennan, J; Shah, T (2000). Quality Assessment and Institutional Change: Experiences From 14 Countries. Higher education, 40(3), 331-349. 10.1023/A:1004159425182

Collado, SP; Garaycochea, RT (2020). An Accreditation Model That Ensures the Quality Improvement of a College Level Study Program. Revista publicaciones, 50(4), 141-156. 10.30827/publicaciones.v50i4.17787

Costa, CAA; Tonolli, EJ; de Oliveira, JR (2016). Bpm And Bpms Avaliation in a Maintenance Sector of an Institution of Higher Education. Sistemas & gestao, 11(2), 133-149. 10.20985/1980-5160.2016.v11n2.699

Chen, Y; Zhang, ZZ (2018). Relationship Between Internationalization of Higher Education and the Further Study Trend of Overseas

Students. Educational sciences-theory & practice, 18(6), 3346-3353. 10.12738/estp.2018.6.239

Da Silva, ALIF; Oliveira, KDD; Mantoan, A; dos Santos, IC (2020). Implementing the Integrated Management System for the Research Labs: Ufabc' Experience Report. Revista gestao & tecnologia-journal of management and technology, 20(2), 280-303. 10.20397/2177-6652/2020.v20i2.1861

Dal Molin, M; Turri, M; Agasisti, T (2017). New Public Management Reforms in The Italian Universities: Managerial Tools, Accountability Mechanisms or Simply Compliance?. International journal of public administration, 40(3), 256-269. 10.1080/01900692.2015.1107737

Debski, M; Cieciora, M; Pietrzak, P; Bolkunow, W (2020). Organizational Culture in Public and Non-Public Higher Education Institutions in Poland: A Study Based on Cameron and Quinn's Model. Human systems management, 39(3), 345-355. 10.3233/HSM-190831

Decramer, A; Smolders, C; Vanderstraeten, A (2013). Employee Performance Management Culture and System Features in Higher Education: Relationship with Employee Performance Management Satisfaction. International journal of human resource management, 24(2), 352-371. doi: 10.1080/09585192.2012.680602

Decramer, A; Smolders, C; Vanderstraeten, A; Christiaens, J (2012). The Impact of Institutional Pressures on Employee Performance Management Systems in Higher Education in the Low Countries. British journal of management, 23(), S88-S103. 10.1111/j.1467-8551.2012.00820.

Decramer, A; Smolders, C; Vanderstraeten, A; Christiaens, J; Desmidt, S (2012). External Pressures Affecting the Adoption of Employee Performance Management in Higher Education Institutions. Personnel review, 41(5-6), 686-704. 10.1108/00483481211263593

Diaz, JAA; Mediano, CM (2015). The Audit Program of Aneca and The International Standards Iso 9000. A Comparative Analysis. Educacion xx1, 18(2), 375-395. 10.5944/educXX1.13938

Diez, F; Iraurgi, I; Villa, A (2018). Quality Management in Schools: Analysis of Mediating Factors. South African journal of education, 38(2), -. 10.15700/saje.v38n2a1388

Drach, II; Lytvynova, SH (2020). Researth Governance in a Modern University in the Conditions of Open Science. Information technologies and learning tools, 80(6), 326-345. 10.33407/itlt.v80i6.4094

Duarte, R; Ramos-Pires, A; Goncalves, H (2014). Identifying At-Risk Students in Higher Education. Total quality management & business excellence, 25(7-8), 944-952. 10.1080/14783363.2014.906110

Escorcia Guzmán, J, & Barros Arrieta, D (2020). Gestión del conocimiento en Instituciones de Educación Superior: Caracterización desde una reflexión teórica. Revista de Ciencias Sociales (Ve), XXVI(3),83-97.

Ferede, B; Elen, J; Van Petegem, W; Hunde, AB; Goeman, K (). Determinants Of Instructors' Educational Ict Use in Ethiopian Higher Education. Education and information technologies, 10.1007/s10639-021-10606-z

Fernandez-Cruz, FJ; Rodriguez-Mantilla, JM; Diaz, MJF (2020). Impact of the Application of Iso 9001 Standards on the Climate and Satisfaction of the Members of a School. International journal of educational management, 34(7), 1185-1202. 10.1108/IJEM-10-2018-0332

Fuchs, P; Raulino, C; Conceicao, D; Neiva, S; de Amorim, WS; Soares, TC; de Lima, MA; De Lima, CRM; Soares, JC; Guerra, JBSODA (2020). Promoting Sustainable Development in Higher Education Institutions: The Use of the Balanced Scorecard as a Strategic Management System in Support of Green Marketing. International journal of sustainability in higher education, 21(7), 1477-1505. 10.1108/IJSHE-02-2020-0079

García García, Griselda. (2016). Administración y gestión en institución de educación superior. RIDE. Revista Iberoamericana para la Investigación y el Desarrollo Educativo, 7(13), 590-606. Recuperado en 17 de marzo de 2022, de http://www.scielo.org.mx/scielo.php?script=sci_arttext&pid=S2007-74672016000200590&lng=es&tlng=es.

Giovanelli, L; Rotondo, F; Marino, L (2017). A Performance Management System to Improve Student Success in Italian Public Universities: Conditions and Critical Factors of an it System. Reshaping accounting and management control systems: new opportunities from business information systems, 20(), 203-219. 10.1007/978-3-319-49538-5_13

Golowko, N; Kopia, J; Geldmacher, W; Forster-Pastor, US (2017). Comparative Study on Quality Management at German Private Universities. Quality-access to success, 18(157), 85-94.

Gonzalez-Aportela, O; Batista-Mainegra, A; Fernandez-Larrea, MG (2020). System Quality Management for the University Extension Process, an Experience of The Havana's University. Revista electronica calidad en la educacion superior, 11(2), 105-134. 10.22458/caes.v11i2.3324

Gonzalez-Sanchez, MB; Gutierrez-Lopez, C; Palanca, MB (sf). How Can Universities Engage Lecturers in Knowledge Transfer? Analyzing the Influence of Performance Management Systems. Journal of knowledge management,. 10.1108/JKM-02-2021-0131

Hamid, S; Ijab, MT; Sulaiman, H; Anwar, RM; Norman, AA (2017). Social Media for Environmental Sustainability Awareness in Higher Education.

International journal of sustainability in higher education, 18(4), 474-491. 10.1108/IJSHE-01-2015-0010

Hofer, Ch. W. y D. Shendel (1978). Strategy formulation: analytical concepts. St. Paul. https://archive.org/details/strategyformulat00char/page/n11/mode/2up

Hoffman, DM; Valimaa, J; Saarinen, T; Soderqvist, M; Raunio, M; Korhonen, M (2013). The International Soletm of Finnish Higher Education: A Virtual Vanishing Act. Ethical technology use, policy, and reactions in educational settings, 107-121. 10.4018/978-1-4666-1882-4.ch009

Jain, S; Pant, P (2010). Environmental Management Systems for Educational Institutions a Case Study of Teri University, New Delhi. International journal of sustainability in higher education, 11(3), 236-249. 10.1108/14676371011058532

Jorgensen, M; Havel, A; Fichten, C; King, L; Marcil, E; Lussier, A; Budd, J; Vitouchanskaia, C (2018). Simply the Best: Professors Nominated by Students for Their Exemplary Technology Practices in Teaching. Education and information technologies, 23(1), 193-210. 10.1007/s10639-017-9594-1

Kallio, KM; Kallio, TJ; Tienari, J; Hyvonen, T (2016). Ethos At Stake: Performance Management and Academic Work in Universities. Human relations, 69(3), 685-709. 10.1177/0018726715596802

Kaplan, R. S. y Norton, D. P. (2007). Usar el Balanced Scored Card como un sistema de gestión estratégica. Harvard Business Review, Julio 2007, pp. 37-47.

Kargyte, V (2015). Application Of Generic Quality Management Models in European Universities. Management theory and studies for rural business and infrastructure development, 37(3), 381-398. 10.15544/mts.2015.33

Kasperaviciute-Cerniauskiene, R; Serafinas, D (2018). The Adoption of Iso 9001 Standard Within Higher Education Institutions in Lithuania: Innovation Diffusion Approach. Total quality management & business excellence, 29(1-2), 74-93. 10.1080/14783363.2016.1164012

Khan, TA; Christensen, T (2021). Challenges of Implementing a Performance and Reward System in Higher Education Institutions in Pakistan: Perceptions of Top Leaders in Contending Regulatory Bodies. Public organization review, 21(2), 243-262. 10.1007/s11115-020-00486-1

Kim, EJ (2021). Changes in North Korea's Higher Education and Education Management System During the Kim Jong Un Era. Asia pacific journal of education, 41(2), 281-298. 10.1080/02188791.2020.1756741

Kultur, C; Yazici, C (2014). Adoption, Diffusion, and Implementation of Course Management Systems a Faculty Focus. Research on course management systems in higher education, 21-46.

Li, L (2018). Current Situation and Improvement Countermeasures for Graduate Education in Public Administration Major in H University. Educational sciences-theory & practice, 18(5), 1424-1431. 10.12738/estp.2018.5.039

Lim, MA (2021). Governing Higher Education: The Pure Data System and the Management of the Bibliometric Self. Higher education policy, 34(1), 238-253. 10.1057/s41307-018-00130-0

Longhurst, B (2009). The Changing Role of the Dean in Higher Education in The UK. Academic administration: a quest for better management and leadership in higher education, 71-82.

Lopez, CRH (2021). Methodological Factors for University Curriculum Environmentalization. Revista contemporanea de educacao, 16(35), 181-209. 10.20500/rce.v16i35.42758

Manatos, MJ; Sarrico, CS; Rosa, MJ (2017). The Integration of Quality Management in Higher Education Institutions: A Systematic Literature Review. Total quality management & business excellence, 28(1-2), 159-175. 10.1080/14783363.2015.1050180

Martinez-Gil, L; Hernandez-Moreno, T (2019). The Quality of the Teaching Process, A System for its Management in the Bachelor's Degree in Economics at the University of Pinar Del Rio, Cuba. Revista electronica calidad en la educacion superior, 10(1), 202-221. 10.22458/caes.v10i1.2051

Martin-Sardesai, A; Guthrie, J (2018). Human Capital Loss in an Academic Performance Measurement Systemhuman Capital Loss in an Academic Performance Measurement System. Journal of intellectual capital, 19(1), 53-70. 10.1108/JIC-06-2017-0085

Martin-Sardesai, A; Irvine, H; Tooley, S; Guthrie, J (2017). Government Research Evaluations and Academic Freedom: A Uk and Australian Comparison. Higher education research & development, 36(2), 372-385. 10.1080/07294360.2016.1208156

Medina, ACH; Cruz, JGS; Castro, WFJ; Cruz, SES (2017). Quality Management and the Formalization of Higher Education Processes: A Descriptive Study of a Transectional Nature in Titling Units of the Province of Tungurahua. Revista publicando, 4(12), 792-805.

Mgaiwa, SJ (sf). Leadership Initiatives in Response to Institutional Quality Assurance Challenges in Tanzania's Private Universities. Journal of further and higher education, (), -. 10.1080/0309877X.2020.1860203

Michael, J; Elser, N (2019). Personal Waste Management in Higher Education: A Case Study Illustrating the Importance of a Fourth Bottom Line. International journal of sustainability in higher education, 20(2), 341-359. 10.1108/IJSHE-03-2018-0054

Mohamed, HAB; Ghani, AMA; Basir, SA (2016). Factors Influencing the Implementation of Islamic Qms in A Malaysian Public Higher Education Institution. Total quality management & business excellence, 27(9-10), 1140-1157. 10.1080/14783363.2015.1064765

Navarro, MAN (2012)[1]. Chapter 10. Quality Audit of The Quality Management System of the Area of Procurement of an Institution of Higher Education (IES). Calidad en los procesos de compras en una institucion de educacion superior, 96-109.

Navarro, MAN (2012)[2]. Chapter 3. Quality Management Systems (Qms). Calidad en los procesos de compras en una institucion de educacion superior, 42-49.

Navarro, MAN (2012)[3]. Chapter 6. Implementation of a Quality Management System. Calidad en los procesos de compras en una institucion de educacion superior, 69-71.

Navarro, MAN (2012)[4]. Chapter 9. Implementation of a Quality Management System in the Area of Procurement of and Institution of Higher Education (IES). Calidad en los procesos de compras en una institucion de educacion superior, 86-95.

Nonaka, I. y Takeuchi, H. (1999). La organización creadora de conocimiento. Oxford University Press.

Osipova, NG; Kolodeznaya, GV; Shevtsov, AN (2018). About the Factors and Reasons of University Student Expulsions and Student Motivation for Educational Activities. Obrazovanie i nauka-education and science, 20(6), 158-182. 10.17853/1994-5639-2018-6-158-182

Pandi, AP; Paranitharan, KP; Jeyathilagar, D (2018). Implementation of Ieqms Model in Engineering Educational Institutions - A Structural Equation Modelling Approach. Total quality management & business excellence, 29(1-2), 29-57. 10.1080/14783363.2016.1154431

Pehlivan, D; Cicek, K (2021). A Knowledge-Based Model on Quality Management System Compliance Assessment for Maritime Higher Education Institutions. Quality in higher education, 27(2), 239-263. 10.1080/13538322.2021.1905654

Perez, SE; Warden, C (2011). Visualising the Hidden Value of Higher Education Institutions: How to Manage Intangibles in Knowledge-Intensive Organisations. Identifying, measuring, and valuing knowledge-based intangible assets: new perspectives, 177-207. 10.4018/978-1-60960-054-9.ch009

Poli, M; Pardini, S; Passarelli, I; Citti, I; Cornolti, D; Picano, E (2015). The 4a's Improvement Approach: A Case Study Based on Uni En Iso 9001:2008. Total quality management & business excellence, 26(11-12), 1113-1130.

Porter, M. E. (1985) Competitive Advantage: Creating and sustaining superior performance. Free Press.

Porter, M. E. (1990) The Competitive advantage of nations. Free Pres.

Prahalad, C. H. y Hamel, G. (1990). La competencia esencial de la corporación. Harvard Bussiness Review, mayo-junio 1990, 79-89. https://hbr.org/archive-toc/3903

Robinson, L (2017). Embracing Online Education: Exploring Options for Success. Journal of marketing for higher education, 27(1), 99-111. 10.1080/08841241.2016.1261978

Romanova, MN; Bortnik, AF; Zakharova, AI; Amanbayeva, LI; Neustroyeva, EN; Romanov, NN; Sidorova, YE; Sokorutova, LV (2019). Continuing Teacher Education in the Secondary College-University System. Dilemas contemporaneos-educacion politica y valores, 7.

Saltos, ACL; Garces, LEG; Cruz, JGS; Garces, LLG (2017). The Management of Capital and The Programmed Savings: A Descriptive Study of Transeccional Cut to The Cooperative Sector of The Province of Tungurahua. Revista publicando, 4(12), 883-904.

Santana, S; Moreira, C; Roberto, T; Azambuja, F (2010). Fighting for Excellence: The Case of the Federal University of Pelotas. Higher education, 60(3), 321-341. 10.1007/s10734-009-9302-1

Santos, AFG (2020). Analysis of Ufrn's Integrated Management Systems from The Perspective of The New Public Management. Navus-revista de gestao e tecnologia, 10, -. 10.22279/navus.2020.v10.p01-13.1363

Sarbu, R; Ilie, AG; Enache, AC; Dumitriu, D (2009). The Quality of Educational Services in Higher Education - Assurance, Management or Excellence?. Amfiteatru economic, 11(26), 383-392.

Sein-Echaluce, ML; Abadia-Valle, AR; Bueno-Garcia, C; Fidalgo-Blanco, A (2017). Interaction of Knowledge Spirals to Create Ontologies for An Institutional Repository of Educational Innovation Best Practices. International journal of human capital and information technology professionals, 8(2), 72-92. 10.4018/IJHCITP.2017040105

Sergeeva, MG; Vlasyuk, IV; Borytko, NM; Podolskaya, MN; Kanishcheva, LN (2021). Regional Aspects of Humanitarization of

University Education. Revista tempos e espacos educacao, 14(33), -. 10.20952/revtee.v14i33.15254

Shelton, C (2017). Giving Up Technology and social media: Why University Lecturers Stop Using Technology in Teaching. Technology pedagogy and education, 26(3), 303-321. 10.1080/1475939X.2016.1217269

Simonova, AA; Fomenko, SL (2017). Evolution of Integrated Quality Management System at Higher School. Quality-access to success, 18(161), 126-134.

Stensaker, B; Hovdhaugen, E; Maassen, P (2019). The Practices of Quality Management in Norwegian Higher Education Collaboration and Control in Study Programme Design and Delivery. International journal of educational management, 33(4), 698-708. 10.1108/IJEM-11-2017-0327

Stensaker, B; Norgard, JD (2001). Innovation and Isomorphism: A Case-Study of University Identity Struggle 1969-1999. Higher education, 42(4), 473-492. 10.1023/A:1012212026597

Stigger, E (2018). Considering the Implications of Internationalization Within Japanese Higher Education. Internationalization within higher education: perspectives from japan, (), 97-107. 10.1007/978-981-10-8255-9_6

Susanj, Z; Jakopec, A; Doric, A (2020). Academics' Effectiveness and Professional Development in Croatia: Challenges for Human Resource Management in Higher Education Institutions. European journal of education, 55(4), 476-488. 10.1111/ejed.12422

Sytnyk, NV; Zinovieva, IS (2021). Modern Nosql Databases for Training Bachelor of Computer Science Specialty. Information technologies and learning tools, 81(1), 255-271. 10.33407/itlt.v81i1.3098

Tapanila, K; Siivonen, P; Filander, K (2020). Academics' Social Positioning Towards the Restructured Management System in Finnish Univsheersities. Studies in higher education, 45(1), 117-128. 10.1080/03075079.2018.1539957

Thunnissen, M; Van Arensbergen, P (2015). A Multi-Dimensional Approach to Talent an Empirical Analysis of the Definition of Talent in Dutch Academia. Personnel review, 44(2), 182-199. 10.1108/PR-10-2013-0190

Vargas, VR; Heyes, G (2016). Scaling Up the Woven Filigree: (Un) Common Systemic Thinking to Embedding Sustainability into The Curriculum in a Large-Scale Higher Education Institution in the UK. Teaching education for sustainable development at university level, (), 299-312. 10.1007/978-3-319-32928-4_21

Voce, J (2015). Reviewing Institutional Policies for Electronic Management of Assessment. Higher education, 69(6), 915-929. 10.1007/s10734-014-9813-2

Wang, M; Morley, MJ; Cooke, FL; Xu, JP; Bian, HM (2018). Scholars, Strategists or Stakeholders? Competing Rationalities and Impact of Performance Evaluation for Academic Managers in Chinese Universities. Asia pacific journal of human resources, 56(1), 79-101. 10.1111/1744-7941.12171

Whitworth, A; Benson, AD (2014). Research on Course Management Systems in Higher Education Introduction. Research on course management systems in higher education, (), XI-XXI.

Wigmore-Alvarez, A; Ruiz-Lozano, M; Fernandez-Fernandez, JL (2020). Management Of University Social Responsibility in Business Schools. An Exploratory Study. International journal of management education, 18(2), -. 10.1016/j.ijme.2020.100382

Yalcin, MA (2012). Communication Barriers in Quality Process: Sakarya University Sample. Turkish online journal of educational technology, 11(4), 65-71.

Yeung, SMC (2018). Linking Iso 9000 (Qms), Iso 26000 (Csr) With Accreditation Requirements for Quality Indicators in Higher Education. Total quality management & business excellence, 29(13-14), 1594-1611. 10.1080/14783363.2017.1282310

Zeledon-Ruiz, MD; Araya-Vargas, Z (2019). From Self-Evaluation to Quality Management and Innovation. The Case of The School of Business Administration (Ucr). Revista electronica calidad en la educacion superior, 10(1), 1-30. 10.22458/caes.v10i1.2447

6

Process Optimization in Industry 4.0: An Analysis of Software Development SMEs in Baja California, Mexico

Roberto Carlos Valdés Hernández, Mónica Claudia Casas Paez, José Luis Arcos Vega, Juan Gabriel López Hernández, Ricardo Ching Wesman, and Adelaida Figueroa Villanueva

Universidad Autónoma de Baja California, Mexico

Abstract

Innovation strategies tend to integrate technology more into SMEs. Thus, showing a trend moving toward definition and continuous process improvement through optimization, strategically helping to achieve organizational goals. Starting from the premise that companies still need to adapt to new market changes, this paper intends to show an analysis of process optimization to develop software in SMEs, looking at innovation as a trigger for growth, and also centered on the industry 4.0. An evaluation is conducted of the correlation between innovation and its incidence in SME competitiveness in the software development sector.

Keywords: Process optimization, industry 4.0, innovation, software engineering

6.1 Introduction

According to Simanca et al. (2016), innovation is a competitive ability for organizations that are able to combine and articulate different aspects of the company organization. This, in addition to a focus on specialization, and of course a motivating orientation toward human talent as a promotor for change. Innovation is an important economic growth promotor both for large companies as well as for SMEs (World Bank, 2013). As a company development strategy, innovation is not only focused on generating new products and processes, but also on optimizing processes that will allow productivity and competitiveness to grow in companies (Balza y Cardona, 2016). According to Sehnem et al., (2022) the most important innovation practices are business models focused on eco-design, product leasing, and collaborative commerce. Therefore, what is sought through innovation is to try to make a sustainable transition from management practices to operative processes.

Innovation-intensive organizations are nowadays a development source for any country as it was mentioned by Schwab (2016) at the International World Forum. Country development has to be designed to promote innovation strategies that will contribute to the growth in the level of competitiveness and to the improvement of the world economy. Hence, companies in Malaysia, Thailand, or the Philippines, as well as in others, such as Hungary, the Czech Republic, and Poland, in addition to Ireland; are innovating their software design processes, starting with the optimization of their processes. They have been able to reach a clear global leadership in the software industry (López et al., 2013). Latin America has started to participate in this dynamic. Many countries in this region are focusing their efforts on competing, especially Argentina, which has a favorable trend toward the software productive sector, through the Center for Transference and Research in Software Engineering (CETIS), which seeks to innovate in software products and services that will add value to this sector (Anacleto et al., 2014).

Due to the aforementioned, according to Faria, Santos, and Zaidan (2021), it is very important that companies have a precise business model that will impact the companyt's performance and competitiveness strategies. This, while also takes into consideration strategic controls to innovate (Wang & Zhang, 2021). For those companies dedicated to developing software and that are looking to implement improvements in the software production process, to automate processes according to Dymora et al. (2019) is a key issue in software engineering and engineering systems nowadays. By optimizing their development processes, and becoming a determining and necessary factor for the implementation of mechanisms to redesign workflows that are basic in the software development process. Companies have to be able to take on new risks to compete in a globalized world; where the role played by innovation and Industry 4.0 these days in companies are key in order to achieve success in SMEs. Industry 4.0 is a term that covers the automation of the industry, robotization, and digitalization. It brings great opportunities in terms of sustainability and increases productivity in industrial production by up to a third (Poor y Basl, 2018).

In that sense, Nakagawa, Antonino, Schnicke, Kuhn, and Liggesmeyer (2021) mentioned that Industry 4.0 requires new ways to develop and operate fabrication processes, since they require to be completely digital. According to Yang and Gu (2021), this industry is adapting and launching new ways of working in organizations from a digital and technological perspective.

6.2 Literature Revision and Hypothesis Formulation

Growth models acknowledge the importance of innovation as a key factor in the companyt's productivity and competitiveness (World Bank, 2013). Innovation and its impact on the company according to Adner y Kapoor (2010) has been a topic that has been studied in the last couple of years, mainly in the global economy. Currently, the quality of software production is directly related to the quality of the process used to obtain, develop, and maintain it; expressed in improvements in project performance, quality increase of the obtained products, and in the success of the organizations.

The importance of improving software processes for performance improvement, usefulness, and effectiveness of the processes in a disciplined way, allowing the measurement of processes through an analysis of potentialities, deficiencies, and based on that, to introduce new changes in the processes that will allow a strategic evolution of the organization (García et al., 2016). Companies that are looking for more profitability through the generation of strategies that are aimed to improve SME competitiveness, but supporting those strategies relies on the innovation capacities that the company has. Taking this into consideration, companies have processes, where work roles are assigned to professionals able to carry out the assigned tasks; where they analyze that processes to be innovated, applying methodology in software development processes. This is one of the most complex in companies dedicated to developing software, where role assignment has a high level of difficulty since when assigning those roles, they must take into consideration the knowledge and skills required at the different levels of the development process. In this sense, optimization is an important part of the productive process, involving different phases that invite creativity into the software production process.

Según (Lahi et al., 2014) la innovación es un proceso dentro de una organización donde su objetivo principal es el de generar nuevas implicaciones estratégicas, que les permitan a las Pymes encontrar nuevos mercados, así como a minimizar sus costos debido a la optimización de sus procesos. Según Argüello, Casanova & Cedaro (2021) se han desarrollado diferentes modelos y estándares para la mejora continua de los proceso de desarrollo de software, partiendo de las habilidades y experiencias de los desarrolladores, en busca de crear un producto de software de mayor calidad, partiendo de aplicar métodos exitosos que contribuyan a satisfacer las expectativas del cliente.

Creative actions will be the ones that enable the optimization of business processes, which directly influence the goals established by the management (Juárez et al., 2016). Likewise, innovation can contribute significantly to the design of measuring instruments for process optimization (Morero et al., 2015). Due to this, in software developing SMEs, client requirement analysis is the initial stage of the development process which is composed of four development stages: specification, design, implementation, and testing. This results in a sole software product, where regardless of the work methodology, assigning the roles in the team is a difficult task. This is taking into consideration that the knowledge and skills that they each possess are different. Likewise, there are different modeling methods, and software product line engineering is one. It suggests a new form of developing the software product, consisting in developing the software by line of products and not software for each product. In this case, this is useful to analysts, designers, and programmers who design software (Benavides et al., 2013). As a result of this, software process improvement seeks to develop high-quality software, considering the capacities of each company, as well as their innovation abilities in the software product development process (Iqbal, Nasir, Khan, Awan, & Farid, 2020).

Considering the aforementioned, we have established the following hypothesis for our research:

H_0: Innovation contributes to new strategic implications and higher profit due to the optimization of the software development process.

H_1: Innovation does not contribute to new strategic implications and higher profit with regard to the quality of the software.

An instrument was designed (questionnaire) to collect data. It is composed of 31 items of the study variables. To design the research instrument, we considered (Hernández, 2014), as well as data collection. Next, we will discuss the analysis of the variables in the study.

- Dimension 1: Considering the degree to which the company manager promotes optimization, and that it leads to generating quality products, considering the commitment and importance given to continuous process improvement by the company management; by assigning resources for applying to obtain certifications and international standards that will facilitate quality assurance in software products.
- Dimension 2: Competitiveness was analyzed by aligning the strategies implemented by the company managers, considering the optimization of the development process, and the level at which the activities impact the strategic priorities of the company. This is by taking into consideration the participation of the management in establishing improvement goals, through process indicators, to measure the feedback and follow-up of the continuous improvement process.

6.2.1 Optimization and software engineering

Baquero and Ciudad (2018) mention that software engineering is a discipline that provides the theoretical and practical knowledge for the specification, design, and implementation of high-quality software, validating it and evolving. Since the 1960s, it has progressively evolved to become a discipline that integrates all the processes associated with software production. According to Martins and Ning (2021), it is important to consider algorithm optimization, by using combinations of design variables considering Software Process Engineering (SPE), which helps software companies to design, model, and improve by using PML: process modelling language. It is considered that these languages in the modeling of processes help develop software. Likewise, models such as SPEM or software process engineering metamodel, which is an OMG (object management group) specification. It is a metamodel that allows you to represent the components of several processes which, according to Menéndez and Castellanos (2015) provides the process modeling elements that lead to describing any software development process of any specific area or discipline. SPEM bases its notation on elements such as work products, work definitions, and roles (Rodríguez et al., 2007). Consequently, this type of modeling allows you to look at software processes from different perspectives, with different levels of abstraction, by using a formally defined language. The adaptation to Figure 6.2 defines the elements known as roles, activities, and knowledge involved in the process. (Humphrey, 2006) mentions that a process model is a structured collection of elements that describe the characteristics of effective and efficient processes. In this sense, ISO established software process standards, or adaptations of them, so that SMEs can apply them in their development processes. Such standards were published under the name ISO/IEC 29110 in 2010 (Pino et al., 2008).

Figure 6.1 shows the adaptation made to the software engineering process defined in norm ISO/IEC 29110. This process is shown under a SPEM v2.0

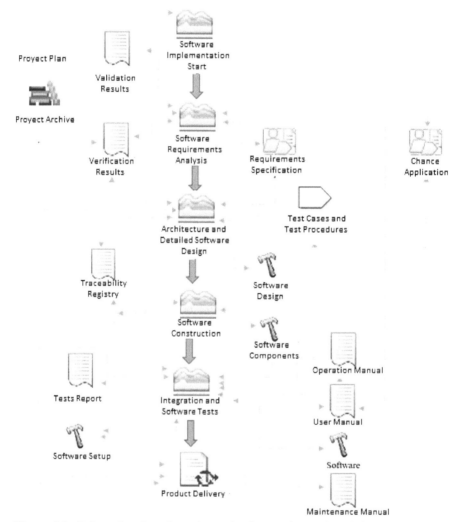

Figure 6.1   Information flow for software implementation. Adapted from the software implementation process and activities (ISO/IEC TR 29110, 2011).

symbology showing the flow of information in activities associated with the process, as well as the most relevant work products and their relations (Object Management Group, 2004). The basic profile of ISO/IEC 29110 is divided into two processes: project management (PM) and software implementation process (SI). Each process is composed of tasks and activities, and the documents (work products or devices) produced (ISO/IEC TR 29110, 2011).

Supposedly, according to Ali et al. (2010), information technologies companies have to improve the quality of their products and services by obtaining certifications that will allow them to optimize processes. They also have to generate products that will satisfy the requirements and needs of their clients, thus achieving a more competitive company. Working on a continuous improvement will be the key factor in the software development process. That is why (Llerena, 2014) mentions that a proper selection of the staff that will be incorporated into the development teams is crucial and has a direct influence on the effectiveness of the process.

As a result of this, software developing companies apply different models to improve their processes. Such is the case of the Swedish company Celsius Tech System AB. The first one is to apply a software product line (SPL). Using systems to control ships, to consider delivery dates with their customers, by applying reutilization techniques in their development processes in different systems; together with a company reorganization. With this, they were able to achieve the development of both systems, build software products with more requirements in shorter periods of time, and improve the design and maintenance.

According to Miranda et al. (2015), SPL engineering centers in developing multiple systems from a common code. Metzger and Pohl (2014) mentioned that it is important to consider costs in development, cost reduction, and managing similar development projects in parallel; since this leads to great benefits when it comes to satisfying specific functionality requirements (Díaz and Trujillo, 2010). Figure 6.2 shows the elements involved such as the role, activity, knowledge, as well as the documents and tools; which are elements that allow to identify whatever it is that could be affecting the activities in the process, as well as knowledge transference between the roles. Likewise, selecting the specific requirements during product development defines the variability of the resulting applications in the software product, based on the devices identified in the process (Martínez et al., 2013).

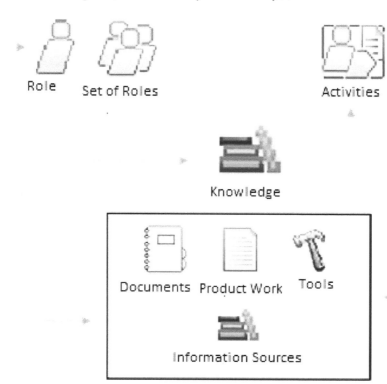

Figure 6.2   Elements involved with adaptation in the process model. Source: Rodríguez et al. (2009).

6.2.2 Innovation and knowledge

Innovation is one of the main pillars of the new economy nowadays. It increases the competitiveness of the company, as well as the efficiency of its processes, in addition to generating added value through the creation of a quality product that will fulfill the highest quality standards (Acuña et al., 2015). Therefore, according to Gallouj and Savona (2009) innovation tends to highlight those attributes related to software services production that affect process optimization and innovation. According to Hernández and Martí (2006), innovative potential starts at human capital: the abilities and knowledge. That is why management needs to pay special attention to identifying and developing knowledge, and it ends up being a fundamental element in the optimization process. Software process improvement is an intensive activity involving knowledge and learning and is key to software development (Chen & Lee, 2022).

In the last couple of years of company management, the importance of knowledge has substantially grown. It has attracted considerable importance among company management since human capital is one of the determining factors for added value in a company. This value increases by reaching goals, and on how willing the company is to develop and take advantage of knowledge. Hence, empowering human resources is the most important factor in innovation development within the company (Narimani, Sahebkar, Khorasani & Sani, 2022). In this sense, human resources and their knowledge play a very important role in new forms of management where human resources are given more weight in the decision-making process, along with leadership, motivation, knowledge, and where the most important thing is to have a strategy for the future.

With regards to this, Foray (2004) mentions that knowledge plays an essential role in the development of a company. It promotes innovation and a culture that is based on the use and transference of information in the company, taking into consideration procedures, experiences, and the knowledge of its employees, considered by (Davenport, 2013) as being essential to have good management of knowledge, integrating strategies, techniques, and procedures, that are aligned with the company strategy. Companies are becoming more interested in implementing development models that will allow them to improve their software development processes. One of the best approaches is software process improvement (SPI), which evaluates the practices and how software products and services are developed. Also, SMART-SPI, which is an SPI data analysis model, that according to Mejía et al. (2017) provides a solution to problems that have been identified in the software product development process. Organizations involved in software development, need to manage the developing activity by modeling the software creation process and trying to improve the quality in the development of their products. In other words, they must guarantee the construction of the software product within the time and cost limits (Domínguez and Bolaños, 2015).

6.2.3 The industry 4.0 and competitiveness

Smart devices and other technologies are pillars of the new industrial revolution, where according to Álvarez and Bernal (2021) they are emerging technologies in the organizational strategy. Innovation is an important economic growth trigger both for large companies as well as for SMEs, who need to adapt to the new market changes in order to remain competitive. Consequently, Industry 4.0, which is a term that includes industry automation, robotization, and digitalization, brings great opportunities in terms of sustainability and an increase in industrial production productivity (Poor and Basl, 2018).

It is called the fourth industrial revolution, which is based on the use of cyber-physics systems to improve information and communication systems (Park and Huh, 2018). Technological development in companies, according to Del Giorgio and Mon (2019) connects the physical and the digital worlds through devices, materials, products, equipment, installations, and communications with the digital world. This is expressed through collaborative systems and software products that are interconnected with a great number of devices to potentialize the development of Industry 4.0, also known as the Intelligent Industry.

This new paradigm, according to Durana et al. (2019) requires continuous innovation and technological design processes in companies. They have to prepare to face the challenges of this new era, and try to successfully adapt to Industry 4.0. According to Hamada (2019), SMEs are not able to adapt to Industry 4.0 because they do not adequately understand how they could change their operation and organization, since product development and test production have benefited from robot automated fabrication, thus shortening production time to satisfy the needs of their clients. This increases the cost of innovation for these companies. Regarding this, Ji et al. (2021) consider that automated robotics are important to reduce robot configuration time and costs, which are involved in operative tasks. Consequently, a good option for a company would be to combine new systems with a strategy established by the management, considering Industry 4.0 factors such as digitalization. However, it is always up to the managers. If the manager is willing to take a risk by introducing new systems and innovations according to the commercial strategy that is a very important part of planning, then personal and professional success will depend on it (Vrchota et al., 2019).

As a result of these technological trends, new products and services become available to clients. There are new business models, new needs, and new challenges; that will definitely lead companies to higher competitiveness (Antúnez, 2019). Software developing companies due to global competitiveness, are forced to reconfigure their productive processes due to very demanding markets, and are supported by digital technologies that are later incorporated into the production process. Other technologies such as mobile computing, the cloud, and Big Data that is present in the banking business and in payment systems, as well as in mobile devices; among other devices and applications that help SMEs to provide added value.

As a result of this, there have been changes in the work systems with the introduction of information technologies, and those SMEs dedicated to software development are no exception. It is evident that as a society we can attest to how much we have evolved. We are now a society where quality holds a very important relevance in the economic world (Gómez et al., 2014).

6.3 Materials and Methods

6.3.1 Materials

The data used in this study serves the purpose to reveal the incidence that innovation in the optimization of the software development process has, as well as in the quality of the analysis of SMEs requirements. We used a series of data to establish the aforementioned hypothesis, specifying which are those factors that influence decision-makers in the optimization of the software development process.

We selected the IT sector, specifically that within SMEs dedicated to developing software. The number of companies was obtained by using information from the economic census collected by the National Institute of Statistics and Geography (INEGI, 2014). The structure of the sample has been formulated and supported under stratified sampling for finite populations. The population is composed of the SMEs established in the state of Baja California, specifically in the cities of Mexicali, Ensenada, and Tijuana. To determine the size of the sample, we considered an error margin lower than 0.03, with a confidence interval of 95%. Data collection was done through an instrument (questionnaire) that was sent by email, and in some cases, we were able to interview the SME manager in person from June to September 2016. Therefore, we obtained a sample of 52 software-developing SMEs. We chose this sector of the industry since it has a great potential for growth as

Table 6.1 Research design.

Characteristics	Research
Population	Small- and mid-size enterprises (86)
Geographical area	Baja California (Mexico)
SME size	SMEs with 5 to 250 employees
Data collection method	Personal and email interviews to SME managers
Sampling method	Proportions
Sample size	86 SMEs
Error of the sample	($\pm 0.03\%$) error, confidence level of 95% ($p = 0.5$)
Fieldwork	June–September 2016

Table 6.2   Sample characteristics.

IT industry	Companies number	Overall percentage
Software development	52	60.5
Software implementation	11	12.8
Consulting and mainte-nance	9	10.5
Website design	7	8.1
Integral consulting	7	8.1
Total	86	100

a development sector for the state of Baja California. Table 6.1 shows the considered research design, as well as the characteristics of the sample used for this study (see Table 6.2).

6.3.2 Method

In the analysis, we assessed the impact of innovation regarding software development optimization, as well as if the company has a defined strategy regarding the SME innovation activity. Another analysis strategy was to consider the size of the company by using the classification proposed by (INEGI, 2014) based on the number of employees in software development companies. In 2016, we conducted a survey in small and medium sized (SME) companies of a sample of 52 SMEs out of a total of 86 in the state of Baja California, for the cities of Mexicali, Tijuana and Ensenada. We analyzed and characterized an organizational phenomenon based on the analysis of the correlation between variables, and how they are significantly related with each other. There was a Spearman's bivariate correlation analysis conducted to determine the degree of relation between the variables in the study, between the variables in the quality of the software, the development of the software and the innovation for development. In this sense, we calculated each analyzed dimension. Table 6.3 shows the obtained results of the Cronbach's alpha, which resulted in an average of 0.84. Therefore, based on those results, we concluded that the instrument was in fact reliable.

Table 6.3   Reliability analysis.

Variable	Cronbach's alpha
Quality of the software	0.852
Development of the software	0.824
Innovation for the development	0.844

Table 6.4 Four-fold contingency table (Budíková et al., 2010).

x	*Y*		nj.
	y [1]	*y* [2]	
x [1]	*a*	*b*	*a + b*
x [2]	*c*	*c*	*c + d*
n.k	*a + c*	*b + d*	*n*

We also tested the hypotheses that suppose the relation between the aforementioned dimensions. The test statistics were based on a quadruple contingency table as shown in Table 6.4, labeled as $n1 = a$, $n2 = b$, $n3 = c$, $n4 = d$ (Freeman, Shoesmith, Sweeney, Anderson, and Williams, 2017; Keller, 2014). There was also a Spearman's bivariate correlation analysis conducted to determine the degree of relation between the variables in the study, between the variables in the quality of the software, the development of the software and the innovation for development. The bivariate correlation is a statistical technique used to determine if two variables hold a common relation.

The statistics of the test can be summarized in Eqn (1). If the hypothesis on the independence of the X and Y applied variables, then K is asymptotically controlled by the distribution $\chi^2(1)$. Rejection hypothesis: $W = (\chi^2_{1-a}(1), \infty)$. The H_1 hypothesis is rejected at the asymptotical significance level α if $K \in W$ under the good approximation condition, tested before the $(K \in W)$ test:

$$k = \frac{n\,(ad - bc)}{2\,(a + b)\,(c + d)\,(a + c)\,(b + d)}.$$

Regarding the results, data were tested by using the Fisher Factorial Test, by a combination of considerations to calculate the probability of marginal frequency tables deviated from the alternative hypothesis. The sum of these probabilities is the p value of the test. The data was analyzed with the exit of the p value for the exact Fisher test. If the value is $p \leq \alpha$, the Independence hypothesis is rejected a significance level of α, established in 0.05 in this document (Devore, 2015).

6.4 Results and Discussion

As Table 6.5 indicates, all the correlation coefficients are significant since they show that $p < 0.01$. Thus demonstrating that there is a significant correlation between the variables. This means that for SMEs, the higher innovation for the development will represent a higher profit for the companies. This, in addition to new strategic implications, and lower costs; which thanks to the innovation in software development processes can be optimized. As a result of the aforementioned, H_1 is rejected. The latter due to the fact that the results in the study show that the adoption of innovation and quality help the company to continue being competitive in a dynamic market, to try to get more profit, by applying strategies focusing on new markets. Also, operative costs are reduced due to the optimization of the process and the improvement in quality indicators. This is a very useful aspect from a competitive perspective since this would be a way to be able to implement new organizational strategies focused on innovation aiming to optimize the software development process which would result in more sophisticated processes that would ultimately impact SME costs and productivity.

Table 6.5 also shows that the variable for software quality has a moderate correlation with the innovation for development level. It is important to highlight that it is the highest correlation at 0.687. When analyzing the software development correlation with software quality and their incidence in SME innovation, explaining why all of the software developing companies seek to continue competing in a dynamic market that is influenced mainly by technological innovation applied to software development processes, always striving to offer quality products. In spite of what was analyzed in this study,

Table 6.5 Results of the correlation analysis.

			Software quality	Software development	Innovation for development
Spearman's	Software quality	Correlation coefficient	1.000	0.631**	0.687**
		Sig. (two-tailed)		0.000	0.005
		N	52	52	52
	Software development	Correlation coefficient	0.631**	1.000	0.503
		Sig. (two-tailed)	0.000		0.563
		N	52	52	52
	Innovation for development	Correlation coefficient	0.687**	0.503	1.000
		Sig. (two-tailed)	0.005	0.563	
		N	52	52	52

**Correlation is significant at the 0.01 level (two-tailed).

there is a need of considering other study variables such as profitability, or client perception. This in order to be able to observe the correlation between the aforementioned variables, and their impact on the company's competitiveness or development. It has been concluded that we must continue researching these topics, since software development for this industry holds a direct impact on the economic development in the northwestern region of Mexico.

6.5 Conclusions

Based on the analysis of 52 software development SMEs, and supported by the theory that innovation focused on the optimization of the development process, results in more profit, as well as new strategic implications, which could motivate SMEs to implement the Industry 4.0 with the purpose of maintaining competitiveness to increase the value of the company. There could be some deterring factors for SMEs, such as financial planning, process management, as well as a lack of investment in new technologies.

In order to analyze the optimization of the software development process to improve software processes, taking innovation into mind, we considered several concluding aspects, such as the correct configuration of the process of introducing innovations and changes in a company, along with the correct configuration of the reference points so that it is possible to continuously monitor and assess process and success. It is also important to consider the high costs of improvement programs, and the high level of failure. All of these elements played an essential role in providing the necessary information to correctly apply the budgets related to SME process improvement. Therefore, the information related to the optimization process is important to consider when deciding where to allocate the improvement efforts in the company. Together with the opinion of experts and specialists when defining the profit, adaptability, relevance, and pertinence of the process for the optimization and improvement.

The results of this research contribute to the importance that optimization and innovation have in the competitiveness of the companies dedicated to developing software. According to the correlation analysis, the level of innovation for the development of software associated to the quality of the software, show the commitment from company owners to promote improvements in the process. It is also related to software development, where implementing improvements in the process will lead to a better knowledge and development of the latter; together with an efficient organizational structure that will support the software development process adequately, resulting in a more competitive company.

Finally, for the management in the software development sector, statistic data shows that the dimensions, quality and competitiveness, are impacted by the level of innovation in the optimization of the development process. As a conclusion, SMEs conduct practices in their processes that support the generation of products with high quality standards, with the purpose of increasing their organizational competitiveness in the strategic and operative part, thus achieving the quality of the software product that is offered to the client resulting in his or her complete satisfaction.

Funding

This research received no external funding.

Conflicts of Interest

The authors declare no conflict of interest.

References

Acuña, C., Cuenca Pletsch, L., Pinto, N., Tomaselli, G., Tortosa, N. (2015). La vinculación Universidad-Industria como instrumento de mejora para la competitividad de las empresas de desarrollo de Software del NEA. JUI 2015, *9° Jornadas de Vinculación Universidad-Industria*, pp. 31-36.

Adner, R, Kapoor, R. (2010). Value creation in innovation ecosystems: How the structure of technological interdependence affects firm performance in new technology generations. *Strategic management journal*, 31(3), 306-333.

Ali, A. J., Islam, M. A., Howe, L. P. (2010). Critical factors impacting sustainability of continuous improvement in manufacturing industries in Malaysia. *World Journal of Management*, 2(3), pp. 65-80.

Alvarez-Aros, E. L., & Bernal-Torres, C. A. (2021). Technological competitiveness and emerging technologies in industry 4.0 and industry 5.0. *Anais da Academia Brasileira de Ciências*, 93.

Anacleto, et al., (2014). Experiencias de I+D+i en productos avanzados para el análisis de software. *8° Jornadas de Vinculación Universidad-Industria, 43 JAIIO*. pp. 37.

Antúnez, A. (2019) La industria 4.0. Análisis y estudio desde el Derecho en la 4ta Revolución Industrial. *Advocatus*, 32, 133-164.

Argüello, M., Casanova, C. A., Cedaro, K. E. (2021). Proposal to Improve Software Testing in Small and Medium Enterprises. In: Florez, H., Pollo-Cattaneo, M. F. (eds) Applied Informatics. ICAI 2021. *Communications in Computer and Information Science*, vol 1455. Springer, Cham. https://doi.org/10.1007/978-3-030-89654-6_35

Balza, V., Cardona, D. (2016). Economías de aglomeración empresarial y políticas públicas de competitividad desde un enfoque global hacia un contexto latinoamericano: Una revisión conceptual. *Revista Espacios*, *37*(36).

Baquero, L., Ciudad, F. (2018). Análisis de tendencias y aplicaciones de la ingeniería de software basada en la búsqueda. *VIII Taller Internacional de Calidad en las Tecnologías de la Información y las Comunicaciones*, la Habana, cuba, 1-7.

Benavides, D., Felfernig, A., Galindo, J. A., Reinfrank, F. (2013). Automated analysis in feature modelling and product configuration. In *International Conference on Software Reuse*, pp. 160-175. Springer, Berlin, Heidelberg.

Budíková, Marie, Maria Králová, and Bohumil Maroš (2010). *Pruvodce základními statistickými metodami*. Praha: Grada Publishing.

Chen, C. Y., & Lee, J. C. (2022). Comparative effects of knowledge-based antecedents in different realms of CMMI-based software process improvement success. *Computer Standards & Interfaces*, 81, 103599.

Davenport, T. H. (2013). *Process innovation:Rreengineering work through information technology*, Cambridge, MA: Harvard Business Press.

De Faria, V. F., Santos, V. P., & Zaidan, F. H. (2021). The Business Model Innovation and Lean Startup Process Supporting Startup Sustainability. Procedia Computer Science, 181, 93-101.

Del Giorgio, H., Mon, A. (2019). Niveles de productos software en la industria 4.0. International *Journal of Information Systems and Software Engineering for Big Companies (IJISEBC)*, 5(2), 53-62.

Devore, Jay L. (2015). Probability and Statistics for Engineering and the Sciences, 9th ed.Boston: Brooks Cole

Díaz, Ó, Trujillo, S. (2010). Línea de Producto de Software. *Publicado en "Fábricas de Software: experiencias, tecnologías y organización" 2° edición, M. G. Piattini y Garzás, J. (editores),* Editorial Ra-Ma.

Dymora, P., Koryl, M., Mazurek, M. (2019). Process Discovery in Business Process Management Optimization. *Information*, *10*(9), 270.

Domínguez, V., Bolaños, M. (2015). SPEM: Software process engineering metamodel. *Revista Latinoamericana de Ingenieria de Software*, 3(2), 92-100.

Durana, P., Kral, P., Stehel, V., Lazaroiu, G., Sroka, W. (2019). Quality Culture of Manufacturing Enterprises: A possible way to adaptation to Industry 4.0. *Social Sciences*, 8(4), 124.

Foray, D. (2004). *Economics of knowledge*, Cambridge, MA: MIT Press.

Freeman, Jim, Eddie Shoesmith, Dennis Sweeney, David Anderson, and Thomas Williams (2017). *Statistics for Business and Economics*, 4th ed. Cengage Learning EMEA: London.

Gallouj, F. Savona, M. (2009). "Innovation in services: a review of the debate and a research agenda", *Journal of Evolutionary Economics*, 19(2), pp. 149-172.

García, A., Trujillo, Y., Perdomo, A. (2016). Optimización de estados en la mejora de procesos de software. *Enl@ ce: Revista Venezolana de Información, Tecnología y Conocimiento*, 13(2), 9-27.

Gómez, G., Aguileta, A., Ancona, G., Gómez, O. (2014). Avances en las Mejoras de Procesos Software en las MiPyMEs Desarrolladoras de Software. Una Revisión Sistemática. *Revista Latinoamericana de Ingeniería de Software*, 2(4), 262–268.

Hamada, T. (2019). Determinants of Decision-Makers' Attitudes toward Industry 4.0 Adaptation. *Social Sciences*, 8(5), 140.

Hernández, S., Martí, L. (2006). Conocimiento organizacional: la gestión de los recursos y el capital humano. Acimed, 34.

Hernández, R. (2014). *Metodología de la investigación*, Sexta Edición. Editorial Mc Graw Hill. México.

Humphrey, W. (2006). *Systems of Systems: Scaling up the Development Program* (No. CMU/SEI-2006-TR-017), Carnegie-Mellon Univ Pittsburgh, Pa. Software Engineering Inst.

INEGI (2014). Instituto Nacional de Estadística, Geografía E informática. Censo Económico del Directorio Estadístico Nacional de UnidadesEconómicas (DENUE), Consultado Enero, 24, 2017, from http://www.beta.inegi.org.mx/app/mapa/denue/default.aspx

Iqbal, J., Nasir, M. H. N., Khan, M., Awan, I., & Farid, S. (2020). Software process improvement implementation issues in small and medium enterprises that develop healthcare applications. *Journal of Medical Imaging and Health Informatics*, 10(10), 2393-2403.

ISO/IEC TR 29110-5-1-2:2011- (2011). Software Engineering - Lifecycle Profiles for Very Small Entities (VSEs) - Part 5-1-2: Management and engineering guide - Generic profile group: Basic profile, International Organization for Standardization/International Electrotechnical Commission: Geneva, Switzerland.

Ji et al., (2021). Learning-based automation of robotic assembly for smart manufacturing. *Proceedings of the IEEE*, 109(4), 423-440.

Juárez, L., Ulloa, R., Escobar, E. (2016). Las TIC, la innovación y los efectos en la competitividad de la PYME. *Revista Internacional Administracion & Finanzas*, 9(7), 87-108.

Keller, G. (2014). Statistics for Management and Economics, 10th ed.Stamford: Cengage Learning, South-Western College Pub.

Lahi, Allan, Elenurm, Tiit. (2014). Catalysts and Barriers of Open Innovation for SMEs in Transition Economy. Paper presented at the *Proceedings of the 2nd International Conference on Innovation and Entrepreneurship: ICIE*, pp 149.

López, A., Niembro, A., Ramos, D. (2013). Cadenas globales de valor, offshoring de servicios y rol de los recursos humanos: Lecciones de la Argentina. *El sistema argentino de innovación: Instituciones, empresas y redes. El desafío de la creación y apropiación de conocimiento*, D. Suárez (ed.), Los Polvorines, Buenos Aires, Ediciones ungs.

Llerena, G. (2014). *Experiencias en la implantación de un sistema de gestión de la calidad para el proceso de producción de software*, Paper presented at the Convención Internacional.1-4.

Martinez, C., Díaz, N., Gonnet, S. M., Leone, H. P. (2013). Representación de la Variabilidad en Líneas de Productos de Software empleando Redes de Petri. *14th Argentine Symposium on Software Engineering (42 JAIIO - ASSE 2013)*, pp. 127-14. http://42jaiio.sadio.org.ar/proceedings/simposios/Trabajos/ASSE/10.pdf

Martins, J. R., & Ning, A. (2021). *Engineering design optimization*. Cambridge University Press. http://flowlab.groups.et.byu.net/mdobook.pdf

Mejía, J., Iñiguez, F., Muñoz, M. (2017). SMART-SPI: A data analysis model proposal for software process improvement. In *2017 12th Iberian Conference on Information Systems and Technologies (CISTI)*, pp. 1-7. IEEE.

Menéndez, V., Castellanos, M. (2015). SPEM: Software process engineering metamodel. *Revista Latinoamericana de Ingenieria de Software*, 3(2), 92-100.

Metzger, A., Pohl, K. (2014). Software product line engineering and variability management: achievements and challenges. In *Proceedings of the on Future of Software Engineering*, pp. 70-84. http://dl.acm.org/citation.cfm?id=2593888.

Miranda, M., Casas, S., Marcos, C. (2015). Análisis de desarrollo de software orientado a Feature-Línea de producto de Software para Aplicaciones de TVDI. *Informes Científicos-Técnicos UNPA*, 7(2), pp. 167-195.

Morero, A., Borrastero, C., Motta, J. (2015). Procesos de innovación en la producción de software en argentina. Un estudio de caso. *Revista de Estudios Empresariales*. Segunda Época, (2), pp. 24-48.

Nakagawa, E. Y., Antonino, P. O., Schnicke, F., Kuhn, T., & Liggesmeyer, P. (2021). Continuous systems and software engineering for Industry 4.0: a disruptive view. *Information and software technology*, 135, 106562.

Narimani, M., Sahebkar, M., Khorasani, M. K., & Sani, I. A. (2022). Designing a Policy Model for Supporting Innovative Human Resources of Knowledge-based Companies in the Specialty Duty System Facility Program. *Journal of Science & Technology Policy*, 14(4).

Object Management Group (2004). "Software Process Engineering Meta-model (SPEM) Specification", version 2.0.

Park, S., Huh, J. (2018). Effect of cooperation on manufacturing it project development and test bed for successful industry 4.0 project: Safety management for security. *Processes*, 6(7), 88.

Pino, F. J., García, F., Piattini, M. (2008). Software process improvement in small and medium software enterprises: a systematic review. En *Software Quality Journal*, 16 (2), pp. 237-261.

Poor, P., Basl, J. (2018). Czech republic and processes of industry 4.0 implementation. *Annals of DAAAM and Proceedings of the International DAAAM Symposium*, 29, 454–59.

Rodríguez-Elias, O. M., Martínez-Garcia, A. I., Vizcaíno, A., Favela, J., Piattini, M. (2007). Organización de Conocimientos en Procesos de Ingeniería de Software por Medio de Modelado de Procesos: una Adaptación de SPEM. JIISIC, 7, 257-265.

Sehnem, S., de Queiroz, A. A. F. S., Pereira, S. C. F., dos Santos Correia, G., & Kuzma, E. (2022). Circular economy and innovation: A look from the perspective of organizational capabilities. *Business Strategy and the Environment*, 31(1), 236-250.

Schwab, K. (2016). The global competitiveness report 2013–2014: Full data edition, World Economic Forum.

Simanca, M. M., Montoya, L. A., Bernal, C. A. (2016). Gestión del conocimiento en cadenas productivas: El caso de la cadena láctea en Colombia. *Información tecnológica*, 27(3), 93-106.

Vrchota, J., Volek, T., & Novotná, M. (2019). Factors Introducing Industry 4.0 to SMES. *Social Sciences*, 8(5), 130.

Wang, T., Yang, J., & Zhang, F. (2021). The effects of organizational controls on innovation modes: An ambidexterity perspective. Journal of Management & Organization, 27(1), 106-130. doi:10.1017/jmo.2018.35

World-Bank (2013). World Bank East Asia and Pacific Economic Update, October 2013: Rebuilding Policy Buffers, Reinvigorating Growth: World Bank Publications.

Yang, F., & Gu, S. (2021). Industry 4.0, a revolution that requires technology and national strategies. *Complex & Intelligent Systems*, 7(3), 1311-1325.

7

The Pandemic Effects and Change Management in Tourism

Diana Cristina Rodríguez-Moreno

Universidad Pedagógica y Tecnológica de Colombia

Abstract

The pandemic caused by COVID-19 spread throughout the world and the measures to deal with it hit the tourism sector in a way that was unimaginable for the sector's agents. Many tourism businesses, especially small ones, did not survive the crisis. The remaining organizations must necessarily change to face the new context. The objective of this paper was to point out some changes that the COVID-19 pandemic generated in the tourism sector and its businesses. The topic of organizational change and change strategies was addressed to suggest ideas for dealing with the crisis. Tourism services can be restructured in the direction of greater customer participation during the service process. The appropriation and application of technology can reduce customer contact and make tourists contribute more resources and improve their skills to increase self-service. Tourism marketing should be oriented to improve the image of destinations, showing how the lives of tourists are protected with appropriate biosecurity protocols. The challenges in the field of human resources management for tourism are wide-ranging; small businesses have significant weaknesses in customer service and difficulties in obtaining trained personnel and hiring them on a permanent basis.

Keywords: COVID-19, tourism sector, change management, strategy, competitiveness

7.1 Introduction

COVID-19, which originated in China, spread throughout the world. Globalization and international travel for tourism or business contributed significantly to the acceleration of infection (Lew, Cheer, Haywood, Brouder, & Salazar, 2020). The measures imposed by national governments to deal with the pandemic have been detrimental to most sectors of the economy, especially services because they depend for the most part on contact between service providers and clients. The tourism sector, which includes lodging, entertainment, transportation, and food companies, among others, is one of the most affected (Mostafanezhad, Cheer, & Sin, 2020).

Tourism companies of all sizes have faced the crisis and have abruptly visualized the need for change within their businesses to cope with the changes imposed by the pandemic. The ability to cope with environmental forces that often drastically alter business dynamics has become a key determinant of competitive advantage and an essential factor for organizational survival. Global crises, such as the COVID-19 crisis, demand changes in companies, which makes the subject of change and its management timely (Bjorn & Kokshagina, 2021). To operate effectively, organizations must align themselves with their environment, making use of their resources, capabilities, skills, and application of technologies to business (Beer, Voelpel, Leibold, & Tekie, 2005).

The objective of this paper was to present some changes generated by the COVID-19 pandemic in the tourism sector and its companies. A review of the scientific literature on the effects of COVID-19 on tourism was conducted, the topic of change and change strategies was reviewed, and then the change approaches were integrated with the business challenges generated by the pandemic.

This work is organized as follows. First, the concept of change, organizational change, and approaches to change are presented, the following is a discussion of the strategy, then the changes in the tourism sector imposed by the COVID-19 pandemic, then the discussion, and finally the conclusions where some ideas on strategies for change in tourism companies that survive the crisis are presented.

7.2 Organizational Change

To change means to move from one state to another, from a circumstance with factors, characteristics, and relationships arranged in a certain way, to an orientation and situation different from the previous one. It is the trans-formation of an entity, subject, situation, or substance into something else. According to Nelson (2003), organizational change has been conceptualized as the passage from a status quo to a new configuration, with the objective of better adapting to the environment, so it can be seen as a deviation from the model due to a natural response to internal and/or environmental conditions. The objective of organizational change is to adapt to changes in the environment, increase efficiency, productivity, and competitiveness (Cheng-Fei & Yu-Fang, 2008).

Organizational change is the result of changes in actions, values, pro-cesses, skills, and contextual situations that produce variations in decision-making (Steinke, Dastmalchian, Blyton, & Hasselback, 2013). The change can be caused by external or internal factors and takes different sizes and shapes (Kotter, Tichi, Simons, & Pound, 1995). Mintzberg and Westley (1992) indicate that change is generated from the inside out or from the out-side in, i.e. deductive or inductive, the first going from the conceptual to the concrete, generally studied in the literature on strategic management, on the other hand, Inductive change leads to tangible variations to generalizations, modifying the organizational vision and culture.

The business organization is an open system and as such constantly interacts with the environment in a symbiotic relationship, generating mutual disturbances and externalities that generate bilateral changes. Organizations are systems in continuous evolution, partly in response to their complex environment with political, economic, social, and technological changes and partly due to internal changes caused by their members (Steinke et al., 2013). Leifer (1989) cited in Nelson (2003) says that the steady state is fictitious because change is consistent with open systems, in which learning occurs, which is an adaptation resulting from experience.

Organizations are structured in terms of archetypes, with qualities and routines that the actors unconsciously accept as the correct way to act, so a radical change implies an abrupt movement from one archetype to another, which can generate problems due to high resistance to change, because of the predominance of ways of thinking and acting; on the other hand, a convergent change is a movement closer to normal, in this case, the pace of change will be more gradual and depends on the conditions of the system and how rigid it is (Greenwood & Hinings, 1996). Change cannot be relied upon to occur in stability; organizations experience periods of incremental change, alternating between periods of more violent change and quieter ones (Nelson, 2003).

Resistance to change includes both organizational and personal factors, the former can be the perceived credibility of the organization, credibility about those leading the change, and the company's history of change; personal factors can lead to judgmental behavior and sabotage (Self & Schraeder, 2009). Resistance to change is also the result of uncertainty, which is one of the most common psychological states in the context of organizational change (Hobman, Jones, Gallois, & Callan, 2004).

Uncertainty is defined as the lack of clear knowledge about something, when information is scarce, uncertain, doubtful, or contradictory, which generates fear of error. In the business context, uncertainty is an aversive state that motivates strategies aimed at reducing or managing it (Hobman et al., 2004). In increasingly complex economic and business environments, uncertainty is growing, due to the increase of agents and interactions, to the lack of understanding of new orders and their operations, and to the increase of randomness in phenomena, all of which leads organizations to generate changes and reconfigurations to ensure their permanence.

Mintzberg y Westley (1992) points out that organizations that do not change eventually lose synchrony with their environment, while those that never stabilize are not able to generate products and services efficiently, so there is always change embedded in stability, as well as stability embedded in change. In the theory of complex thought order and disorder, stability and change are part of the organizational dynamics (Morin, 1998). Apparently, according to the academic literature, there are two perspectives for change management, the planned and the emergent approach (Bamford & Forrester, 2003). The planned approach aims to generate economic value for the companies' shareholders, where change is planned, focused on formal systems and organizational structure; from the other perspective, change is emergent, less planned and programmatic, aimed at developing a culture of high commitment based on people's ability to implement the strategy and learn in the process of change (Beer & Nohria, 2001).

The planned change approach is substantially based on the contributions of Kurt Lewin, initiated around the 1950s, with his work on action research and the three-step change model, planned change assumes organizational change as a process of moving from one fixed state to another, through a series of planned moves, using a three-stage model, the first being holding on to the known (freeze), the second being the exploration of ideas (unfreeze) and finally identifying and utilizing desired skills and values and refreezing (Burnes, 1996; Bamford & Forrester, 2003).

A successful change project must, in accordance with the planned change perspective, comprise the three steps of unfreezing the current level, moving to the new level, and refreezing this new level (By, 2007). According to Lewin, when a change occurs in the performance of a group, this usually has a short duration and returns to the previous standard, then the achievement itself is not enough, it is necessary to stay at the new level, so to adopt a new behavior, the previous one must be discarded (Burnes, 1996).

In the planned change approach there is a tendency to replace choice with certainty and preference or lesson with prescription, however, the change progresses continuously and openly (Burnes, 1996); the planned approach assumes that people in the organization agree to work in one direction without disagreement, however, differences usually occur (Bamford & Forrester, 2003). The planned perspective ignores situations in which rapid transformations are required, it also tends to overlook organizational politics and conflicts or assumes that they can be easily identified and resolved; on the other hand, the emergent approach takes into account the unpredictable nature of change, sees it as a continuous and open process of adaptation to variable conditions (Burnes, 1996) the environment and the company.

The emerging change approach states that change should not be assumed as a series of linear events that occur in a set period, on the contrary, it should be understood as an unpredictable process, with multiple relationships between multiple variables; the emerging view of change is more concerned with preparing for and facilitating change rather than providing specific, planned steps for change initiatives (By, 2007). An important development of emergent change is the emphasis on action (from the bottom up) rather than control (from the top down) (Bamford & Forrester, 2003).

Dunphy and Stace (1993) suggest that a more holistic approach to organizational change management is required, one that is transformative, incremental, and adapts to the use of both coercive and participatory means to achieve change, a contingent model is needed that allows change strategies to be modified according to changes in the environment. The contingent approach proposes that the structure and performance of organizations depends on the situational variables they face; companies do not face the same challenges, their situations are different, so their structures and operations must be different as well (Burnes, 1996). If the operations and structures of the company are arranged according to contingencies, then it is possible that the opposite occurs, that is, that the influence is not exerted on the organizational structure but on the situational variables, thus the organizations can manipulate and modify them according to its structure, ways of working and management style, then sometimes the environment variables are the ones that should be changed (Burnes, 1996).

There seems to be a consensus that organizations are facing unprecedented levels of change and consequently the ability to manage change should be a core competency (Burnes, 2005). Understanding change management is critical, regardless of company size or purpose (By & Dale, 2008). Given the need for change in organizations, changes can be discontinuous, reactive, ad hoc or triggered by crisis situations (By, 2007; Burnes, 2005; Nelson, 2003). In any case and whatever the need and the strategies for change, the challenge of organizational change is to improve the ability to learn how to respond more effectively to the changing environment as well as the ability to shape that environment (Steinke et al., 2013).

There is no doubt how important, for organizations, their ability to identify where they want to be in the future and how to manage the changes necessary to get there, as a consequence, organizational change cannot be separated from strategy, just as strategy cannot. can exist without implying change (By, 2007; Burnes, 2005). Not only is there a relationship between strategy and organizational change, but other variables of change are also structure, technology, culture, objectives, effectiveness, efficiency, and human resources (Sadeghi, 2011). Next, strategy is studied as a dependent and independent variable of change, that is, generating organizational change requires strategies, but dealing with change in the environment also requires change strategies in organizations.

7.3 Strategy and Competitive Advantage

Mintzberg y Waters (1985) establish, as a result of a decade of research on the process of strategy formation, that strategy is a pattern in a flow of decisions. Strategy is a path to a goal, it is also defined as the art of directing military operations and hence its adaptation to organizational discourse. Grant (1991) specifies strategy as the combination that a company implements between its internal resources and skills, as well as the opportunities and threats generated by the environment.

Mintzberg (1994) states that strategy is not a plan, it is a vision, its essence lies in its construction as a learning process, through trial and experimentation, thus, those that work gradually converge into viable patterns that converge into strategies. During the 1980s, the study of the strategy focused on the link between strategy and the environment in which the company operates (Grant, 1991), thus the concept of sustained competitive advantage as the basis of the company's performance has been one of the bases for the study of strategy (Cheng-Fei & Yu-Fang, 2008).

Porter (1980) suggests that the performance of companies depends on the characteristics of the industry in which organizations operate, so the competitive strategy must consider five forces that exert pressure on the sector: existing competitors, potentials, bargaining power of suppliers, customers, and the existence of substitute products. Porter (1985) also establishes three generic competitive strategies: cost leadership, differentiation, and market focus. Although extensive literature on competitive strategy emphasizes strategic positioning issues through the choice between cost and differentiation, broad and narrow market, it is essential to recognize the existence and situation of the company's resources (Grant, 1991). However, the presence of productive resources does not fully clarify the competitiveness of sectors, efficiency in the use of resources is also very important (Porter, 1991), as a possibility of economies of scale, with ownership of resources with plant capacity and efficiency, superior process technologies, economical labor, low-cost raw materials, etc., or on the differentiation side, the reputation of the brand or logistics networks (Grant, 1991).

The vision of resources and capabilities expresses that competitive advantage is the result of the resources and capabilities controlled by the company, it considers the company as the main unit of analysis (Dyer & Singh, 1998); for resource theory, environmental exploration is only half the story, understanding sources of competitive advantage requires internal company analysis (Barney, 1995) argues that the differential performance of the companies is due more to the heterogeneity of the companies than to the structure of the industry (Rumelt, 1991). The resource-based model deals primarily with the internal accumulation of resources (Peteraf, 1993), which, to be a source of competitive advantage, must be valuable, scarce, imperfectly imitable, and non-substitutable (Barney, 1991). Not only the asset endowment counts, but also the capabilities that the company possesses are essential to achieve objectives (Rumelt, Schedel, & Teece, 1991). From the perspective of capabilities, these must be built and the strategy implies choosing between paths of skills development (Teece, Pisano, & Shuen, 1997; Teece, 2007)

Another approach, on the formation of competitive advantages, is the relational one, which not only considers the industrial environment and the company with its resources and capabilities, the critical resources of a company can go beyond its limits and can be integrated into routines and processes. Between companies, a business network can develop relationships that result in sustained competitive advantage, so the relational view is useful to examine the links between organizations that create value (Dyer & Singh, 1998). To increase the chances of successful strategy implementation, it is essential to improve understanding of the complex interactions between structural change efforts and organizational networks (Lynch & Louise, 2019).

7.4 Changes in Tourism Generated by the Pandemic

In December 2019, COVID-19 hit Wuhan, the World Health Organization notified the world of the existence of the virus in January 2020 and in March declared the contagion of the virus as a pandemic (Yang, Zhang, & Chen, 2020; Gössling, Scott, & Hall, 2020; Brouder, 2020). The measures to contain the contagion of the virus in all the countries of the world have been basically social distancing, mandatory quarantine, suspension of non-essential activities and restriction in the movement of people (Gretzel et al., 2020; Williams, 2020; Qiu, Park, Li, & Song, 2020). These actions had a negative impact on most lines of the economy, especially activities related to services because they normally require interpersonal contact.

One of the sectors that bring together several services is tourism, which was completely paralyzed (Couto et al., 2020; Niewiadomski, 2020) with the consecutive demand crisis (Zenker & Kock, 2020); because the fear of contagion led to the closure of cities in most countries (Bae & Chang, 2020), hotels, museums, beaches, transportation, cruises, restaurants, among others, were closed, sporting and cultural events, festivals, fairs were postponed and canceled (Gössling et al., 2020; Ioannides & Gyimóthy, 2020). The COVID-19 pandemic generated a crisis of greater proportions in world tourism. The pandemic has had a significant impact on the tourism industry (Motevalli-taher & Paydar, 2021), and has generated shock and unprecedented changes (González-Torres, Rodríguez-Sánchez, & Pelechano-barahona, 2021). It is health and epidemiological crisis that has a sustained and devasting duration (Radic et al., 2020). The final impact on the economies will depend on the measures taken at the national, regional, and local levels (Cepal, 2020). Sigala (2020) points out that the circumstances and impact of the COVID-19 pandemic show signs that the crisis is not only different from others, but can also generate deep and long-term structural social and cultural transformations in tourism activity; it is a major event scale with interconnected and multi-dimensional shocks that challenge values and worldviews and lead to a sustained recession.

The World Tourism Organization calculated that with the crisis in the sector caused by measures to cope with the pandemic, the industry contracted by approximately 80% by 2020; The World Travel and Tourism Council assumes that the losses of the tourism industry will be around US $ 22 billion and a reduction of 75 million direct jobs; the International Air Transport Association indicates that bankruptcy reached US 119 billion in 2020 (Polyzos, Samitas, & Spyridou, 2020; Tatum, 2020; Zhu & Deng, 2020; Rutynskyi & Kushniruk, 2020; Zenker & Kock, 2020).

The opinion of academics on tourism and crises is framed in two contexts, supply and demand, the first demands crisis management at the collective level, and the second is based on the perception of individual risk (Qiu et al., 2020), They also indicate that when the pandemic is overcome, even if travel restrictions are lifted, the psyche and behavior of tourists will have changed (Kock, Nørfelt, Josiassen, Assaf, & Tsionas, 2020); in the same way, they indicate that when the pandemic is overcome, even if travel restrictions are lifted, the psyche and behavior of tourists will have changed (Tremblay-huet, 2020).

Restrictions on international, regional, and local travel or displacement immediately affected all economies, especially businesses immersed in tourism such as accommodation, air and land transportation; cruises, cafes and restaurants, conventions, festivals, fairs, sporting events, etc. (Gössling et al., 2020). Museums, hotels, and beaches were also closed and events of all types and sizes were postponed or canceled (Ioannides & Gyimóthy, 2020).

The environment has a decisive influence on tourism, likewise tourism generates externalities that affect its environment (Uğur & Akbıyık, 2020). The COVID-19 spread throughout the planet traveling on the transport networks used by the tourism industry, so precisely the trips, many with tourist reasons, contributed to the virus spread (Lew, Cheer, Haywood, Brouder, & Salazar, 2020; Maditinos & Vassiliadis, 2008). Tourism involves activities that are greatly affected by unexpected events such as wars, terrorism, diseases, economic crises, etc.

The crisis in tourism generated by the pandemic affected the operating capacity of related services (Chen, Huang, & Li, 2020). The difficulties to which the tourist services businesses have been subjected are unprecedented, although it is not the first crisis, if it is the largest (Rutynskyi & Kushniruk, 2020; (Kock, Nørfelt, Josiassen, Assaf, & Tsionas, 2020; Tadini & Piva, 2020; Mariolis, Rodousakis, & Soklis, 2020)

In thousands of places, businesses of all sizes, which depend directly or indirectly on the economy of the visitors, have suspended operations and it is foreseen that many will probably never reopen (Ioannides & Gyimóthy, 2020). It was suggested that around 75% of small businesses in the hotel sector will not reopen after the pandemic in the United States and Europe (Baum & Nguyen, 2020). In Latin America, around 99% of the companies are MSMEs and the forced suspension of activities due to the quarantine, meant an accelerated and abrupt reduction in sales, which forced numerous companies to definitively close (Cepal, 2020).

The hotels sought different functionalities due to the pandemic, such as places for quarantine, temporary accommodation for health workers, hospital extensions for mildly ill patients, infirmaries such as quarantine places with associated services (Rogerson & Baum, 2020). The pandemic severely affected the airline industry, airlines such as Virgin, Flybe, Trans States Airlines, Compass Airlines, etc., have collapsed and face serious financial problems (Tsionas, 2020). Air transport is an essential component of tourism, the repercussions on tourist activity derived from reductions in air traffic, in recent history there have been impacts that have had a pandemic event in air transport, the Sars that was limited to the areas of North America and Asia produced negative effects on passenger air traffic, with COVID-19 the impact has been much greater (Tadini & Piva, 2020).

In terms of consumer behavior, tourism consumers are very sensitive to crises of local and global dimensions. Nothing scares the average tourist more than the threat of contracting a virus or illness while traveling (Rutynskyi & Kushniruk, 2020). On the day of the news of the pandemic, many travelers made the decision to cancel or postpone their trips and began to discuss issues related to travel insurance guarantees; people were affected by anxiety and fear (Uğur & Akbıyık, 2020).

The threat of COVID-19 modifies the behavior of tourists, it is possible that they become more ethnocentric, thus choosing national destinations first and more frequently over foreign ones, having as motivation the support of the local economy (Zenker & Kock, 2020). In this way, tourists contribute to the recovery of national tourism (Arbulú, Razumova, Rey-maquieira, & Sastre, 2021). There is a greater preference for the group to which one belongs, when there is a pathogenic threat, it becomes more attractive to interact with the members of the group because this behavior presents fewer health risks, and the group also provides support in case of illness (Navarrete & Fessler, 2006, cited by Kock et al., 2020).

7.5 Discussion

Due to the pandemic caused by COVID-19, the tourism sector has been affected to such an extent that many of the micro, small and medium-sized companies dedicated to tourism were forced to definitively close (Cepal, 2020). the same will happen with 75% of small tourism businesses in the United States and Europe (Baum & Nguyen, 2020). With the trips suspended, the tourism businesses lost clients for a period of more than a year (Lapointe, 2020), without income and with the permanence of labor and financial obligations, among others. Traces of the pandemic suggest that the crisis for tourism is unprecedented and will lead to severe socio-cultural changes (Sigala, 2020).

Crises provide opportunities for change for companies and their leaders. Change management is an exercise in choosing what to change and the approach to use, according to the circumstances in which the change occurs (Burnes, 1996), which should be viewed holistically and contextually, as well as retrospectively (Mintzberg & Westley, 1992). The business system must adapt its structure according to the context of change (Bagnaresi et al., 2019). In the company, the changes verify in its architecture that, according to the new states, it is necessary to rearrange elements within the system, so that it preserves its external structure, remains alive, and develops.

The management of the COVID-19 crisis is presented in two contexts, first that of supply that requires collective management by the network of agents involved in tourism and the second of demand focused on tourists and their behavior (Qiu et al., 2020), which has changed and continues to transform. The changes for the tourism sector and its companies will be permanent and mandatory. The companies, which still exist, must, first of all, recognize the change to configure strategies to adapt or face it (Self & Schraeder, 2009).

In the case of the tourism crisis due to COVID-19, the environment has forced change and imposed its need. As Mintzberg y Waters (1985) said the environment is dictating the guidelines for the actions that organizations must undertake. Companies have the need to achieve an adjustment to the environment, to maintain their balance and survive; they usually aim to achieve this adjustment through their competitive strategy, the success of which also determines the success of the company. To survive and thrive in a rapidly changing environment, companies must use strategies of various types and levels (Cheng-Fei & Yu-Fang, 2008).

To manage change, in tourism companies, it is clear that the planned perspective is not applicable, as a rapid transformation is required, on the other hand, the emerging change that emphasizes action may be more relevant. It is necessary for companies to recognize their resources and manage their capabilities by developing different competencies in human resources, competencies that meet the new needs of customers.

7.6 Conclusions

The demand for tourism businesses will not recover in the short term, a situation accentuated by the outbreaks of the virus and the time it took to obtain effective vaccines and their distribution. Tourist services, in many countries, must operate at medium capacity, which will generate an increase in prices in this way but will also increase due to the costs that companies must incur for biosecurity measures. Tourism companies will face this change by designing differentiation strategies and segmenting the target market more specifically. Services can now be restructured with greater customer participation, in the service process, the use of technology can reduce contact and make the tourist support and contribute more resources, such as time and training to increase self-service.

The marketing of tourism businesses must also change, the characteristics of the service are necessarily different, there are fewer clients, the tourist may perceive that the service improves, that the quality increases, due to the greater attention of the staff, for example, in Restaurants advertising should be aimed at improving the images of tourist destinations, promoting and showing how the lives of tourists are protected with the appropriate biosafety protocols.

The challenges in the field of human resource management for tourism are broad, especially because small companies have significant weaknesses in customer service, due to the financial difficulty in obtaining trained and permanently hired personnel. Tourism is a sector that is characterized by labor informality, by hiring people in shifts and for short periods due to the seasonality of demand, with the COVID-19 crisis the situation seems to worsen for companies and workers. Joint work with the government and academia is required to achieve training in human resource competencies for the sector.

References

Arbulú, I., Razumova, M., Rey-maquieira, J., & Sastre, F. (2021). Journal of Destination Marketing & Management Can domestic tourism relieve the COVID-19 tourist industry crisisă? The case of Spain. Journal of Destination Marketing & Management, 20(July 2020), 100568. https://doi.org/10.1016/j.jdmm.2021.100568

Bae, S. Y., & Chang, P. (2020). Current Issues in Tourism The effect of coronavirus disease-19 (COVID-19) risk perception on behavioural intention towards ' untact ' tourism in South Korea during the first wave of the pandemic (March 2020). Current Issues in Tourism, 1–19. https://doi.org/10.1080/13683500.2020.1798895

Bagnaresi, D., Barbini, F. M., Battilani, P., Bagnaresi, D., Barbini, F. M., & Battilani, P. (2019). Organizational change in the hospitality industryă: The change drivers in a longitudinal analysis. Business History, 0(0), 1–22. https://doi.org/10.1080/00076791.2019.1676230

Bamford, D. R., & Forrester, P. L. (2003). Managing planned and emergent change within an operations management environment. International Journal of Operations & Productivon Management, 23(5), 546–564. https://doi.org/10.1108/01443570310471857

Barney, J. (1991). Firm Resources and Sustained Competitive Advantage. Journal of Management, 17(1), 99–120. https://doi.org/10.1177/014920639101700108

Barney, Jay. (1995). Looking inside for Competitive Advantage. Academy of Management, 9(4), 49–61. Retrieved from https://www.jstor.org/stable/4165288?seq=1#metadata_info_tab_contents

Baum, T., & Nguyen, T. (2020). Hospitality, tourism, human rights and the impact of COVID-19. International Journal of Contemporary Hospitality Management, 32(7), 2397–2407. https://doi.org/10.1108/IJCHM-03-2020-0242

Beer, M., & Nohria, N. (2001). Breaking the Code of Change. Research and Ideas, April, 1–4.

Beer, M., Voelpel, S. C., Leibold, M., & Tekie, E. B. (2005). Strategic Management as Organizational Learning: Developing Fit and Alignment through a Disciplined Process. Long Range Planed, 38, 445–465. https://doi.org/10.1016/j.lrp.2005.04.008

Bjorn, J., & Kokshagina, O. (2021). How firms undertake organizational changes to shift to more-exploratory strategiesă: A process perspective.

Research Policy, 50(July 2019). https://doi.org/10.1016/j.respol.2020.10 4118

Brouder, P. (2020). Reset reduxă: possible evolutionary pathways towards the transformation of tourism in a COVID-19 world. Tourism Geographies, 0(0), 1–7. https://doi.org/10.1080/14616688.2020.1760928

Burnes, B. (1996). No such thing as … a " one best way " to manage organizational change. Management Decision, 34(10), 11–18.

Burnes, B. (2005). Complexity theories and organizational change. International Journal of Management Reviews, 7(2), 73–90.

By, R. (2007). Organisational change management: A critical review Organisational. Journal of Change Management, 5(4), 369–380. https://doi.org/ 10.1080/14697010500359250

By, Rune, & Dale, C. (2008). The Successful Management of Organisational Change in Tourism SMEs: Initial Findings in UK Visitor Attractions. International Journal of Tourism Research, 10(April), 305–313.

Cepal. (2020). COVID-19 América Latina y el Caribe ante la pandemia del COVID-19. Efectos económicos y sociales.

Chen, H., Huang, X., & Li, Z. (2020). A content analysis of Chinese news coverage on COVID-19 and tourism. Current Issues in Tourism, 0(0), 1–8. https://doi.org/10.1080/13683500.2020.1763269

Cheng-Fei, T., & Yu-Fang, Y. (2008). A model to explore the mystery between organizations' downsizing strategies and firm performance. Journal of Organizational Change Management, 21(3), 367–384.

Couto, G., Castanho, R. A., Pimentel, P., Carvalho, C., Sousa, Á., & Santos, C. (2020). The Impacts of COVID-19 Crisis over the Tourism Expectations of the Azores Archipelago Residents. Sustainability, 12(7612), 1–14.

Dunphy, D., & Stace, D. S. M. of C. C. (1993). The Strategic Management of Corporate Change. Human Relations, 46(8), 905–920. Retrieved from https://journals.sagepub.com/stoken/rbtfl/2W8RG6JILEGDPU7ZK6CY EC/pdf/10.1177/001872679304600801

Dyer, J. H., & Singh, H. (1998). The Relational View: Cooperative Strategy and Sources of Interorganizational Competitive Advantage. Academy of Management Review, 23(4), 660–679. https://doi.org/0.2307/259056

González-Torres, T., Rodríguez-Sánchez, J.-L., & Pelechano-barahona, E. (2021). Managing relationships in the Tourism Supply Chain to overcome epidemic outbreaksă: The case of COVID-19 and the hospitality industry in Spain. International Journal of Hospitality Management, 92, 1–11. https: //doi.org/10.1016/j.ijhm.2020.102733

Gössling, S., Scott, D., & Hall, C. M. (2020). Pandemics, tourism and global changeǎ: a rapid assessment of COVID-19. Journal of Sustainable Tourism, 1–20. https://doi.org/10.1080/09669582.2020.1758708

Grant, R. M. (1991). The Resource-Based Theory of Competitive Advantage: Implications for Strategy Formulation. Knowledge and Strategy (Vol. 33). Butterworth-Heinemann. https://doi.org/10.1016/B978-0-7506-7088-3.5 0004-8

Greenwood, R., & Hinings, C. R. (1996). Understanding Radical Organizational Changeǎ: Bringind Together the Old and the New Institutionalism. Academy of Management Review, 21(4), 1022–1054. https://doi.org/10.2 307/259163

Gretzel, U., Fuchs, M., Baggio, R., Hoepken, W., Law, R., Neidhardt, J., … Xiang, Z. (2020). e-Tourism beyond COVID-19: a call for transformative research. Information Technology & Tourism, 22(2), 187–203. https://doi. org/10.1007/s40558-020-00181-3

Hobman, E., Jones, E., Gallois, C., & Callan, V. J. (2004). Uncertainity During Organizational change: Types, Consequences and Magement Strategies. Journa of Business and Psychology, 18(4), 507–532.

Ioannides, D., & Gyimóthy, S. (2020). The COVID-19 crisis as an opportunity for escaping the unsustainable global tourism path. Tourism Geographies, 0(0), 1–9. https://doi.org/10.1080/14616688.2020.176344 5

Kock, F., Nørfelt, A., Josiassen, A., Assaf, A. G., & Tsionas, M. G. (2020). Understanding the COVID-19 tourist psycheǎ: The Evolutionary Tourism Paradigm. Annals of Tourism Research, 85(May), 1–13. https://doi.org/10 .1016/j.annals.2020.103053

Kotter, J., Tichi, N., Simons, R., & Pound, J. (1995). Leading Change: Why Transformation Efforts Fail the Promise of the Governed Corporation. HarvardBusinessReview.

Lapointe, D. (2020). Reconnecting tourism after COVID-19ǎ: the paradox of alterity in tourism areas. Tourism Geographies, 0(0), 1–6. https://doi.org/ 10.1080/14616688.2020.1762115

Lew, A., Cheer, J., Haywood, M., Brouder, P., & Salazar, N. (2020). Visions of travel and tourism after the global COVID-19 transformation of 2020. Tourism Geographies, 0(0), 1–12. https://doi.org/10.1080/14616688.2020. 1770326

Lynch, S. E., & Louise, M. (2019). Strategy implementation and organizational changeǎ: How formal reorganization affects professional networks.

Long Range Planning, 52(2), 255–270. https://doi.org/10.1016/j.lrp.2018 .02.003

Maditinos, Z., & Vassiliadis, C. (2008). Crises and Disasters in Tourism Industry: Happen locally - Affect globally. Mibes - e book. Retrieved from http://mibes.teilar.gr/e-books/2008/maditinos_vasi-liadis67-76.pdf

Mariolis, T., Rodousakis, N., & Soklis, G. (2020). The COVID-19 multiplier effects of tourism on the Greek economy. Tourism Economics, 1–8. https: //doi.org/10.1177/1354816620946547

Mintzberg, H. (1994). La caída y el auge de la planificación estratégica. Harvard Business Review, 16. Retrieved from https://hbr.org/1994/01/ the-fall-and-rise-of-strategic-planning?language=es

Mintzberg, H., & Waters, J. (1985). Of Strategies, Deliberate and Emergent. Strategic Management Journal, 6(3), 257–272. Retrieved from https://ww w.jstor.org/stable/2486186?origin=JSTOR-pdf&seq=1

Mintzberg, H., & Westley, F. (1992). Cycles of Organizational Change. Strategic Management Journal, 13, 39–59. Retrieved from http://www. jstor.org/stable/2486365.

Morin, E. (1998). Introducción al pensamiento complejo (Gedisa). Barcelona. Retrieved from http://cursoenlineasincostoedgarmorin.org/images/descar gables/Morin_Introduccion_al_pensamiento_complejo.pdf

Motevalli-taher, F., & Paydar, M. M. (2021). Supply chain design to tackle coronavirus pandemic crisis by tourism management. Applied Soft Computing Journal, 104, 107217. https://doi.org/10.1016/j.asoc.2021.1072 17

Nelson, L. (2003). A case study in organisational change: implications for theory. The Learning Organization, 10(1), 18–30. https://doi.org/10.1108/ 09696470310457478

Niewiadomski, P. (2020). COVID-19ă: from temporary de-globalisation to a re- discovery of tourism? Tourism Geographies, 0(0), 1–6. https://doi.org/ 10.1080/14616688.2020.1757749

Peteraf, M. (1993). The Cornerstones of Competitive Advantage: A Resource Bases View. Strategic Management Journal, 14(3), 179–191.

Polyzos, S., Samitas, A., & Spyridou, A. E. (2020). Tourism demand and the COVID-19 pandemică: an LSTM approach. Tourism Recreation Research, 1–13. https://doi.org/10.1080/02508281.2020.1777053

Porter, M. (1985). Competitive Advantage - Creating and Sustaining Superior Performance. New York: FreePress. https://doi.org/10.1182/blood-2005-1 1-4354

Porter, M. (1991). La ventaja competitiva de las naciones. Ed Vergara. Argentina (Vergara). Buenos Aires, Argentina.Porter, M. E. (1980). Competitive strategy: Techniques for analyzing industries and companies. New York.

Qiu, R. T. R., Park, J., Li, S., & Song, H. (2020). Social costs of tourism during the COVID-19 pandemic. Annals of Tourism Research, 84(July), 1–14. https://doi.org/10.1016/j.annals.2020.102994

Radic, A., Law, R., Lück, M., Kang, H., Ariza-montes, A., Arjona-fuentes, J. M., & Han, H. (2020). Apocalypse Now or Overreaction to Coronavirusă: The Global Cruise Tourism Industry Crisis. Sustainability, 12(6968), 1–19.

Rogerson, C. M., & Baum, T. (2020). Covid-19 and African tourism reasearch egendas. Development Southern Africa, 37(5), 727–742. https://doi.org/10.1080/0376835X.2020.1818551

Rumelt, R. P. (1991). Does industry matter? Strategic Management Journal, 185(February 1990), 167–185.Rumelt, R., Schedel, D., & Teece, D. (1991). Strategic Mangement and Economics. Strategic Management Journal, 12, 5–29. Retrieved from https://www.jstor.org/stable/2486431?seq =1

Rutynskyi, M., & Kushniruk, H. (2020). The impact of quarantine due to COVID-19 pandemic on the tourism industry in Lviv (Ukraine). Problems and Perspectives in Management, 18(2), 193–205. https://doi.org/10.215 11/ppm.18(2).2020.17

Sadeghi, D. (2011). Social and Alignment of organizational change strategies and its relationship with increasing organizations ' performance. Procedia - Social and Behavioral Sciences, 20, 1099–1107. https://doi.org/10.1016/ j.sbspro.2011.08.119

Self, D. R., & Schraeder, M. (2009). Enhancing the success of organizational change resistance. Leadership & Organization Development Journal, 30(2), 167–182. https://doi.org/10.1108/01437730910935765

Sigala, M. (2020). Tourism and COVID-19ă: Impacts and implications for advancing and resetting industry and research. Journal of Business Research, 117(June), 312–321. https://doi.org/10.1016/j.jbusres.2020 .06.015

Steinke, C., Dastmalchian, A., Blyton, P., & Hasselback, P. (2013). Organizational change strategies within healthcare. Healthcare Management Forum, 26(3), 127–135. https://doi.org/10.1016/j.hcmf.2013.05.002

Tadini, M., & Piva, E. (2020). Impatto del Covid-19 su Trasporto Aereo e Turismo: Possibili Scenari Evolutivi. Documento Geografici, 1(35), 565–578. https://doi.org/10.19246/DOCUGEO2281-7549/202001

Tatum, M. (2020). Will medical tourism survive covid-19? BMJ, 370, 1–3. https://doi.org/10.1136/bmj.m2677

Teece, D. J. (2007). Explicating Dynamic Capabilities: The Nature and Microfoundatios of (sustainable) Enterprise Performance. Strategic Management Journal, 1350(June), 1319–1350. https://doi.org/10.1002/smj

Teece, D., Pisano, G., & Shuen, A. (1997). Dynamic Capabilities and Strategic Management. Strategic Management Journal, 18(7), 509–533.

Tremblay-huet, S. (2020). COVID-19 leads to a new context for the " right to tourism ": a reset of tourists ' perspectives on space appropriation is needed appropriation is needed. Tourism Geographies, 0(0), 1–4. https://doi.org/10.1080/14616688.2020.1759136

Tsionas, M. G. (2020). COVID-19 and gradual adjustment in the tourism, hospitality, and related industries. Tourism Economics, 1–5. https://doi.org/10.1177/1354816620933039

Uğur, N. G., & Akbıyık, A. (2020). Impacts of COVID-19 on global tourism industryǎ: A cross-regional comparison. Tourism Management Perspectives, 36(September), 1–13. https://doi.org/10.1016/j.tmp.2020.100744

Yang, Y., Zhang, H., & Chen, X. (2020). Coronavirus pandemic and tourism: Dynamic stochastic general equilibrium modeling of infectious disease outbreak. Annals of Tourism Research, 83(February), 1–6. https://doi.org/10.1016/j.annals.2020.102913

Zenker, S., & Kock, F. (2020). The coronavirus pandemic – A critical discussion of a tourism research agenda. Tourism Management, 81(May), 104164. https://doi.org/10.1016/j.tourman.2020.104164

8

Sustainable Tourism in Mountain Biking Events in Michoacan, Mexico: The Vision of the Organizers

Abraham Nuñez-Maldonado[1], Martha Beatriz Flores-Romero[1], Miriam Edith Pérez Romero[1], and José Álvarez-García[2]

[1]Faculty of Accounting and Management,
Universidad Michoacan de San Nicolas de Hidalgo, Mexico
[2]Universidad de Extremadura, Spain

Abstract

This chapter presents the vision that organizers of mountain biking events have of the sustainable tourism generated by the participants, from the four dimensions of sustainability. The analysis was carried out employing a survey of 12 organizers from different municipalities in the state of Michoacán, where the minimum selection requirements were to have held the event for at least 5 consecutive years, to ensure continuity, and to have at least 400 participants in each of the events, to subsequently analyze the responses through the experton theory, giving as a result what each of the questions asked represents for them, The conclusion is that the environmental, economic and social dimensions of sustainable tourism are of great relevance for the organizers of these sporting challenges, with areas of opportunity in the generation of public policies for both environmental protection and restrictions to be respected by the participants of the various mountain biking events in Michoacán, as well as little or no information on governmental websites.

Keywords: Experton, sustainable tourism, mountain bike events

8.1 Introduction

The present research is carried out from the point of view of the organizers of mountain biking events, in which a fuzzy logic technique called expertons is applied, which has not been used from this perspective, it must be taken into account that the organizers lack important knowledge about the tourism sector, which would normally allow them to make appropriate decisions and implement the relevant improvements (Hugaerts et al., 2021) and if we add to this the fact that they are not a homogeneous group, but take various forms, such as associations, commercial companies and professional clubs (Peris-Ortiz, Álvarez-García, and Del Río-Rama, 2017), which primarily use the events as a means to perpetuate their commitment to sport and reinforce the connection to the natural environment in which they operate (Dobson and McLuskie, 2020), where it would also be important to know what kind of sporting events fulfill certain social functions and whether these have a positive impact on sport tourists (Malchrowicz-Mośko and Chlebosz, 2019), organizers could therefore design event venues and activities to promote and maximize value for the host communities (Filo, Lock, Sherry, and Quang Huynh, 2017).

According to the International Cycling Union (2020) the reasons for organizers to hold an event are as follows: Emotional reasons, which are mainly to share their love for cycling; Social reasons, to respond to demand and offer young people the opportunity to compete; Cultural reasons, it is very common for them to be organized during local festivities; Promotional reasons; as they allow them to discover a locality or city. This is why the guidance and training that is emerging is an important opportunity for organizers to offer a valuable service in this growing market (Dobson and McLuskie, 2020), taking into account that the various research carried out on mountain bike events focuses on various issues such as the visual content published (Taberner and Juncà, 2021), visitor spending (Buning, Cole, and McNamee, 2016), travel experiences (Hagen and Boyes, 2016), landscape damage (Yeh, Lin, Hsiao, and Huang, 2021), the tourism market (Buning, Cole, and Lamont, 2019), environmental impacts (Farías-Torbidoni and Sallent, 2009), tourism development (Taylor, Frost, and Laing, 2019), motivation (Getz and McConnell, 2014), among many other topics.

Nowadays, millions of people use bicycles as an efficient and sustainable vehicle for mobility, transport, leisure, and sport, which has become a very useful tool to get to know tourist sites, these conditions can be exploited to develop mountain bike tourism in destinations with suitable geographical environments (Gómez, Mantilla, Posso, and Maldonado, 2018; Gutiérrez, 2016) since, in recent years, mountain tourism has become increasingly popular among tourists, some tourist destinations have developed a range of tailor-made facilities and packages for mountain biking (Del Río-Rama, Maldonado-Erazo, Durán-Sánchez, and Álvarez-García, 2019; Pröbstl-Haider, Lund-Durlacher, Antonschmidt, and Hödl, 2018), as the physical-sports activity becomes a complementary tourism offer for the area where it is carried out (Lisbona, Medina, and Sánchez, 2008).

8.2 Theoretical and Conceptual Framework

To define sustainable tourism we have to understand that tourism is a social, cultural and economic phenomenon that contributes to economic growth, social development and mutual understanding worldwide (UNWTO, 2005), while the term "sustainability" is ambiguous because it applies to production, ecology, economy, environment, society or development (Dourojeanni, 2000). As a result, the World Tourism Organisation (2019) describes sustainable tourism as *"tourism that takes into account its current and future economic, social and environmental impact, addressing the needs of visitors, the industry, the environment and host communities"*. In the same vein, environmental, economic and sociological aspects are marked as the three pillars of sustainability (Hansmann, Mieg, y Frischknecht, 2012), although several theorists agree in identifying four basic dimensions (Achkar et al., 2005; Brito Rodríguez and Cànoves Valiente, 2019; Orozco Alvarado and Núñez Martínez, 2013), because it requires strong political leadership (Organización Mundial del Turismo, 2005), thus emerging as the fourth pillar called public policies.

The tourism industry is moving towards development and many kinds of research on sports tourism have been released (Yang, Chuang, Lo, and Lee, 2020), this universe of physical-sports practices linked to the use and enjoyment of the natural environment, which are developed in natural spaces for their enjoyment, experimentation and discovery of nature and landscapes, receives several denominations among the most significant we have: adventure sports, nature sports, alternative sports, extreme sports to mention just a few (Durán-Sánchez, Álvarez-García, and Del Río-Rama, 2020; Silva et al., 2021). Cycle tourism has established itself at the intersection of sport and adventure tourism as a tourism segment (Buning et al., 2019), where the organizers should be aware of how sports events have a positive impact on participants (Malchrowicz-Mośko and Chlebosz, 2019), therefore, the following questions listed below in Table 8.1 were asked:

Currently, in Europe, there is a network of sites promoting biodiversity, known as *"Natura 2000"*, which requires organizers of such events to assess the effects of environmental pollution and whether they are promoting respect for nature (International Cycling Union, 2020), for this reason, questions A1 and A2 were asked to identify whether the organizers in Michoacán take into consideration the regulations that are being implemented in other parts of the world, which is where global efforts are being directed. These sporting activities have been seen as a powerful tool for the modernization and development of a rural or local area, improving and differentiating the tourist offer (Medina and Sánchez Martín, 2005), which is why it is important to know whether local consumption takes place at these events (E1) because the expenditure made on products from the place of origin can be beneficial for both the organizers and the participants (Sims, 2009), where it is also important to know whether local consumption is promoted at this type of event (S1). Both purchases and participation in other activities are related to the structure of the event (Gibson, Kaplanidou, and Kang, 2012), which is why it is important to know whether participants visit tourist sites in the area of the event (E2), as well as to identify whether the organizers think that holding these events promotes tourism in the different regions of Michoacán (S2).

Table 8.1   Instrument.

Nomenclature	Question
A1	Sporting event participants generate pollution to host cities?
A2	Participants in sporting events promote respect for nature?
E1	Participants in sporting events consume local products?
E2	Do participants get to know the tourist resources of the city where the event takes place?
P1	Do you know if there are any tourism policies for the protection of the environment that must be respected during a sporting event?
P2	Do participants have access to event information on the various government websites?
P3	Are you aware of government-implemented sporting restrictions that participants must respect during sporting events (e.g., no headphones, clothing, etc.)?
S1	Is local consumption promoted at the event?
S2	Do you think that holding sporting events in rural areas is an efficient way of promoting the different regions of Michoacán?

Source: Own elaboration.

Government sports policies contribute to sustainable growth (Yu, Jeong, and Kim, 2021), as public policies to create safe routes for bicycles increase their use of them in the area where they are implemented (Serra i Serra, 2016), this is why there is a need to train tourism companies (event organizers) to adopt sustainability-oriented policies (Islam, Zhang, and Hasan, 2019), in the regulations that the International Cycling Union (2021) has in its chapter 15 Cycling for all, in its Section 15.1.015 *"The organiser shall take all appropriate measures for the protection of the environment"*, giving rise to the question of whether the local government has any similar regulations (P1), the implementation of an official website (P2) is also necessary, as it is a basic tool to facilitate tourists access to information about the destination (Molinillo, Liébana-Cabanillas, Anaya-Sánchez, and Buhalis, 2018). It is worth mentioning that bicycle clothing and accessories are often necessary, such as shoes with or without clips, technical clothing, full-face helmets, tools, hydration, among other things (Hagen and Boyes, 2016), hence the importance of public policies in this regard (P3).

Expert testimony, referrals from friends and consumer behavior (mobile phones, clothing, etc.) are communications that inform the consumer (Santesmases, Sánchez, and Valderrey, 2014), it is therefore desirable to incorporate models, which are structured on the basis of expert consultation and can be evaluated by experts, and which contain a certain degree of uncertainty (Bastar Gómez, 2014; Ferrer-Comalat, Linares-Mustarós, and Rigall Torrent, 2021), in which a panel of experts is oriented to assess a branch of knowledge (Salgado-Barandela, Barajas, and Sánchez-Fernández, 2017), taking into account that when experts advocate the same solutions for the same problems, it will not cause any problems. But when several experts propose different solutions, it is difficult to check which is the most appropriate answer (Hara, 2008).

The tool applied to analyze the experts' opinions was the "experton theory", which is based on fuzzy logic, aggregating the opinion of several experts through confidence intervals (Ferrer-Comalat, Linares-Mustarós, and Corominas-Coll, 2018; Gámez González, Rondan Cataluña, Diez de Castro, and Navarro-Garcia, 2010), defined differently is the generalization of the probability when the cumulative probabilities are replaced by monotonically decreasing intervals (Bartkowiak and Rutkowska, 2020; Sirbiladze, Khutsishvili, and Ghvaberidze, 2014), which was created by Kaufmann and Gil Aluja (1988), the main advantage being the full consideration of all individual opinions and the production of a single final result (Alfaro-García, Gil-Lafuente, and Alfaro-Calderón, 2017), which allows us to make an assessment of a variable without excluding the degree of imprecision that characterizes human reasoning, it should be clarified that the assessment is subjective data provided by one or more persons (Gil-Lafuente et al., 2017), where the analysis of the subjectivity of the managers, is using a confidence interval of confidence "[$a1$, $a2$]", with $0 \leq a1 \leq a2 \leq 1$ (Yepes-Baldó, Romeo, Bòria-Reverter, Pérez, and Guàrdia-Olmos, 2016), thanks to this process of expert aggregation, reliable information is obtained, so that the values given are as close to reality as possible (Gil Lafuente, 2010).

It is also important to mention that if the assessments provided by the experts are accurate, they are called "singleton", and in case of using intervals, "experton" (Gámez-González et al., 2010). Expertons are used when it is a matter of bringing together the opinion of several experts into a single, comprehensive opinion, since expert consultation is nowadays a topic of scientific interest with different lines of research available (Gámez-González et al., 2010; Linares-Mustarós, Ferrer-Comalat, Corominas-Coll, and Merigó, 2019).

As Pröbstl-Haider (2018) mentions, all selected experts were willing to participate. This high level of cooperation demonstrates the relevance and importance of the topic, as tourism researches aspects associated with pro-environmental attitudes among tourists (Falk and Hagsten, 2019), the great economic potential for a host site (Daniels and Norman, 2003), the harnessing of social impacts through events, which has created the need for organizers to think creatively about the use of all resources at their disposal (Filo et al., 2017), as well as the analysis of the political dimension, which involves identifying the direct or indirect involvement of government structures (Carpinetti and Esponda, 2013).

8.3 Method

The various event organizers were selected from the various municipalities of the State of Michoacán, such as Angangueo, Etúcuaro, Huetamo, Morelia, Paracho, Pátzcuaro, Tafetán, Uruapan, and Zacapu, those events met two requirements, at least 5 years of having organized an event, to ensure continuity and, having had a minimum of 400 participants in each of the events, obtaining 12 responses to the questionnaire made on google forms and sent electronically through a link on WhatsApp, the questions were asked using an endecadary scale, the content validity of the questionnaire was determined through the Cronbach's alpha coefficient of univariate analysis of the SPSS

25 statistical programme, giving us a result of 0.829, taking as a starting point the lower number of the survey confidence intervals, the scale is higher than the recommended minimum of 0.8 (Álvarez-García, Fraiz Brea, and Del Río-Rama, 2013). As shown in Table 8.2, there is no significant variation if any of the survey items are removed, which is why all items are left in the research.

The starting point for constructing an experton, consists of providing an eleven-point semantic scale as shown in Table T10.3, to evaluate a statement or assertion, including the lower and upper bounds of the interval (Ferrer-Comalat et al., 2021; López, Linares-Mustarós, and Viñas, 2020; Yepes-Baldó et al., 2016), where "0" corresponded to totally disagree and "10" to totally agree since the opinions obtained are usually elaborated with this scale (Alarcón, Caques, and Lafuente, 2014), the expertons are constructed with the help of an Excel sheet.

Table 8.2   Total element statistics.

	Cronbach's alpha if the item has been removed
A1	0.824
A2	0.837
E1	0.790
E2	0.847
P1	0.806
P2	0.788
P3	0.791
S1	0.786
S2	0.819

Source: Own elaboration in SPSS 25.

Table 8.3   Endecadary scale.

Degree	Meaning
0	Totally disagree
0.1	Almost disagree
0.2	Nearly disagree
0.3	Rather disagree
0.4	More disagree than agree
0.5	Neither agree nor disagree
0.6	More agree than disagree
0.7	Rather agree
0.8	Nearly agree
0.9	Almost agree
1	Totally agree

Source: Adapted from Kaufmann (1990).

8.4 Results

The criteria of the experts involved in the process were transformed into values on a scale from 0 to 10, in decimal places, to subsequently take the first step in calculating expertons is to determine the frequencies of assessments (Gil-Lafuente et al., 2017), where the absolute frequency tables are made in order to subsequently calculate the relative frequencies as shown in Table 8.4, where we can start to find interesting results, in which experts consider that the participants generate pollution in the cities, but the majority also consider that they promote environmental protection, it can also be noted that on the economic side they agree that participants consume local products and visit the tourist attractions around the event, in terms of public policies, it can be noted that in some municipalities within the state there are rules for environmental protection, but in the majority there are none, in terms of the publication of events in the various government webpages we see a total lack of interest, as well as the fact that there are no policies that regulate what the athletes should and should not do while the event is taking place, while socially most agree that local consumption is promoted within the event and that participants enjoy the tourist attractions of the area, demonstrating that for experts this type of event is fundamental for the knowledge and development of the various communities where they are held.

A widely used concept and the most common way to evaluate the information and reduce the randomness of an experton can be obtained by calculating the mathematical expectation of the probabilistic set (Alfaro-García et al., 2017; López et al., 2020), which is obtained by adding the lower extremes of each level (except 0) and dividing the result by 10 (Gil-Lafuente, 2005):

$$\varepsilon(A1) = [0.83 + 0.83 + 0.83 + 0.83 + 0.83 + 0.58 + 0.58 + 0.42 + 0.25$$
$$+ 0.25; 0.92 + 0.83 + 0.83 + 0.83 + 0.83 + 0.83 + .067 + 0.58$$
$$+ 0.42]/10$$
$$= [0.3; 0.70]$$

The experton can be interpreted as a Φ-fuzzy subset indicating the degree of agreement among the group of experts in assessing whether a sentence is met with a degree of confidence (Linares-Mustarós, Ferrer-Comalat, Corominas-Coll, and Merigó, 2021), if we look at the results for the experton in Table 8.5, it informs us that the percentage of experts who are in favor of the claim being true that the participants create pollution in the cities are at least to the α-cut of 0.6 is between 58% and 83%, while the mathematical

Table 8.4 Relative frequencies.

Valuation scale	Sustainable tourism								
	Environmental		Economic		Public policies			Social	
	A1	A2	E1	E2	P1	P2	P3	S1	S2
0.00	0.17	0.08	0.08	0.08	0.58	0.33	0.42	0.00	0.00
0.10	0.00	0.08	0.00	0.00	0.00	0.17	0.00	0.00	0.00
0.20	0.00	0.00	0.00	0.00	0.00	0.08	0.00	0.08	0.00
0.30	0.00	0.00	0.00	0.08	0.00	0.25	0.08	0.00	0.08
0.40	0.00	0.00	0.08	0.17	0.17	0.00	0.17	0.00	0.08
0.50	0.25	0.00	0.08	0.17	0.17	0.08	0.00	0.25	0.08
0.60	0.00	0.17	0.00	0.08	0.08	0.00	0.08	0.08	0.08
0.70	0.17	0.08	0.00	0.08	0.00	0.00	0.08	0.08	0.08
0.80	0.17	0.17	0.08	0.00	0.00	0.00	0.00	0.08	0.17
0.90	0.00	0.17	0.08	0.08	0.00	0.00	0.00	0.17	0.00
1.00	0.25	0.25	0.58	0.25	0.08	0.08	0.17	0.25	0.42

Source: Own elaboration.

Table 8.5 Complementary cumulative frequencies.

Valuation scale	Sustainable tourism				Public policies			Social	
	Environmental		Economic						
	A1	A2	E1	E2	P1	P2	P3	S1	S2
0.00	1.00	1.00	1.00	1.00	1.00	1.00	1.00	1.00	1.00
0.10	0.83	0.92	0.92	0.92	0.42	0.67	0.58	1.00	1.00
0.20	0.83	0.92	0.92	0.92	0.42	0.50	0.58	1.00	1.00
0.30	0.83	0.92	0.92	0.92	0.42	0.42	0.58	0.92	1.00
0.40	0.83	0.92	0.92	0.83	0.42	0.17	0.58	0.92	0.92
0.50	0.83	0.92	0.83	0.67	0.42	0.17	0.50	0.92	0.83
0.60	0.58	0.75	0.75	0.50	0.25	0.08	0.33	0.67	0.75
0.70	0.58	0.67	0.75	0.42	0.17	0.08	0.33	0.58	0.58
0.80	0.42	0.50	0.75	0.33	0.08	0.08	0.25	0.50	0.58
0.90	0.25	0.50	0.67	0.33	0.08	0.08	0.17	0.42	0.42
1.00	0.25	0.33	0.58	0.25	0.08	0.08	0.17	0.25	0.42
Sum	6.25	7.33	8.00	6.08	2.75	2.33	3.67	7.17	7.50
M.E.	0.63	0.73	0.80	0.61	0.28	0.23	0.37	0.72	0.75

Source: Own elaboration, based on Gil Lafuente (2017).

expectation for the same construct is between 63% and 70%, as can be seen, the information contained in the experton is much richer than simply reducing it to a mathematical expectation (Ferrer-Comalat et al., 2018).

However, an analysis of the results obtained with the mathematical expectations shows that: construct A1 [0.63;0.70] indicates that for the organizers of the events, the participants generate pollution but in construct A2 [0.73;0.80], it can be seen that they also believe that the participants are promoting respect for nature to a greater extent than in question A1. In terms of their opinions regarding local consumption E1 [0.80;0.83] we can presume that participants mostly go shopping in the host cities but are less likely to be aware of the tourism resources on offer, as indicated by E2 [0.61;0.60]. According to the opinions of the organizers, the greatest area of opportunity in the survey is public policies, where there is very little chance of having them for the protection of the environment P1 [028;0.31], having information about the events on government websites P2 [0.23;0.29], as well as measures implemented by the government that the participants must respect during the event P3 [0.37;0.42]. Concerning social issues, we can mention that even though local consumption is promoted in the events S1 [0.72;0.78], the one carried out by the participants is higher in percentage as mentioned in E1 [0.80;0.83], it can also be mentioned that for the organizers, this type of events can be an efficient way to promote the different regions of the State as observed in S2 [0.75;0.81].

8.5 Conclusion

Many countries are actively pursuing strategies to attract domestic and foreign tourists, one way of increasing this is to use sporting events (Yang et al., 2020), although mountain biking events are considered a growing phenomenon worldwide, there is a lack of research and data on the organizers involved in these activities (Peris-Ortiz et al., 2017), even though the importance of sporting events for the development and economic and social reactivation of tourist destinations is increasingly growing (Malchrowicz-Mośko and Chlebosz, 2019). In the present study, the opinions of mountain bike event organizers have been taken into account and they have expressed their opinions with the freedom given by confidence intervals using the experton theory, this is because it is one of the most robust and widely used tools for analyzing the opinions of a group of experts under uncertainty (Ferrer-Comalat et al., 2018), which has finally established itself as a mathematical entity in scientific thought (Gil-Lafuente, 2005; Linares-Mustarós et al., 2021), this, due to the difficulty experts have in determining a precise numerical valuation, has led them to ask for a closed interval rather than a single value (López et al., 2020).

Among the results obtained, we can mention that: the environmental, economic, and social variables of sustainable tourism have great relevance in the organization of mountain bike events, as it is the organizer's task to identify potential environmental problems in advance and to address them in three stages: before, during and after the race (International Cycling Union, 2020), not losing sight of the economic and social aspects in the same phases of the process. Having a great area of opportunity in the creation of public policies that promote the events within the official government pages, that encourage the protection of the environment, and that regulate the participation of sportsmen and women during the event, sustainability can be measured by the results of its public policies in the three dimensions of development: economic, social and environmental (Alfaro-Calderón, Godinez-Reyes, Gomez-Monge, Alfaro-García, and Gil-Lafuente, 2019).

Since this study was conducted in Mexico, in particular with mountain bike event organizers in Michoacán, its conclusions cannot be generalized. Future research should be further investigated in other destinations and at different types of events (Taberner and Juncà, 2021), to demonstrate the suitability of these methods using different sources and cultural contexts, as it is one of the first studies using the method of "expertons" to the organizers of mountain bike events on the sustainable tourism they generate.

Acknowledgments

We would like to thank the Doctorate studies in Administration, Saint Nicholas and Hidalgo Michoacán State University (UMSNH), and the National Quality Postgraduate Program of the National Council of Science and Technology (CONACyT) in México, is gratefully acknowledged.

References

Achkar, M., Canton, V., Cayssials, R., Dominguez, A., Fernández, G., and Pesce, F. (2005). Indicadores de Sustentabilidad. In Comisión Sectorial de Educación Permanete (Ed.), DIRAC, Facultad de Ciencias. Montevideo.
Alarcón, C. N., Caques, A. G., and Lafuente, J. G. (2014). Propuestas Para El Desarrollo De Indicadores Éticos Difusos En Marketing. Recta, 15(1), 1–12.

Alfaro-Calderón, G. G., Godinez-Reyes, N. L., Gomez-Monge, R., Alfaro-García, V. G., and Gil-Lafuente, A. M. (2019). Forgotten Effects in the Valuation of the Social Well-Being Index in Mexico'S Sustainable Development. Fuzzy Economic Review, 24(01), 67–81. https://doi.org/10.25102/fer.2019.01.04

Alfaro-García, V. G., Gil-Lafuente, A. M., and Alfaro-Calderón, G. G. (2017). A fuzzy methodology for innovation management measurement. Kybernetes, 46(1), 50–66. https://doi.org/10.1108/K-06-2016-0153

Álvarez-García, J., Fraiz Brea, J. A., and Del Río-Rama, M. D. L. C. (2013). Implantación de un sistema de gestión de la calidadă: beneficios percibidos. Revista Venezolana de Gerencia, 18(63), 379–407.

Bartkowiak, M., and Rutkowska, A. (2020). Vague expert information/recommendation in portfolio optimization-an empirical study. Axioms, 9(2), 1–12. https://doi.org/10.3390/AXIOMS9020038

Bastar Gómez, S. (2014). Metodología De La Investigación. In Metallurgia Italiana. https://doi.org/10.1017/CBO9781107415324.004

Brito Rodríguez, M., and Cànoves Valiente, G. (2019). El desarrollo turístico en Mazatlán, México: evaluación de la sostenibilidad por medio de indicadores. Cuadernos de Turismo, (43), 187–213. https://doi.org/10.6018/turismo.43.08

Buning, R. J., Cole, Z. D., and McNamee, J. B. (2016). Visitor expenditure within a mountain bike event portfolio: Determinants, outcomes, and variations. Journal of Sport and Tourism, 20(2), 103–122. https://doi.org/10.1080/14775085.2016.1239547

Buning, R. J., Cole, Z., and Lamont, M. (2019). A case study of the US mountain bike tourism market. Journal of Vacation Marketing, 1–13. https://doi.org/10.1177/1356766719842321

Carpinetti, B., and Esponda, A. (2013). Introducción al desarrollo sustentable (Segunda). Florencio Varela: Universidad Nacional Arturo Jauretche.Daniels, M. J., and Norman, W. C. (2003). Estimating the economic impacts of seven regular sport tourism events. Journal of Sport and Tourism, 8(4), 214–222. https://doi.org/10.1080/1477508032000161528

Del Río-Rama, M. D. L. C., Maldonado-Erazo, C. P., Durán-Sánchez, A., and Álvarez-García, J. (2019). Mountain tourism research. A review. European Journal of Tourism Research, 22(2019), 130–150.

Dobson, S., and McLuskie, P. (2020). Performative entrepreneurship: identity, behaviour and place in adventure sports Enterprise. International Entrepreneurship and Management Journal, 16(3), 879–895. https://doi.org/10.1007/s11365-020-00661-2

Dourojeanni, A. (2000). Procedimientos de gestion para el desarrollo sustentable. Retrieved from https://repositorio.cepal.org/handle/11362/556 4

Durán-Sánchez, A., Álvarez-García, J., and Del Río-Rama, M. D. L. C. (2020). Nature sports: state of the art of research. Annals of Leisure Research, 23(1), 52–78. https://doi.org/10.1080/11745398.2019.1584535

Falk, M., and Hagsten, E. (2019). Ways of the green tourist in Europe. Journal of Cleaner Production, 225, 1033–1043. https://doi.org/10.1016/J.JCLE PRO.2019.04.001

Farías-Torbidoni, E. I., and Sallent, O. (2009). El impacto ambiental de las actividades físico-deportivas en el medio natural. El caso de la práctica del Mountain Bike o bicicleta todo terreno. RETOS. Nuevas Tendencias En Educación Física, Deporte y Recreación, (16), 31–35.

Ferrer-Comalat, J. C., Linares-Mustarós, S., and Corominas-Coll, D. (2018). A Generalization of the Theory of Expertons. International Journal of Uncertainty, Fuzziness and Knowlege-Based Systems, 26, 121–139. https://doi.org/10.1142/S021848851840007X

Ferrer-Comalat, J. C., Linares-Mustarós, S., and Rigall Torrent, R. (2021). Incorporating fuzzy logic in harrod's economic growth model. Mathematics, 9(18), 1–20. https://doi.org/10.3390/math9182194

Filo, K., Lock, D., Sherry, E., and Quang Huynh, H. (2017). 'You belonged to something': exploring how fundraising teams add to the social leverage of events. European Sport Management Quarterly, 18(2), 216–236. https://doi.org/10.1080/16184742.2017.1368684

Gámez-González, J., Rondan-Cataluña, F. J., Diez-de Castro, E. C., and Navarro-Garcia, A. (2010). Toward an international code of franchising. Management Decision, 48(10), 1568–1595. https://doi.org/10.1108/0025 1741011090333

Getz, D., and McConnell, A. (2014). Comparing Trail Runners and Mountain Bikers: Motivation, Involvement, Portfolios, and Event-Tourist Careers. Journal of Convention and Event Tourism, 15(1), 69–100. https://doi.org/10.1080/15470148.2013.834807

Gibson, H. J., Kaplanidou, K., and Kang, S. J. (2012). Small-scale event sport tourism: A case study in sustainable tourism. Sport Management Review, 15(2), 160–170. https://doi.org/10.1016/j.smr.2011.08.013

Gil-Lafuente, A. M. (2005). Fuzzy logic in financial analysis. Berlin: Springer International Publishing.

Gil-Lafuente, A. M., Garcia, I., Souto, L., Blanco, B. E., Ortíz, M., and Zamora, T. (2017). La gestión y toma de decisiones en el sistema empresarial cubano. Barcelona: Real Academia de Ciencias Económicas y Financieras.

Gil Lafuente, J. (2010). Marketing, Finanzas y Gestión del Deporte (Publicaciones de la Real Academia de Ciencias Económicas y Financieras, Ed.). Barcelona.

Gómez, J. A., Mantilla, J. M., Posso, M. A., and Maldonado, X. (2018). Ciclismo de Montaña como Motor del Desarrollo Sostenible del Turismo Local en Ecuador. Información Tecnológica, 29(5), 279–288. https://doi.org/10.4067/s0718-07642018000500279

Gutiérrez, F. R. (2016). Cicling as a vector of a territorial development. Boletin de La Asociacion de Geografos Espanoles, 70. https://doi.org/10.21138/bage.2177

Hagen, S., and Boyes, M. (2016). Affective ride experiences on mountain bike terrain. Journal of Outdoor Recreation and Tourism, 15(2013), 89–98. https://doi.org/10.1016/j.jort.2016.07.006

Hansmann, R., Mieg, H. A., and Frischknecht, P. (2012). Principal sustainability components: Empirical analysis of synergies between the three pillars of sustainability. International Journal of Sustainable Development and World Ecology, 19(5), 451–459. https://doi.org/10.1080/13504509.2012.696220

Hara, T. (2008). QuantitativeTourism Industry Analisis. Introduction to Input-Output, Social Accounting Matriz Modelling and Tourism Satellite Accounts.

Hugaerts, I., Scheerder, J., Helsen, K., Corthouts, J., Thibaut, E., and Könecke, T. (2021). Sustainability in participatory sports events: The development of a research instrument and empirical insights. Sustainability (Switzerland), 13(11), 1–16. https://doi.org/10.3390/su13116034

International Cycling Union. (2020). Organiser's guide to road events. Retrieved from https://archive.uci.org/docs/default-source/publications/uci-guide-orga-2020-eng.pdf

Islam, M. F., Zhang, J., and Hasan, N. (2019). Assessing the adoption of sustainability practices in tourism industry: Insights from a developing country. Bottom Line, 33(1), 94–115. https://doi.org/10.1108/BL-09-2019-0113

Kaufmann, A., and Gil Aluja, J. (1988). Modelo para la gestion de los efectos olvidados. Gandariña: Milladoiro.Kaufmann, A. J. (1990). Expert appraisements and counter-appraisements with experton processes. [1990]

Proceedings. First International Symposium on Uncertainty Modeling and Analysis, 619–624. https://doi.org/10.1109/ISUMA.1990.151326

Linares-Mustarós, S., Ferrer-Comalat, J. C., Corominas-Coll, D., and Merigó, J. M. (2019). The ordered weighted average in the theory of expertons. International Journal of Intelligent Systems, 34(3), 345–365. https://doi.or g/10.1002/int.22055

Linares-Mustarós, S., Ferrer-Comalat, J. C., Corominas-Coll, D., and Merigó, J. M. (2021). The weighted average multiexperton. Information Sciences, 557(xxxx), 355–372. https://doi.org/10.1016/j.ins.2020.08.029

Lisbona, M., Medina, X., and Sánchez, R. (2008). El turismo deportivo: visiones críticas sobre posibilidades de desarrollo local en España y México. In Actualidad en el deporte: Investigación y aplicación (pp. 165–179). Retrieved from http://www.ankulegi.org/wp-content/uploads/2012/03/01 12

Lisbona.pdfLópez, C., Linares-Mustarós, S., and Viñas, J. (2020). The use of fuzzy mathematical tools for local public services outsourcing according to typology. Journal of Intelligent and Fuzzy Systems, 38(5), 5379–5389. https://doi.org/10.3233/JIFS-179631

Malchrowicz-Mośko, E., and Chlebosz, K. (2019). Sport Spectator Consumption and Sustainable Management of Sport Event Tourism; Fan Motivation in High Performance Sport and Non-Elite Sport. A Case Study of Horseback Riding and Running: A Comparative Analysis. Sustainability, 11(7), 2178. https://doi.org/10.3390/su11072178

Medina, F. X., and Sánchez Martín, R. (2005). Actividad físico-deportiva, turismo y desarrollo local en España. PASOS Revista de Turismo y Patrimonio Cultural, 3(1), 97–107. https://doi.org/10.25145/j.pasos.2005.03.0 07

Molinillo, S., Liébana-Cabanillas, F., Anaya-Sánchez, R., and Buhalis, D. (2018). DMO online platforms: Image and intention to visit. Tourism Management, 65, 116–130. https://doi.org/10.1016/j.tourman.2017.09.021

Organización Mundial del Turismo. (2005). Indicadores de desarrollo sostenible para los destinos turísticos Guía práctica (Primera). Madrid: OMT.

Orozco Alvarado, J., and Núñez Martínez, P. (2013). Las teorías del desarrollo en el analisis sustentable. Intersedes: Revista de Las Sedes Regionales, 14(27), 144–167. Retrieved from http://www.redalyc.org/ articulo.oa?id=66627452008

Peris-Ortiz, M., Álvarez-García, J., and Del Río-Rama, M. D. L. C. (2017). Sports management as an emerging economic activity: Trends and best practices. In Sports Management as an Emerging Economic Activity: Trends and Best Practices (1st ed.). https://doi.org/10.1007/978-3-31 9-63907-9

Pröbstl-Haider, U., Lund-Durlacher, D., Antonschmidt, H., and Hödl, C. (2018). Mountain bike tourism in Austria and the Alpine region–towards a sustainable model for multi-stakeholder product development. Journal of Sustainable Tourism, 26(4), 567–582. https://doi.org/10.1080/09669582.2 017.1361428

Salgado-Barandela, J., Barajas, A., and Sánchez-Fernández, P. (2017). Impacto económico del deporte: tema de interés creciente en la literatura científica / Economic Impact of Sport: Topic of Growing Interest for the Scientific Literature. Revista Internacional de Medicina y Ciencias de La Actividad Física y Del Deporte, 68(2017), 729–755. https://doi.org/10.153 66/rimcafd2017.68.010

Santesmases, M., Sánchez, A., and Valderrey, F. (2014). Fundamentos de Mercadotecnia (Primera). Retrieved from https://www.academia.edu/8 889213/Fundamentos_del_Marketing_Kotler_11va_ed?auto=download

Serra i Serra, M. (2016). El cicloturismo y las vías verdes como ejemplo de turismo sostenible. Revista CIDOB d'Afers Internacionals, 2016(113), 187–209.

Silva, G., Correia, A., Rachão, S., Nunes, A., Vieira, E., Santos, S., ... Fernandes, P. O. (2021). A Methodology for the Identification and Assessment of the Conditions for the Practice of Outdoor and Sport Tourism-Related Activities: The Case of Northern Portugal. Sustainability, 13(13), 7343. https://doi.org/10.3390/su13137343

Sims, R. (2009). Food, place and authenticity: Local food and the sustainable tourism experience. Journal of Sustainable Tourism, 17(3), 321–336. https://doi.org/10.1080/09669580802359293

Sirbiladze, G., Khutsishvili, I., and Ghvaberidze, B. (2014). Multistage decision-making fuzzy methodology for optimal investments based on experts' evaluations. European Journal of Operational Research, 232(1), 169–177. https://doi.org/10.1016/j.ejor.2013.06.035

Taberner, I., and Juncà, A. (2021). Small-Scale Sport Events as Place Branding Platforms: A Content Analysis of Osona's Projected Destination Image through Event-Related Pictures on Instagram. Sustainability, 13(21), 12255. https://doi.org/10.3390/su132112255

Taylor, P., Frost, W., and Laing, J. (2019). Exploring how entrepreneurial actors shape tourism development: the case of mountain bike tourism at

Rotorua. Tourism Recreation Research, 44(4), 479–491. https://doi.org/10 .1080/02508281.2019.1615769

Union Cycliste Internationale. (2021). UCI Cycling Regulations. Retrieved 23 September 2021, from http://www.uci.ch/mm/Document/News/Rulesa ndregulation/16/80/73/1-GEN-20160101-E_English.pdf

UNWTO. (2005). Measuring Sustainable Tourism. Madrid.UNWTO. (2019). Tourism and the Sustainable Development Goals-Journey to 2030. https: //doi.org/10.18111/9789284419401

Yang, J. J., Chuang, Y. C., Lo, H. W., and Lee, T. I. (2020). A two-stage MCDM model for exploring the influential relationships of sustainable sports tourism criteria in Taichung City. International Journal of Environmental Research and Public Health, 17(7). https://doi.org/10.3390/ijerph 17072319

Yeh, C.-C., Lin, C. J.-Y., Hsiao, J. P.-H., and Huang, C.-H. (2021). Landscape Damage Effect Impacts on Natural Environment and Recreational Benefits in Bikeway. Diversity, 13(2), 52. https://doi.org/10.3390/d13020052

Yepes-Baldó, M., Romeo, M., Bòria-Reverter, S., Pérez, F. J., and Guàrdia-Olmos, J. (2016). Uncertain averaging operators: a new way to study the psychosocial organizational phenomena. Quality and Quantity, 50(6), 2725–2739. https://doi.org/10.1007/s11135-015-0286-x

Yu, J. G., Jeong, Y. D., and Kim, S. K. (2021). Verifying the effectiveness of sports event policies for a city's sustainable growth: Focusing on the multiple effects. Sustainability (Switzerland), 13(6), 1–15. https://doi.org/ 10.3390/su13063285

9

Innovation Capabilities in Business Models for Agricultural Organizations: Theoretical Approaches

Daniela Niño-Amézquita and Diana María Dueñas Quintero

Universidad Pedagógica y Tecnológica de Colombia, Colombia

Abstract

Small-scale agricultural production manages its improvement alternatives in associative-type organizations to improve producers' conditions. Its performance is limited in developing sustainable strategies that can be linked to business models oriented toward innovation. Considering this, a content and bibliometric analysis is carried out to identify capabilities that contribute to innovation in agricultural organizations. Forty-two scientific publications were prioritized, identifying six capabilities that contribute to innovation, finding that the relationship capacity is decisive to generate co-creation processes and the closing of gaps to absorb knowledge and generate value to its stakeholders, in accordance with the contexts and powers of its members.

Keywords: Innovation capabilities, business models, agricultural organizations

9.1 Introduction

The theory of resources and capabilities provides a study framework to generate competitive advantages that are sustainable over time (Barney, 1991). As organizations have evolved to join and stay in the markets, these capabilities are transformed and energized, and others are created, requiring

159

the incorporation of new knowledge that can lead to innovation in different contexts. In the agricultural sector, as in other sectors, innovation is determined by the presence or absence of favorable conditions and linked to human, organizational, or environmental knowledge and capabilities (French et al., 2014).

In the agricultural context, organizations are constituted as associative units that allow producers to gain negotiating power, reduce production costs, improve productivity and marketing, and eliminate price uncertainty (Francesconi & Heerink, 2011; An et al., 2015). These organizations face challenges related to sustainability focused on productive efficiency, poverty reduction, and agricultural development. Innovation contributes to these purposes with processes that improve the productivity and modernization of rural economies (Teece, 2007; Ramírez et al., 2020).

Jiménez et al. (2020) ratify this position on the relationship between knowledge management and innovation, finding that there are better ways of adding value and taking advantage of the opportunities in the market at a higher level of innovation in agricultural organizations. However, innovations do not emerge spontaneously; they result from cumulative processes where expectations, interests, knowledge, capabilities, and needs are exchanged, adjusted, and negotiated as constituent elements of business models (Quinonez Zuniga & Laverde Urrea, 2019; Rossi & Chia, 2020).

This process can be difficult to materialize and adjust to the context. Faced with this restriction, this study arises from questioning what elements allow to recognize the innovation capabilities in agricultural organizations to design pertinent business models, understanding that these organizations have different characteristics from the companies of other economic activities.

A content analysis is presented on the theoretical and conceptual constructs in the measurement of innovation capabilities in agricultural organizations, relating them to the specific characteristics that describe this type of organization to define elements that contribute to inclusive and sustainable business models. The document presents the theoretical framework of the research, the methodology used for the analysis, the description of the results, discussion, and conclusions about the findings.

9.2 Theoretical Framework

9.2.1 Resources and capabilities

For several decades, researchers have tried to understand the sources of sustainable competitive advantages in organizations and found mainly on the bases suggested by Porter (1985) in using strengths and neutralizing threats to build sustainable competitive advantages. However, Barney's (1991) study mentions that models focused on competitive advantages assume that companies in an industry are identical in terms of relevant and strategic resources. Contrary to this perspective, the theory based on resources and capabilities assumes that companies can be heterogeneous between the industry regarding their resources and be sustainable over time.

From this perspective, Barney (1991) broadly explains the scope of resources and capabilities in organizations. Resources refer to the assets, skills, attributes, information, and knowledge, among others, that an organization possesses, while its capabilities describe what the organization can do. These are understood as companies' power to use their resources as a competitive advantage. Capabilities emerge as a company takes advantage of its strategic resources, and its value is determined by the market context in which it operates. Sustained in evolutionary economics, the performance of organizations is established by the development and adaptation of capabilities in complex and changing environments, which is why the resource-based theory is based on this premise.

9.2.2 Dynamic capabilities

The dynamic capabilities approach seeks to provide a coherent and evolving framework on how companies develop a competitive advantage and maintain it over time (Teece & Augier, 2008). In this approach, the term "capabilities" is linked to the role of strategic management in the adaptation, integration, and reconfiguration of internal and external organizational skills. In contrast, the term "dynamic" is empowered to renew skills to adapt to the environment and the market (Teece et al., 1997).

Teece (2007) explains that it is necessary to equip oneself with capabilities to create, expand, and update the organization's asset base to achieve sustainable competitive advantage. They suggest dividing dynamic capabilities into three groups: sensing, seizing, and transforming. Sensing implies identifying opportunities and threats; seizing is linked to taking advantage of opportunities; transforming refers to maintaining competitiveness through the reconfiguration of intangible assets. Additionally, they argue that efficiency in these capabilities is supported by capturing value through innovation to have long-term benefits.

Lawson et al. (2001) also point out how dynamic capabilities contribute to the increase of management capacity and the use of resources oriented to innovation and technological development, learning processes, product development, and process improvement (p. 379).

9.3 Innovation Capabilities and Agricultural Organizations

The capacity for innovation is defined as the competence to exploit knowledge from internal or external sources to turn it into ideas that can give rise to new products and services, process improvement through technology, organizational and market skills dynamically adapted to the environment (Lichtenthaler & Lichtenthaler, 2009; Blanco-Mesa et al., 2019).

It also involves integration capabilities to incorporate skills, competencies, and capabilities with key resources to improve their performance. These can also be determined by whether organizations have innovative characteristics and by their ability to manage the resources and knowledge necessary to maintain their competitive position. This vision based on dynamic resources and capabilities as a basis for talking about innovation also has restrictions that for Lawson et al. (2001) are related to the identification of the key resources that contribute value, how they can be an impediment if there is no clarity about the competencies, and if limitations are identified that can be modified over time. This situation is common in the agricultural sector because of the way in which these capabilities are conceived in the management structures of grassroots organizations.

In the agricultural context on a smaller scale, these elements are commonly developed by associative structures with bargaining power in the market and integrate productive units and their families, commonly living and working in the field on agricultural goods and services (Flores & Naranjo, 2006). Innovation has a community, participatory, democratic, and social connotation in these agricultural organizations, culturally marked by a lack of trust and limitations caused by decades of social marginalization. For this reason, the importance of generating trust lies in the fact that small farmers achieve capabilities to experiment and contribute to the solution of their technological, productive, and business problems (Gutiérrez, 2010).

In this regard, the study by Castro, Flores, and Rajadel (2018) analyzes the relevance of implementing innovation processes to strengthen productive management in these types of organizations. It finds gaps in their comparative advantages and the low provision of infrastructure to adapt knowledge and technology, requiring capabilities that stimulate innovation as a facilitator and driver of productivity and, therefore, the strengthening of the national and family economy.

In this sense, the capacity for innovation from dynamic capacity is divided into three stages: sensing, seizing, and transforming (Teece, 2007). It is possible to identify criteria and constructs that various authors have proposed to understand the dynamics of innovation in organizations. Understanding that agricultural organizations have different dynamics and that the dynamic capability framework offers elements, it is possible to analyze, relate, and measure innovation capabilities in business, rural, agro-industrial, and associative contexts.

9.4 Business Model in Rural Organizations

A business model is determined by the bases or foundations on which an organization creates, provides, and captures value (Osterwalder & Pigneur, 2013). The business model is established by the logic of an organization's value and its people. It is found that it is possible to generate and retain value by the design, validation, and use of tools and practices (Foss & Saebi, 2018). In that sense, conceptually, it allows making implicit assumptions about customers' behavior, income, costs, competitors, and the environment (Teece, 2010).

In agricultural organizations, the business model becomes a process that involves the relationship of individuals who work together to solve problems in a community. Associative business models are characterized by assuming an increase in individual capabilities for marketing and generating value-added products (Francesconi & Heerink, 2011; Fischer & Qaim, 2012). Agricultural organizations must face challenges that imply rigor in generating equitable conditions and using resources that sustain competitive advantages.

Although these organizations have knowledge and experience from their productive work, they are unaware of aspects that would facilitate their direct articulation with the market through innovative, inclusive, and profitable negotiation models (Quinonez Zuniga & Laverde Urrea, 2019). Therefore, the theoretical approaches facilitate the structuring of business models that enable the approach of these instruments to the realities of rural organizations (Quinonez Zuniga & Laverde Urrea, 2019). It is highlighted that the success factors on identified and studied cases refer to marketing schemes and modalities based on the existence of a support institution and policy instruments to achieve the necessary and essential elements in the implementation of good management practices (Rodriguez, 2017).

9.5 Methodology

The research is qualitative and descriptive because it addresses subjective realities as objects of study. During the development of the study, patterns are perceived that become generalities to finally infer trends that allow the analysis of a state of knowledge about the issue raised (Sampieri, 2014). At the same time, it will enable identifying the interaction between theoretical constructs and raising generalities from this.

A content analysis is carried out through the theoretical review about constructs or variables that determine the innovation capabilities in agricultural organizations and their relationship with business models. For this purpose, a search is carried out in databases such as Web of Science, Scopus, Taylor and Francis, and Google Scholar, as repositories of quality information in the social sciences and specifically in management.

The criteria to limit the search for information, as indicated in Table 9.1, is determined by the search equations: "Innovation capabilities" AND "business model" OR "smallholders farmers" OR "partial least squares," which were established by the relevance and scope of the topic, such as the need to show observable variables that will explain them. The search period was concentrated between 2010 and 2021 due to the growth in scientific production during this time. On the other hand, it was limited to the area of study in business and management, finally taking 48 articles that stood out for their relevance.

The 48 selected articles were analyzed using the qualitative analysis software Atlas.ti 9 in order to identify the innovation capabilities relevant to the characteristics of agricultural organizations. Through coding, the constructs that explain the capacity for innovation, innovation in the business model, and the relevance of these elements were established in relation to the main characteristics of the agricultural organizations identified through the literature.

Table 9.1   Search string.

Scopus, WOS, Taylor & Francis, and Google Scholar	
Search criteria	**Results**
"Innovation capabilities" AND "business model" OR "smallholders farmers" OR "partial least squares"	1306
2010−2021	1237
Business, management, and accounting	636
Relevance	42

Source: Own elaboration.

In this way, it was possible to generate logs that describe the elements and a matrix of co-occurrences on the relationship between constructs. Consequently, the semantic network that allowed us to understand the interaction of the concepts in the different investigations was generated, thus identifying trends about their study and observation.

9.6 Results

The studies generated about the innovation capabilities in agricultural organizations are based on the theoretical constructs of the dynamic capabilities to understand the innovation process. Figure 9.1 shows the main concepts developed in the investigations taken for the study. It highlights characteristics of agricultural organizations such as their social and family character, the formation of networks to increase productivity and their performance, and the integration of knowledge, technology, and management as central elements for the development of markets, thanks to innovation.

On these constructs, six innovation capabilities related to the characteristics of agricultural organizations were identified, as indicated in Table 9.2. The link between resources and capabilities was established on the fulfillment of objectives and the generation of competitive advantages of these organizations, being an essential and strategic element influenced by the market context in which the organization operates (Barney, 2001). In this sense, innovation capabilities can be explained and classified based on

Figure 9.1   Word cloud.
Source: Own elaboration with Atlas.ti 9.

dynamic capabilities raised by Teece (2007), focused on sensing, seizing, and transforming.

The sensing capacity implies identifying opportunities and threats through learning processes and relationships with interested parties. In the investigations found, these concepts are applied in the manufacturing (Robledo et al., 2010; Ribau et al., 2017), industrial (Battistella et al., 2017), service (Kiani et al., 2019), environmental (Behnam et al., 2018), and agricultural (Sachitra & Chong, 2018; Cummings, 2013; Ramos-Sandoval et al., 2019; Björkdahl & Börjesson, 2012) sectors, and in SMEs from different sectors (Moreno Rojas & García Carrillo, 2014).

Likewise, seizing is linked to taking advantage of opportunities in the environment in accessing knowledge, changes mediated by the culture of innovation, defined as the generalized attitude of the organization toward the exploration and generation of knowledge from successes or failures (Björkdahl & Börjesson, 2012). This is how culture is incorporated into the strategic direction in stages of adjustments and adaptation. These capabilities have been analyzed in the manufacturing (Robledo et al., 2010; Ribau et

Table 9.2 Innovation capabilities.

Dynamic capabilities	Innovation capabilities	Authors
Sensing(Teece, 2007)	Learning orientation capability	Robledo et al., 2010; Moreno Rojas & García Carrillo, 2014; Sachitra & Chong, 2018; Ribau et al., 2017; Battistella et al., 2017; Kiani et al., 2019; Cummings, 2013; Ramos-Sandoval et al., 2019
	Relationship capacity	Robledo et al., 2010; Behnam et al., 2018; Sachitra & Chong, 2018; Björkdahl & Börjesson, 2012
Seizing(Teece, 2007)	Capability to develop an innovative culture	Cummings, 2013; Ramos-Sandoval et al., 2019; Björkdahl & Börjesson, 2012; Alfaro-García et al., 2017
	Strategic management capability	Robledo et al., 2010; Ribau et al., 2017; Alfaro-García et al., 2017; Björkdahl & Börjesson, 2012
Transforming (Teece, 2007)	Capability to develop and improve products or services	Ramos-Sandoval et al., 2019; Setyawati et al., 2020; Bastanchury-López et al., 2020; Donate et al., 2016; Freije et al., 2021; Christa et al., 2020; Björkdahl & Börjesson, 2012
	Adaptive capability	Battistella et al., 2017

Source: Own elaboration based on cited authors.

al., 2017) and agricultural sectors (Cummings, 2013; Ramos-Sandoval et al., 2019; Velázquez-Casarez et al., 2021) and in small and medium enterprises (Alfaro-García et al., 2017).

Velazquez-Casarez et al. (2021) state that the culture of innovation is incorporated in organizations if there is the presence of leaders who manage sources of resources and markets to increase their performance and establish strategies and actions that help them to improve their competitiveness (p. 386). In that order of ideas, culture permeates the organization through commitment and leadership created by a shared and robust vision throughout the organizational structure (Alfaro-García et al., 2017).

Finally, the transformation is understood as the reconfiguration of intangible assets to develop or improve products or services and the ability to adapt to change. The authors identify these processes from sectors such as industrial (Battistella et al., 2017), manufacturing (Freije et al., 2021), financial (Christa et al., 2020), technological (Donate et al., 2016), artisanal (Setyawati et al., 2020), and agricultural (Ramos-Sandoval et al., 2019; Bastanchury-López et al., 2020; Velázquez-Casarez, et al., 2021).

Thus, the performance of organizations is determined by marketing strategies focused on innovation. However, in the case of grassroots agricultural organizations, characterized by a more social than business approach, transformation will depend on the extent to which they generate capacities to strengthen the productive systems of their associates (Velázquez-Casarez et al., 2021). To the extent that results are generated, the culture of innovation will be visible and will become part of the actions of the organizations.

In this sense, innovation can occur in the business model by considering elements of the organization's architecture on the value proposition (Teece, 2010). For practical purposes, Clauss (2017) defines three dimensions of the business model, listed in Table 9.3, which include value creation, understood as the way in which companies generate differentiating elements that are appreciated by the market throughout the supply chain; the value proposition with a portfolio of solutions for clients; and finally the capture of value that generates income, which is reinvested in the organization to continue obtaining benefits that ensure sustainable performance.

Velazquez-Casarez et al. (2021) affirm these conditions in the need for organizational strategies to increase competitiveness through the development of innovation capabilities at the level of the business model and production systems in new processes, products, and marketing (Table 9.3).

In the case of agricultural organizations, due to their characteristics, internal dynamics are different, making it necessary to analyze the relevance of innovation capacities in their business model. Its main characteristics are related to its associative and community nature, cooperation networks, leadership management, and trust between individuals and institutions (Akhavan & Mahdi Hosseini, 2016; FAO, 2020; Fischer & Qaim, 2012; Terrazas et al., 2019; Espinosa et al., 2018; Vargas-Prieto & Sanchez-Álvarez, 2020).

In addition, dependence on government policies for the development of projects, obtaining technical assistance, the search for environmental sustainability, and the co-creation of products and services to face a volatile market was found (Shiferaw et al., 2009; Murendo et al., 2011; Turner et al., 2017; Saumett et al., 2018). Due to the type of actors that make up these organizations from their educational level and technological development, there are gaps in access to financial resources and a low capacity to access and adapt research. This implies restrictions on the performance of organizations and, therefore, their effects on productivity and competitiveness of the sector

Table 9.3 Business model innovation.

Business model innovation	Observable variables	Authors
Innovation in value creation(Clauss, 2017)	New technologies	Moreno Rojas & García Carrillo, 2014; Clauss, 2017; Bocken et al., 2014
	New processes	Clauss, 2017
	New associations	Clauss, 2017; Saumett et al., 2018; Mutenje et al., 2016; Francesconi & Heerink, 2011
Innovation in the value proposition(Clauss, 2017)	New relationships with consumers	Clauss, 2017
	New clients and markets	Clauss, 2017; Francesconi & Heerink, 2011; Barrett et al., 2012
Innovation in capturing value (Clauss, 2017)	New cost and revenue structures	Clauss, 2017
	Resource management	Cummings, 2013

Source: Own elaboration based on cited authors.

(Barrera et al., 2017; Ramos-Sandoval et al., 2019; Muhic & Bengtsson, 2021).

As evidenced in Table 9.4 and Figure 9.2, innovation capabilities such as sensing, seizing, and transforming processes are related to the characteristics and dynamics of agricultural organizations, from the detection in the learning capacity with the organizational performance and the associative nature of the organizations. Likewise, the relationship capacity is established by cooperation networks, these two capacities being essential for the development of this type of organization (Sachitra & Chong, 2018).

In sensing capabilities such as culture toward innovation, there is the incidence of traditional practices with technological development in agricultural organizations (Flores & Naranjo, 2006). It is also linked to the strategic direction to strengthen associative processes, requiring that leaders have more training and experience in these processes for better results (Espinosa et al., 2018; Barrera et al., 2017). The above is consistent with the fact that the culture incorporated into the organizational strategy allows mediating inefficiencies in the processes (Alfaro-García et al., 2017).

The transformation capabilities are determined by developing or improving products and services through collaboration networks, understanding that these organizations hardly have the resources to develop products independently. For this reason, alliances with government entities, universities, or technological development centers play an essential role in this type of capability (Ramos-Sandoval et al., 2019). Regarding the capability to adapt, organizations define and implement strategies to face the complexity and volatility of the markets, also associated with the development of sustainable projects and initiatives in the sector as an alternative to take advantage of natural resources in a responsible way (Shiferaw et al., 2009; Murendo et al., 2011).

Understanding that there are models adapted to the conditions of organizations, we present elements that could be considered to assess the way innovation is measured. This is the case of models focused on how value is added from the optimization of resources for innovation in products or services, but which have a wider scope by considering not only economic but also social objectives of organizations. The above allows bringing up the concept of light innovation, being a more holistic look at innovation, which is defined by Blanco-Mesa and Baier-Fuentes (2017) as follows:

"is a process that optimizes existing resources for the generation of differentiated and affordable products and services aimed at specific and unattended markets, which are based on creativity and the transfer and

Table 9.4   Table of code co-occurrences.

	AdaptabilityGr = 10	Innovative culture development capacityGr = 10	Learning capacityGr = 30	Product or service development capacityGr = 19	Relationship capacityGr = 32	Strategic direction capacityGr = 14
AssociativityGr=23	0	2	3	2	4	4
Co-creationGr = 4	0	0	1	0	3	1
Community participationGr = 6	0	0	1	0	3	1
ConfidenceGr = 6	0	0	0	0	2	1
Cooperation networksGr = 20	0	0	3	3	7	1
Environmental sustainabilityGr = 14	4	1	1	0	2	0
Financial exclusionGr = 3	0	0	1	0	0	1
Government policiesGr = 9	1	0	0	0	0	0
Insufficient R&DGr = 4	0	0	0	1	2	0
LeadershipGr = 3	0	0	1	0	0	1
Low educational levelGr = 7	0	0	1	0	2	3
Low technological levelGr = 6	0	2	0	0	0	0
Market volatilityGr = 6	1	0	2	0	1	0
PerformanceGr = 13	0	0	5	4	4	2
Productivity and competitivenessGr = 6	0	0	2	0	0	0
Projects managementGr = 3	0	0	2	0	1	0
Technical assistanceGr = 4	0	0	2	0	0	0

Source: Own elaboration with Atlas.ti 9.

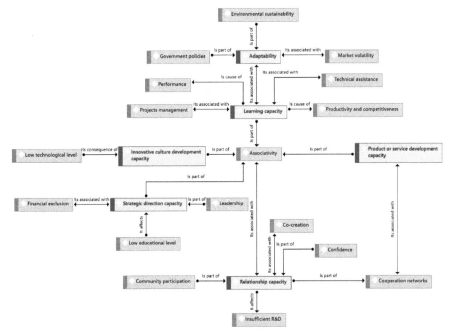

Figure 9.2 Semantic network of innovation capacities in agricultural organizations.
Source: Own elaboration with Atlas.ti 9.

dissemination of knowledge among different stakeholders in order to create value through the solution of social and organizational problems and needs." (p. 101)

As Lawson et al. (2001) point out, there are lessons learned about the use of dynamic capabilities in the development of innovative business models. In agricultural organizations, elements such as the use of basic capacities based on the experience and trajectory of the producers, in their management focused on the management of resources, mainly knowledge of good agricultural practices and participation in institutional spaces are considered. It is not very visible in the content analysis as to how the management of these spaces achieves technological and market resources as a permanent requirement of the members of the organizations.

It is possible that this behavior responds to the way agricultural organizations are conceived mainly in the Latin American context. Its orientation and scope is based on managing resources to strengthen learning capacities in training processes that are not followed up in the implementation of such knowledge. This results in the use of external knowledge without significant impact on the productive units, which limits the measurement of performance. For this reason, performance is determined by the institutional framework without assessing the internal effects on these organizations. As indicated by Saunila et al. (2014), the use of external knowledge is determined by the ability to impact the performance of innovation capabilities that can be validated by tools that monitor the results of this interaction.

9.7 Discussion

From the perspective of the theory of resources and capabilities, organizations require developing dynamic capabilities that allow them to configure and reconfigure the base of their assets to respond to ever-changing technologies and markets (Teece & Augier, 2008). In this sense, the development of innovation capacity is established by its potential to generate sustainable competitive advantages in agricultural organizations through the ideation and creation of new ventures that take advantage of the challenges and opportunities in the economic environment by means of management skills focused on strengthening their internal processes and their response capacity (Flores & Naranjo, 2006; Lawson & Samson, 2001).

It is highlighted that measuring the capabilities of organizations to introduce and maintain continuous changes is relevant to identify competitive advantages (Alfaro-García et al., 2017). The ability to innovate is a determinant in organizations, which generates and fosters new ideas, identifies opportunities, requirements, and solutions on identified constraints taking advantage of their resources, knowledge, and capabilities (Blanco-Mesa et al., 2019). In this sense, dynamic capabilities contribute to the identification of innovation capabilities in the agricultural context, due to the connection with the elements that make up the business model, these elements being indispensable for an organization to be considered dynamically capable (Teece, 2010).

Therefore, the study of innovation capabilities and their relevance in consolidating organizations' business models from the agricultural context results in the consolidation of six capabilities based on the theory of dynamic capabilities proposed by Teece (2007). During the sensing process, the organization seeks to take advantage of the opportunities generated in the context where it develops its activity. It establishes its priorities through learning and relationship processes.

For agricultural organizations, learning is permanent, mainly through exploring and exchanging knowledge related to using technologies in the production system (Kiani et al., 2019). However, agricultural organizations rely primarily on their knowledge and resources, with a low capacity to take and adapt knowledge that can mobilize the technical and economic support necessary to innovate in improving their performance (Cummings, 2013).

Therefore, managing alliances for acquiring, adapting, and using knowledge is a routine practice, allowing greater dissemination and mobilization of economic resources (Barrera et al., 2017). In other words, the relationship capability facilitates alternatives to manage restrictions in the incorporation of research and development processes, in order to co-create products and services and network management, in response to the link generated by the alliances between innovative institutions and producers (Vargas-Prieto & Sanchez-Álvarez, 2020; Turner et al., 2017; Cepeda & Arias-Pérez, 2019). Therefore, it could be considered that for this type of organizations, the open innovation approach proposed by Chesbrough (2003) is the most appropriate for the exchange and appropriation of knowledge.

Likewise, it allows organizations to reduce problems derived from their scope: strengthening their associates' economic development and the community's social well-being (Best et al., 2021). The relationship capability is essential in sensing because it facilitates identifying opportunities by government programs and policies to generate value in the transformation stage (De Silva et al., 2021). Understanding that the relationship is external, it is implied that the participation of the associates is decisive in the productive units, considering that it is the peasants themselves who exchange ideas and spaces of social and productive cohesion for the organization (Espinosa et al., 2018; Flores & Naranjo, 2006).

In the retention stage, the organization recombines and builds new competencies to take advantage of emerging opportunities. This process requires culturally strengthening the organization members to reduce resistance to change in transition periods and promote collaboration, creativity, and the flow of information for the creation and accumulation of knowledge (Donate et al., 2016; De Silva et al., 2021). For agricultural organizations, the culture toward innovation is reactive, causing restrictions for adopting technologies in production systems, making their productivity and profitability lower. This behavior translates into the lack of coordination and establishment of agreements, an obstacle to technological development (Flores & Naranjo, 2006; Muhic & Bengtsson, 2021).

Consequently, the capacity for strategic direction management capacity of a company is restored by the knowledge that the leaders of the organizations have in administrative, financial, and management processes, which facilitate interaction with the members or associates about their commitments, benefits, and integration processes for the development of initiatives that promote social and economic well-being (Barrera et al., 2017). Thus, it is the natural leaders who assume the responsibility of directing the work of the organizations, which is often a job with low formal incentives (Saumett et al., 2018; FAO, 2020).

Later, in the transformation stage, it is necessary to maintain profitable and sustained growth, recombining assets and organizational structures as markets and technologies change (Teece, 2007). Therefore, the development and improvements in the products or services of organizations are crucial to performance by understanding consumer needs (Christa et al., 2020). In agricultural organizations, this process requires cooperation networks to generate and absorb the necessary knowledge to develop new products, techniques, or markets (Ramos-Sandoval et al., 2019).

This open business model encourages further exploration of radically new products or services, reducing incremental innovations (Cheng, 2011). These conditions facilitate the transformation stage and can adapt for sustainability over time (Ahmad et al., 2020). Therefore, the characteristics of the production systems and the members of the organizations make them resilient due to the way in which they cope with agricultural production processes and changes in the environment (Murendo et al., 2011).

For this condition to be viable, flexible policies are required. Sociocultural conditions establish the need for approaches that can be tested, validated, and adapted to productive environments for incorporating different technologies and management practices (Shiferaw et al., 2009; Rajala et al., 2012). In this sense, accompaniment and learning are essential for the success of this type of organization in their search to adapt and sustain themselves (Sachitra & Chong, 2018).

Innovation for agricultural organizations is a dynamic process, which adjusts to the stages of creation, proposal, and capture of value through the absorption of knowledge (Chesbrough & Rosenbloom, 2002; Clauss, 2017). Therefore, not only the capabilities must have the dynamism to generate competitive advantages such as the structure of the management model in addition to its flexibility and relationship capacity (Teece, 2010).

The behavior of agricultural organizations is determined by environmental variables, mainly institutional, in which there are opportunities for access to resources focused on the improvement of productive units, mainly access to knowledge and technologies that strengthen production systems. There are important limitations identified in this study regarding the capacity to manage new markets for products with a differentiated offer, increasing the gaps in the approach of its members and confidence in the management of inclusive businesses.

9.8 Conclusions

The analysis of research related to innovation capabilities in rural organizations shows the use of elements that contribute to how knowledge is sensed, seized, and transformed based on the addition of value and social development of the communities linked to agricultural production systems.

On the theoretical foundations of Teece (2007), it is found that, in the agricultural context, innovation involves learning capabilities and external relations for the acquisition of knowledge, which, in turn, require an innovative culture and adequate direction for the generation of products and services with the ability to adapt to the change.

Likewise, the business model in agricultural organizations can be explained through the elements of creation, proposal, and capture of value as indicated by Clauss (2017), understanding that the structures must be as dynamic as the development of capabilities for adjustment and positioning in the environment. Therefore, how the sensing, seizing, and transformation processes are developed in the organization will impact the addition of value.

The analysis generated in this research shows the interest of the elements that allow recognizing the innovation capabilities in agricultural organizations to establish sustainable business models. These organizations have particularities that differentiate them from commonly studied companies, which in their associative and community nature configure their business model and their aptitudes for innovation differently.

The contribution of future research is based on validating constructs or categories of analysis that validate the way in which innovation capacities are managed in agricultural organizations made up of local actors that depend on smaller-scale production systems. In addition, it questions whether the identification of alternatives focused on innovation strengthens the capacities of this type of organizations, with a different conception of resource and market management in highly competitive environments. In this regard, it is important to rethink whether the way in which these types of organizations are encouraged corresponds to inclusive and sustainable business models.

References

Ahmad, S., Omar, R., & Quoquab, F. (2020). Family firms' sustainable longevity: the role of family involvement in business and innovation capability. Journal of Family Business Management, 11(1), 86–106. https://doi.org/10.1108/JFBM-12-2019-0081

Akhavan, P., & Mahdi Hosseini, S. (2016). Social capital, knowledge sharing, and innovation capability: an empirical study of R&D teams in Iran. Technology Analysis and Strategic Management, 28(1), 96–113. https://doi.org/10.1080/09537325.2015.1072622

An, J., Cho, S. H., & Tang, C. S. (2015). Aggregating Smallholder Farmers in Emerging Economies. Production and Operations Management, 24(9), 1414–1429. https://doi.org/10.1111/poms.12372

Alfaro-García, Victor G., Gil-Lafuente, A. M., & Alfaro Calderón, G. G. (2017). A fuzzy methodology for innovation management measurement. Kybernetes, 46(1), 50–66. https://doi.org/10.1108/K-06-2016-0153

Barney, J. (1991). Firm Resources and Sustained Competitive Advantage. In Journal of Management (Vol. 17, Issue 1, pp. 99–120). https://doi.org/10.1177/014920639101700108

Barney, J. B. (2001). Resource-based theories of competitive advantage: A ten-year retrospective on the resource-based view. Journal of Management, 27(6), 643–650. https://doi.org/10.1016/S0149-2063(01)00115-5

Barrera, A., Cuevas, V., Ramírez, A., & Espejel, A. (2017). Identification of organizational innovation components to consolidate rural associative enterprises. Revista de Geografía Agrícola, 59, 127–144.

Barrett, C. B., Bachke, M. E., Bellemare, M. F., Michelson, H. C., Narayanan, S., & Walker, T. F. (2012). Smallholder participation in contract farming: Comparative evidence from five countries. World Development, 40(4), 715–730. https://doi.org/10.1016/j.worlddev.2011.09.006

Bastanchury-López, M. T., De-Pablos-Heredero, C., Montes-Botella, J. L., Martín-Romo-Romero, S., & García, A. (2020). Impact of dynamic capabilities on performance in dairy sheep farms in Spain. Sustainability (Switzerland), 12(8), 2015–2020. https://doi.org/10.3390/SU12083368

Behnam, S., Cagliano, R., & Grijalvo, M. (2018). How should firms reconcile their open innovation capabilities for incorporating external actors in innovations aimed at sustainable development? Journal of Cleaner Production, 170, 950–965. https://doi.org/10.1016/j.jclepro.2017.09.168

Best, B., Miller, K., McAdam, R., & Moffett, S. (2021). Mission or margin? Using dynamic capabilities to manage tensions in social purpose organisations' business model innovation. Journal of Business Research, 125(January), 643–657. https://doi.org/10.1016/j.jbusres.2020.01.068

Blanco-Mesa, F., & Baier-Fuentes, H. (2017). Towards an Integral View of Light-Innovation: Conceptual Analysis of Non-Intensive Innovations. Cuadernos Del Cimbage, 19(2), 79–103.

Blanco-Mesa, F., León-Castro, E., Cifuentes-Valenzuela, Marlenne Velázquez-Cázares, J., & Sánchez-Ovalle, V. (2019). Medición de las capacidades de innovación en tres sectores primarios en Colombia. Efectos olvidados de las capacidades de innovación de la quínoa, la guayaba y apícola en Boyacá y Santander. Real Academia de Ciencias Económicas y Financieras. Observatorio de Investigación Económico- Financiera. https://racef.es/archivos/publicaciones/mo60_19_web_racef.pdf

Bocken, N. M. P., Short, S. W., Rana, P., & Evans, S. (2014). A literature and practice review to develop sustainable business model archetypes. Journal of Cleaner Production, 65, 42–56. https://doi.org/10.1016/j.jclepro.2013.1 1.039

Cepeda, J., & Arias-Pérez, J. (2019). Information technology capabilities and organizational agility: The mediating effects of open innovation capabilities. Multinational Business Review, 27(2), 198–216. https://doi.org/10.1 108/MBR-11-2017-0088

Cheng, C. (2011). Dynamic service innovation capability, radical service innovation and open business models. International Journal of Services, Technology and Management, 16(3–4), 229–242. https://doi.org/10.1504/ IJSTM.2011.044357

Chesbrough, H. (2003). Open Innovation The New Imperative for Creating and Profiting from Technology. In Harvard business school press. Harvard Business School Publishing Corporation Chesbrough, H., & Rosenbloom, R. S. (2002). The role of the business model in capturing value from innovation: Evidence from Xerox Corporation's technology spin-off companies. Industrial and Corporate Change, 11(3), 529–555. https://doi.org/ 10.1093/icc/11.3.529

Christa, U. R., Wardana, I. M., Dwiatmadja, C., & Kristinae, V. (2020). The role of value innovation capabilities in the influence of market orientation and social capital to improving the performance of central Kalimantan bank in Indonesia. Journal of Open Innovation: Technology, Market, and Complexity, 6(4), 1–14. https://doi.org/10.3390/joitmc6040140

Clauss, T. (2017). Measuring business model innovation: conceptualization, scale development, and proof of performance. R and D Management, 47(3), 385–403. https://doi.org/10.1111/radm.12186

Cummings, A. (2013). Construyendo capacidades de innovación en iniciati-
vas asociativas de pequeñas agroindustrias rurales en El Salvador. Revista
Iberoamericana de Ciencia, Tecnología y Sociedad - CTS, 8(24), 295–319.

De Silva, M., Al-Tabbaa, O., & Khan, Z. (2021). Business model innovation
by international social purpose organizations: The role of dynamic capabilities. Journal of Business Research, 125(December), 733–749. https:
//doi.org/10.1016/j.jbusres.2019.12.030

Donate, M. J., Peña, I., & Sánchez de Pablo, J. D. (2016). HRM practices for
human and social capital development: effects on innovation capabilities.
International Journal of Human Resource Management, 27(9), 928–953.
https://doi.org/10.1080/09585192.2015.1047393

Espinosa, H. R., Gómez, C. J. R., & Betancur, L. F. R. (2018). Factores
determinantes de la sostenibilidad de las agroempresas asociativas rurales.
Revista de Economia e Sociologia Rural, 56(1), 107–122. https://doi.org/
10.1590/1234-56781806-94790560107

FAO, O. de las N. para la alimentación. (2020). Smallholders and family
farms in Albania - Country study report 2019. In Smallholders and family
farms in Albania - Country study report 2019. https://doi.org/10.4060/ca
7450en

Fischer, E., & Qaim, M. (2012). Linking Smallholders to Markets: Determinants and Impacts of Farmer Collective Action in Kenya. World Development, 40(6), 1255–1268. https://doi.org/10.1016/j.worlddev.2011.11.0
18

Flores, R., & Naranjo, C. (2006). Uso del capital social en la generación de
asociatividad en pequeñas organizaciones familiares campesinas. Revista
de Trabajo Social, 73, 99–109. https://doi.org/10.7764/rts.73.99-109

Foss, N. J., & Saebi, T. (2018). Business models and business model innovation: Between wicked and paradigmatic problems. Long Range Planning,
51(1), 9–21. https://doi.org/10.1016/j.lrp.2017.07.006

Francesconi, G. N., & Heerink, N. (2011). Ethiopian agricultural cooperatives
in an era of global commodity exchange: Does organisational form matter?
Journal of African Economies, 20(1), 153–177. https://doi.org/10.1093/ja
e/ejq036

Freije, I., de la Calle, A., & Ugarte, J. V. (2021). Role of supply chain
integration in the product innovation capability of servitized manufacturing
companies. Technovation, xxxx. https://doi.org/10.1016/j.technovation.2
020.102216

French, J., Montiel, K., & Palmieri, V. (2014). Posicionamiento institucional
- la innovación en la agricultura: un proceso clave para el desarrollo

sostenible. Iica, 20. http://opackoha.iica.int/cgi-bin/koha/opac-detail .pl?biblionumber=45

Kiani, M. N., Ahmad, M., & Gillani, S. H. M. (2019). Service innovation capabilities as the precursor to business model innovation: a conditional process analysis. Asian Journal of Technology Innovation, 27(2), 194–213. https://doi.org/10.1080/19761597.2019.1654398

Lawson, B., Samson, D., 2001. Developing innovation capability in organisations: a dynamic capabilities approach. Int. J. Innov. Manag. 05, 377-400. https://doi.org/10.1142/S1363919601000427

Lichtenthaler, U., & Lichtenthaler, E. (2009). A capability-based framework for open innovation: Complementing absorptive capacity. Journal of Management Studies, 46(8), 1315–1338. https://doi.org/10.1111/j.1467-6486. 2009.00854.x

Muhic, M., & Bengtsson, L. (2021). Dynamic capabilities triggered by cloud sourcing: a stage-based model of business model innovation. Review of Managerial Science, 15(1), 33–54. https://doi.org/10.1007/s11846-019-0 0372-1

Murendo, C., Keil, A., & Zeller, M. (2011). Drought impacts and related risk management by smallholder farmers in developing countries: Evidence from Awash River Basin, Ethiopia. Risk Management, 13(4), 247–263. https://doi.org/10.1057/rm.2011.17

Mutenje, M., Kankwamba, H., Mangisonib, J., & Kassie, M. (2016). Agricultural innovations and food security in Malawi: Gender dynamics, institutions and market implications. Technological Forecasting and Social Change, 103, 240–248. https://doi.org/10.1016/j.techfore.2015.10.004

Ochoa Jiménez, S., Cervantes Hurtado, G. V., Jacobo Hernández, C. A., & Flores López, J. G. (2020). Knowledge and Innovation in Mexican Agricultural Organizations. Economies, 8(4), 103. https://doi.org/10.3 390/economies8040103

Osterwalder, A., & Pigneur, Y. (2013). Generación de modelos de negocio (T. Clark (ed.)). DEUSTO.Quinonez Zuniga, C., & Laverde Urrea, L. E. (2019). Construction of business models in rural organizations. Telos-Revista Interdisciplinaria En Ciencias Sociales, 21(3), 776–794.

Rajala, R., Westerlund, M., & Möller, K. (2012). Strategic flexibility in open innovation - designing business models for open source software. European Journal of Marketing, 46(10), 1368–1388. https://doi.org/10.1108/030905 61211248071

Ramírez, C. J., Robledo, J., & Aguilar, J. (2020). Trust networks and innovation dynamics of small farmers in Colombia: An approach from territorial system of agricultural innovation. Revista de La Facultad de Ciencias Agrarias, 52(2), 253–266.

Ramos-Sandoval, R., García Álvarez-Coque, J. M., & Mas-Verdú, F. (2019). Innovative capabilities of users of agricultural R&D services. Regional Science Policy and Practice, 11(2), 295–305. https://doi.org/10.1111/rs p3.12152

Ribau, C. P., Moreira, A. C., & Raposo, M. (2017). SMEs innovation capabilities and export performance: an entrepreneurial orientation view. Journal of Business Economics and Management, 18(5), 920–934. https://doi.org/10.3846/16111699.2017.1352534

Rodriguez, D. (2017). Esquemas de comercialización que facilitan la vinculación de productores agricolas con los mercados (Issue December 2016).

Rossi, V., & Chia, E. (2020). Innovation in social studies of agricultural processes evolution and emphasis on Latin America. Agrociencia Uruguay, 24(1). https://doi.org/10.31285/agro.24.346

Sachitra, V., & Chong, S. C. (2018). Resources, capabilities and competitive advantage of minor export crops farms in Sri Lanka: An empirical investigation. Competitiveness Review, 28(5), 478–502. https://doi.org/10.1108/CR-01-2017-0004

Sampieri, R. H. (2014). METODOLOGIA DE LA INVESTIGACION (6th ed.). McGraw-Hill / Interamericana Editores SA.

Saumett, H., Osorio, E.-C., Estrada, T.-H., & Carrillo, L.-C. B. (2018). Caracterización de Organizaciones del sector agropecuario.Saunila, M., Pekkola, S., & Ukko, J. (2014). The relationship between innovation capability and performance. International Journal of Productivity and Performance Management, 63(2), 234-249. doi:http://dx.doi.org/10.1108/IJPPM-04-20 13-0065

Setyawati, H. A., Suroso, A., & Adi, P. H. (2020). Examining the impact of entrepreneurial orientation on marketing performance: the mediating role of entrepreneurial networking and innovation capability. International Journal of Scientific and Technology Research, 9(2), 1895–1904.

Shiferaw, B. A., Okello, J., & Reddy, R. V. (2009). Adoption and adaptation of natural resource management innovations in smallholder agriculture: Reflections on key lessons and best practices. Environment, Development and Sustainability, 11(3), 601–619. https://doi.org/10.1007/s10668-007-9 132-1

Teece, D. J. (2007). Explicating dynamic capabilities: The nature of micro-foundations of (sustainable) enterprise performance. Strategic Management Journal, 28, 1319–1350. https://doi.org/10.1002/smj.640

Teece, D. J. (2010). Business models, business strategy and innovation. Long Range Planning, 43(2–3), 172–194. https://doi.org/10.1016/j.lrp.2009.07.003

Terrazas, A., De la Garza, S., & Cruz, R. (2019). Las Organizaciones Rurales, Opciones Para La Integración De Los Pequeños Productores Rurales Del Sector Agrícola En San Buenaventura, Cohauila. Revista Mexicana de Agronegocios, 45, 285–298.

Turner, J. A., Klerkx, L., White, T., Nelson, T., Everett-Hincks, J., Mackay, A., & Botha, N. (2017). Unpacking systemic innovation capacity as strategic ambidexterity: How projects dynamically configure capabilities for agricultural innovation. Land Use Policy, 68(July), 503–523. https://doi.org/10.1016/j.landusepol.2017.07.054

Vargas-Prieto, A., & Sanchez-Álvarez, C. (2020). Análisis de evolución de la asistencia técnica y el fomento de cooperativas rurales en Colombia. Cooperativismo \& Desarrollo, 1–22. https://revistas.ucc.edu.co/index.php/co/article/view/3127

Velazquez-Cazares, M. G., Gil-Lafuente, A. M., Leon-Castro, E. et al. Innovation capabilities measurement using fuzzy methodologies: a Colombian SMEs case. Comput Math Organ Theory 27, 384–413 (2021). https://doi-org.ezproxy.unal.edu.co/10.1007/s10588-020-09321-w

10

A Multicriteria Ranking of Stocks for Portfolio Selection Considering Investor Preferences

Pavel A. Alvarez[1], Maria Bernal[1], Manuel Muñoz[2], Ernesto León-Castro[3], and Cuitláhuac Valdez[1]

[1]Universidad Autónoma de Occidente, Unidad Regional Culiacan, Mexico
[2]Management Department, Universidad de Sonora, Mexico
[3]Unidad Navojoa, Instituto Tecnologico de Sonora, Mexico

Abstract

The objective of this work is to present a new approach to evaluate stock. In the stock market, there are a large number of stocks, so the investor faces the problem of choosing the ones that make up a portfolio. The ELimination Et Choix Traduisant la REalité (ELECTRE)-III method was applied to evaluate and generate a ranking that orders the stocks of the Mexican Stock Exchange (MSE) from best to worst according to the preferences of the investors. The top 20 firms shown in the ranking mostly coincide with the best firms of the Price and Quotation Index from the MSE. The ranking generated can be helpful to the investor in the selection of a satisfactory portfolio, since their preferences were considered in the stock evaluation phase.

Keywords: Portfolio selection, multicriteria ranking, ELECTRE-III, Mexican Stock Exchange

10.1 Introduction

Portfolio selection is a problem addressed mainly in financial topics based on Markowitz's contribution in his seminal article "Portfolio Selection" by Markowitz (1952). Markowitz introduced the term investment diversification.

He defined the portfolio selection problem as determining an investment portfolio that maximizes return given a certain level of risk or minimizes risk given a considering a given return (Boonjing and Boongasame, 2016). The risk of a stock is associated with various factors, and its effect can be offset by buying shares of various firms so that an investment portfolio reduces risk due to diversification.

Different studies (Hurson and Zopounidis, 1997; Zopounidis and Doumpos, 1998, 2002; Bouri, Martel, and Chabchoub, 2003; Mansour, Cherif, and Abdelfattah, 2019) have proposed to address the portfolio selection problem through the following stages: stage 1 – the evaluation of various stocks measured by the result of financial indicators to select the most attractive according to the evaluation criteria and the investors' preferences. Stage 2 – the definition of the proportions of capital allocated to each stock to construct the portfolio that meets the risk and return conditions. Both phases are critical and require the intervention of the investor to obtain efficient investment portfolios.

The most critical portfolio selection stage is stock selection (Xidonas, Doukas, and Hassapis, 2021). Two fundamental elements of this stage are: 1) In portfolio management decision making generally only two criteria are used, profitability and risk. This represents a limitation that is frequently mentioned in the literature, since it does not incorporate other important evaluation criteria for the investor (Aouni et al., 2018) The use of other relevant financial information leads to a different investment decision (Vuković, 2020); 2) The diversification strategy is related to the investor's risk profile, that is, their preferences (Mansour, Cherif, and Abdelfattah, 2019). The traditional portfolio selection methods cannot incorporate the individual goals of the decision maker, personal preferences, and attitude toward risk (Xidonas, Doukas, and Sarmas, 2021). The decision-maker preferences are not considered; the relative valuation of the criteria can be very different between one decision-maker and another. These two fundamental elements can generate a ranking, stock list eligible, which does not satisfy the investor.

The selecting stock is clearly a multicriteria problem due to its multi-dimensional nature and multicriteria decision. Its methods have the advantage of including user preferences. There is a need to use a Multicriteria Decision-Making method to prioritize the stocks. It is a ranking of these that makes it possible to identify the best-performing stocks which can be used in the second stage to generate investment portfolios with the stocks located in the top positions of the global ranking generated, instead of considering all the shares of the Mexican stock market. Optimization processes can be used to obtain attractive portfolios for the investor.

This set of procedures multicriteria decision-making, known as MCDM, includes four main approaches and these, in turn, various methods. The full aggregation, outranking, goal, aspiration or reference level, and non-classical MCDM are the representative approaches (Alvarez, Ishizaka, and Martínez, 2021). The multicriteria aggregation procedure of ELECTRE-III is adequate in the presence of heterogeneous scales. In this method, they do not allow for compensation of performances among criteria (Figueira, Greco, S., and B., Slowinski, 2013). Because the performance indicators used as criteria to evaluate actions are presented on different scales, in the present work, the ELECTRE-III method proposed by Roy (1978) is applied in the first stage to evaluate stock with various financial performance indicators based on book values and market values. The ELECTRE-III method allows the generation of a global stock ranking regarding the complete set of indicators.

The portfolio selection problem is applied to 120 firms listed on the Mexican Stock Exchange (MSE). We consider this implementation as a practical alternative approach to support the investor in making investment decisions about traditional portfolio theory, since it considers several criteria at the same time and whose results integrate the preferences of the decision-maker.

This chapter is divided into five sections. It starts with Section 12.1 which gives the presentation of the topic. A literature review of multicriteria methods used in portfolio selection is included in Section 12.2. Section 12.3 provides the ELECTRE-III method as a multicriteria decision-making method for the ranking of shares. In Section 12.4, the main results are reflected and, finally, Section 12.5 generates some closures and points out possible lines of future work.

10.2 Literature Review

Globalization and advances in information technology make it easier to obtain a large amount of data, information, and economic and financial news that affect stocks. However, it also makes it more complex for the decision-maker to decide between a great number of alternatives. In addition to the above, markets are increasingly competitive, and an incorrect decision can cause substantial financial losses, so multicriteria decision-making (MCDM) methods are alternatives that help decision-makers deal with these circumstances. The MCDM methods consider several criteria simultaneously to evaluate the stocks; that is, they assume that this problem must be evaluated from different dimensions. They are also able to consider the specific preferences of investors.

Recently the selection of portfolios has gained importance since there are many investigations focused on this topic. The analysis carried out in a paper (Almeida-Filho, de Lima Silva, and Ferreira, 2021) found 657 articles on MCDM methods applied to financial issues, of which 185 focus on portfolio selection, in contrast with Aouni et al. (2018) just 3 years ago found 116 published studies, some oriented in the evaluation or selection of assets for the construction of portfolios, while others focused on the construction of investment portfolios and optimization approaches with budgetary restrictions. It is also based on modern portfolio theory. To learn more about the MCDM methods applied to portfolio selection, you can also consult (Xidonas, Doukas, and Hassapis, 2021).

A literature review was carried out finds that the number and variety of criteria used have recently increased, identifying the need to develop new decision-making models to improve existing ones with approaches closer to reality (Aouni et al., 2018; Aouni et al., 2018). In one case, the Tehran Stock Exchange (TSE) was studied. Specific criteria were selected, and a fuzzy analytical network process (FANP) was developed to evaluate and select portfolios at the TSE (Galankashi, Rafiei, and Ghezelbash, 2020). Another work (Erdemlioglu and Joliet, 2019) studied optimal equity portfolios with a long-term horizon under heterogeneous levels of risk aversion, focusing on European stocks.

Vuković (2020) performs a comparative analysis of stock selection using a hybrid approach of MCDM and modern portfolio theory. Since the MCDM methods used may yield different rating results, a hybrid stock rating is calculated. With the results of this study, it can be concluded that investment portfolio decisions benefit from including more financial information.

In Mohammed (2021), multicriteria decision-making techniques are applied in fuzzy environments in the selection of projects for portfolio management. In this study, the preference weights of the criteria were identified using fuzzy AHP. Then, the weights were embraced in fuzzy techniques to improve the gaps in alternatives and achieve the organization's objectives. Other research (Zare Mehrjerdi, 2021) bases stock selection on risk–benefit study through the MCDM methods in a fuzzy environment, allowing decision-makers to identify the list of acceptable portfolios where they can allocate some portions of their assets.

A method was introduced to select stocks based on financial index data before forming the portfolio based on their financial performance through the Technique for Order of Preference by Similarity to Ideal Solution (TOPSIS) model. The optimal portfolio was generated using the Markowitz model (Aqilah, Fauzi, and Ismail, 2019). Another article also shows the use of the MCDM method to address the integrated portfolio problem with the fuzzy AHP fuzzy TOPSIS multicriteria model (ALDALOU and PERÇİN, 2018).

Kao and Steuer (2016) proposed a method for estimating information values, arguing that, in the mean-variance model, the process to specify the expected returns of individual assets is based on the information. It is decisive for the capital allocations that the different stocks be corrected. The model is tested on Taiwan stocks.

In Mansour, Cherif, and Abdelfattah (2019), the possibility theory, as well as a goal programming model, is used. It allows for considering trade-offs between investors' preferences concerning diverse objectives difficult to measure in an imprecise context. The portfolio selection approach presented in this study is multi-objective, involving fuzzy parameters, where the fuzzy numbers give the distributions of possibilities, and the investor's preferences are treated through satisfaction functions.

In Egypt, specialists were consulted to identify the most important aspects to create a portfolio management model to be applied in the stock market of that country (Elselmy, Ghoneim, and Elkhodary, 2019). The survey concluded that the factors to consider are fair value, liquidity, sales growth, net profit growth, industry growth, bank interest rate, market capitalization, the price per profit, dividends, cash dividend, volatility, and Beta ratio portfolio market.

Hadhri and Ftiti (2019) investigated the feasibility of investing in countries whose markets with growth potential. They focus on the third classic moment used in asset allocation: realized bias. It uses an analysis based on asymmetry in the markets focused on the potential opportunities for diversification and the portfolio's investment strategy.

The work developed by Jeong and Kim (2019) compared six online portfolio strategies' effectiveness and tested them in the Korea Stock Market.

Zhu (2019) analyzed the Markowitz and Arrow-Pratt risk remuneration models and the Jia and Dyer standard risk model. The study generated an investment optimization proposal through a model that combines the mean entropy and portfolio model with transaction cost.

10.3 The ELECTRE-III Method for the Ranking Generation

The ELECTRE-III method is an outranking approach, which compares each pair of alternatives in the set $(a, b) \in A \times A$ to assess the credibility of the statement "*a* is at least as good as *b*" denoted by aSb (Roy, 1978). The partial concordance index in (1) is defined by $C_j(a,b)$, evaluating the difference between two alternatives by the criterion $g_j.$, using the preference of the decision-maker defined in the indifference q_j and preference p_j thresholds:

$$C_j(a, b) = \frac{p_j(g_j(a)) - [g_j(b) - g_j(a)]}{p_j(g_j(a)) - q_j(g_j(a))}. \tag{10.1}$$

The comprehensive index $C(a,b)$ (eqn (10.2)): Is the sum of the partial concordance indices $C_j(a,b)$ on each criterion, considering the weights of each criterion w_j. The value of $C(a,b)$ expresses to what extent the performance of all the criteria is following the statement "*a* outranks *b*":

$$C(a, b) = \frac{\sum\limits_{j=1}^{n} w_j C_j(a, b)}{\sum\limits_{j=1}^{n} w_j}. \tag{10.2}$$

The index of discordance index $D_j(a,b)$ (eqn (10.3)): In this index, the discrepancy of criterion g_j indicates the extent to which this criterion disagrees with the statement "*a* outranks *b*." The discordance index D_j reaches its maximum value when the criterion g_j adds its veto to the outranking relation. The index obtains its minimum value when the criterion g_j does not discordance with the relationship:

$$D_j(a, b) = \min \left\{ 1, \max \left\{ 0, \frac{[g_j(b) - g_j(a)] - p_j(g_j(a))}{v_j(g_j(a)) - p_j(g_j(a))} \right\} \right\} \tag{10.3}$$

The relationship about fuzzy classification is defined for each pair of alternatives (a,b) as a credibility index. The relationship $\sigma(a, b)$ fully expresses to what extent "*a* outranks *b*" considering the comprehensive concordance index and the discordance index for each criterion g_j. Credibility is reduced in the presence of one or more discordant criteria when $D_j(a, b) > C(a,b)$. Under the veto effect, $\sigma(a, b) = 0$ if $\exists j \mid D_j(a, b) = 1$ regardless of the relative importance w_j of the criterion. The credibility index in eqn (10.4) is computed based on eqn (10.2) and (10.3):

$$\sigma(a, b) = \begin{cases} C(a, b) & if \ \overline{F}(a, b) = 0 \\ C(a, b) \times \prod\limits_{J \in \overline{F}(a,b)} \frac{1 - D_j(a,b)}{1 - C(a,b)} & if \ \overline{F}(a, b) \neq 0, \end{cases} \tag{10.4}$$

where $\bar{F}(a, b) = j\epsilon F/D_j(a, b) > C(a, b)$.

The value of $\sigma(a, b)$ is an interval [0,1]. The index excludes the possibility that a significant loss in a criterion can be compensated by a small number of gains from the remaining criteria.

10.3.1 The ELECTRE-III method for the ranking generation of Mexican Stock Exchange (MSE)

This section will explain the process for implementing the ELECTRE-III method for prioritizing the shares of the Mexican Stock Exchange (MSE). In Figure 10.1, the methodology developed in three stages is illustrated. In the first stage, the description of the data is carried out; in the second stage, stocks evaluation is carried out to obtain the ranking, and in the third, the 20 best-evaluated companies in the second stage are compared with the companies that make up the MSE Price and Quotation Index.

10.3.1.1 Data description

In this research, financial indicators are used as decision criteria. These indicators are the most used in the papers on portfolio selection. Because decision-making implies profit but also the possibility of losing money, the calculation of volatility and profitability becomes a complex problem. Therefore, the need to include all these indicators as criteria has been generated. (Fernandez et al., 2019). To measure the results of the companies in this research, the following groups of ratios were used: profitability, asset

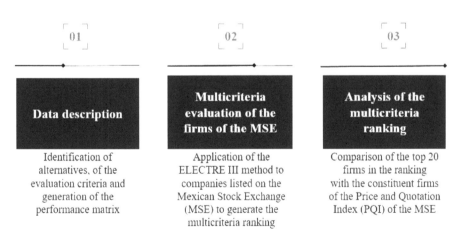

Figure 10.1 Methodology for generating a multicriteria ranking of MSE companies with the ELECTRE-III method.

turnover, financial leverage, liquidity, market value, and risk (Bodie and Merton, 2003; Besley and Brigham, 2001; Ortega, 2008). These financial indicators are presented in Table 10.1. The 22 ratios are grouped into six categories as criteria for evaluating stocks: profitability (5 ratios), financial leverage (5 ratios), asset turnover (5 ratios), liquidity ratios (2 ratios), market ratios (3 ratios), and risk (2 ratios). For a more detailed description of the indicators, see Bernal, Alvarez, Muñoz, and Leon-Castro (2020).

The alternatives that will be evaluated correspond to the listed MSE companies. The MSE includes a list of 140 companies; however, only 120 companies for this research have the required information available. These firms represent the alternatives that must be evaluated considering several

Table 10.1   Financial indicators are used as decision criteria.

Label	Ratio
Profitability	
(11,A)	Return on capital (ROE) (%)
(11,B)	Return on sales (ROS)
(11,C)	Return on assets (ROA) ($)
(11,D)	Economic value added (EVA) ($)
(11,E)	Dupont identity (DI) (%)
Financial leverage	
(12,A)	Debt
(12,B)	Long-term debt
(12,C)	Debt to capital
(12,D)	Multiplied of capital
(12,E)	Interest coverage ratio
Assets turnover	
(13,A)	Turnover stocks
(13,B)	Accounts receivable turnover
(13,C)	Asset turnover
(13,D)	Fixed asset turnover
(13,E)	Asset turnover frequency
Liquidity	
(14,A)	Current ratio
(14,B)	Quick ratio or acid test
Market	
(21,A)	Price-earnies
(21,B)	Market-books
(21,C)	Earnings per share
Risk	
(22,A)	Beta
(22,B)	Volatility

selected criteria. Additionally, the MSE generates the Price and Quotation Index (PQI) made up of the top 35 of the best companies selected for their results in certain indicators (BMV, 2015). Table 10.2 shows the partial data gathered corresponding to companies in the MSE. For the valuation of the complete set of indicators; see Bernal, Alvarez, Muñoz, and Leon-Castro (2020).

Multicriteria evaluation of firms in the MSE is developed. Some parameters are necessary for the multicriteria evaluation with the ELECTRE-III method. Determining the parameters allows the decision-maker to express their preferences concerning alternatives' performance in each criterion: the indifference threshold (q_j), the preference thresholds (p), veto threshold (v_j), and the weight (w_j) for each criterion (g_j). Table 10.3 shows the parameters defined for each established criterion. For example, the criterion labeled as g(11,A) has values 0.01 and 0.05 of indifference and preference, respectively (see row 1 in Table 10.3). The value of these thresholds means that there is indifference between two stocks in criterion $g(11,A)$ when the stock value is less than or equal to 0.01 with respect to another stock, and a strict preference when its value is more significant than 0.05 in the criterion. For the portfolio selection problem, the veto threshold was not defined. Thus, in these models, the veto condition is not used.

With these inputs, the decision model is carried out in two steps, firstly the valued improvement matrix is obtained, and then the distillation process is applied to obtain the multicriteria ranking of the stocks of the Mexican Stock Exchange (MSE).

10.4 Results

The current section is meant to analyze the ranking generated by the multicriteria decision-making method. Table 10.4 shows the top 20 companies in the ranking generated by ELECTRE-III. The complete ranking can be seen in Annex A. In Table 10.4 the ranking generated by the current study is compared with the ranking of the MSE's Price and Quotation Index. The generated ranking with ELECTRE-III shows 13 companies from the first places on the MSE's Price and Quotation Index. It corresponds to 70% of the total number of companies in the index.

This result shows that when considering multiple criteria for the evaluation of stocks and taking into account the preferences of the investor, the ranking generated mainly coincides with the companies selected for the reference Mexican stock index in the first places; However, some other firms

Table 10.2 Performance matrix of firms in the Mexican Stock Exchange (MSE).

Firm	A1	A2	A3	A4	A5	...	A117	A118	A119	A120	A121
Criterion	IENOVA	VISTA	ACCELSA	AEROMEX	AGUA	...	RASSINI	RLH	SPORT	VASCONI	SITES
g(11,A)	0.09	−0.06	0.14	−0.19	0.05	...	0.21	−0.05	0.05	0.03	−0.01
g(11,B)	0.47	0.16	0.1	0	0.11	...	0.12	−0.15	0.07	0.05	0.32
g(11,C)	0.07	0.05	0.12	0	0.07	...	0.16	−0.02	0.06	0.05	0.05
g(11,D)	−1595671	−1158094	627347	−864514	−216280	...	886766	−2740763	−8766	−37510	−349681
g(11,E)	0.13	0.11	0.19	0.01	0.12	...	0.34	−0.04	0.13	0.11	0.2
g(12,A)	0.46	0.56	0.36	1.27	0.42	...	0.53	0.43	0.54	0.53	0.77
g(12,B)	0.27	0.38	0.15	0.42	0.3	...	0	0.31	0.4	0.26	0.69
g(12,C)	0.84	1.26	0.55	9.69	0.74	...	1.12	0.75	1.15	1.12	3.36
g(12,D)	1.84	2.26	1.55	7.63	1.74	...	2.12	1.75	2.15	2.12	4.36
g(12,E)	4.14	1.24	29.11	0.07	2.95	...	−9.71	−0.45	1.45	1.97	1.06
g(13,A)	109.72	11.69	6.94	37.62	4.57	...	13.12	360	360	2.98	360
g(13,B)	6.38	3.85	5.11	11.12	3.31	...	10.98	3.59	21.87	3.57	33.99
g(13,C)	0.16	0.31	1.24	0.92	0.66	...	1.37	0.15	0.9	0.95	0.15
g(13,D)	0.16	0.37	2.11	1.22	1.09	...	2.13	0.19	1.04	2.16	0.15
g(13,E)	2339	1196	295	399	557	...	266	2450	404	384	2512
g(14,A)	0.32	1.38	1.91	0.45	2.95	...	1.1	2.2	0.62	1.58	1.15
g(14,B)	0.18	0.42	1.33	0.38	2.12	...	0.74	1.71	0.48	0.76	1.1
g(21,A)	13.32	−14.44	6.97	8.22	27.96	...	5.55	20.56	62.58	41.37	−391.33
g(21,B)	1.21	1204.37	0.65	1.52	1.51	...	1.14	−1.09	3.08	1.22	3.65
g(21,C)	0.28	−0.53	2.05	2.7	0.79	...	7.6	0.9	0.33	0.58	−0.03
g(22,A)	0.01	0.04	0.01	0.02	0.02	...	0.02	0	0.01	0.01	0.02
g(22,B)	0.47	0.27	0.21	0.55	0.55	...	0.18	0.13	0.03	−0.07	0.16

Table 10.3 Parameters of decision model.

No.	Criteria	Min/Max	Weight	Indifference thresholds	Preference thresholds
				qt	pt
1	g(11,A)	Max	0.024055	0.01	0.05
2	g(11,B)	Max	0.019244	0.05	0.1
3	g(11,C)	Max	0.014433	0.05	0.1
4	g(11,D)	Max	0.028866	10000	20000
5	g(11,E)	Max	0.009622	0.01	0.05
6	g(12,A)	Min	0.015402	0.1	0.15
7	g(12,B)	Min	0.007701	0.1	0.15
8	g(12,C)	Min	0.012835	0.1	0.15
9	g(12,D)	Max	0.005134	0.5	1
10	g(12,E)	Max	0.010268	0.5	1
11	g(13,A)	Max	0.007344	0.5	1
12	g(13,B)	Max	0.011016	0.5	1
13	g(13,C)	Max	0.014688	0.5	1
14	g(13,D)	Max	0.01836	1	2
15	g(13,E)	Min	0.022032	180	360
16	g(14,A)	Max	0.064974	0.3	0.5
17	g(14,B)	Max	0.054026	0.2	0.4
18	g(21,A)	Max	0.07296696	3	5
19	g(21,B)	Max	0.054945	0.5	1
20	g(21,C)	Max	0.09186804	0.3	1.2
21	g(22,A)	Min	0.19985988	0.002	0.005
22	g(22,2B)	Min	0.24036012	0.2	0.5

such as VESTA, BACHOCO, and GPROFUT also appear in this ranking and are not part of this index. Those shares belonging to the MSE's Price and Quotation Index not shown in the ranking of the current study present low values in criteria related to book indicators. It is highlighted that investors considered those indicators as relevant, and not only those related to profitability and risk.

The resulting ranking may differ from the application of other methods in the sense that some actions may appear in different positions but close to those they occupy in this ranking because each method treats the preferences of the decision maker differently and may have variations in the evaluation criteria. This does not mean that one method is better than another. There are several methods, but the one that should be used is the one that is most user-friendly for the investor and analyst.

Table 10.4   Top 20 firms in the ranking.

Position	Label	Firm
1	a39	**PINFRA**
2	a26	**GRUMA**
3	a65	**OMA**
4	a24	**GAP**
5	a13	**ASUR**
6	a9	VESTA
7	a32	**BOLSA**
8	a88	BACHOCO
9	a57	**WALMEX**
10	a73	GPROFUT
11	a96	**KIMBER**
12	a67	**KOF**
13	a68	**FEMSA**
14	a63	**CUERVO**
15	a61	CERAMIC
16	a11	MINSA
17	a71	**MEGA**
18	a83	CYDSASA
19	a42	POSADAS
20	a116	**AC**

Note: Companies with bold type are included in the MSE's Price and Quotation Index (PQI).

10.5 Conclusions

In this research, a methodology applied to the problem of portfolio selection is proposed. One hundred twenty-one shares of the Mexican Stock Exchange (MSE) are evaluated through the ELECTRE-III method, therefore, a ranking is generated which orders stocks according to their performance, 21 financial indicators, and the preferences of the investor.

The MCDM can be an alternative to treat problems where many factors intervene. The comparison of alternatives is linked to investment decisions in shares whose markets are increasingly complex.

The case study applied in the current research a comparative analysis between the ELECTRE-III and the Price and Quotation Index (PQI) of the MSE is presented. It was observed that the top 20 companies in the generated multicriteria ranking have a meaningful coincidence with the PQI of the MSE, but some firms that are not in the PQI also appear in this ranking. In this sense, the multicriteria ranking generated can be helpful to the investor for guiding the selection of stock to their satisfaction and making up their investment portfolio, since the evaluation process includes their preferences.

A limitation of this work is that this method is useful for the selection of stocks, but it is not possible to allocate the available budget to each of these. To complete the portfolio selection process, it must be combined with some optimization method to obtain an efficient portfolio that meets the risk and return objectives. Another limitation is that the ranking obtained may have small differences compared to other methods, and some of the shares may occupy a different position.

In future lines of research, the construction of models that convert preferences into fuzzy preferences is contemplated. The use of fuzzy variables for the evaluation of stocks can also be included. Likewise, the methodology used could be applied to other stock markets considering different performance criteria of the company and the market, and thus demonstrate its efficiency in said markets.

References

ALDALOU, E. and PERÇİN, S. (2018) 'Financial Performance Evaluation of Turkish Airline Companies Using Integrated Fuzzy Ahp Fuzzy Topsis Model*', Uluslararası İktisadi ve İdari İncelemeler Dergisi, 18(EYI Special Issue), pp. 583–598. doi: 10.18092/ulikidince.347925.

Almeida-Filho, A. T. de, de Lima Silva, D. F. and Ferreira, L. (2021) 'Financial modelling with multiple criteria decision making: A systematic literature review', Journal of the Operational Research Society. Taylor & Francis, 72(10), pp. 2161–2179. doi: 10.1080/01605682.2020.1772021.

Alvarez, P. A., Ishizaka, A. and Martínez, L. (2021) 'Multiple-criteria decision-making sorting methods: A Survey', Expert Systems with Applications, 183. doi: https://doi.org/10.1016/j.eswa.2021.115368.

Aouni, B. et al. (2018) 'On the increasing importance of multiple criteria decision aid methods for portfolio selection', Journal of the Operational Research Society. Taylor & Francis, 69(10), pp. 1525–1542. doi: 10.1080/01605682.2018.1475118.

Aqilah, N., Fauzi, M. and Ismail, M. (2019) 'Applicability of TOPSIS Model and Markowitz Model', Journal of Physics: Conference Series, 1212(012032). doi: 10.1088/1742-6596/1212/1/012032.

Bernal, M. R., Alvarez P. A., Muñoz M., Leon-castro E. A., G.-C. D. A. (2020) 'Multicriteria hierarchical aproach for portfolio selection in stock exchange', Journal of Intelligent & Fuzzy Systems, 40, pp. 1945–1955.

Besley, S. and Brigham, E. F. (2001) Fundamentos de Admnistración Financiera. 12a. ed. México.BMV (2015) Tipos de índices. Available at: https://www.bmv.com.mx/es/indices/principales/ (Accessed: 15 August 2019).

Bodie, Z. and Merton, R. (2003) Finanzas. México: Pearson Eduación.Boonjing, V. and Boongasame, L. (2016) 'Combinatorial Portfolio Selection with the ELECTRE III method: Case study of the Stock Exchange of Thailand (SET)', Proceedings of the 2016 Federated Conference on Computer Science and Information Systems, 8(4), pp. 719–724. doi: 10.15439/2016f228.

Bouri, A., Martel, J. M. and Chabchoub, H. (2003) 'A Multi-criterion Approach for Selecting Attractive Portfolio', Journal of multicriteria decision analysis, II(February), pp. 269–277. doi: 10.1002/mcda.334.

Elselmy, H. S., Ghoneim, A. and Elkhodary, I. A. (2019) 'Portfolio selection factors: Egypt equity market case study', ACM International Conference Proceeding Series, pp. 212–216. doi: 10.1145/3328833.3328858.

Erdemlioglu, D. and Joliet, R. (2019) 'Long-term asset allocation, risk tolerance and market sentiment', Journal of International Financial Markets, Institutions and Money. Elsevier B. V., 62, pp. 1–19. doi: 10.1016/j.intfin.2019.04.004.

Fernandez, E. et al. (2019) 'A novel approach to select the best portfolio considering the preferences of the decision maker', Swarm and Evolutionary Computation. Elsevier Ltd, 46(February), pp. 140–153. doi: 10.1016/j.swevo.2019.02.002.

Figueira, J. R., Greco, S., R. and B., Slowinski, R. (2013) 'An overview of electre methods and their recent extensions', Journal of Multi-Criteria Decision Analysis, (20), pp. 61–85. doi: ttps://onlinelibrary.wiley.com/doi/pdf/10.1002/mcda.1482.

Galankashi, M. R., Rafiei, F. M. and Ghezelbash, M. (2020) Portfolio selectionă: a fuzzy-ANP approach. Financial Innovation.Hadhri, S. and Ftiti, Z. (2019) 'Asset allocation and investment opportunities in emerging stock markets: Evidence from return asymmetry-based analysis', Journal of International Money and Finance. Elsevier Ltd, 93, pp. 187–200. doi: 10.1016/j.jimonfin.2019.01.002.

Hurson, C. and Zopounidis, C. (1997) 'On The Use Of Multicriteria Decision Aid Methods To Portfolio Selection', in Clímaco J. (eds) Multicriteria Analysis. Springer, Berlin, Heidelberg, pp. 496–507. doi: https://doi.org/10.1007/978-3-642-60667-0_47.

Jeong, T. and Kim, K. (2019) 'Effectiveness of F-SCORE on the Loser Following Online Portfolio Strategy in the Korean Value Stocks Portfolio', American Journal of Theoretical and Applied Business, 5(1), pp. 1–13. doi: 10.11648/j.ajtab.20190501.11.

Kao, C. and Steuer, R. E. (2016) 'Value of information in portfolio selection, with a Taiwan stock market application illustration', European Journal of Operational Research. Elsevier B. V., 253(2), pp. 418–427. doi: 10.1016/j.ejor.2016.02.011.

Kaucic, M. (2019) 'Portfolio optimization by improved NSGA-II and SPEA 2 based on different risk measures', Financial Innovation. Financial Innovation, 5, pp. 5–26. doi: https://doi.org/10.1186/s40854-019-0140-6.

Mansour, N., Cherif, M. S. and Abdelfattah, W. (2019) 'Multi-objective imprecise programming for financial portfolio selection with fuzzy returns', Expert Systems With Applications. Elsevier Ltd. doi: 10.1016/j.eswa.2019.07.027.

Markowitz, H. (1952) 'Portfolio Selection', The Theory and Practice of Investment Management: Asset Allocation, Valuation, Portfolio Construction, and Strategies, Second Edition, 7(1), pp. 77–91. doi: 10.1002/9781118267028.ch3.

Mohammed, H. J. (2021) 'The optimal project selection in portfolio management using fuzzy multi-criteria decision- making methodology', Journal of Sustainable Finance & Investment. Taylor & Francis, 0(0), pp. 1–17. doi: 10.1080/20430795.2021.1886551.

Ortega, A. (2008) Planeación financiera estratégica. Mc Graw Hill.Qi, Y. and Steuer, R. E. (2018) 'On the analytical derivation of efficient sets in quad-and-higher criterion portfolio selection', Annals of Operations Research. Springer US, 293(2), pp. 521–538. doi: 10.1007/s10479-018-3101-y.

Roy, B. (1978) 'ELECTRE III: un algorithme de classement fondé sur une représentation floue des préférences en présence de critères multiples', Cahiers du CERO, 20.Vuković, M. (2020) 'Comparative analysis of stock selection using a hybrid MCDM approach and modern portfolio theory', Croatian Review of Economic, Business and Social Statistics, 6(2), pp. 58–68. doi: 10.1515/crebss.

Xidonas, P., Doukas, H. and Hassapis, C. (2021) 'Grouped data, investment committees & multicriteria portfolio selection', Journal of Business Research. Elsevier Inc., 129(February), pp. 205–222. doi: 10.1016/j.jbusres.2021.02.044.

Xidonas, P., Doukas, H. and Sarmas, E. (2021) 'A Python-based Multicriteria Porfolio Selection Dss', RAIRO Operations Research, 55, pp. 3009–3034.

doi: https://doi.org/10.1051/ro/2020140.

Zare Mehrjerdi, Y. (2021) 'A novel metohodology for portfolio selection in fuzzy multi criteria environment using risk-benefit analysis and fractional stochastic', Numerical Algebra Control & Optimization, (2), pp. 1–23. doi: 10.3934/naco.2021019.

Zhu, J. (2019) 'Theoretical and Empirical Study on Risk Measurement Method Statistics and Portfolio Model Theoretical and Empirical Study on Risk Measurement Method Statistics and Portfolio Model', Journal of Physics: Conference Series 1213 042009. doi: 10.1088/1742-6596/1213/4/042009.

Zopounidis, C. and Doumpos, M. (1998) 'Developing a multicriteria decision support system for financial classification problems: The FINCLAS system', Optimization Methods and Software, 8(3–4), pp. 277–304. doi: 10.1080/10556789808805680.

Zopounidis, C. and Doumpos, M. (2002) 'Multi-criteria Decision Aid in Financial Decision Makingă: Methodologies and Literature Review', Journal of multicriteria decision analysis, II(December), pp. 167–186.

Anex A

A multicriteria ranking of stocks of the Mexican Stock Exchange (MSE)

Position	Label	Firm	Position	Label	Firm	Position	Label	Firm
1	a39	PINFRA	41	a12	DINE	80	a48	MEXCHEM
2	a26	GRUMA	42	a50	PAPPEL	81	a97	INVEX
3	a65	OMA	43	a25	PASA	82	a109	GFAMSA
4	a24	GAP	44	a38	CEMEX	83	a43	ELEMENT
5	a13	ASUR	45	a6	ALEATIC	84	a35	AHMSA
6	a9	VESTA	46	a53	SIMEC	85	a94	GFINBUR
7	a32	BOLSA	47	a5	AGUA	86	a40	COLLADO
8	a88	BACHOCO	47	a58	BAFAR	87	a107	CMR
9	a57	WALMEX	48	a95	GFNORTE	88	a77	MEDICA
10	a73	GPROFUT	49	a33	VINTE	89	a18	GMXT
11	a96	KIMBER	50	a46	ICH	90	a80	AZTECA
12	a67	KOF	51	a23	KUO	91	a99	PROCORP
13	a68	FEMSA	52	a76	LAB	92	a86	ACTINVR
14	a63	CUERVO	53	a78	AMX	93	a54	TEAK
15	a61	CERAMIC	54	a8	ARA	94	a91	FINDEP
16	a11	MINSA	55	a100	Q	95	a115	NEMAK
17	a71	MEGA	56	a104	ALSEA	96	a19	GSANBOR
18	a83	CYDSASA	57	a7	ALFA	97	a81	CABLE
19	a42	POSADAS	58	a15	GICSA	98	a30	TRAXION
20	a116	AC	59	a66	HERDEZ	99	a34	VOLAR
21	a56	CIE	60	a119	SPORT	100	a4	AEROMEX
22	a106	LIVEPOL	61	a17	GMD	101	a69	LACOMER
23	a114	VITRO	62	a105	CIDMEGA	102	a20	HOMEX
24	a55	GCC	63	a27	PLANI	103	a92	GBM
25	a44	GMEXICO	64	a101	R	104	a121	SITES
26	a45	GCARSO	65	a62	CULTIBA	105	a49	MFRISCO
27	a14	GIGANTE	66	a117	RASSINI	106	a79	AXTEL
28	a64	UNIFIN	67	a70	LALA	107	a10	CADU
29	a102	TLEVISA	68	a72	SORIANA	108	a89	BSMX
30	a85	LAMOSA	69	a118	RLH	109	a112	HIMEXSA
31	a47	GENTERA	70	a36	ALPEK	110	a52	POCHTEC
32	a93	ELEKTRA	71	a120	VASCONI	111	a2	VISTA
33	a108	ACCELSA	72	a59	BIMBO	112	a98	MONEX
34	a3	GPH	73	a84	RCENTRO	113	a103	VALUEGF
35	a110	GPH	74	a21	IDEAL	114	a87	BBAJIO
36	a51	PE&OLES	75	a113	HOTEL	115	a82	MAXCOM
37	a90	CREAL	76	a111	HCITY	116	a37	AUTLAN
38	a75	FRAGUA	77	a29	TMM	117	a41	CONVER
39	a16	GISSA	78	a1	IENOVA	118	a28	SARE
40	a22	JAVER	79	a60	CHDRAUI	119	a31	URBI
						120	a74	BEVIDES

11

Cost–Benefit Analysis of Solar Energy Usage in the Wine-making Industry in Valle de Guadalupe, Ensenada, Baja California, Mexico

Olivia Denisse Mejia Victoria, Karla Janette López Mercado, and José Manuel Valencia Moreno

Facultad de Ciencias Administrativas y Sociales, Universidad Autónoma de Baja California, Mexico

Abstract

The purpose of this paper is to carry out a cost–benefit analysis (CBA) of a photovoltaic system within the wine-making industry for self-generating electrical energy, through financial techniques such as the net present value (NPV), internal rate of return (IRR), payback period (PP), and cost–benefit analysis (CBA). A mixed methodology was used in this research: a quantitative method was used for the investment project's assessment and a qualitative method was used for the analysis and interpretation of the participants' discourse.

Keywords: Cost–benefit, solar energy, winemaking

11.1 Introduction

Implementing processes in favor of environmental protection is currently necessary in face of the different phenomena of climate change and global warming. There are renewable and environmentally-friendly technologies which are sources of unlimited resources. Power generation from fossil-based resources affects the environment in different ways, accelerating the "greenhouse effect" phenomenon, which involves infrared terrestrial radiation being trapped, causing an increase in the planet's temperature and a rising sea level (Bolaños & Chivelet, 2004).

Furthermore, energy consumption is one of the main environmental concerns regarding wine production and distribution (Christ & Burrit, 2013). For every bottle of wine, an ecological footprint of 100 grams of CO_2 is generated due to the electrical energy demand used in the machinery and processes, as well as the air emissions due to the use of fossil fuels.

Góngora (2016) mentions in his study that wine production in Baja California emits around 0.47 kg of CO_2 into the atmosphere per bottle produced. Additionally, it is believed that there are significant amounts of solid residue generated in the production, packaging, and marketing stages. According to Gargallo and García (2018), the wine-making industry must change its processes, including cultivation and wine production to reduce greenhouse gas emissions and thus contribute to improving the environment.

In the last decades, the electric power industry restructuring has seeked to transition from a model of generation from fossil-based resources to a model with renewable resources, representing one of the most important economic transformations (SEMARNAT, 2018).

In view of this situation, it is worth noting that Mexico has vast possibilities of generating renewable energy due to its geographic and climate conditions. This profusion will strengthen energy security and will promote a greater energy independence for most states (SENER, 2018).

It is important to note that over the years, the production of electrical energy with renewable energies has been increasing globally from 2010 to 2018, which has allowed renewable energies to integrate into the world energy matrix in an integrated way. important and even more so for the future. Thus, it is obtained that for the year 2018 the production was 6,586,124 GWh, it was an increase of 6.06% with respect to the year 2017, it means that there was an increase of 376 GWh (International Renewable Energy Agency [IRENA], 2020)

Based on the above, this study is intended to reveal the new approach winemakers have regarding the use of renewable energy in their companies in contrast with preview research on the region, it also analyze the cost–benefit obtained by investing in this technology, and assesses if the benefits have increased and the costs have decreased. The literature reviewed argues that it is beneficial for companies both to reduce their operating expenses, as well as to enhance the company's image for public perception.

This chapter presents the theoretical and conceptual framework about the renewable energy cost financial analysis, and Mexican regulation, next the Methodology describes the mixed method that is used in this research. Finally, it describes the conclusions, the CBA's results indicate that investing in a photovoltaic system project is feasible, however, it is not very profitable. The interviews show the new approach winemakers on using renewable energy in this industry, and 100% of the participants are interested and in favor of using a photovoltaic system for both economic benefits and environmental protection.

11.2 Theoretical and Conceptual Framework

In accordance with the Guide for Programs to Promote Energy Generation with Natural Resources, renewable energy is "obtained from natural sources which are considered as endless", (SEMARNAT, 2015, p. 13). These are considered unlimited sources due to the immense amount of energy they contain or because they are capable of regenerating through natural means. On the other hand, the Energy Transition Act (Ley de Transición Energética, LTE) Article 3, Section 16 defines renewable energy as "energy whose source resides in nature's phenomena, processes, or matters prone to be transformed into energy usable by humans which are naturally generated, therefore, they are continuously or regularly available and do not emit pollutants when being generated" (SENER, 2017, pg. 3).

There are two main categories of renewable energy sources: non-polluting or clean sources, and polluting sources. The first category consists of solar energy, wind energy, hydraulic energy, geothermal energy, tidal energy, and wave energy. The second category consists of sources that transform organic matter or biomass (SEMARNAT, 2015, p. 13).

This research focuses on solar energy, that is, energy that is directly obtained from the sun through electromagnetic radiation, which is used to generate electricity. The sun's potential is unlimited, as it is capable of producing four thousand times more energy than what we are capable of consuming. Solar energy can be transformed into electricity through photovoltaic panels, which are made up of several cells that allow light to be converted into electricity (Kannan & Vakeesan, 2016). To measure the solar resource, its unit in terms of energy is commonly the kilowatt-hour per square meter per day (kWh/m^2-day), while that of power is the watt per square meter ($watt/m^2$).

It is through a photoelectric cell that solar energy can be converted into electrical energy, the light that arrives in the form of photons, impacts on a surface made mainly of silicon, which emits electrons that, when captured, produce an electric current. Some of the equipment necessary for the production of electrical energy through solar energy are photovoltaic cells, photovoltaic module, bidirectional meter, energy accumulators, inverter (device that converts direct current into alternating current), transmission lines, electrical panel (wiring, transformer, rectifier, and controller) equipped with voltmeter and ammeter, fuses and switches (Hernández, 2017).

Electricity generated by solar energy can be used in independent or separate facilities or in commercial photovoltaic parks. In the first case, the purpose is to leverage the electricity generated at night, therefore, it must be stored in batteries. In the second case, distribution lines are installed and these conduct the electricity generated in the grid to a company that offers electrical energy, such as Comisión Federal de Electricidad (CFE) in Mexico, where it is stored.

To effectively use solar energy and other renewable energy, and to reduce greenhouse gases that impact global warming, some agreements have been reached, such as the United Nations Framework Convention on Climate Change (UNFCCC) and the Kyoto Protocol. The UNFCCC was created in 1992 with the purpose of "achieving the stabilisation of atmospheric concentrations of greenhouse gases to a level that prevents dangerous anthropogenic interference in the climate system" (United Nations, 2021). This is the purpose of reducing the impact of climate change and looking for solutions to adapt to the impacts that already seem inevitable, committing nations, both developed and underdeveloped, to work together to limit the global temperature increase below 1.5°C.

To carry out this initiative, on December 11, 1997, the Kyoto Protocol was approved; however, it did not become effective until February 16, 2005. This protocol ensures industrialized countries' commitment toward the UNFCCC and limits and reduces greenhouse gases based on the individual goals agreed upon. The agreement only allows these countries to adopt mitigation policies and measures and they must report them regularly.

The Kyoto Protocol and the Paris Agreement required industrialized countries to carry out activities, negotiations, and investments in clean technology projects that would meet the goal of reducing greenhouse gas emissions promoting the generation of sustainable development by leveraging renewable energy to reduce global warming (SENER, 2019).

In accordance with the above-mentioned, it is extremely important for countries to promote the use of renewable energy to fulfill the commitment toward environmental protection. This is why they develop new energy reform acts, financing programs, and tax deductions, among other ways of promoting this commitment, so the percentage of electrical energy production through renewable sources can increase every year.

To enforce support programs, projects, and negotiations that encourage the use of renewable energy (RE), an economic assessment must be carried out to calculate the investment projects' profitability. The most common methods used are the net present value (NPV), internal rate of return (IRR), payback period (PP), and ultimately, the cost–benefit analysis (CBA).

The CBA is a technique widely used by the private sector to determine whether a project can be started or not (Cervone 2010). For Snell (2011), it is a formal technique adapted and clear, systematic, and rational decisions, applied, especially when faced with complex alternatives or uncertain times. Lara and Orly (2017) define the cost–benefit analysis as a technique used to evaluate investment projects that consist of comparing the costs associated with carrying out a project versus the financial benefits that the project will produce.

Additionally, it is important to consider some benefits that the Mexican legislation provides in support of investment projects in renewable energy such as the Income Tax Act, Article 34, Section XIII. Internationally, several researches have been developed with the purpose of verifying the feasibility of deploying photovoltaic systems in organizations (Sanabria, 2016; Pikas, Kurnitski, Thalfeldt, and Korkela, 2017; Higuera and Carmona, 2017; Bitar and Chamas, 2017) have demonstrated that the benefits of a photovoltaic system are feasible, however, the government still needs to continue to grant incentives to promote these projects and not cancel them, otherwise the projects are profitable in the longer term.

Studies carried out in Mexico (Hernández, 2017; Escalante, 2017; Armendáriz, Luna, and González, 2017; Benito and Ruíz, 2018) reinforce that using solar energy as a source of electrical energy is feasible; because positive impacts are obtained in the nation's financial, environmental, and social areas which give way to continuously carrying out studies in science and technology so that solar panels are increasingly more efficient and less expensive. There have been few regional studies, however, López, Marín, and Alcalá, (2011) and Rodríguez (2013) show that it is important to continue carrying out studies to promote the deployment of solar energy.

11.3 Methodology

This present research uses mixed methods, it presents the CBA of investing on photovoltaic systems and the results of the interview applied to winemakers to know their opinion about investing in this kind of innovation. The spatial context of the study was referred to Valle de Guadalupe (Baja California, Mexico), contemplating only the wineries. Valle de Guadalupe is located 25 kilometers north of the city of Ensenada, in the interior of the Baja California peninsula; It is an extension of rocky-mountainous zone of approximately 66,353 thousand hectares on the banks of the Arroyo de Guadalupe with a height above sea level of 1,100 feet (355 meters). The Mediterranean climate that Valle de Guadalupe has makes it ideal for wine activities (Ruiz, Valderrama and Maldonado, 2012). The study was carried out in the period from May to September 2020.

A techno-economic study was carried out regarding the electrical energy generation project through a photovoltaic system connected to the Comisión Federal de Electricidad's electrical grid with the purpose of analyzing if this type of investment is profitable for wine-making companies in Valle de Guadalupe, Ensenada, Baja California. The return on investment technique was also used to determine the estimated savings by deploying this technology and the awareness of the benefits it provides for companies and the environment. The analysis considered the methodology used in the Bitar and Chamas (2017) study, applying formulas to calculate the net present value (NPV), internal rate of return (IRR), payback period (PP), and cost–benefit Analysis.

Within the quantitative method, a semistructured interview was carried out which was applied to a group of participants. The participants were managers and owners of wine-making companies in the region. The purpose of conducting the interview to this group of participants was to determine the awareness they have regarding the use of renewable energy in their company. The instrument was developed based on the study carried out by López, Marín, and Alcalá (2011). The instrument is made up of a group of 55 questions divided into nine sections.

Taking into account these questions, it is important to mention that only three of the nine sections were taken into account. These sections were awareness, costs, and barriers to entry. Given that the literature reviewed mainly argues that investment projects in generating energy from renewable sources are not carried out due to a lack of society's awareness, high costs, and a lack of governmental incentives. The participants were six owners of wine-making companies in Valle de Guadalupe, Ensenada, Baja California, Mexico.

11.4 Results

To carry out the cost–benefit analysis, here is a breakdown of the investment project's costs and benefits. Given the information from the vendor, the quote would be as follows:

The consumption of watts was calculated from the last receipt of a winery, which shows the use of energy from the last year, then we calculate the dairy consumption of 282.3 kWh.

To determine the ideal size or power of the photovoltaic system required, we divided the daily consumption by the minimum peak solar hours.

The minimum peak solar hours were taken from Database NASA (2020), according to the coordinates we take the worst-case scenario, 3.73 hours.

So we obtained 75.7 kW, then with the adjustment of system incorporating the losses system, considering a normal losing power it would be 75.7 × 1.20 = 90.84 kW.

To calculate the number of modules to be required for sizing, the size of the system is taken into account and divided by the power of the module to be used. But first, we convert the Kilowatts of the system to watts, which is how the power of the solar panel comes from, for this we just multiply 75.7 kW × 1000= 75,700 W.

Then to know how many modules will be needed, according to the Greenova supplier, they recommend using a monocrystalline module with better efficiency 405 W, than the other options that the two others suppliers we consulted.

Number of modules= 75700 W/405 W = 187 modules.

Considering the losses, the system would be 90.84 kW, so the total of modules would be 224 solar panels, we decide to round to 200 solar panels, so it does not increase the investment too much, generating a total of 81,000 W.

So the investment budget would be US$93,960, considering the process of the watt.

Investment budget		
System size: 81,000 watts	US$	MXN$
Price per watt	$1.00	$20.00
Subtotal	$81,000.00	$1,620,000.00
VAT	$12,960.00	$259,200.00
Grand total	$93,960.00	$1,879,200.00

Maintenance costs were not considered because this solar panel system's maintenance is very low, water and soap are carefully applied to the panels' surface, then it must be gently scrubbed in a way that will not damage the modules, so this cost is zero pesos.

Regarding the benefits, the annual savings intended to be achieved through the installed solar panels were considered as one of the project's benefits, therefore, the information provided by the Greenova vendor in the quote was considered, which shows a previous electrical energy consumption projection and the payments made to Comisión Federal de Electricidad (CFE) without solar panels.

The same chart shows the new electrical energy consumption generated by the system and the new payments that will be made to CFE with solar panels. This projection shows the savings (benefit) that will be achieved with the photovoltaic system, giving an annual total of $203,027.77.

It is important to note that the photovoltaic system has a 25-year durability, therefore, the benefits were projected in this period in the following chart.

Benefits	
1 year	25 years
$203,027.77	$5,075,694.20

To calculate the NPV, the annual cash flows ($203,027.77) were taken into consideration in a 25-year projection considering average inflation of 4% (Banxico, 2020) and a 1% interest rate ($i = 0.05$) (see chart).

Year	Amount	Year	Amount
1	$203,027.77	14	$338,056.16
2	$211,148.88	15	$351,578.41
3	$219,594.84	16	$365,641.54
4	$228,378.63	17	$380,267.21
5	$237,513.77	18	$395,477.89
6	$247,014.33	19	$411,297.01
7	$256,894.90	20	$427,748.89
8	$267,170.69	21	$444,858.85
9	$277,857.52	22	$462,653.20
10	$288,971.82	23	$481,159.33
11	$300,530.70	24	$500,405.70
12	$312,551.92	25	$520,421.93
13	$325,054.00		

Based on the cash flow projection, the 25 years composition process was carried out in the following table. The value considered for interest was 5% ($i = 0.5$).

Year	Amount	Year	Amount
1	$193,286.15	14	$169,833.31
2	$191,372.42	15	$168,151.79
3	$189,477.65	16	$166,486.92
4	$187,601.63	17	$164,838.54
5	$185,744.19	18	$163,206.47
6	$183,905.14	19	$161,590.57
7	$182,084.29	20	$159,990.66
8	$180,281.48	21	$158,406.59
9	$178,496.51	22	$156,838.21
10	$176,729.22	23	$155,285.36
11	$174,979.43	24	$153,747.88
12	$173,246.96	25	$152,225.62
13	$171,531.64		

Finally, to obtain the photovoltaic system's NPV, the values were substituted in the formula:

$$NPV = \sum_{n=1}^{n} \frac{FED_n}{(1+i)^{\wedge n}} - I_0$$

$$NPV = \$4,299,338.64 - \$1,879,200$$

$$NPV = \$2,420,138.64$$

Regarding the IRR, the "trial and error" technique is used, that is, if with 10% interest (in this case) the project generates a \$672,026.52 profitability, then the IRR must be above 10% so that the NPV equals ZERO. After trying different percentages finally, the IRR was 13.62105%.

To verify this, the values are substituted in the formula:

$$NPV = \sum_{n=1}^{n} \frac{FED_n}{(1+?)^{\wedge n}} - I_0 = 0$$

$$NPV = \$1,879,352.21 - \$1,879,200$$

$$NPV = \$0.49$$

$$IRR = 13.62\%$$

Regarding the payback period (PP), the following elements are taken into account:

- Total investment amount: \$1,879,200.00.
- Capital cost (CC) or minimum acceptable rate of return (MARR): 5% (Grupo Tegra 2020).
- Investment assessment frame or period: 25 years.
- Expected cash flows:

$$PP= \text{Year prior to complete payback}$$
$$+ \left(\frac{\text{Unrecovered costs at the beginning of the year}}{\text{Cash flow throughout the year}} \right)$$

$$PP = 10 + \left(\frac{\$30,221.80}{\$174,979.43} \right)$$
$$= 10.17 \text{ years}$$

In summary, the payback period is obtained approximately 10.17 years:

$$\textbf{Benefits} = 14.83 \text{ years}$$

$$\textbf{Benefits} = \$2,420,138.15$$

$$\textbf{Costs} = \$1,879,200.00$$

Applying the following formula

$$CBA = \frac{\text{Total benefits}}{\text{Total costs}}$$

$$CBA = \frac{\$2,420,138.15}{\$1,879,200.00} = 1.29$$

For this result's interpretation, Jacome and Carvache (2017) mention that if the result of the cost–benefit ratio is over 1, the project is profitable, in other words, if the income exceeds the expenses, consequently, the project will gain profits. Therefore, the result achieved (1.29) means the investment project is profitable.

Regarding the qualitative analysis, considering the three sections used in the semistructured interviews, the following results were obtained:

- In regard to the awareness section, questions that would offer us a guideline to understand the level of awareness the participants have concerning RE, which also includes revealing the most commonly known types of RE and which RE they would be interested in deploying in their company, this was precisely the starting point for a fluent interview.

Most of the participants at least know three types of existing renewable energy (wind energy, solar energy, and hydraulic energy); respondent 1 and respondent 4 mentioned more than three types of energy. Respondent 1 (R1) mentioned solar energy, wind energy, hydraulic energy, and geothermal energy, while Respondent 2 (R2) mentioned the same energies as respondent 1, but added bioenergy.

When asked if the respondents had ever been interested at some point in deploying one of the existing RE, at least five of the six respondents had been interested in using RE (R1, R2, R3, R4, and R5) only one of them had never considered it (R6). The respondents were asked which of the existing types of RE would they be willing to use in their company, most of them answered solar energy and some of the respondents are already using it to generate electrical energy at their company.

- They were asked questions regarding their perception of the costs involved in a photovoltaic system investment project, as well as if they were interested in deploying it in their company. What this revealed was that, despite years having passed and this type of technology has decreased its prices, it is still expensive to invest in this type of project. Precisely because it is through an immediate payment (R1, R2, R3, and R6).

Two of the respondents mentioned that they are already working on a project to cover a percentage of the electrical energy consumption with a photovoltaic system, because even though it is expensive, they believe in the long run it will offer saving benefits and overall, they are looking for ways to help improve climate change's impact (R3 and R4). On the other hand, other respondents mentioned that they had previously been interested in installing solar panels in their company, which was when a program called Solarízate, a state-wide program that helped with 50% of the project's total investment, was in place, but one of them was denied access and decided not to pursue the project. It was somewhat impossible for the other respondent to purchase the photovoltaic system because it entailed investing approximately four million pesos and he had to consider other costs this type of project would incur (R1 and R2).

- Regarding barriers to entry, they were asked questions that would assess the obstacles they have or had had to implement renewable energy in their companies; whether it had been due to a lack of interest or information, a lack of government incentives, or institutional constraints. Within this section two subsections were established: 1) capital requirements where the following categories were identified: governmental grants and 2) social environment.

For the first case, some respondents stressed that to be able to invest in renewable energy projects for their company, they would need a large sum of money, this has led them to decide not to purchase a photovoltaic system. In addition, they mentioned that the vendors who provide this product do not offer financing options. The only payment option they offer is to pay a percentage before starting the project, and the rest of the payment must be settled before finalizing the installation and for this reason, they decide to prioritize other vineyard expenses. Furthermore, they ensure that they do not have the funds available solely for this type of project.

On the other hand, some of the respondents are already investing in a photovoltaic system, it is worth noting that they are medium-sized companies, that had previously analyzed this concern, however, at the time it was not possible to invest in solar panels due to the costs because they did not have the capital, but they are currently considering this type of investment in view of the long-term benefits (R3 and R4).

The respondents argue that the lack of governmental grants or programs has also caused them to not be interested in investing in renewable energy projects because they believe that the government is against or places limitations for these projects, but they mention that there should be programs to encourage them to adopt renewable energy (R1, R3, R4, and R5).

Regarding the social environment, the participants' perception concerning the use of renewable energy in their company may also be due to the environment or groups they belong to and may vary due to personal o third-party experiences. Three categories were identified in this subsection: a) information, b) health emergency, and c) lack of interest.

11.5 Conclusions

It was found in the cost–benefit analysis (CBA) that investing in a photovoltaic system project is feasible, however, it is not very profitable. It is feasible due to the system's lifespan (25 years), which is enough time to allow an investment payback period. However, it is not considered very profitable due to the return on investment which is achieved after 10 years.

Due to the time, it takes to recover from the project's investment, the project can be considered unappealing, since other studies have shown that the return on investment can be in less time, from 3 to 8 years. It is worth mentioning that this varies according to the benefits and the costs are taken into account when carrying out the CBA and the information that is accessible (Armendáriz, 2017; Bitar and Chamas, 2017; Benito and Ruíz 2018; Bello and Paez, 2018).

On the other hand, in the interviews, an approachability with the owners of vineyards in Valle de Guadalupe was achieved, which allowed an understanding of their perception of the use of RE in their company. It can be emphasized that with the passing of time, it is clearer, comparing it with the study carried out by López et al. (2011) in Baja California which mentions that most entrepreneurs had no idea how a solar cell works and there was still a need for more awareness regarding this subject. Whereas this study's respondents had more awareness, they were more familiar with the subject, and most of them had asked for a quote with a solar energy equipment vendor.

What was significantly noted is that they still perceive this type of technology as something expensive and they mention that if they had payment options to purchase a solar panel system they would do so. This confirms the results obtained by Bitar and Chamas (2017) in their study, due to the fact that there are no financial options available that encourage the purchase of the photovoltaic system, although the entrepreneurs are more aware and interested in the subject, the significant capital expenditure they would have to take to invest in this technology is still what hinders them from doing so.

Furthermore, the content analysis from the interviews confirms that investing in a photovoltaic system is not very profitable for vineyard owners due to the long period that it takes for them to earn savings or a return on investment. They mention that they would prefer to invest in projects that will create short-term profitability or benefits (less than 5 years).

For future investigations, we recommend to carry out feasibility analyzes because solar panels continue to improve their efficiency and have been reducing costs. Likewise, apply all the tax benefits that exist and in the event that government financing support is reactivated, also apply them so that the return on investment is less than 9 years.

For society, that they continue to be interested in companies that carry out activities that are in favor of caring for the environment so that they continue to worry about adapting activities that help care for the environment, as well as companies that manufacture solar panels that carry out more research with new products that generate cost reduction for their production, which will have the consequence that when they are introduced to the market they are less expensive; On the other hand, if they are produced with new materials that generate greater efficiency in each solar panel, the number of solar panels needed in each project can also be reduced, which can reduce the total cost of the investment.

References

Abella, M. (2017). Dimensionado de sistemas fotovoltaicos [Photovoltaic Systems' Aspects]. Retrieved from: https://static.eoi.es/savia/docume nts/componente45301.pdf

Aguilera, A. (2017). El costo-beneficio como herramienta de decisión en la inversión en actividades científicas [Cost-Benefits as a Decision Tool for the Investment in Scientific Activities]. Retrieved from: http://scielo.sld.c u/scielo.php?script=sci_arttext&pid=S2073-60612017000200022

Armendáriz, J., Luna, A. and González, M. (2017). Costo-beneficio de sistemas fotovoltaicos en el sector residencial en la ciudad de Chihuahua [Photovoltaic Systems' Cost-Benefit in Residential Area in the City of Chihuahua]. Retrieved from: https://www.researchgate.net/publication /322784870_Costo-Beneficio_de_Sistemas_Fotovoltaicos_en_el_Secto r_Residencial_en_la_Ciudad_de_Chihuahua

Baca, G. (2013). Evaluación de proyectos (7ma Ed) [Proyects' Assessment (Seventh Edition)]. Mexico. McGraw Hill. Retrieved from: https://www.ac

ademia.edu/39204599/Evaluacion_de_Proyectos_7ma_Ed_Gabriel_Bac
a_Urbina

Badii, M. H., Guillen, A., Abreu, J. L. and UANL, S. (2016). Renewable Energies and Energy Conservation. Daena: International Journal of Good Conscience, 11(1), 141-155. Retrieved from: http://www.spentamexico.o rg/v11-n1/A12.11(1)141-155.pdf

Bello, A. M. and Páez, D. N. (2018). Estudio de viabilidad financiera de la generación de energía eléctrica a partir de paneles solares para puestos de salud en Colombia [Financial Feasibility Study: Electrical Energy from Solar Panels for Health Centers in Colombia]. Retrieved from: https://repo sitory.unilibre.edu.co/handle/10901/15473

Benito, G. M. and Ruíz, K. J. (2018). Análisis beneficio-costo de la imple-mentación de un sistema de energía solar fotovoltaica en el campus aguas claras de la universidad santo Tomás sede Villavicencio, meta [Cost-Benefit Analysis: Deployment of Photovoltaic Solar Energy System in Aguas Claras Campus, Universidad Santo Tomás Sede de Villavicencio, Meta]. Retrieved from: https://repository.usta.edu.co/bitstream/handle/11 634/13714/2018ginnabenito.pdf?sequence=1&isAllowed=y

Bitar, S. M. and Chamas, F. (2017). Estudio de factibilidad para la imple-mentación de sistemas fotovoltaicos como fuente de energía en el sector industrial de Colombia [Feasibility Study: Deployment of Photovoltaic Systems as an Energy Source in Colombia's Industrial Sector]. Retrieved from:https://repository.cesa.edu.co/bitstream/handle/10726/1572/MBA00 499.pdf?sequence=1&isAllowed=y

Bolaños, J. I. and Chivelet, M. (2004). Cambios climáticos. Una aproxi-mación al sistema Tierra [Climate Change. An Approach to Earth's Sys-tem]. Biblio 3W, Revista Bibliográfica de Geografía y Ciencias Sociales, Universidad de Barcelona, Vol. IX, n° 492,1. Retrieved from: http://www. ub.es/geocrit/b3w-492.htm

Canal, R. (2019). Cuidar el ambiente para incrementar el valor de las empre-sas [Environmental Protection to Increase a Company's Value]. Retrieved from: https://www2.deloitte.com/mx/es/pages/dnoticias/articles/empresa s-sustentables.html

Christ, K. L. and Burritt, R. L. (2013). Critical environmental concerns in wine production: an integrative review. Retrieved from: https://www.scie ncedirect.com/science/article/pii/S0959652613002084#!

Coello de Portugal, M. C. (2019). La ventaja competitiva de las energías ren-ovables [Competitive Advantage of Renewable Energy]. Retrieved from: https://repositorio.comillas.edu/xmlui/bitstream/handle/11531/27736/TF

G%20-%20Coello%20de%20Portugal%20MagallAn,%20MarAa%20del
%20Carmen.pdf?sequence=1

Consejo Mexicano Vitivinícola (CMV). (2010). Consejo Mexicano Vitivinícola. Retrieved from: http://vinoclub.com.mx/index.php?module=Articulo
s&aid=67

Dickson, M. H., and Fanelli, M. (2004). Pisa: Istituto di Geoscienze e
Georisorse, CNR. Retrieved from: http://www.lis.edu.es/uploads/812fe
7d1_d505_4825_9db3_8438d78a406c.PDF

Escalante, F. I. (2017). Análisis de los retos y oportunidades la imple-
mentación de energía solar en pequeña escala en baja california sur
[Challenges and Oportunities Analysis of Deploying Solar Energy at a
Small Scale in Baja California Sur]. Retrieved from: http://biblio.uabcs
.mx/tesis/te3891.pdf

Flórez, R. O. (2011). Hidráulica. Generación de energía. [Hydraulics. Energy
Generation]. Ediciones de la U. Retrieved from: https://books.google.com
.mx/books?hl=es&lr=&id=FTOjDwAAQBAJ&oi=fnd&pg=PA15&dq=en
erg%C3%ADa+hidraulica+concepto&ots=_3UKD7-pVq&sig=RpqpgtO
OzrGkohhvk69PLEcpjqc#v=onepage&q=energ%C3%ADa%20hidraulica
%20concepto&f=false

Fuenmayor, G. and Villasmil, Y. (2008). La percepción, la atención y la
memoria como procesos cognitivos utilizados para la comprensión textual
[Perception, Attention and Memory as Cognitive Processes in Reading
Comprehension]. Retrieved from: https://www.redalyc.org/pdf/1701/1
70118859011.pdf

Gargallo, P. and García, N. (2018). Impactos ambientales y medidas de
mitigación en el sector vitivinícola español [Environmental Impacts and
Mitigation Measures in the Spanish Wine Sector]. Retrieved from: https:
//www.researchgate.net/publication/327158572_Impactos_ambientales_y
_medidas_de_mitigacion_en_el_sector_vitivinicola_espanol

Góngora, M. A. (2016). Propuestas de prácticas sustentables en la industria
vitivinícola de baja california, México [Proposals of Sustainable Practices
for the Winemaking Industry in Baja California, Mexico]. Retrieved from:
https://www.colef.mx/posgrado/wp-content/uploads/2016/12/TESIS-G
%C3%B3ngora-Rosado-Marvin-Addiel.pdf

González, M. E., Beltrán, L. F., Diéguez, E. T. and Ortega, A. (2006). Poten-
cial de aprovechamiento de la energía eólica para la generación de energía
eléctrica en zonas rurales de México [Potential for Use of Wind Energy
for Electrical Energy Generation in Rural Areas in Mexico]. Interciencia,

31(4), 240-245. Retrieved from: https://www.redalyc.org/pdf/339/339115 02.pdf

Hernández, F. (2016). Teoría de la percepción (ingredients) [Perception Theory (ingredients)]. Retrieved from: https://core.ac.uk/download/pdf/1294 86119.pdf

Hernández, R., Fernández, C. and Lucio, Pilar. (2014). Metodología de la investigación [Research Methodology]. México D. F.: McGraw-Hill. Retrieved from: https://www.uca.ac.cr/wp-content/uploads/2017/10/I nvestigacion.pdf

Hernández, R. (2017). Análisis de factibilidad para la instalación de un sistema de energía limpia mediante celdas fotovoltáicas para la alimentación eléctrica del edificio 4 en el ITSLV [Analysis of Feasibility: Installation of Clean Energy System through Photovoltaic Cells for Electric Feeding in Building 4 in ITSLV]. Retrieved from: https://www.repositorionacionalcti .mx/recurso/oai:ciateq.repositorioinstitucional.mx:1020/97

Higuera, L. H. and Carmona, H. (2017). Análisis de factibilidad de un proyecto de autogeneración eléctrica fotovoltaica en Colombia para áreas productivas menores de 10.000m2 [Feasibility Analysis: Photovoltaic Electric Self-Generation Project in Colombia in Productive Areas Smaller than 10.000m2]. Retrieved from: https://repository.eafit.edu.co/handle/1 0784/11690

International Renewable Energy Agency (IRENA). (2020). Renewable Energy Statistics 2020. Retrieved from: https://irena.org/-/media/Files/ IRENA/Agency/Publication/2020/Jul/IRENA_Renewable_Energy_Statist ics_2020.pdf

Kannan, N. and Vakeesan, D. (2016). Solar energy for future world: A review. Renewable and Sustainable Energy Reviews, 62, 1092-1105. Doi:10.1016/j.rser.2016.05.022.

Lara, I. J. and Orly, F. (2017). Análisis del Costo – Beneficio una Herramienta de Gestión [Cost-Benefit Analysis: Management Tool Benefit]. Revista Contribuciones a la Economía. Retrieved from: http://eumed.net/ce/201 7/2/costo-beneficio.html

LISR. (2013). Ley del Impuesto Sobre la Renta [Income Tax Act]. Retrieved from: http://www.diputados.gob.mx/LeyesBiblio/pdf/LISR_230421.pdf

López, V. G., Marín, M. E. and Alcalá, M. C. (2011). El uso de las energías renovables solar y eólica: la percepción de los empresarios de baja california [Solar and Wind Renewable Energy Use: Baja Californian Entrepreneurs' Perception]. Retrieved from: http://acacia.org.mx/busque da/pdf/06_04_Energias_Renovables.pdf

Mankiw, N. (2017). Principles of Economics (7th. Ed.) CENGAGE Learning.

Martinez, M. R., and Lora, E. S. (2015). Bioenergía: Fuentes, conversión y sustentabilidad [Bioenergy: Sources, Conversion, and Sustainability]. José María Rincón Martínez, Electo Eduardo Silva Lora. Retrieved from: https://books.google.com.mx/books?hl=es&lr=&id=YpnxCAAAQBAJ&oi=fnd&pg=PA7&dq=bioenergia&ots=q33BybF7-n&sig=cwJwc7_bCsoEZO-tu2pbIQbl1tE#v=onepage&q&f=false

Olin, J. (2013). Contabilidad de costos (4a. ed.) [Accounting Costs (Fourth Edition)]. McGraw Hill.

Oxford Economics. (2019). Global SME Pulse 2019. Retrieved from: https://www.oxfordeconomics.com/recent-releases/SME-Pulse-2019

Pikas, E., Kurnitski. J., Thalfeldt, M. and Korkela, L. (2017). Cost-Benefit Analysis of nZEB Energy Efficiency Strategies with On-Site Photovoltaic Generation. Retrieved from: https://www.sciencedirect.com/science/article/abs/pii/S0360544217305558?via%3Dihub

Rodríguez, J. C. (2013). El uso y aprovechamiento de las energías renovables en la agroindustria de maneadero, B. C., análisis costo beneficio [Cost-Benefit Analysis: Renewable Energy Usage in Agroindustry in Maneadero, Baja California].

Sanabria, A. F. (2016). Análisis costo/beneficio de la implementación de tecnologías de energía con paneles solares en la ese hospital San Cristóbal [Cost-Benefit Analysis: Solar Energy Panel Techonolgy Deployment in ESE Hospital in San Cristobal]. Retrieved from: https://repository.unimilitar.edu.co/bitstream/handle/10654/14931/SanabriaOrozcoAndresFelipe2016.pdf;jsessionid=68EAA8D547C3680C40F13E2D7F90FDBD?sequence=1

Secretary of Natural Resources and the Environment (Secretaría de Medio Ambienta y Recursos Naturales, SEMARNAT). (2018). Guía de programas de fomento a la generación de energía con recursos renovables [Guide for Programs to Promote Energy Generation with Natural Resources]. Retrieved from: https://www.gob.mx/publicaciones/es/articulos/guia-de-programas-de-fomento-a-la-generacion-de-energia-con-recursos-renovables-142904?idiom=es

Secretary of Energy (Secretaría de Energía, SENER). (2017). Reporte de avance de energías limpias 2017 [Clean Energy Progress Report, 2017]. Retrieved from: https://www.gob.mx/cms/uploads/attachment/file/354379/Reporte_de_Avance_de_Energ_as_Limpias_Cierre_2017.pdf

Secretary of Energy (SENER). (2018). Reporte de avance de Energías Limpias, primer semestre 2018, México 2018 [Clean Energy Progress

Report, First Semester 2018, Mexico 2018]. Retrieved from: https://ww w.gob.mx/cms/uploads/attachment/file/418391/RAEL_Primer_Semestr e_2018.pdf

Secretary of Energy (SENER). (2018). Desarrollo del Sistema Eléctrico Nacional *2018-2032* [National Electric System Development 2018-2032]. Retrieved from: https://www.gob.mx/cms/uploads/attachment/file/331770 /PRODESEN-2018-2032-definitiva.pdf

Secretary of Energy (SENER). (2018). Desarrollo del Sistema Eléctrico Nacional 2019-2033 [National Electric System Development 2019-2033]. Retrieved from: http://www.gob.mx/sener/documentos/prodesen-2019-20 33

Snell, M. (2011). Cost-Benefit Analysis. A Practical Guide, 2nd ed., Thomas Telford, London.

United Nations (2021). Retrieved from: https://unfccc.int/files/essential_bac kground/background_publications_htmlpdf/application/pdf/conveng.pdf

12

The Rubik's Cube of Emerging Technologies and Stock Volatility

Laura Arenas and Ana M. Gil-Lafuente

Universidad de Barcelona, España

Abstract

It is argued that emerging technologies lead to increased stock volatility. However, the empirical results are mixed, and the causes are unclear. This paper analyses the topic by applying a systematic literature review. We find that stock volatility has increased overall because of emerging technologies and identify the main drivers as the uncertain nature of emerging technologies, greater complexity to calculate fundamental values, the idiosyncratic nature of over-enthusiastic and novice investors, and intangible asset-driven emerging technologies. Additionally, some properties of emerging technologies are explored.

Keywords: Emerging technologies, stock markets, stock return, stock volatility.

12.1 Introduction

Understanding the behavior of time series of stock returns is one of the key research lines in finance. Perhaps one of the most intriguing findings in this area, is that stock returns may be related to the fast-changing and growing technological environment. Since the 4th industrial revolution is leading to an overall transformation of the system, driven by emerging technologies, stocks return, and stock return volatility reacts quickly.

Emerging technologies include disruptive technologies resulting from radical innovations (e.g., genetic engineering) and evolutionary technologies, derived from long trajectories in different research fields (e.g., wireless technologies and the Internet) (Day and Schoemaker, 2000). Emerging technologies include significant uncertainties and novel features that can potentially have a dramatic impact on the socio-economic system (Boon and Moors, 2008; Martin, 1995, Porter, Roessner, Jin, and Newman, 2002; Small, Boyack, and Klavans, 2014; Rotolo and Hicks, 2015) that can be linked to the *"techno-economic paradigm"* (Pérez, 1983), (Pérez, 1985) as introduced by the socio-economist and historian Carlota Pérez.

On the other hand, investments in emerging technologies are considered risky due to the implicitly high degree of uncertainty regarding their future performance. They have been defined as technologies developed and produced in a research environment, but that have necessarily been fully deployed in the market.

Radical or breakthrough innovation, as per the contextualization of emergence, comes as a surprise (Leydesdorff and Rafols, 2011), which in this context are uncovered by their relevant ex-post impact on future technological development (Ahuja and Morris, 2001; Schoenmakers and Duysters, 2010) and adoption. The uncertainty concerning the performance of emerging technologies may be associated with the surprise effect, costs of future ownership, the provision of complementary inputs, the establishment of dominant standards, and possible related obsolescence (Hall and Rosenberg, 2010).

From a single firm perspective, adopting emerging technologies might be beneficial to stakeholders. Investing and adopting emerging technologies is stimulating mainstream interest for investors, since it promotes process efficiency and a means to improve firm performance, thus shareholders would expect the firm to improve their economic performance in the future, being reflected in increasing returns.

Regarding the overall market perspective, advances and new technologies, make information available on a timelier basis, thus emerging technologies should improve the quality and flow of data used for asset valuation purposes, while decreasing stock return volatility.

However, contradictory as it might appear at a first glance, uncertainty about new technologies tends to increase stock market volatility, particularly due to the option effect, that is when the value increases with the uncertainty proxied by the risk of the underlying asset. The last suggests that innovation increases the complexity of transactions (Allen, 2012). West (1988), Shiller (1981a), and Leroy and Porter (1981) explain that despite improved information about future cash flows, these are more substantially discounted, since the news are arriving timelier, increasing stock price, and stock return volatility.

The stability of the market valuation from a market system perspective is also being impacted by the new economy, resulting in an overall increased stock price and stock return volatility (Campbell, Lettau, Malkiel, and Xu, 2001; Iraola and Santos, 2007; Kearney and Potì, 2008).

A different matter is the contradiction of the exponential growth of new technologies versus a slowdown in productivity (Brynjolfsson, Rock, and Syverson, 2019) which may shed light on the potential inability of current productivity measures to reflect the real benefits of the new technological wave.

Moreover, technologies emerging in finance are providing new market opportunities, which entail novel volatility patterns. The linkage of emerging technologies and market return volatility should be explored by connecting long-term economic structure with short-term financial market behavior to uncover unrevealed intersections.

This review suggests to analyzes whether emerging technologies lead to an increase in stock return volatility and suggests what the main drivers behind this might be.

From a Knightian standpoint, the outcomes of an investment in an emerging technology can be considered uncertain, and since volatility is commonly used as a proxy for uncertainty, the notion of exploring emerging technologies in the context of stock return and stock return volatility is aligned with the theoretical notion of uncertainty.

The chapter document several potential explanations as to why emerging technologies drive stock volatility. The rationales proposed are motivated principally by:

- the uncertain nature of emerging technology that shapes specific stock volatility patterns,
- the greater complexity of calculating fundamental values,
- over-enthusiastic and novice investors leading to noise around the markets, and
- emerging technologies are driven by idiosyncratic features and intangible assets.

Also, specific features of emerging technologies can be described as diffusive, persistent, heterogeneous, and momentum oriented.

This review takes the form of an agenda and is organized as follows: Section 14.2 discusses the concept of emerging technology. In Section 14.3, the rationales for the linkage between emerging technologies and stock volatility are examined. In Section 14.4, certain properties related to emerging technologies are discussed and in Section 14.5, a closer look at recent empirical evidence on the link between emerging technologies and stock return volatility is provided, examining phenomena such as FinTech, AI, blockchain, cloud computing, and so on. Section 14.6 ends with some concluding remarks.

We use the specification of "emerging technology" as proposed by Rotolo and Hicks (2015) and which is attributed to radical novelty, relatively fast growth, coherence, prominent impact, and uncertainty and ambiguity.

12.2 The Concept of Emerging Technologies

The concept of "emerging technologies" has been the subject of much discussion in the academic and professional literature, with frequently casual and ambiguous usage of the term for a specific technology (Li, Porter, and Suominen, 2018; Fan, Lau, and Leon, 2015; Linton and Walsh, 2008), mainly due to the wide range of different views and domains the concept was adopted. Li, Porter, and Suominen (2018) found the existence of multiple theoretical lines of research on technological change, disruption, and emergence promotes conceptual cross-fertilization and consideration of interdisciplinary approaches to technological emergence.

Reviewing the literature, from a science policy perspective, Martin (1995) was quick to position the concept of "emerging technology" in relation to broad economic and societal impacts. Porter, Roessner, Jin, and Newman (2002) redefined this vision by adding that "emerging technologies" improve economic leverage in the coming (roughly) 15-year horizon, and Boon and Moors (2008) highlight the role of aspects, regarding emerging technologies, that are still uncertain and non-specific. Hung and Yee-Yeen (2006) and Porter et al. (2002) start from the emergence and focus on the economic influence and impact of competition driven by novel technologies, looking at the concept from the macro-level perspective.

Another view of emerging technology arises in the management literature, where emergence is often observed from the perspective of technological adoption. There is also extensive literature connecting emerging technologies to innovation management. Cozzens, Gatchis, Kang, Kim, and Lee (2010) place the term in the context of contemporary innovation theory.

A micro-level view is offered by Riordan and Salant (1994), who proposes a micro-level angle of the concept, looking at company dynamics when introducing new technologies to their portfolios. Li (2005) stresses the impacts of network externalities on emerging technology markets. Srinivasan (2008) conceptualizes it in terms of the sources, characteristics, and effects of emergent technologies, highlighting the effect of shifting value chains, digitalization of goods, and the changing locus of innovation. Halaweh (2013) defines the characteristics of emerging (IT) technologies as uncertainty, network effect, unseen social and ethical concerns, cost, limitation on countries, and a lack of investigation and research.

In a literature review, Rotolo and Hicks (2015) present a conceptual framework of emerging technologies by integrating previous works. The framework consists of five characteristics of radical novelty, relatively fast growth, coherence, prominent impact, and uncertainty and ambiguity. This is the definition that is used in this article.

An emerging technology could fail over time, become a generalized technology, or even a disruptive technology (Li, Porter, and Suominen, 2018).

The concept of emerging technology targets various characteristics, including significant uncertainties, novel features (Boon and Moors, 2008; Martin, 1995; Porter et al. 2002; Small, Boyack, and Klavans, 2014), and the potentially dramatic impact on socio-economic systems (Rotolo and Hicks, 2015), latter might be aligned within the frame of the "techno-economic paradigm" (Pérez, 1983; Pérez, 1985) introduced by socio-economist and historian Carlota Perez.

12.3 Emerging Technologies as Drivers of Stock Return Volatility

In the following section, we will discuss certain drivers of stock return volatility spreading from the emerging technology phenomena.

12.3.1 Uncertain nature of emerging technology

Uncertainty about the future is the main reason for performing a risk analysis, identifying, and anticipating factors or situations that will reduce or result in investment losses and thus, anticipating how an investment will perform considering certain states. It was Knight who first determined that risk and uncertainty are relevant for economic analysis (Knight, 1921) to entail the evaluation of cost and benefits. However, Knight also highlighted the distinction between two concepts that are often used to express the same notion. Uncertainty refers to events that cannot be expressed mathematically in probabilistic terms, while risk can be quantified by assigning subjective probabilities to a state of risk. Uncertainty and risk are not mutually exclusive. Risk management may reduce uncertainty, but uncertainty never will be completely managed away.

The efficient market hypothesis state that new information randomly arriving in the market drives price volatility. The weak form of the efficient market hypothesis links stock price and return volatility and relates stock price volatility with technical analysis and calendar effect, and the semi/strong version of the efficient market hypothesis relates stock price volatility with fundamentals and corporate announcements. Empirical studies such as (1981a) and Schwert (1989) suggest that volatility is driven by more factors then solely changes in fundamentals. For example, irrational investors doing noise trading participate significantly in stock price volatility. In this context, volatility can be defined as the sum of transitory volatility caused by noise trading and unobserved fundamental volatility caused by the arrival of stochastic information (Hwang and Satchell, 2000).

Emerging technology is characterized as a radical novelty that is uncertain and ambiguous, and indeed not all novel inventions will result to be successful (Fleming, 2001) and result in profits for its investors.

Stock markets critical roles for inventions and for emerging technologies. significant role in promoting new technologies and inventions. First, the stock market channel funds from investors expecting to gain from innovation to firms involved in emerging technology and second, as a platform to monitor the progress and performance of emerging technologies by tradable financial asset behavior. Without the stock market platform, no tradable financial assets, tracks the supply, demand, progress, adoption and performance of the emerging technology via financial behavior, no market fluctuation, or indeed stock return volatility can be monitored as representative of investors' expectations. In this context, the stock market is especially relevant for making the innovation-intensive, high-tech industries uniquely suited for financing technology-led growth (Brown, Martinsson, and Petersen, 2017) and information source of emerging technology adoption as investments vehicle.

The implication of a high level of capital fluidity is twofold. It facilitates attracting investments, however, it makes it easier to withdraw capital. With previous notions, funding, and trading of emerging have been associated with the speculative type of funding and venture capital financing (Bartholomew,

1997; Gompers and Lerner, 2003; Ranciere, Tornell, and Westermann, 2008). Traders may be drawn to speculative stocks due to their higher volatility, which creates an opportunity to generate greater returns—albeit at greater risk.

Pástor and Veronesi (2006), Gharbi, Sahut, and Teulon (2014), and Schwert (2002) provided evidence of new or frontier technology firms that exhibit unjustifiably high stock return and volatility. Some authors associate stock price behavior during the technological revolution with a bubble-like pattern (Shiller, 2000; Pérez, 2003; Pástor and Veronesi, 2009). Bubbles may also be provoked by technology in presence of uncertainty, narratives related to new technologies, the entrance of novice investors, and the pure play[1] implemented by tech-firms to engage investors as argued by Goldfarb and Kirsch (2019). Shiller (2000) and Pérez (2003) attributed this behavior to market irrationality and Pástor and Veronesi (2009), for example, relate the uncertainty around new technologies to expectations about future productivity and the time-varying nature of this uncertainty itself.

The literature that covers the linkage between technological innovation and stock prices in levels, onboard this topic mostly from an aggregate macro perspective to the economy and the overall contention, is that new technologies cause the stock market to drop (Greenwood and Jovanovic, 1999; Hobjin and Jovanovic, 2001; Laitner and Stolyarov, 2003; Manuelli, 2000).

The expectation of lower future profits by firms that purchase a soon-to-be-obsolete technology drives their market value down (Manuelli, 2000) and raises future returns on new investments (Laitner and Stolyarov, 2019). When the novel technology becomes available, it is gradually adopted by new firms, leading to a period of high investment that gradually adapts to evolving back to an equilibrium.

Pástor and Veronesi (2009) state that it is the time-varying nature of risk, which is initially idiosyncratic and becomes systematic as the new technology is adopted, that leads new economy stocks to initially command a high market value. As the probability of adoption increases, systematic risk pushes discount rates up and hence drives stock prices down in both the new and old economies.

Greenwood and Jovanovic (1999) and Manuelli (2000) study the behavior of macroeconomic variables and the stock market, given major technological

---

[1] 'Pure play' firms are defined by Goldfarb and Kirsch (2019) as firms whose fortunes are tightly coupled with the commercialization of the innovation.

changes. Pástor and Veronesi (2009) present a macroeconomic model where the productivity of new technology is uncertain, and its learning process drives a boom-bust pattern in the stock market.

Benner (2007) found that incumbent firms' stock prices will decline and there will be negative reactions from the stock market, the subsequent response hence being penalized due to institutional pressures from financial markets.

Laitner and Stolyarov (2019) develop a suitable model for studying risk premia and asset-pricing phenomena related to technology diffusion. When examining the diffusion of an emerging technology, most models suggest that this diffusion drives some degree of uncertainty reduction, which to a certain extent is a perpetuating feature of uncertainty reduction (Mansfield, 1968), since uncertainty will never be eliminated.

Iraola and Santos (2007) provide a model of technology adoption to analyze different channels of technological innovation that impact stock prices. The ration behind is that the value of the stock market absorbs the option value of the emergence and adoption of future technology.

The environment related to emerging technologies must also be accounted for in the form of obsolescence risk. Competitive advantages of firms with new technology may replace traditional firms, emerging with a dominant market share, which may result in initially signaling to the market competing traditional firm stocks are being negatively impacted. This scenario may suggest that investors with profile outside emerging technologies, will go toward a long-term strategy to overcome volatility that may be induced by their initial entrance. Thus, the demand for long-term investment increases. Evidence indicates, for example, that the average maturity of US corporate bonds increased from 9.5 years in 1996 to more than 15 years in 2017 (US Corporate Bond Issuance), and the average European 10-year bond yield, dropped from 10.78% in January 1993 to 5.73% in January 2000 and 1.15% in January 2019 (European Central Bank, 2022) followed by a negative yield scenario afterward, this suggests an overall scenario away from short term volatility toward long term safety.

This may also be linked to several aspects of the digital era and comprehensively the emergence of technology waves. The flagship technologies of the most recent waves were brought into the market mainly by small, and young firms. This suggests that the narrative of the IT revolution is about the entrance, and since entrance survival rates are low and may take decades to grow (O'Reilly III and Tushman, 2011; Stubbart and Knight, 2006), it might also sum to the uncertain nature of emerging technologies. Corporate longevity is declining, according to Innosight's biennial corporate longevity reports (Viguerie, Calder, and Hindo, 2021). As the economy transitions from the industrial age to the digital age, firms will survive for shorter periods (Berente, Lee, Potts, and Srinivasan, 2020).

Investors additionally must incorporate regulatory uncertainty in their evaluation of new technologies and opportunities. Governments are still exploring how to regulate the fast-growing emerging technology environment. However, at this point, it is unclear if technology-driven firms will self-regulate or as traditionally, imposed by a regulatory entity (PGIM, 2018). Emerging technologies themselves could facilitate regulatory compliance and supervision as RegTech alternatives, smart regulation which incorporates traditional regulators' objectives, with boarding decentralized ledger or crypto economics incentives to implement the rule-based protocols.

To sum up, we reviewed the difference between uncertainty and risk, indicating that emerging technologies are naturally uncertain due to various circumstances.

First, evidence from the past is limited or inexistent. It is not possible to perform a solid risk analysis, preventing getting light on the future outcome of emerging technology and its associated investment. Second, emerging technologies nature can be associated to bubble like patterns, obsolescence risk that comes along with any emerging technology by displacing traditional ones, and regulatory risk, since emerging technology will be regulated by governments, however, it is not clear, yet which structural approach will be the usual frame implemented. Considering the foregoing, investors may look to overcome the increased volatility facing in the short-term, adjusting their portfolios to the more safe long-term horizons.

12.3.2 Greater complexity for calculating fundamental values

There are still questions to be asked as to how new technology may relate to macroeconomic factors and sources of uncertainty that could explain asset market phenomena such as driving the risk premia.

Short-term volatility among stock markets is well recognized, whereby firms seek to optimize investment opportunities (Pyka and Burghof, 2013) driven by the short-term pressure on them to generate economic returns for their investors (Hopkins, Crane, Nightingale, and Baden-Fuller, 2013; Martin and Scott, 2000; Salter and Martin, 2001) while monitoring their fundamentals in quarterly reporting (Aggarwal and Hsu, 2014; Manso, 2011; Noda and Bower, 1996).

With this rational, it seems difficult to link short-term stock market fluctuation with long-term economic theory, since the market value of a stock should be explained by fundamentals such as profit, dividend, and output growth, these doses do not fluctuate as much (Peralta-Alva, 2007). Some literature, for example, Kydland and Prescott (1982), has proposed technology shocks that impact the macroeconomy, channeled by the stock market, as an explanation for short-term fluctuations. Jovanovic and Rosseau (2002) associate fluctuations in the stock market with three technological revolutions: Electricity, World War II, and IT. These authors document long lags in the operation and diffusion of new technologies. During radical technological changes, excess volatility peaks associated with the related uncertainty (Shiller, 2000), and therefore, fundamental information is less useful for making estimations about future values (Tushman and O'Reilly III, 1996).

However, to better understand how technological shocks might be channeled and translated into stock market fluctuations, it is insightful to recall such a basic financial concept as the notion that asset prices should equal expected discounted cashflows. Stock valuation is, *per se*, forward-looking since the value of an asset is mainly defined as the present value of the actual future payoffs (dividend) that the investor will receive. Therefore, stock prices may also reflect the expectations regarding the emerging technology, since expected cashflows for investors in emerging technologies will also be considered.

The common component and forward-looking feature of asset valuation are the interest or growth rates that are used to discount future payoffs. However, when looking at the fluctuations in those rates, stock valuation models are expected to imply significant volatility driven by those economic components. The perception of an economic slowdown in this regard is enough to generate big changes in stock market prices (Peralta-Alva, 2007). Some literature shows that real stock price indexes move much more than the present value of the corresponding real dividend series and that the present value seems to behave much more like a trend over time (Shiller, 1981a; Shiller, 1981b; Leroy and Porter, 1981; West, 1984; Mankiw, Romer and Shapiro, 1985; Brooks and Katsaris, 2003; Capelle-Blancard and Raymond, 2004). In the efficient-market literature, the valuation error is explained by "anomalies," otherwise known as "small" departures from market efficiency. For an integral discussion on the topic of discount rates, see Cochrane (2011).

Meanwhile, psychology and perceptions are being recovered that attribute most price variations to the field of behavioral finance, see Kahneman and

Tversky (1979), Bovi (2009), Sahni (2012), Tauni, Fang, and Iqbal (2016), Riccardi and Simon (2000). The recent line of argument is that the long-term behavior of stock prices is consistent with fundamentals, while their short-run evolution reflects unobserved behavioral factors (Gallagher and Taylor, 2001; Manzan, 2007; Coakley and Fuertes, 2006).

A different discussion in this area is the contradiction between the astonishing growth of new technologies, versus a slowdown of productivity in recent decades. Brynjolfsson, Rock, and Syverson (2019) studied this *Modern Productivity Paradox* applied to artificial intelligence technology and highlight that a mismeasurement of output and productivity may be prevailing due to a pessimistic reading of the empirical past, rather than optimism about the future, implying that productivity has already absorbed the benefits of new technologies but has yet to be accurately measured (e.g., Mokyr, 2014; Feldstein, 2015).

One factor may be the availability of new predictive technologies to evaluate investment opportunities. Allen (2012) finds empirical evidence suggesting that financial innovation often increases the complexity of transactions. More data availability and more complex predictive analytics techniques increase the chances of data mining, whereby spurious patterns are observed when, in fact, there are none (Siegel, 2021). Data mining is easier than ever now that computing power has become so cheap (Lo and Mackinlay, 1990).

Recapturing, financial analysis is forward-looking, starting with the notion that the present value of an asset equals the future value of their future cash flows discounted. Emerging technologies bear greater complexity in identifying or calculating fundamental values. Radical new technologies and inventions are identified only by their *ex-post* impact on technological development (Ahuja and Morris Lampert, 2001), (Schoenmakers and Duysters, 2010), product performance (Leifer, O'Connor and Rice, 2001), or market structure (Mascitelli, 2000), making it much more difficult to integrate associated features in financial forward-looking value frame.

12.3.3 Overenthusiastic and novice investors

Stock markets and market volatility cannot only be driven by stock and associated firms' fundamental information. Significant market volatility is impacted by different factors that shape investors' decisions, for example, overreaction and underreaction, irrational exuberance, overconfidence, bandwagon effect trend-chasing, regretting, and fear of missing out, among others.

Investors may induce volatility in the market by interpreting arriving stochastic information and noise trading. Several behavioral biases direct investors toward their decisions.

Investment in emerging technology provides more space for behavioral biases due to the uncertainty there are surrounded and more complexity of objectively value financial information as discussed in the previous section The future of the unknown, and potential surprise effect or outcome that may result from an emerging technology is particularly attractive for certain investor profiles. In the case of new emerging technologies, no past references or historical reference is available to be used as a guideline to follow, not only in terms of development, and market acceptance but also in financial market behavior and investor profiling. As stated by Kucharavy and De Guio (2008), forecasting emerging technologies with no past are difficult since they have not passed the *infant mortality threshold.* when the S-shaped curve is applied to forecast their trajectory.

Thus, and recalling the notion, that stock prices are formed based on the expected optimal forecast on available information, we can argue that the expectations about future profits from an emerging technology will also be reflected, including expectations, and signaling from overenthusiastic and novice investors.

Investment in new emerging technology may increase overenthusiasm and the influx of novice investors, who are more likely to be influenced by external and subjective factors. Pérez (2012) states that it is when old technology is replaced by new technology that excess funds flood the market driven by over-excitement, decoupling the temporary price from its fundamental valuation.

To understand better the linkage between emerging technologies, stock return volatility, and investor profiling, we may recall the context of new technologies and the rationale of bubble patterns.

Behavioral biases significantly influence the emergence of bubbles. Anderson (1787) as early as more than two centuries ago argued that investment will increase by potential gains, resulting in an assets price appreciation, while attracting new investors, leading to further price and so on, creating a certain buckle driven by greed and profit-seeking attitude.

The financial press commonly endorsed the view that individual investors as being largely responsible for the technology bubbles.[2] When investors are

---

[2] "Economists and market experts say (individual) investors ... not the so-called 'smart money' on Wall Street – are the reasons behind the greatest bull market in history" ("Little

inexperienced and less financially literate, they may be guided by opportunities that are new and seem exciting, as is often the situation with new technologies (Goldfarb and Kirsch, 2019). New emerging technology, which may be associated with a surprise effect of emergence, makes this problem more impactful.

As indicated by Griffin, Harris, and Topalog (2005) there are three theoretical models in the bubble literature that target investor interaction and that can be linked with specific new technology investment scenarios. The first is the rational market view which states that sophisticated traders (arbitrageurs) quickly trade against irrational agents, eliminating deviation from the economic value as represented by Friedman (1953) and Fama (1965). The second argument states that changes in economic value are driven by bay noise traders, preventing sophisticated traders to eliminate deviations from the fundamental value. The third, argues that rational speculators may drive a bubble, whereby arbitrageurs, knowing that the market is overvalued, maximize profits by riding the bubble (Abreu and Markus, 2002), (Abreu and Brunnermeier, 2003). As a result, market prices may be self-driven based on prophecies (Merton, 1968), also known as "rational bubbles" (Froot and Obstfeld, 1991).

From a more empirical perspective, Frehen, Goetzmann, and Rouwenhorst (2013) revisit the first global financial bubbles that occurred in 1720 in France, Great Britain, and the Netherlands and found evidence against irrational exuberance and in favor of speculation about fundamental financial and economic innovations in the European economy (Prendergast and Stole, 1996). Whereby young managers hope to acquire a reputation for quick learning, they tend to exaggerate their own information and via their attitude and trading behavior, impact the market. Benner and Ranganathan (2013), study the reactions of securities analysts as important sources of institutional pressure on firms to respond to industry convergence through relevant technological change, such as that between wireline telecom and cable industries. They found that analysts' reactions depend on investor preferences, which are more positive or negative toward "growth" and "margin" preferences, respectively. Harrison, Scheinkman, and Xiong (2008), found that young managers intentionally assume excessive positions regarding technology stocks to signal to smart investors that they understand the new

---

guy becomes market's big mover; professionals lose their lock on Wall St. trading," The Washington Post, February 2, 1999, E01). See also "Market savvy," Los Angeles Times, November 17, 1998, C4, and "Where no investor has gone before: Amateurs steered the ship through a spacey year, The Washington Post, January 3, 1999, H01.

technology, as opposed to old managers. Griffin, Harris, Shu, and Topaloglu (2011) examine the daily trading behavior of different investor groups and evidence that institutional investors drove and burst the technology bubble. Greenwood and Nagel (2009) observe that during the technology bubble, young managers increased their technology holdings during the run-up and decreased them during the downturn. Furthermore, young managers, exhibit trend-chasing behavior in their technology stock investments. Also, during the run-up to the technology bubble, venture capital rose from 10% to 40% share of investment, as calculated by Goldfarb and Kirsch (2019). On the other hand, Zuckerman and Rao (2004) found that co-movement among internet and other stock categories is less common during periods of price appreciation than during erosion, which may suggest that the endogenous driven mechanism is being driven by the buckle of price appreciation.

During the technology bubble between 1997 and 2000, technology stock rose more than five times and institutional investors reportedly bought more than individual investors (Griffin et al., 2011). Lewellen (2003) detected that almost all internet stocks in March 2000 had an extremely high price-to-sale ratio, compared with other stocks, indicating that investors were more likely to pay more for internet stock compared to others. Corbet, Sensoy, and Yarovaya (2020a) documented that companies that use "crypto-exuberant" naming practices become more volatile and offer substantial and persistent stock market premiums. Greenwood and Nagel (2009) claim that younger managers outperformed before the peak in March 2000, and significantly underperformed after the peak, averaging out to about zero. Siegel (2021) adds that the failure of analysts to adapt their earnings forecasts to the technology sector despite the negative views of the industry was particularly pronounced among analysts in the Internet sector. Dealing with news that does not correspond to one's worldview creates what is called *cognitive dissonance*. The distinguished paper by Cooper, Dimitrov, and Rau (2001) found that during the period of the internet hype from the late 1990s into the 2000s, there was a tendency among investors to bid up the stock prices just for changing domain names to ".com". In contrast, the paper by Lee (2001) related the event to a potential misinterpretation of the fundamentals. Akyildirim, Brunnermeier, and Nagel (2004) document that hedge funds, considered among the most sophisticated investors, did not exert a correcting force on stock prices during the technology bubble. Instead, they were heavily invested in technology stocks.

Recapturing, overall sentiments or feelings are experienced constantly on the markets. The excitement or overenthusiasm of something new and the potential outcome of a surprise, as an emerging technology, impact the market via decisions taken by overenthusiastic investors. Young and less experienced investors are more likely to follow behavioral biases. Hence it makes sense that enthusiastic and novice investors will bid up the stock price, since the future course of emerging technology will be especially impacted by investors' expectations. From a different point of view, investors will learn from the past and the newer emerging technologies there are available to invest in, the greater leeway there is for risk diversification, even among the same sectors.

12.3.4 The idiosyncratic nature of emerging technologies

Volatility can be categorized as market and firm-specific or idiosyncratic volatility. Idiosyncratic volatility (Campbell et al., 2001; Kearney and Potì, 2008) is attributed by some literature to the IT revolution (Campbell et al., 2001; Mazzucato, 2002; Mazzucato and Tancioni, 2008), and the economy is increasingly induced by intangible assets (Bagella, Becchetti, and Adriani, 2005), (Kearney and Potì, 2008), (Chan, Lakonishok and Sougiannis, 2001).

As stated by Cao, Timothy, and Zhao (2008), much of the literature has attempted to characterize the rising trend in idiosyncratic risk. First, the idiosyncratic risk may be related to profitability level and variance (Pástor and Veronesi, 2003; Wei and Zhang, 2006). Second, it is positively related to expected earnings growth and institutional ownership (Xu and Malkiel, 2003). Third, idiosyncratic risk is negatively related to firm age (Pástor and Veronesi, 2003). Fourth, it is negatively related to expected returns in the cross-section (Ang, Hodrick, Xing, and Zhang, 2006). Fifth, it is correlated with the business cycle (Brown and Ferreira, 2003) and sixth, it is a stronger predictor of a cross-section of return than of liquidity (Spiegel and Wang, 2005).

A large body of the literature provides evidence that innovative sectors are more exposed to idiosyncratic risk than traditional markets do (Chan, Lakonishok, and Sougiannis, 2001; Schwert, 2002; Domanski, 2003), thus emerging technology. Technology, and specifically new technology developing sectors, have a unique setting that is systematically different from that of traditional firms. A broad range of industry participants, including public research organizations, entrants, and incumbent firms, contribute to the advancement of emerging technologies ecosystem (Kapoor and Klueter, 2020; Powell, Koput, and Smith-Doerr, 1996; Rosenberg and Nelson, 1994).

The flagship technologies of the most recent waves were mainly brought into the market by small, young firms, which may explain the overall uncertainty related to emerging technologies and be aligned (Pástor and Veronesi, 2003) with the notion that idiosyncratic risk is negatively related to firm age which we already reviewed in the previous section.

Often these firms are defined as knowledge-based organizations since they are human capital intense (Ahmed and Alhadab, 2020), which entails a higher level of unreported assets compared to traditional firms (Brown, Martinsson, and Petersen, 2017; Junttila, Kallunki, Kärja, and Martikainen, 2005; Kwon and Yin, 2006; Kwon and Yin, 2015; Lim, 2015; Watanabe, Hur, and Lei, 2006).

Net assets of a form should be reflected by the stock market value of the firm. However, it is more complicated in a firm with a relevant share of intangible assets as R&D. Explaining the real asset base of companies by including soft assets or intangible assets and being able to explain asset valuation of tech giants and loss-making unicorns is still controversial, and as expected, leading to a certain level of uncertainty. In the last decades an increase in R&D expenditures. While predictable earnings and returns in highly innovative tech firms are generated by intangible assets, they are associated with a higher degree of uncertainty (Chan, Lakonishok, and Sougiannis, 2001; Kothari, Laguerre, and Leone, 2002), whereby earnings volatility related to R&D expenditure is three times larger than earnings volatility associated to tangible assets. The positive relationship between the share of intangible assets (as a proxy for IT-related changes) and the increase in idiosyncratic risk in the 1990s is consistent with the view that IT increases uncertainty with respect to firm valuation (Domanski, 2003).

Since intangible assets are highly transferable, for example qualified scientific knowledge, these firms are more exposed to underinvestment (Hall, 2002), since the possibility to retain its value is less secure, which provokes higher risk levels (Borah, Pan, Chul Park, and Shao, 2018). Thus, it makes sense that it is more complicated for these firms or projects to obtain external funding, especially from risk-adverse investment profiles, for their R&R activities. Small-cap stocks outperformed large-cap stocks based on the size effect and value stocks, stocks with low market value relative to its fundamentals, outperform the market in the long run as the value effects states. Yu, Liu, Fung, and Kin (2020) state that R&D intensity in firms adds another important dimension to the size and value effects market anomalies, when describing stock returns, especially for small technology firms.

At the stock level, highly innovative stocks are growth stocks but are also considered riskier because they do not typically offer dividends. For example, Tesla stated in their dividend policy that there is a non-dividend-paying stock. One big reason is technology firms generally need to keep growing by adopting the best and brightest new innovations. If Alphabet, Amazon, and Facebook along with Berkshire Hathaway would pay shareholder dividends it would increase the S&P index's overall yield by 7.6 percent (Inbert, 2017). Aboody and Lev (2000) on the other hand, show that insiders in high-tech firms make more generous profits than their colleagues. Additionally, technology companies are known as growth stocks, stocks that demonstrate to gain better than average earnings and with market expectations to deliver relevant profit growth. The momentum of growth stocks may be higher (Bagella, Becchetti, and Adriani, 2005), as the inertia of a price trend continues for a particular length of time.

A wide range of literature (Greenwood and Jovanovic, 1999; Hobjin and Jovanovic, 2001; Laitner and Stolyarov, 2003; Peralta-Alva, 2007), study the effects of technology on the values of old or traditional and new companies. Lin, Palazzo, and Yang (2017) found that higher risk and higher expected returns are reported by firms that operate with old capital, since old capital firms are more likely to upgrade soon and are therefore more exposed to shocks resulting from competing for frontier technologies. Rubera and Kirca (2012) found that the effect of firm innovativeness is stronger on market position for firms with innovativeness output and radical innovation.

Projects, and projects related to emerging technologies, can generate greater degree of asymmetric information, since managers have the insights and more knowledge about the state of the outcome (Blazenko, 1987), resulting in an increased, stock return volatility. Particularly High-tech firms, suffer from the asymmetric information problem (Gharbi, Sahut, and Teulon, 2014; Gu and Li, 2007; Gu and Wang, 2005; Barron, Byard, Kile and Riedl, 2002). Idiosyncratic volatility can be used as an alternate measure or proxy of information asymmetry as it measures the amount of price volatility due to firm-specific information (Abdul-Baki, 2013).

R&D intensity can be linked to asymmetric information in explaining volatility. Gharbi, Sahut, and Teulon (2014) show how firm generates information asymmetry with regard to its firm's prospects. Andi, Jaafar, and Torluccio (2015) state that mispricing can occur if investors are unable to correctly estimate the long-term benefits of R&D investment or determine if R&D firms are riskier than others. On the downside, stocks listed on markets in continental Europe and operating in high-tech sectors are more prone to undervaluation due to information asymmetries that are more severe in bank-based countries.

Technology firms with the objective to close the gap of lacking information, hold conference calls and provide the public with additional information about financial conditions (Tasker, 1988; Dell'Acqua, Perrini, and Caselli, 2010). Dell'Acqua, Perrini, and Caselli (2010) additionally found that these actions made by technology firms can decrease idiosyncratic volatility. This can be strategic for firms to overcome the initial burden of high idiosyncratic risk by launching emerging technologies. Another shade is external expert criteria about firm performance. Barron et al. (2002) studied analysts' forecasts consensus and found that it is negatively associated with firm's intangible asset share. On the other hand, lower levels of analyst consensus are associated with high-technology manufacturing companies.

Arenas and Gil-Lafuente (2021a) found that the price return of high−tech Exchange Traded Funds (ETFs) is negatively associated with idiosyncratic risk in high-volatility regimes and positively related to low-volatility regimes. These results suggest that idiosyncratic risk can penalize or reward investors' investment in emerging technologies based on certain circumstances. Darby, Liu, and Zucker (2004) suggest that knowledge capital intensity explains price jumps of underlying knowledge base firm stocks, since firms with two standard deviations more in knowledge capital, are valued by 10−50% in excess.

Resuming, the different shades of the idiosyncratic nature of emerging technologies, idiosyncratic risk increased in the last decades and an overall argument suggests that this increase in idiosyncratic risk, is related to the new economy as driving force of economic growth. Technology firms are holding more idiosyncratic risk, than other sectors, due to asymmetric information related to invention and developments, their knowledge intensity, and high level of R&D expenditures, since these features are highly transferable, complex to measure, and difficult to integrate into contemporaneous valuation frameworks, adding uncertainty. Nevertheless, idiosyncratic risk is conditional or time-varying in its proportions zooming into the emergence of new technologies. During technological revolutions, the nature of this uncertainty quantified by risk, shifts from being idiosyncratic, to become systemic, as the likelihood of a large−scale adoption is increasing over time.

12.4 Certain Properties of Emerging Technologies

Financial time series comprehend features known as stylized factors, such as volatility clustering, heteroscedastic variance, non-normal leptokurtic distribution, and the leverage effect. Stylized factors originated in financial time series by the rate of information arriving in the market (Lamoureux and Lastrapes, 1990); errors in the learning processes of economic agents (Mizrach, 1995); and the artificial calendar timescale in lieu of a perceived operational timescale (Stock, 1988). Stylized factors are related to technological change and often associated with bubble-like patterns during technological revolutions attributing more irrationality to the market.

The trajectory of the progress of emerging technology has been studied by, for example, Anderson and Tushman (1990), Dosi (1982), and Sahal (1985). A stylized description for an emerging technology is that there is a slow but gradual improvement in the technology's performance, as reflected by the canonical S-shaped pattern (Dosi, 1982; Foster, 1986; Henderson, 1995; Sahal, 1985; Stoneman, 2002). The S-shape curve[3] depicts the normal evolution of a system in accordance with the laws of natural growth over a period. It begins with slow change, followed by rapid change, and ends with slow change again until the asymptote is reached. These phases can be interpreted as periods of birth, growth, maturity, decline, and death for any system and represent the characteristic features of the pattern followed by emerging technology. The S-shape represents cumulative growth whereas a bell-shaped curve is usually applied to represent the rate of growth within a time span.

The idea of paradigms and trajectories can account for the observable phenomenon of cumulativeness of technical advances (within an established trajectory), also defined as the cumulative feature of the *progress* upon a technological trajectory and detailed by Dosi (1982) as the probability of future advances related to the position of firms or countries. The previous description coincides with the presentation of technical progress by Nelson and Winter, which applied Markovian chains at firm and industry levels (Nelson and Winter, 1977). The advantages of Markovian chains are that if one knows the current state of the process, then no additional information on its past states is needed to make the best possible prediction of its future, which make sense for the study of emerging technology patterns.

Multiple technological trajectories, for different digital technologies and applications, can develop, clash, and evolve over time, and at different speeds, industry-dependent (Martinelli, Mina, and Moggi, 2021).

The diffusion of emerging technology may be also considered in the evolutionary context. Rogers (1995) defines diffusion as a process in which

---

[3] The S-shape curve is also known in different context as the Logistic curve, Verhulst-Pearl equation, Pearl curve, Richard's curve (Generalized Logistic), Growth curve, Gompertz curve, S-curve, S-shaped pattern, Saturation curve, Sigmoid(al) curve, Foster's curve and Bass model, among other names used.

innovations are spread among the members of a social system over time. From this perspective, diffusion is defined as the process by which innovations, new products, new processes, or new management methods spread within and across economies (Stoneman, 1986). In turn, adoption is a decision to implement innovations based on knowledge, and persuasion by individuals within a given system. On the other hand, social adoption and contagion influences adoption. Adoptions of new technologies, fads, and many other human activities spread among individuals through social interactions (Goffman and Newill, 1964; Leskovec, 2007).

Three theoretical approaches have been widely adopted to define the diffusion process and they are worth mentioning at this point. The first is known as the epidemic approach, which considers diffusion to result from the spread of information (Griliches, 1975; Mansfield, 1961; Mansfield, 1989; Mansfield, 1968). The second is the rank approach (Davies, 1979; Karshenas and Stoneman, 1993; Stoneman and Diederen, 1994), in which empirical Probit models are used to rank firms by their characteristics. The third is the game theory approach. Adoption is based on firms' strategic interactions, more precisely *on order* and *stock effects* (Reinganum, 1981a; Reinganum, 1981b; Stoneman, 1986; Fudenberg and Tirole, 1985). The rank and *game theory* approaches are based on the explicit treatment of the firm's adoption decision. However, technology diffusion also influences technology adoption due to complementarity effects between prevailing strategies, organizations, and information technologies (Bocquet, 2007). For example, the introduction of low energy consumption to sensors, and their declining costs, drove their diffusion; advanced machine learning and deep learning began to drive automation; cloud connectivity is delivering low-cost processing power and pervasive interconnection; and new ways to connect monitoring and management systems (so-called "digital twins") (Martinelli, Mina, and Moggi, 2021). Several studies (Berman, Bound, and Griliches, 1994; Berman, Bound, and Machin, 1997; Greenan and Guellec, 1998; Brynjolfsson and Hitt, 2000; Brynjolfsson and Hitt, 2003; Bresnahan, Brynolfsson, and Hitt, 2000) have highlighted the fact that since the information technology (IT) revolution, the mere adoption of IT may no longer be enough to gain competitiveness, which also requires a cluster of related innovations in the organization, new customer and supplier relationships and new product designs.

The complementarity perspective suggests that the adoption of new technology only generates better firm performance if it fits with other complementary choices made by the firm. Empirical studies have shown that the adoption of new technology is strongly linked to firms' strategies, to their organizational practices, and to their competitive environments (Bocquet, 2007). Therefore, diffusion should be analyzed from a multivariate and multipartite perspective, as stated by Grübler (1991).

When technology is subject to increasing returns, this sets the scenario for a distinctive pattern of diffusion. Pezzoni, Veugelers, and Visentini (2019) provided new evidence on technological diffusion and found that the highest-impact novel technologies need longer to be legitimized, particularly the riskier types of new inventions involving new combinations of dissimilar, unfamiliar, and science-based components.

One feature of diffusion may be driven by positive feedback loops in terms of adoption and the associated "bandwagon" effects (Abrahamson and Rosenkopf, 1997; Arthur, 1996; Shapiro and Varian 1998; Fichman, 2000), also known as *irrational exuberance* in the context of investors in stock markets, and which refers to the tendency to adopt a certain attitude simply because everyone else is doing it.

The *bandwagon* phenomenon can be viewed as a bull market situation and the emergence of bubbles. See, for example, the IPO of SNAP Inc. in 2017, which led to appreciation among technology companies driven by the technology rally and evidenced the existence of an inherent correlation apparatus, which can be understood as emerging technologies *self-organizing* their growth. In the context of technology evolution, the trajectory is linked to the autonomous momentum (Dosi, 1982), which is the momentum that seems to be maintained by its own (Nelson and Winter, 1977; Rosenberg, 1976) technical progress or trajectory. However, from the stock market perspective, *momentum* is commonly related to investor irrationality (Daniel, Hirshleifer, and Subrahmanyam, 1997; Barberis, Andrei, and Vishny, 1998) since investors miss to integrate new arriving information and thus under-react. Nevertheless, also perfectly rational investors may follow momentum (Crombez, 2001). High/tech firms generate greater momentum as shown by Ahmed and Alhadab (2020), notwithstanding this response is asymmetric for low-tech stocks. Jaggia and Thosar (2004) found similar evidence as the momentum is important, while fundamental has at best weak explanatory power in the medium-term in emerging tech US IPOs.

Industrial revolution is revealed as a stochastic process, meaning that its evolution follows a succession of random variables that evolve in function of other variables, generally time. The rate of change of this succession has similar shades as of complex system dynamics. Heavy tails, for example, are increasingly related dynamics originating from innovation and are viewed as evidence of lumpy growth, suggesting the absence of a single rational expectation (Dosi, 2005). Instead, it suggests the occurrence of extreme events due to greater probabilities for dynamic innovation (Axtell, 2001).

While many studies have looked at innovation and the adoption of technologies separately, they are linked. Advances (and expected advances) in a single technology should affect both its adoption rate and the adoption of alternative technologies.

Gold, Peirce, and Rosegger (1970) find that the rate of adoption is relatively slow and that technologies for which it is slow to take off as standard technologies. Recent surveys show that although the rate of adoption for many digital technologies is relatively low and skewed toward larger firms, it has a hierarchical pattern in which the most sophisticated technologies are most frequently accepted only after more basic applications (Zolas, Kroff, Brynjolfsson, McElheran, Beede, Buffington, . . . Dinlersoz, 2021). The direction of change in adoption can also be affected by unexpected events, as highlighted and exemplified by Ciarli, Kenney, Massini, and Piscitello (2021) for the COVID-19 pandemic that, in a very short time, forced in-person events to go online and in a matter of weeks fostered the use of digitalization in such fields as telemedicine, which had previously only had limited impact (Mann, Chen, Chunara, Testa, and Nov, 2020). Changes that might have taken years to be adopted were accelerated by an unexpected event (Ciarli, Kenney, Massini, and Piscitello, 2021).

Significant heterogeneity is seen in the recombination and development of emerging technologies that cannot be fully explained by adoption. For example, many firms develop their digital technologies in-house for their own use (Montobbio, 2020).

The persistence over time is also being addressed in the literature as a distinct feature of innovation dynamics (Alfranca, Rama, and Von Tunzelmamm, 2002; Cefis, 2003; Malerba, Orsenigo, and Peretto, 1997; Dosi, 2005). Technologies mature (Christensen, 1992) and firms that have invested in innovative technologies in the past are more probable to continue in this line, investing in the future (Cohen and Levinthal, 1989), as an endogenous pattern. This procyclical and endogenous pattern is consistent with the cyclical patterns of diffusion. Since new technologies take time to catch on, the cyclical response to news shocks is highly persistent (Comin, 2009). High persistence in a process may be related or exemplified by a random walk, which recalling certain numerical properties refers to an $I(1)$ process, where the series in level is not weakly dependent (iid) but its first difference is.

Also, the establishment of extensive new technological trajectories might explain a "clustering" of new technological innovations and their economic impact in time (Dosi, 1982), forming the evolutionary curve of emerging technology. However, evidence exists that a certain clustering of innovations can apparently be identified at a statistically significant level (Kleinknecht, 2016) and returns (Arenas and Gil Lafuente, 2021a) and that the clustering effect is more focused on the end of the diffusion life cycle also known as "season of saturations" (Grübler, 1991).

Dosi (2005) attributed mentioned heterogeneous to different capability to innovate and adopt innovation, developed elsewhere due to differentiation.

Discontinuity in technological change can be associated with the emergence of extraordinary innovative and radical technology (Dosi, 1982) that induces major discontinuities in the statistics that describe structures (Dosi, 1995), particularly (i) different organizational arrangements and (ii) different production efficiencies. Since the work by Mensch (1975), the debate on the discontinuous nature of technological change has been dominated by discussion of the Schumpeterian hypothesis of the discontinuous rate of the appearance of innovations. There has been under debate that the evolution of emerging technologies does not cohere to a smooth pattern of cumulative progress but is, often disorderly and punctuated by episodes of setbacks (Freeman, 2013; Kapoor and Klueter, 2020; Kline and Rosenberg, 1986; Rotolo and Hicks, 2015). A setback is defined as *a reversal or check in progress* and is a relatively common feature of technology emergence, as detailed and exemplified by Kapoor and Klueter (2020) and made evident by such examples as ballpoint pens (Cooper and Smith, 1992), biogas (Geels and Raven, 2006), electric cars (Garud and Gehman, 2012), fuel cells (Bakker, 2010) and semiconductor lithography equipment (Adner and Kapoor, 2016).

12.5 Recent Empirical Evidence

Recent empirical evidence of the link between stock prices, stock price returns and stock return volatility is still lacking in order to provide further insight into the little-known intersection between economic and financial measures. However, below some articles that shed some light on different nuances related to the constellation of emerging technologies and the stock market are reviewed.

Fintech developments, for example, can be seen as disruptive innovations, particularly automation of financial services providing alternatives for traditional financing and trading. In the context of disruptive technologies and stock market returns, recent studies have attempted to provide evidence on the value creation side due to FinTech. Navaretti, Calzolari, Mansilla-Fernande, and Pozzolo (2018) found that FinTech increases liquidity demand uncertainty in the financial market, which may augment market volatility and, *per se,* additional return to compensate. Majid, Sultana, Abid, and Elahi (2021) studied the impact of innovation on the S&P100 firms and found that innovation is an resource enabler to obtaining positive abnormal returns for firms, remaining steady under noise trading and investor biasedness. Low and Wong (2021) studied the varying effects of disruptive FinTech growth across six ASEAN countries on incumbent banks' stock returns and found that the results vary across respective geographical areas and may be considered when studying the impact of innovation on stock market performance.

AI is transforming the way financial services are delivered to customers and almost daily new developments are being deployed, from research and new libraries for Python, R, Julia and others. Lui, Lee, and Ngai (2022) studied the impact of 119 AI-related announcements on 62 listed firms that have invested in AI. The result indicates a 1.77% decline in firms' stock prices. However, negative impact was observed for firms with weak information technology capabilities or low credit ratings. Setiawan, Cavaliere, Koti, Ogunmola, ...Singh (2021) found, that artificial intelligence programs led to greater financial performance for the banking industry.

The World Economic Forum (World Economic Forum, 2016) identified Bitcoin-based blockchain technology as among the top 10 emerging technologies. A relevant concern here is volatility spillovers in the cryptocurrency market spreading to the financial system. Some researchers such as Baek and Elbeck (2015) and Glaser, Zimmermann, Haferkorn, Weber, and Siering (2014) claim that Bitcoin is mainly used as a speculative vehicle due to its volatility. Hassani, Huang, and Silva (2018) argued that a "stable coin" have low price volatility since there are being tied to some underlying fiat currency. Andersson and Styf (2020) identified a slight increase in systematic risk on stock return and a slight reduction in terms of the total risk of the stock return of the Swedish OMX PI Index due to the introduction of blockchain technology. Based on 175 firm announcements between 2015 and 2019, Klöckner, Schmidt, and Wagner (2021) conducted an international study to estimate the impact of blockchain initiatives on the market value of firms and found that engagement in a blockchain project attenuates a positive stock market reaction. Akyildirim, Corbet, Lucey, and Sensoy (2020b) studied the link between a range of cryptocurrencies and the implied volatility of both United States and European financial markets as measured by the VIX and VSTOXX respectively. The results indicated the existence of a varying positive interrelationship between the conditional correlations of cryptocurrencies and financial market stress, which increases during periods of high stress because of contagion from the market to cryptocurrencies. Umar, Rizvi, and Naqvi (2021) examine risk, return and volatility spillovers originating from the cryptocurrency market that is transmitted into the global financial system using Baba-Engle-Kraft-Kroner (BEKK) methodology. The result shows that in the case of shock emitted by the crypto market, the spillover effect is channeled to the financial markets; while from the contrarian perspective, does not hold. Once the shock is incorporated or absorbed, equity and high-yield hedged bond markets persist to the subsequent volatility spillovers originating from the crypto market.

Cloud computing is powerful extensive and will continue to grow in the future since it is extremely cost-effective. Mahmood, Arslan, Dandu, and Udo (2014) studied how the public business is impacted by cloud computing adoption in terms of stock performance and found that the impact results in a positive cumulative abnormal return at the time of an event announcement. This study also highlights that cloud-adopting and non-cloud-adopting companies suffer from higher stock risk during the announcement, but the risk is not statistically significant. Parameswaran, Venkatesan, Gupta, Sharman, and Rao (2011) studied cloud computing announcements regarding stocks listed in the New York Stock Exchange (NYSE), American Stock Exchange (AMEX), and NASDAQ and found that they have a significant positive impact on stock price, albeit a few days later than the day of the announcement. The same results are found by Son, Lee, Lee and Bong (2014), who also observe that market reactions to cloud computing initiatives depend on three key characteristics of the latter, namely firm-specific, resource-specific, and vendor-specific factors. Parameswaran, Venkatesan, and Gupta (2013) study this topic from the perspective of the competitor and find that cloud security breach announcements have a significant negative impact on the stock value both of firms and of their competitors. Nicholas-Donald, Mahmood, and Trevino (2018) used a resource-based view, the efficient market hypothesis, to analyze 136 companies that adopted cloud computing and are listed in one of the US stock exchanges and found that cloud computing announcements increase the trading volume and risk of these companies.

IoT is another technology that has become widespread. Tang, Huang, and Wang (2018) found positive impacts of this on firms' Tobin's q and financial performance, particularly in terms of improving return on assets (ROA).

Ba, Lisic, Liu, and Stallaert (2013) found that the stock market reacted positively to announcements of global green vehicle innovation and that overall green product development decisions, such as innovation type and market segment choices, exert a direct influence on a firm's market value.

Arenas and Gil Lafuente (2021b) investigated emerging technology as a factor that captures the volatility of the Spanish banking sector using the GARCH and diagonal BEKK approach and found evidence of significant stock return volatility clustering, spillover, and persistence.

The study by Agrawal, Bharath, and Viswanathan (2004) shows that there is a significant increase in idiosyncratic and total stock return volatility when a firm initiates e-commerce, accompanied by positive abnormal returns of stock prices.

12.6 Conclusion

The chapter presents a review of research to provide new insights into the linkage of emerging technology and stock price and stock return volatility. The chapter takes the form of an agenda and is based on secondary information.

The baseline notion for this review is that emerging technologies should be examined in the context of stock return and stock return volatility. Risk is commonly used as a proxy for uncertainty, and innovation is an example of true uncertainty (Knight, 1921) thus emerging technology should be studied under the lens of stock return and stock return volatility.

After offering a general overview in Section 14.1, the concept of emerging technology is discussed in Section 14.2. In Section 14.3, some key areas to shed some light on the link between emerging technologies and stock volatility are examined. Section 14.4 defined certain properties of emerging technology, such as diffusive, persistent, heterogeneous, and momentum-oriented are defined, which brought us back to the historical considerations of technology bubbles, booms, and busts. In Section 14.5 recent empirical evidence on FinTech, AI, blockchain, cloud computing, and other technologies is reviewed.

The main conclusion is that emerging technologies increase systemically stock return and stock return volatility.

One important implication of this review is that similar terms are used in the literature to refer to emerging technology.

After reviewing theoretical arguments on economic growth, and how these arguments relate and link to stock market fluctuations and irrational expectations, we observe a connection within the framework of the New Economy.

Since emerging technologies can be interpreted as being derived from radical innovation and may be consolidated within what Carlota Perez introduced as the "techno-economic paradigm" (Pérez, 1983), the stock market will reflect the economic conditions, which are ultimately related to technological change.

Risk is mainly generated by uncertain individual events concerning emerging technology, whose overall aggregated impact generates stock market volatility. The main drivers of risk in the presented scenario are the uncertain nature of emerging technologies, greater difficulty to calculate fundamental values, over-enthusiastic novice investors and the idiosyncratic nature of emerging technologies being driven by intangible assets.

Emerging technologies can be defined as diffusive, persistent, heterogeneous, and momentum-oriented, which can be regarded as the natural pattern those systems evolve.

The premise brings us back to the historical implications of technology bubbles, idiosyncratic risk, and indeed the fact that the overall risk resulting from the emerging technology environment is conditional or time-variant, initially mostly idiosyncratic nature later becomes more systematic as large-scale adoption and the effects of social contagion take place.

The review of recent empirical evidence supports the premise that there is a link between emerging technology dynamics and stock return and volatility. However, direction and tertiary circumstances have to be considered, from a unique perspective as are still not able to deliver a generalized statement.

Future research should integrate empirical finance evidence with social science theory, update the evidence in fast-changing circumstances, distinct based geographically, broaden our understanding of time series behavior, focus on the distinction between risk and uncertainty, and seek to close the wide gap between long-term economic and short-term financial measures.

References

Abdul-Baki, R. (2013). Do information asymmetry proxies measure information asymmetry? Doctoral Thesis. Concordia University.

Aboody, D., Lev, B. (2000). Information asymmetry, R&D, and insider gains. The journal of Finance, 2000, 55(6), 2747-2766. doi: https://doi.org/10.1111/0022-1082.00305

Abrahamson, E., Rosenkopf, L. (1997). Social network effects on the extent of innovation diffusion: A computer simulation. Organization science, 8(3), 289-309. doi:https://doi.org/10.1287/orsc.8.3.289

Abreu, D., Brunnermeier, M. (2003). Bubbles and crashes. Econometrica, 71, 173-204. doi:https://doi.org/10.1111/1468-0262.00393

Abreu, D., Markus K. B. (2002). Synchronization risk and delayed arbitrage. Journal of Financial Economics, 66, 341-360. doi:https://doi.org/10.1016/S0304-405X(02)00227-1

Adner, R., Kapoor, R. (2016). Innovation ecosystems and the pace of substitution: Re-examining technology S-curves. Strategic management journal, 37(4), 625-648. doi: https://doi.org/10.1002/smj.2363

Aggarwal, V. A., Hsu, D. H. (2014). Entrepreneurial exits and innovation. Management Science, 2014, vol. 60, no 4, p. 867-887, 60(4), 867-887. doi:https://doi.org/10.1287/mnsc.2013.1801

Agrawal, D., Bharath, S., Viswanathan, S. (2004). Technological change and stock return volatility: Evidence from eCommerce adoptions. doi:http://dx.doi.org/10.2139/ssrn.3099337

Ahmed, M. S., Alhadab, M. (2020). Momentum, asymmetric volatility, and idiosyncratic risk-momentum relation: Does technology-sector matter? The Quarterly Review of Economics and Finance, 78, 355-371. doi:https://doi.org/10.1016/j.qref.2020.05.005

Ahuja, G., Morris L. C. (2001). Entrepreneurship in the large corporation: A longitudinal study of how established firms create breakthrough inventions.

Strategic management journal, 22(6-7), 521-543. doi:https://doi.org/10.1002/smj.176

Akyildirim, E., Corbet, S., Sensoy, A., Yarovaya, L. (2020a). The impact of blockchain related name changes on corporate performance. Journal of Corporate Finance. 65(101759). doi:https://doi.org/10.1016/j.jcorpfin.2020.101759

Akyildirim, E., Corbet, S., Lucey, B., Sensoy, A. (2020b). The relationship between implied volatility and cryptocurrency returns. Finance Research Letters, 33(101212). doi:https://doi.org/10.1016/j.frl.2019.06.010

Alfranca, O., Rama, R., Von Tunzelmamm, N. (2002). A patent analysis of global food and beverage firms: the persistence of innovation. Agribusiness: An International Journal, 18(3), 349-368. doi: https://doi.org/10.1002/agr.10021

Allen, F. (2012). Trends in financial innovation and their welfare impact:an overview. European Financial Management, 18(4), 493-514. doi:https://doi.org/10.1111/j.1468-036X.2012.00658.x

Anderson, A. (1787). A Historical and Chronological Deduction of the Origin of Commerce, From the Earliest. Volume III. (London: J. Walter).Anderson, P., Tushman, M. L. (1990). Technological discontinuities and dominant designs: A cyclical model of technological change. Administrative science quarterly, 604-633. doi:https://doi.org/10.2307/2393511

Andersson, K., Styf, A. (2020). Blockchain Technology & Volatility of Stock Returns: A Quantitative Study that Examines Blockchain Technology's Impact on Volatility in Swedish Stock. Master Thesis, Umeå University, Faculty of Social Sciences, Umeå School.

Andi, D., Jaafar, A., Torluccio, G. (2015). Mispricing and risk of R&D investment in European firms. The European Journal of Finance, 21(5), 444-465. doi:https://doi.org/10.1080/1351847X.2013.838185

Ang, A., Hodrick, R., Xing, Y., Zhang, X. (2006). The cross-section of volatility and expected returns. The Journal of Finance, 61(1), 259-299. doi: https://doi.org/10.1111/j.1540-6261.2006.00836.x

Arenas, L., Gil-Lafuente, A. M. (2021a). Regime Switching in High-Tech ETFs: Idiosyncratic Volatility and Return. Mathematics, 9(7), 742. doi:https://doi.org/10.3390/math9070742

Arenas, L., Gil Lafuente, A. M. (2021b). Impact of emerging technologies in banking and finance in Europe: A volatility spillover and contagion approach. Journal of Intelligent and Fuzzy Systems, 40(2), 1903-1919. doi:https://doi.org/10.3233/JIFS-189195

Arthur, W. B. (1996). Increasing returns and the new world of business. Harvard business review, 74(4), 100-109.Axtell, R. L. (2001).

Zipf distribution of US firm sizes. Science, 293(5536), 1818-1820. doi:10.1126/science.1062081

Ba, S., Lisic, L., Liu, Q., Stallaert, J. (2013). Stock market reaction to green vehicle innovation. Production and Operations Management, 22(4), 976-990. doi: https://doi.org/10.1111/j.1937-5956.2012.01387.x

Baek, C., Elbeck, N. (2015). Bitcoins as an investment or speculative vehicle? A first look. Applied Economics Letters, 22(1), 30-34. doi:https://doi.org/10.1080/13504851.2014.916379

Bagella, M., Becchetti, L., Adriani, F. (2005). Observed and "fundamental" price–earning ratios: A comparative analysis of high-tech stock evaluation in the US and in Europe. Journal of International money and finance, 24(4), 54. doi:https://doi.org/10.1016/j.jimonfin.2005.03.004

Bakker, S. (2010). The car industry and the blow-out of the hydrogen hype. Energy Policy, 38(11), 6540-6544. doi:https://doi.org/10.1016/j.enpol.2010.07.019

Barberis, N., Andrei, S., Vishny, R. (1998). A model of investor sentiment. In R. Thaler, Advances in Behavioral Finance, Volume II (pp. 307-343). Princeton: Princeton University Press. doi:https://doi.org/10.1515/9781400829125-015

Barron, O. E., Byard, D., Kile, C., Riedl, E. J. (2002). High-technology intangibles and analysts' forecasts. Journal of Accounting Research, 40(2), 289-312. doi:https://doi.org/10.1111/1475-679X.00048

Bartholomew, S. (1997). National systems of biotechnology innovation: complex interdependence in the global system. Journal of international business studies,, 28(2), 241-266. doi:https://doi.org/10.1057/palgrave.jibs.8490100

Benner, M. J. (2007). The incumbent discount: Stock market categories and response to radical technological change. Academy of Management Review, 32(3), 703-720. doi:https://doi.org/10.5465/amr.2007.25275206

Benner, M., Ranganathan, R. (2013). Divergent reactions to convergent strategies: Investor beliefs and analyst reactions during technological change. Organization Science, 24(2), 378-394. doi:https://doi.org/10.1287/orsc.1120.0755

Berente, N., Lee, J., Potts, A., Srinivasan, N. (2020). Do "Digital" Firms Live Longer as Fields Converge? A Survival Analysis of the S&P 500. En AMCIS.Berman, E., Bound, J., Machin, S. (1997). Implications of skill-biased technological hange: International evidence. Centre for Economic Performance, Discussion Paper No. 24. doi:https://doi.org/10.1162/003355398555892

Berman, E., Bound, J., Griliches, Z. (1994). Changes in the demand for skilled labor within U.S. manufacturing: Evidence from the annual survey of manufactures. Quarterly Journal of Economics, 109, 367-97. doi:https://doi.org/10.1162/003355398555892

Blazenko, G. W. (1987). Managerial preference, asymmetric information, and financial structure. The journal of finance, 42(4), 839-862. doi:https://doi.org/10.1111/j.1540-6261.1987.tb03915.x

Bocquet, R. B. (2007). Complementarities in organizational design and the diffusion of information technologies: An empirical analysis. Research Policy, 36(3), 367-386. doi:https://doi.org/10.1016/j.respol.2006.12.005

Boon, W., Moors, E. (2008). Exploring emerging technologies using metaphors–a study of orphan drugs and pharmacogenomics. Social science & medicine, 66(9), 1915-1927. doi:https://doi.org/10.1016/j.socscimed.2008.01.012

Borah, N., Pan, L., Chul Park, J., Shao, N. (2018). Does corporate diversification reduce value in high technology firms? Review of Quantitative Finance and Accounting, 51(3), 683-718. doi:https://doi.org/10.1007/s11156-017-0685-2

Bovi, M. (2009). Economic versus psychological forecasting. Evidence from consumer confidence surveys. Journal of Economic Psychology, 30(4), 563-574. doi:https://doi.org/10.1016/j.joep.2009.04.001

Bresnahan, T. F., Brynolfsson, E., Hitt, L. M. (2002). Information Technology, Workplace Organisation and the Demand for Skilled Labour; Firm-Level evidence. Quarterly Journal of Economics, 117, 339-376. doi:https://doi.org/10.1162/003355302753399526

Brooks, C., Katsaris, A. (2003). Rational speculative bubbles: an empirical investigation of the London Stock Exchange. Bulletin of Economic Research, 55(4), 319-346. doi:https://doi.org/10.1111/1467-8586.00179

Brown, D. P., Ferreira, M. A. (2003). The Information in the Idiosyncratic Volatility of Small Firms. Working paper, University of Wisconsin-Madison.Brown, J. R., Martinsson, G., and Petersen, B. C. (2017). Stock markets, credit markets, and technology-led growth. Journal of Financial Intermediation, 32, 45-59. doi:https://doi.org/10.1016/j.jfi.2016.07.002

Brunnermeier, M., Nagel, S. (2004). Hedge funds and the technology bubble. The journal of Finance, 59(5), 2013-2040. doi:https://doi.org/10.1111/j.1540-6261.2004.00690.x

Brynjolfsson, E., Hitt, L. M. (2000). Beyond Computation: Information Technology, Organizational Transformation and Business Performance. Journal of Economics Perspective, 14(4), 23-48. doi:http://dx.doi.org/10.1257/jep.14.4.23

Brynjolfsson, E., Hitt, L. M. (2003). Computing Productivity: Firm-level Evidence. Review of Economics and Statistics, 85(4), 793-808. doi:https://doi.org/10.1162/003465303772815736

Brynjolfsson, E., Rock, D., Syverson, C. (2019). 1. Artificial Intelligence and the Modern Productivity Paradox: A Clash of Expectations and Statistics. In The Economics of Artificial Intelligence (pp. 23-60). University of Chicago Press. doi:https://doi.org/10.7208/9780226613475-003

Campbell, J. Y., Lettau, M., Malkiel, B. G., Xu, Y. (2001). Have individual stocks become more volatile? An empirical exploration of idiosyncratic risk. The journal of finance, 56(1), 1-43. doi: https://doi.org/10.1111/0022-1082.00318

Capelle-Blancard, G., Raymond, H. (2004). Empirical evidence on periodically collapsing stock price bubbles. Applied Economics Letters, 11(1), 61-69. doi:https://doi.org/10.1080/1350485042000187480

Cefis, E. (2003). Is there persistence in innovative activities? International Journal of Industrial Organization, 21(4), 489-515. doi:https://doi.org/10.1016/S0167-7187(02)00090-5

Chan, L. K., Lakonishok, J., Sougiannis, T. (2001). The stock market valuation of research and development expenditures. The Journal of finance, 56(6), 2431-2456. doi: https://doi.org/10.1111/0022-1082.00411

Christensen, C. M. (1992). Exploring the limits of the technology S-curve. Part I: component technologies. Production and operations management, 1(4), 334-357. doi:https://doi.org/10.1111/j.1937-5956.1992.tb00001.x

Ciarli, T., Kenney, M., Massini, S., Piscitello, L. (2021). Digital technologies, innovation, and skills: Emerging trajectories and challenges. Research Policy(104289). doi:https://doi.org/10.1016/j.respol.2021.104289

Coakley, J., Fuertes, A.-M. (2006). Valuation ratios and price deviations from fundamentals. Journal of Banking & Finance, 30(8), 2325-2346. doi:https://doi.org/10.1016/j.jbankfin.2005.08.004

Cochrane, J. H. (2011). Presidential address: Discount rates. The Journal of finance, 66(4), 1047-1108. Cohen, W., Levinthal, D. (1989). Innovation and learning: the two faces of R & D. The Economic Journal, 99(397), 569-596. doi:https://doi.org/10.2307/2233763

Comin, D. (2009). On the integration of growth and business cycles. Empirica, 2009, 36(2), 165/176. doi:https://doi.org/10.1007/s10663-008-9079-y

Cooper, A., Smith, C. (1992). How established firms respond to threatening technologies. Academy of Management Perspectives, 6(2), 55-70. doi:https://doi.org/10.5465/ame.1992.4274396

Cooper, M., Dimitrov, O., Rau, P. (2001). A rose. com by any other name. The journal of Finance, 56(6), 2371-2388. doi:https://doi.org/10.1111/0022-1082.00408

Cozzens, S., Gatchair, S., Kang, J. J., Kim, K. S., Lee, H. J. (2010). Emerging technologies: quantitative identification and measurement. Technology

Analysis & Strategic Management, 22(3), 361-376. doi:https://doi.org/10
.1080/09537321003647396

Crombez, J. (2001). Momentum, rational agents and efficient markets. The
Journal of Psychology and Financial Markets, 2(4), 190-200. doi:https:
//doi.org/10.1207/S15327760JPFM0204_3

Daniel, K. D., Hirshleifer, D. A., Subrahmanyam, A. (1997). A theory of overconfidence, self-attribution, and security market under-and
over-reactions. Self-Attribution, and Security Market Under-and Over-
Reactions. doi:http://dx.doi.org/10.2139/ssrn.2017

Darby, M. R., Liu, Q., Zucker, L. G. (2004). High stakes in high technology:
High-tech market values as options. Economic Inquiry, 2004, vol. 42, no
3, p. 351-369., 42(3), 351-369. doi:https://doi.org/10.1093/ei/cbh066

Davies, S. (1979). The diffusion of process innovation. Cambridge: Cambridge University Press.Day, G., Schoemaker, P. (2000). Avoiding the
pitfalls of emerging technologies. California management review, 42(2),
8-33.

Dell'Acqua, A., Perrini, F., Caselli, S. (2010). Conference calls and stock
price volatility in the post-reg FD era. European Financial Management,
16(2), 256-270. doi:https://doi.org/10.1111/j.1468-036X.2008.00444.x

Domanski, D. (2003). Idiosyncratic Risk in the 1990s: Is it an IT Story?
WIDER Discussion Paper.Dosi, G. (1982). Technological paradigms and
technological trajectories: a suggested interpretation of the determinants
and directions of technical change. Research policy, 11(3), 147-162. doi:ht
tps://doi.org/10.1016/0048-7333(82)90016-6

Dosi, G. (1995). Learning, market selection and the evolution of industrial
structures. Small Business Economics, 7(6), 411-436. doi:https://doi.org/
10.1007/BF01112463

Dosi, G. (2005). Statistical regularities in the evolution of industries: a guide
through some evidence and challenges for the theory. LEM working paper
series.Fama, E. F. (1965). The behavior of stock-market prices. Journal of
Business, 38, 34-105. Retrieved from https://www.jstor.org/stable/23507
52

Fan, S., Lau, R. Y., Leon, Z. J. (2015). Demystifying big data analytics
for business intelligence through the lens of marketing mix. Big Data
Research,, 2(1), 28-32. doi:https://doi.org/10.1016/j.bdr.2015.02.006

Feldstein, M. (2015). The U.S. Underestimates Growth. Wall Street Journal,
18, 2015.Fichman, R. G. (2000). The diffusion and assimilation of information technology innovations. Framing the domains of IT management:
Projecting the future through the past, 105127, 105-128.

Fleming, L. (2001). Recombinant uncertainty in technological search. Management science, 47(1), 117-132. doi:https://doi.org/10.1287/mnsc.47.1.
117.10671

Foster, R. (1986). Innovation: The Attacker's Advantage. Summit Books New York.Freeman, C. (2013). Economics of industrial innovation. Routledge.

Frehen, R., Goetzmann, W., Rouwenhorst, G. (2013). New Evidence on the First Financial Bubble. Unpublished NBER Working Paper Series 15332, Cambridge-UK. doi:https://doi.org/10.1016/j.jfineco.2012.12.008

Friedman, M. (1953). The case for flexible exchange rates. (U. o. Press, Ed.) in M. Friedman, ed> Essays in Positive Economics.Froot, K., Obstfeld, M. (1991). Intrinsec bubble: the case of stock prices. American Economic Review, 81, 1189-1217. doi:https://doi.org/10.3386/w3091

Fudenberg, D., Tirole, J. (1985). Preemption and rent equalization in the adoption of new technology. The Review of Economic Studies, 52(3), 383-401. doi:https://doi.org/10.2307/2297660

Gallagher, L. A., Taylor, M. P. (2001). Risky arbitrage, limits of arbitrage, and nonlinear adjustment in the dividend-price ratio. Economic Inquiry, 39(4), 524-536. doi:https://doi.org/10.1093/ei/39.4.524

Garud, R. R., Gehman, J. (2012). Metatheoretical perspectives on sustainability journeys: Evolutionary, relational and durational. Research policy, 41(6), 980-995. doi:https://doi.org/10.1016/j.respol.2011.07.009

Geels, F., Raven, R. (2006). Non-linearity and expectations in niche-development trajectories: ups and downs in Dutch biogas development (1973–2003). Technology Analysis & Strategic Management, 18(3-4), 375-392.

Gharbi, S., Sahut, J.-M., Teulon, F. (2014). R&D investments and high-tech firms' stock return volatility. Technological Forecasting and Social Change, 88, 306-312. doi:https://doi.org/10.1016/j.techfore.2013.10.006

Glaser, F., Zimmermann, K., Haferkorn, M., Weber, M., Siering, M. (2014). Bitcoin-asset or currency? revealing users' hidden intentions. Revealing Users' Hidden Intentions. ECIS. Retrieved from https://ssrn.com/abstract=2425247

Goffman, W., Newill, V. (1964). Generalization of epidemic theory. Nature, 204(4955), 225-228.Gold, B., Peirce, W. S., Rosegger, G. (1970). Diffusion of major technological innovations in US iron and steel manufacturing. The Journal of Industrial Economics, 218-241. doi:https://doi.org/10.2307/2097611

Goldfarb, B., Kirsch, D. A. (2019). Bubbles and crashes: The boom and bust of technological innovation. Stanford University Press.Gompers, P., and Lerner, J. (2003). Short-term America revisited? Boom and bust in the venture capital industry and the impact on innovation. Innovation Policy and the Economy,, 3, 1-27. doi:https://doi.org/10.1086/ipe.3.25056151

Greenan, N., Guellec, D. (1998). Firm Organization, Technology and Performance: An Empirical Study. Economics of Innovation and New

Technology, 6(4), 313-347. doi:https://doi.org/10.1080/104385998000 00024

Greenwood, J., Jovanovic, B. (1999). The information-technology revolution and the stock market. American Economic Review, 89(2), 116-122. doi:ht tps://doi.org/10.1257/aer.89.2.116

Greenwood, R., Nagel, S. (2009). Inexperienced investors and bubbles. Journal of Financial Economics, 93(2), 239-258. doi:https://doi.org/10.1016/j. jfineco.2008.08.004

Griffin, J., Harris, J., Shu, T., Topaloglu, S. (2011). Who drove and burst the tech bubble? The Journal of Finance, 66(4), 1251-1290. doi:https://doi.or g/10.1111/j.1540-6261.2011.01663.x

Griffin, J., Harris, J., Topalog, S. (2005). Who Drove and Burst the Tech Bubble? working paper, University of Texas. doi:https://doi.org/10.111 1/j.1540-6261.2011.01663.x

Griliches, Z. (1975). Hybrid corn: an exploration in the economics of technological change. Econometrica, 48, 501-522.Grübler, A. (1991). Diffusion: long-term patterns and discontinuities. In Diffusion of technologies and social behavior. Berlin, Heidelberg.: Springer. doi:https://doi.org/10.1007/ 978-3-662-02700-4_18

Gu, F., Li, J. Q. (2007). The credibility of voluntary disclosure and insider stock transactions. Journal of Accounting Research, 45(4), 771-810. doi: https://doi.org/10.1111/j.1475-679X.2007.00250.x

Gu, F., Wang, W. (2005). Intangible assets, information complexity, and analysts' earnings forecasts. Journal of Business Finance & Accounting, 32(9-10), 1673-1702. doi:Intangible assets, information complexity, and analysts' earnings forecasts.

Halaweh, M. (2013). Emerging technology: What is it. Journal of technology management & innovation, 8(3), 108-115. doi:http://dx.doi.org/10.4067/S 0718-27242013000400010

Hall, B. (2002). The financing of research and development. Oxford review of economic policy, 18(1), pp. 35-51. doi:https://doi.org/10.1093/oxrep/18 .1.35

Hall, B., Rosenberg, N. (2010). (Eds.), Handbook of the Economics of Innovation. Amsterdam: North Holland.Harrison, H., Scheinkman, J., Xiong, W. (2008). "Advisors and Asset Prices: A Model of the Origins of Bubbles,". Journal of Financial Economics, 89(2), 268-287. doi:https://doi.or g/10.1016/j.jfineco.2007.09.001

Hassani, H., Huang, X., Silva, E. (2018). Banking with blockchain-ed big data. Journal of Management Analytics, 5(4), 256-275.

Henderson, R. (1995). Of life cycles real and imaginary: the unexpectedly long old age of optical lithography. Research Policy, 24(4), 631–643. doi:ht tps://doi.org/10.1016/S0048-7333(94)00790-X

Hobjin, B., Jovanovic, B. (2001). The information-technology revolution and the stock market: Evidence. American Economic Review, 91(5), 1203-1220. doi:https://doi.org/10.1257/aer.91.5.1203

Hopkins, M. M., Crane, P. A., Nightingale, P., Baden-Fuller, C. (2013). Buying big into biotech: scale, financing, and the industrial dynamics of UK biotech, 1980–2009. Industrial and Corporate Change, 22(4), 903-952. doi:https://doi.org/10.1093/icc/dtt022

Hung, S.-C., Yee-Yeen, C. (2006). Stimulating new industries from emerging technologies: challenges for the public sector. Technovation, 26(1), 104-110. doi:https://doi.org/10.1016/j.technovation.2004.07.018

Hwang, S., Satchell, S. E. (2000). Market risk and the concept of fundamental volatility: measuring volatility across asset and derivative markets and testing for the impact of derivatives markets on financial markets. Journal of Banking & Finance. doi:https://doi.org/10.1016/S0378-4266(99)00065-5

Inbert, F. (2017, Octobrer 6). https://www.cnbc.com.Retrievedfromhttps://www.cnbc.com/2017/10/06/investors-are-losing-out-on-billions-because-tech-dont-pay-dividends.html

Iraola, M. A., Santos, M. (2007). Technological waves in the stock market.Jaggia, S., Thosar, S. (2004). The medium-term aftermarket in high-tech IPOs: Patterns and implications. 28(5), 931-950. doi:https://doi.org/10.1016/S0378-4266(03)00040-2

Jovanovic, B., Rosseau, P. L. (2002). Stock markets in the new economy.Junttila, J., Kallunki, J.-P., Kärja, A., Martikainen, M. (2005). Stock market response to analysts' perceptions and earnings in a technology-intensive environment. International review of financial analysis, 14(1), 77-92. doi:https://doi.org/10.1016/j.irfa.2004.06.005

Kahneman, D., Tversky, A. (1979). Prospect theory: An analysis of decision under risk. Econometrica: The Econometric Society, 47(2), 263-291. doi:https://doi.org/10.1142/9789814417358_0006

Kapoor, R., Klueter, T. (2020). Progress and setbacks: The two faces of technology emergence. Research Policy, 49(1), 103874. doi:https://doi.org/10.1016/j.respol.2019.103874

Karshenas, M., Stoneman, P. (1993). Rank, stock, order, and epidemic effects in the diffusion of new process technologies: An empirical model. Rand Journal of Economics, 24(4), 503-528. doi:https://doi.org/10.2307/2555742

Kearney, C., Potì, V. (2008). Have European stocks become more volatile? An empirical investigation of idiosyncratic and market risk in the Euro area. European Financial Management, 14(3), 419-444. doi:https://doi.org/10.1111/j.1468-036X.2007.00395.x

Kleinknecht, A. (2016). Innovation patterns in crisis and prosperity: Schumpeter's long cycle reconsidered. London: Springer.

Kline, J., Rosenberg, N. (1986). ńAn overview of innovationż, in Landau R., Rosenberg N.(eds) The positive sum strategy: harnessing technology of economic growth. Washington: National Academic Press.

Klöckner, M., Schmidt, C., Wagner, S. (2021). When Blockchain Creates Shareholder Value: Empirical Evidence from International Firm Announcements. Production and Operations Management. doi:https://doi.org/10.1111/poms.13609

Knight, F. H. (1921). Risk, uncertainty and profit. Houghton Mifflin.Kothari, S. P., Laguerre, T. E., Leone, A. J. (2002). Capitalization versus expensing: Evidence on the uncertainty of future earnings from capital expenditures versus R&D outlays. Review of accounting Studies, 7(4), 355-382. doi:https://doi.org/10.1023/A:1020764227390

Kucharavy, D., De Guio, R. (2008). Technological forecasting and assessment of barriers for emerging technologies. In 17th International Conference on Management of Technology (IAMOT 2008), (pp. 14-2). Dubai. Retrieved from https://hal.archives-ouvertes.fr/hal-00282751

Kwon, S. S., Yin, J. (2015). A comparison of earnings persistence in high-tech and non-high-tech firms. Review of Quantitative Finance and Accounting, 44(4), 645-668. doi:https://doi.org/10.1007/s11156-013-0421-5

Kwon, S. S., Yin, J. (2006). Executive compensation, investment opportunities, and earnings management: High-tech firms versus low-tech firms. Journal of Accounting, Auditing & Finance, 21(2), 119-148. doi:https://doi.org/10.1177/0148558X0602100203

Kydland, F. E., Prescott, E. C. (1982). Time to build and aggregate fluctuations. Econometrica: Journal of the Econometric Society, 1345-1370. doi:https://doi.org/10.2307/1913386

Laitner, J., Stolyarov, D. (2003). Technological change and the stock market. American Economic Review, 93(4), 1240-1267. doi:https://doi.org/10.1257/000282803769206287

Laitner, J., Stolyarov, D. (2019). Asset Pricing Implications of Disruptive Technological Change. University of Michigan working paper.

Lamoureux, C. G., Lastrapes, W. D. (1990). Heteroskedasticity in stock return data: Volume versus GARCH effects. The journal of finance, 45(1), 221-229. doi:https://doi.org/10.1111/j.1540-6261.1990.tb05088.x

Lee, P. M. (2001). What's in a name. com?: The effects of '. com'name changes on stock prices and trading activity. Strategic Management Journal, 22(8), 793-804. doi:https://doi.org/10.1002/smj.177

Leifer, R., O'Connor, G. C., Rice, M. (2001). Implementing radical innovation in mature firms: The role of hubs. Academy of Management Perspectives, 15(3), 102-113. doi:https://doi.org/10.5465/ame.2001.5229646

Leroy, S., Porter, R. (1981). The Present-Value Relation: Tests Based on Variance Bounds. Econometrica, 49, 555-574. doi:https://doi.org/10.2307/1911512

Leskovec, L. A. (2007). The dynamics of viral marketing. In Proceedings of the 7th ACM conference on Electronic commerce (págs. 228-237). Adamic, and BA Huberman.

Lewellen, J. (2003). Discussion of "The Internet Downturn: Finding Valuation Factors in Spring 2000". Journal of Accounting and Economics, 34, 237-247. doi:https://doi.org/10.1016/S0165-4101(02)00089-7

Leydesdorff, L., Rafols, I. (2011). How do emerging technologies conquer the world? An exploration of patterns of diffusion and network formation. Journal of the American Society for Information Science and Technology, 62(5), 846-860.

Li, M., Porter, A. L., and Suominen, A. (2018). Insights into relationships between disruptive technology/innovation and emerging technology: A bibliometric perspective. Technological Forecasting and Social Change, 129, 285-296. doi:https://doi.org/10.1016/j.techfore.2017.09.032

Li, X. (2005). Cheap talk and bogus network externalities in the emerging technology market. Marketing Science, 24(4), 531-543.

Lim, E. N. (2015). The role of reference point in CEO restricted stock and its impact on R&D intensity in high-technology firms. Strategic Management Journal, 36(6), 872-889. doi:https://doi.org/10.5465/ambpp.2013.10053abstract

Lin, X., Palazzo, D., Yang, F. (2017). The risks of old age: Asset pricing implication of technology adoption. Working Paper, Ohio State University.

Linton, J. D., Walsh, S. T. (2008). Acceleration and extension of opportunity recognition for nanotechnologies and other emerging technologies. International Small Business Journal, 26(1), 83-99. doi:https://doi.org/10.1177/0266242607084660

Lo, A. W., Mackinlay, A. C. (1990). Data-snooping biases in tests of financial asset pricing models. The Review of Financial Studies, 3(3), 431-467. doi:https://doi.org/10.1093/rfs/3.3.431

Low, C., Wong, M. (2021). The Effect of FinTech on the Financial Institution in Six ASEAN Countries: Fama-French Five-Factor Asset Pricing Model Approach. In Ninth International Conference on Entrepreneurship and Business Management (ICEBM 2020) (pp. 224-232). Atlantis Press.

Lui, A., Lee, M., Ngai, E. (2022). Impact of artificial intelligence investment on firm value. Annals of Operations Research, 308, 373–388. doi:https://doi.org/10.1007/s10479-020-03862-8

Mahmood, M., Arslan, F., Dandu, J., Udo, G. (2014). Impact of cloud computing adoption on firm stock price–an empirical research. Twentieth Americas Conference on Information Systems. Savannah.

Majid, S., Sultana, N., Abid, G., Elahi, A. (2021). The Impact of Corporate Innovation on Abnormal Stock Returns: The Moderating Role of Investor Sentiment. Academy of Strategic Management Journal, 20, 1-16.

Malerba, F., Orsenigo, L., Peretto, P. (1997). Persistence of innovative activities, sectoral patterns of innovation and international technological specialization. International Journal of Industrial Organization, 15(6), 801-826. doi:https://doi.org/10.1016/S0167-7187(97)00012-X

Mankiw, N., Romer, D., Shapiro, M. (1985). An Unbiased Reexamination of Stock Price Volatility. Journal of Finance, 40, 677-687. doi:https://doi.org/10.1111/j.1540-6261.1985.tb04990.x

Mann, D., Chen, J., Chunara, R., Testa, P., Nov, O. (2020). COVID-19 transforms health care through telemedicine: evidence from the field. Journal of the American Medical Informatics Association, 1132-1135. doi:https://doi.org/10.1093/jamia/ocaa072

Mansfield, E. (1961). Technological change and the rate of imitation. Econometrica, 29, 741-766. doi:https://doi.org/10.2307/1911817Mansfield,E.(1968).IndustrialResearchandTechnologicalInnovation.NewYork:Norton.

Mansfield, E. (1989). The diffusion of industrial robots in Japan and United States. Research Policy, 18, 183-192.Manso, G. (2011). Motivating innovation. The Journal of Finance, 66(5), 823-1860. doi:https://doi.org/10.1111/j.1540-6261.2011.01688.x

Manuelli, R. E. (2000). Technological Change, the Labor Market and the Stock Market. Working Paper 8022. National Bureau of Economic Research. doi:https://doi.org/10.3386/w8022

Manzan, S. (2007). Nonlinear mean reversion in stock prices. Quantitative and Qualitative Analysis in Social Sciences, 1(3), 1-20.Martin, B. (1995). Foresight in science and technology. Technology analysis & strategic management, 7(2), 139-168. doi:https://doi.org/10.1080/09537329508524202

Martin, S., Scott, J. T. (2000). The nature of innovation market failure and the design of public support for private innovation. Research policy, 29(4-5), 437-447. doi:https://doi.org/10.1016/S0048-7333(99)00084-0

Martinelli, A., Mina, A., Moggi, M. (2021). The enabling technologies of industry 4.0: Examining the seeds of the fourth industrial revolution. Industrial and Corporate Change, 30(1), 161-188. doi:https://doi.org/10.1093/icc/dtaa060

Mascitelli, R. (2000). From experience: harnessing tacit knowledge to achieve breakthrough innovation. Journal of Product Innovation Management: an International Publication of the Product Development & Management Association, 17(3), 179-193. doi:https://doi.org/10.1111/1540-5885.1730179

Mazzucato, M. (2002). The PC industry: New economy or early life-cycle? Review of Economic Dynamics, 5(2), 318-345. doi:https://doi.org/10.100 6/redy.2002.0164

Mazzucato, M., Tancioni, M. (2008). Innovation and idiosyncratic risk: an industry-and firm-level analysis. Industrial and Corporate Change, 17(4), 779-811. doi:https://doi.org/10.1093/icc/dtn024

Mensch, G. (1975). Das technologische Putt: Innovationen iiberwinden die Depression. Frankfurt: Umschau Verlag.

Merton, R. (1968). The self-fulfilling prophecy [1948]. in Social Theory and Structure, 1968 Enlarged Edition. New York: The Free Press.Mishkin, F. S. (2016). The Economics of Money, Banking, and Financial Markets. Pearson.

Mizrach, B. (1995). Learning and conditional heteroscedasticity in asset returns. na.Mokyr, J. (2014). Secular stagnation? Not in your life. Secular Stagnation: Facts, Causes and Cures. 83.

Montobbio, F. S. (2020). IZA Discussion Papers, No. 12967. Retrieved from https://www.iza.org/publications/dp/12967/robots-and-the-origin-of-their -labour-saving-impact

Navaretti, G., Calzolari, G., Mansilla-Fernande, J., Pozzolo, A. (2018). Fintech and banking. Friends or foes?. Friends or Foes. Friends or Foes. doi:http://dx.doi.org/10.2139/ssrn.3099337

Nelson, R. R., Winter, S. G. (1977). Dynamic competition and technical progress. Amsterdam: North-Holland.Nicholas-Donald, A., Mahmood, M., Trevino, L. (2018). Does adoption of cloud computing matter? The economic worth of cloud computing implementation. International Journal of Information Systems and Management, 1(4), 328-342.

Noda, T., Bower, J. L. (1996). Strategy making as iterated processes of resource allocation. Strategic management journal, 17(S1), 159-192. doi: https://doi.org/10.1002/smj.4250171011

O'Reilly III, C. A., Tushman, M. L. (2011). Organizational ambidexterity in action: How managers explore and exploit. California management review, 53(4), 5-22. doi:https://doi.org/10.1525/cmr.2011.53.4.5

Parameswaran, S., Venkatesan, S., Gupta, M. (2013). Cloud computing security announcements: assessment of investors' reaction. Journal of Information Privacy and Security, 9(1), 17-46. doi:https://doi.org/10.1 080/15536548.2013.10845671

Parameswaran, S., Venkatesan, S., Gupta, M., Sharman, R., Rao, H. (2011). Impact of Cloud Computing Announcements on Firm Valuation. In AMCIS.

Pástor, Ľ., Veronesi, P. (2003). Stock Valuation and Learning about Profitability. Journal of Finance, 58(5), 749-1789. doi:https://doi.org/10.1111/1540 -6261.00587

Pástor, Ľ., Veronesi, P. (2006). Was there a Nasdaq bubble in the late 1990s? Journal of Financial Economics, 2006, 81(1), 61-100. doi:https://doi.org/10.1016/j.jfineco.2005.05.009

Pástor, Ľ., Veronesi, P. (2009). Technological revolutions and stock prices. American Economic Review, 99(4), 1451-1483. doi:https://doi.org/10.1257/aer.99.4.1451

Peralta-Alva, A. (2007). The information technology revolution and the puzzling trends in Tobin's average q. International Economic Review, 48(3), 929-951. doi: https://doi.org/10.1111/j.1468-2354.2007.00450.x

Pérez, C. (1983). Structural change and assimilation of new technologies in the economic and social systems. Futures, 15(5), 357-375. doi:https://doi.org/10.1016/0016-3287(83)90050-2

Pérez, C. (1985). Microelectronics, long waves and world structural change: New perspectives for developing countries. World Development, 14, 441-463. doi:https://doi.org/10.1016/0305-750X(85)90140-8

Pérez, C. (2003). Technological revolutions and financial capital. Cheltenham, UK: Edward Elgar Publishing.

Pérez, C. (2012). Financial bubbles, crises and the role of government in unleashing golden ages. FINNOV Milton Keynes, UK: Open University.

Pezzoni, M., Veugelers, R., Visentini, F. (2019). Technology diffusion trajectories: New evidence.PGIM. (2018). "The End of Sovereignty". Retrieved from PGIM: https://www.pgim.com/insights/megatrends/sovereignty

Porter, L., Roessner, J., Jin, X.-Y., Newman, N. (2002). Measuring national 'emerging technology'capabilities. Science and Public Policy, 29(3), 189-200. doi:https://doi.org/10.3152/147154302781781001

Powell, W. W., Koput, K. W., Smith-Doerr, L. (1996). Interorganizational collaboration and the locus of innovation: Networks of learning in biotechnology. Administrative science quarterly, 116-145. doi:https://doi.org/10.2307/2393988

Prendergast, C., Stole, l. (1996). Impetuous youngsters and jaded old-timers: Acquiring a reputation for learning. Journal of political Economy, 104(6), 1105-1134. doi:https://doi.org/10.1086/262055

Pyka, A., Burghof, H.-P. (2013). Innovation and Finance. Routledge.

Ranciere, R., Tornell, A., and Westermann, F. (2008). Systemic crises and growth. The Quarterly Journal of Economics, 123(1), 359-406. doi:https://doi.org/10.1162/qjec.2008.123.1.359

Reinganum, M. (1981a). Misspecification of capital asset pricing: Empirical anomalies based on earnings' yields and market values. 19(1), 19-46. doi:https://doi.org/10.1016/0304-405X(81)90019-2

Reinganum, M. (1981b). The arbitrage pricing theory: Some empirical results. The journal of finance, 36(2), 313-321. doi:https://doi.org/10.1111/j.1540-6261.1981.tb00444.x

Riccardi, V., Simon, H. (2000). What is behavioral finance? Business, Education & Technology Journal, 2(2), 1-9. Retrieved from https://ssrn.com/abstract=256754

Riordan, M. H., Salant, D. J. (1994). Preemptive adoptions of an emerging technology. The journal of industrial economics, 247-261. doi:https://doi.org/10.2307/2950568

Rogers, E. M. (1995). Diffusion of Innovations.[Google Scholar]. New York: The Free Press. Rosenberg, N. (1976). Perspectives on technology. Cambridge University Press.

Rosenberg, N., Nelson, R. R. (1994). American universities and technical advance in industry. Research policy, 23(3), 323-348. doi:https://doi.org/10.1016/0048-7333(94)90042-6

Rotolo, D., Hicks, D. (2015). What is an emerging technology? Research policy, 44(10), 1827-1843. doi:https://doi.org/10.1016/j.respol.2015.06.006

Rubera, G., Kirca, A. H. (2012). Firm innovativeness and its performance outcomes: A meta-analytic review and theoretical integration. Journal of Marketing, 76(3), 130-147. doi:https://doi.org/10.1509/jm.10.0494

Sahal, D. (1985). Technological guideposts and innovation avenues. Research policy, 14(2), 61-82. doi:https://doi.org/10.1016/0048-7333(85)90015-0

Sahni, D. (2012). Behavioral finance: Testing applicability on Indian investors. International Journal of in Multidisciplinary and Academic Research, 1(2), 1-12.

Salter, A. J., Martin, B. R. (2001). The economic benefits of publicly funded basic research: a critical review. Research policy, 30(3), 509-532. doi:https://doi.org/10.1016/S0048-7333(00)00091-3

Schoenmakers, W., Duysters, G. (2010). The technological origins of radical inventions. Research Policy, 39(8), 1051-1059. doi:https://doi.org/10.1016/j.respol.2010.05.013

Schwert, G. (1989). Why does stock market volatility change over time? The journal of finance, 44(5), pp. 1115-1153. doi:https://doi.org/10.1111/j.1540-6261.1989.tb02647.x

Schwert, G. (2002). Stock volatility in the new millennium: how wacky is Nasdaq? Journal of Monetary Economics, 49(1), 3-26. doi:https://doi.org/10.1016/S0304-3932(01)00099-X

Setiawan, R., Cavaliere, L., Koti, K., Ogunmola, G., ... Singh, S. (2021). The Artificial Intelligence and Inventory Effect on Banking Industrial Performance. Turkish Online Journal of Qualitative Inquiry (TOJQI), 12(6), 8100-8125.

Shapiro, C., Varian, H. R. (1998). Networks and Positive Feedback. In Information rules: A strategic guide to the network economy. Harvard Business Press.

Shiller, R. C. (2000). Irrational exuberance. Philosophy and Public Policy Quarterly, 20(1), 18-23. doi:http://dx.doi.org/10.13021/G8pppq.202000. 333

Shiller, R. J. (1981a). Do Stock Prices Move Too Much to Be Justified by Subsequent Changes in Dividends? American Economic Review, 71(3), 421-436. doi:https://doi.org/10.3386/w0456

Shiller, R. J. (1981b). Alternative Tests of Rational Expectation Models: The Case of the Term Structure. Journal of Econometrics, 16, 71-78.

Siegel, J. J. (2021). Stocks for the long run: The definitive guide to financial market returns & long-term investment strategies. (5th, Ed.) McGraw-Hill Education, 2021.

Small, H., Boyack, K., Klavans, R. (2014). Identifying emerging topics in science and technology. Research policy, 43(8), 1450-1467. doi:https://doi.org/10.1016/j.respol.2014.02.005

Son, I., Lee, D., Lee, J.-N., Bong, Y. (2014). Market perception on cloud computing initiatives in organizations: An extended resource-based view. Information & Management,, 51(6), 653-669. doi:https://doi.org/10.1016/j.im.2014.05.006

Spiegel, M. I., Wang, X. (2005). Cross-sectional variation in stock returns: Liquidity and idiosyncratic risk. Working Paper, Yale School of Management. Retrieved from https://ssrn.com/abstract=709781

Srinivasan, R. (2008). Sources, characteristics, and effects of emerging technologies: Research opportunities in innovation. Industrial Marketing Management, 37(6), 633-640. doi:https://doi.org/10.1016/j.indmarman.2007.12.003

Stock, J. H. (1988). Estimating continuous-time processes subject to time deformation: an application to postwar US GNP. Journal of the American Statistical Association, 83(401), 77-85. doi:https://doi.org/10.1080/01621459.1988.10478567

Stoneman, P. (1986). Technological diffusion: the viewpoint of economic theory. Ricierche Economiche, 4, 585/606.Stoneman, P. (2002). The Economics of Technological Diffusion. Oxford: Blackwell.

Stoneman, P., Diederen, P. (1994). Technology diffusion and public policy. The Economic Journal, 104(425), 918-930. doi:https://doi.org/10.2307/2234987

Stubbart, C. I., Knight, M. B. (2006). The case of the disappearing firms: empirical evidence and implications. Journal of Organizational Behavior: The International Journal of Industrial, Occupational and Organizational Psychology and Behavior, 27(1), 79-100. doi: https://doi.org/10.1002/job.361

Tang, C., Huang, T., Wang, S. (2018). The impact of Internet of things implementation on firm performance. Telematics and Informatics, 35(7), 2038-2053. doi:https://doi.org/10.1016/j.tele.2018.07.007

Tasker, S. C. (1988). Bridging the information gap: Quarterly conference calls as a medium for voluntary disclosure. Review of Accounting Studies, 3(1), 127-167. doi:https://doi.org/10.1023/A:1009684502135

Tauni, M., Fang, H., Iqbal, A. (2016). Information sources and trading behavior: does investor personality matter? Qualitative Research in Financial Markets., 8(2), 94-117. doi:https://doi.org/10.1108/QRFM-08-2015-0031

Tushman, M., O'Reilly III, C. A. (1996). Ambidextrous organizations: Managing evolutionary and revolutionary change. California management review, 38(4), 8-29. doi:https://doi.org/10.2307/41165852

Umar, M., Rizvi, S., Naqvi, B. (2021). Dance with the devil? The nexus of fourth industrial revolution, technological financial products and volatility spillovers in global financial system. Technological Forecasting and Social Change, 163(120450). doi:https://doi.org/10.1016/j.techfore.2020.120450

US Corporate Bond Issuance, ". S. (n.d.). https://www.sifma.org/resources/research/us-corporate-bonds-statistics/.

Viguerie, P., Calder, N., Hindo, B. (2021, May 01). 2021 Corporate Longevity Forecast. Retrieved 2021, from innosight.com: https://www.innosight.com/insight/creative-destruction/

Watanabe, C., Hur, J. Y., Lei, S. (2006). WATANABE, Chihiro; HUR, Jae Yong; LEI, Shanyu. Converging trend of innovation efforts in high technology firms under paradigm shift—a case of Japan's electrical machinery. Omega, 34(2), 178-188. doi:https://doi.org/10.1016/j.omega.2004.09.002

Wei, S. X., Zhang, C. (2006). Why did individual stocks become more volatile? The Journal of Business, 2006, 79(1), 259-292. doi:https://doi.org/10.1086/497411

West, K. (1988). Dividend innovations and stock price volatility. Econometrica: Journal of the Econometric Society, 27-61. doi:https://doi.org/10.2307/1911841

West, K. (1984). Speculative Bubbles and Stock Price Volatility. In Memo No.54, Financial Research Center. Princeton, N. J.: Princeton University.

World Economic Forum. (2016). These are the top 10 emerging technologies of 2016. Retrieved from https://www.weforum.org/agenda/2016/06/top-10-emerging-technologies-2016

Xu, Y., Malkiel, B. G. (2003). Investigating the behavior of idiosyncratic volatility. The Journal of Business, 2003, 76(4), 613-645. doi:https://doi.org/10.1086/377033

Yu, L., Liu, X., Fung, H.-G., Kin, W. (2020). Size and value effects in high-tech industries: The role of R&D investment. The North American Journal of Economics and Finance, 51, 100853. doi:https://doi.org/10.1016/j.naje f.2018.10.001

Zolas, N., Kroff, Z., Brynjolfsson, E., McElheran, K., Beede, D., Buffington, C., . . . Dinlersoz, E. (2021). Advanced technologies adoption and use by U.S. firms: Evidence from the Annual Business Survey. National Bureau of Economic Research, Working Paper No 28290. Retrieved from https: //www.nber.org/system/files/working_papers/w28290/w28290.pdf

Zuckerman, E., Rao, H. (2004). Shrewd, crude or simply deluded? Comovement and the internet stock phenomenon. Industrial and Corporate Chang, 13(1), 171-212. doi:https://doi.org/10.1093/icc/13.1.171

13

Managerial Decision-making Factors in SMEs: Supplier Companies in the Construction Industry Analysis

Nancy Camargo[1], Fabio Blanco-Mesa[1], Ernesto Leon-Castro[2], and Beatriz Callejas-Cuervo[1]

[1]Universidad Pedagógica y Tecnológica de Colombia, Colombia
[2]Unidad Navojoa, Instituto Tecnologico de Sonora, Mexico

Abstract

Organizations currently live facing an increasingly changing, complex, and hostile environment, in this sense, it is interesting to understand how they direct decision-making based on adequate management and planning. In this sense, the main aim is to analyze the process carried out in the decision-making of the managers of SMEs that provide construction product suppliers. A qualitative and descriptive approach is used to interpret the experience of six managers of SMEs that provide construction products. The semi-structured survey is used as a collection instrument and content analysis is used to interpret the opinions given. A decision-making process is identified that highlights a preliminary evaluation of scenarios, the decision is made through intuition and reason, and the results are evaluated in the short term by observing the behavior of the company. The elements that intervene in the decision-making process fall into four groups: available information, manager characteristics, evaluative and strategic framework, and organizational prospects.

Keywords: Strategy, management, organization, decision-making

13.1 Introduction

In organizational development, the importance and benefits of decision-making, whether individual or group, lie in giving adequate management to the intuition of decision-makers through analysis, techniques, or rational models to improve this process (Antunes & Costa, 2012). Managers and companies in the organizational context present diverse situations that require time and dedication to choose the most appropriate among the different alternatives. In fact, managers strive for appropriate decision-making for the different conditions that arise in the organization, so they must understand the need to study, analyze and significantly improve their knowledge in this process; this includes theory and related approaches, methods and techniques, and the development of advanced personal skills at a higher level (Al-Tarawneh, 2012)

The objective of this work is to analyze the factors that influence the decision-making process of managers in SMEs that supply construction materials in the city of Tunja. For this purpose, a theoretical review of the different approaches to managerial decision-making was carried out and the key elements involved in the process were identified based on applied surveys. Methodologically, a descriptive qualitative approach was used to approach the experiences of six managers and to carry out an interpretation process to understand their characteristics and common features within the decision-making process. A semi-structured interview is applied, and a content analysis supported by Atlas Ti is performed, defining seven categories: managerial coordination, managerial skills, organizational leadership, organizational strategy, managerial challenges, decision-making, and organizational foresight.

This chapter is organized into five sections. The first describes the review of the state-of-the-art and theoretical framework on the evolution, process, models, and elements involved in managerial decision-making. The second section describes the method, participants, research categories, data collection instruments, and analysis strategies. The third section describes the findings and interpretation of the managers' opinions. The fourth section presents the discussion and finally, the conclusions of the research are established.

13.2 Theoretical Framework

Business leaders face different situations every day which are directly related to decision-making, since during these decisions there are factors that involve risks; for which there are studies that show how companies can use risk management in a concrete way to achieve better risk-reward decisions under uncertainty (Burke & Demirag, 2019). One of the main challenges facing managers today is to respond in a timely manner to the situations that may arise in their environment, and through a clear and strategic vision, they must guide their company to another level during a changing market. Strategic decision-making has been described as the process of developing the organizational mission and objectives and deciding on the course of action a company should follow (Sajjad & Francesca, 2016). Decision-making has been a fundamental factor in management; therefore, it is essential to analyze the evolution of decision-making, its process both at the intuitive and managerial levels and the models that have contributed to strengthening it and making it more practical.

Around 1950, pioneers in the field of decision-making work in the field of decision analysis, whose strength lies in the hard sciences that support its analysis: mathematics and statistics. (Gigante, 2017). During the industrial revolution, decision-making was characterized by individualistic management, only business owners were the ones who, based on their knowledge, decided on organizational aspects. At the beginning of the 20th century, the individual made decisions based primarily on operational statistics and internal information, but this method lacked the sophistication necessary to deal with the multitude of factors related to organizational decisions. (Moody, 1983). During World War II the military field began to develop operations research techniques related to problem-solving in decision-making (Rodríguez & Pinto, 2019). Thus, the need to evaluate decision-making grew and they began to shape this process through scientific studies. In the business field, the concern was about production and how to face the large new companies. And it is here where the need to develop models and approaches to guide managerial thinking starts, among which the decision-making models begin to develop.

13.2.1 Management decision-making

Decision-making is one of the main interests of many researchers and is conceptualized as a process of problem identification and resolution (Daft, 2007). When it talks about decision-making, it refers to the process of choosing between one or the different alternatives that may arise during different uncertain events (Beatrice Kovacs, 1990). According to Mckenzie et al. (2011), decision-making is a knowledge-intensive activity. On the one hand, content knowledge keeps decisions relevant to the circumstances and rooted in experience; while, process knowledge, such as skills and organizational structures to support better decision-making. This is the activity that almost epitomizes the behavior of managers and the one that clearly distinguishes managers from other occupations in society (Harrison & Francisco, 1996). In the same sense, Fierro Celis (2014) affirms that "decision making is the process by which managers respond to opportunities and threats by analyzing options and making decisions related to organizational goals and courses of action." (p. 79). From another perspective, Hess et al. (2011), one of the dichotomies in contemporary thinking about decision-making is the apparent conflict between the roles of emotion and rationality. Likewise, (Stanovich, & West, 2000) suggests taking cognitive functions and dividing them according to their relevance; the faster, effortless, implicit, and emotional compared to those that were slower, conscious, explicit, and logical.

In the above aspects of how to decide, information is taken as the main basis. Information is not, of course, an end in itself; it is the basic input for decision-making. This information is used to carry out actions that benefit daily operations within organizations. Citroen (2011) states that "Information about the internal and external environment of the organization is a crucial factor in the decision-making process by industry executives" (p. 493); that is, this process plays a transcendental role, since having sufficient information minimizes uncertainty.

Decision-making is made for a single purpose to solve any type of problem in even the most predictable environments. Decision-makers need both the experience to recognize and respond appropriately to different contexts, as well as sensitivity to the way problems are presented and their own norms, habits, and expectations (Mckenzie et al., 2011).

Decisions can be classified as routine, adaptive, and innovative (Cabeza et al., 2004). Routine decisions are systematized choices that respond to already known situations; adaptive decisions are those responses to moderately unusual or partially known problems; and innovative decisions arise as alternative, creative and exceptional solutions to unusual problems.

13.2.2 The managerial decision-making process

Decision-making is a human process in which one chooses between several options, in these decision-making processes there are stages. The need to make decisions quickly in the different situations that arise is becoming increasingly complex. The efficient action with which decisions are carried out is an important factor in decision-making, as well as which are the steps to be followed; also the construction of broader and more accurate views about the reality of the business and better planning and decision-making processes (Pulgarín & Rivera, 2012).

Decision-making never stops, and it is important to evaluate how important the decision is; Moody (1991) recommends evaluating five important factors: size and duration of the commitment, flexibility, certainty, control variables, and finally the human impact of the decisions. Rationality in decision-making requires insight into organizations and a selection of preferred alternatives according to a value system, whose behavioral consequences can be evaluated (Daft, 2007).

In managerial decision-making, decision-makers study, analyze, accept or reject the different options that may be presented, according to Mintzberg (1889) "the manager plays the main role in a decision-making system, since only the manager possesses the complete information to proceed to make the decisions which will follow the strategy" (p. 19). The decision-making style of a manager in an organization not only affects the personal lives of his or her subordinates but also affects their work-related attitudes (Riaz et al., 2014). According to Mintzberg (1889) without outside information, the manager is unable to make effective decisions.

It has been stated that "many organizations are eliminating levels of management and decentralizing decision-making. There is a shift toward more horizontal structures, with teams of front-line workers who have the authority to make decisions and solve problems on their own" (Daft, 2007, p. 428). In this sense, delegation has begun, segmenting those decisions that are characteristic of the managerial function and others that are of a more operative nature. The decision-maker intentionally deliberates on moral dilemmas and makes a rational choice. This is ethical decision-making.

13.2.3 Decision-making process models

Decision-making models can be used for problem-solving in a wide variety of circumstances and contingencies, and decisions can be made individually or among representatives of multiple organizations or among several individuals within the same organization (Lambarry et al., 2010). Some models are described in Table 13.1.

The above models allow for a simple decision-making process and are used depending on the type of organization. In each of the models' certain steps are followed according to what needs to be organized, and demand certain managerial skills that are achieved with experience and knowledge.

Table 13.1   Decision-making models.

Models	Description
Rational	Rational decision-making; the idea of the behavior of individuals is emphasized since human beings are inherently emotional and rational choice is based on the assumption that cumulative social behavior is derived from individual decisions (Uzonwanne, 2016).
Economic rationality	In this model, people can identify all the alternatives and consider the consequences of each one. A person needs to have all the necessary information to be able to process it and thus identify the different alternatives to be evaluated (Cabeza et al. 2004).
Limited rationality	Decision-makers are cognitively limited to handle, use, and interpret large amounts of information or relatively complex information, due to representational issues that require more personal effort (Rodríguez, 2018). It focuses on thought processes that guide the individual in making decisions, and in this rationality, the search for and satisfaction of the individual's needs are important (Simón, 1987).
Political rationality	It is composed of key actors and dynamics among which the following stand out players, positions, influence, and movements. The model emphasizes the processes of perception, search and selection, access, and control of information, as well as bargaining and persuasion. It is associated with the adequate processing and analysis of information.
Organizational behavior	It is the study of the performance and attitudes of people in organizations. Effectiveness and productivity depend on the employees and their contribution to the work (Dailey Robert, 1990). This model proposes that organizations must resolve the potential for conflict given by the different individual interests and assume the need to define the organization's purpose (Cabeza et al., 2004).
Garbage cans	Four basic variables are considered, each of which is a function of time (Cohen et al., 2011). The model is based on the fact that organizations, being very complex, present deficiencies in terms of information, interpersonal relationships, and methods used; therefore, it is to be expected that their decision-making processes also present inconsistencies on some occasions (Cabeza et al., 2004).
Kepner-Tregoe	It aims to analyze the problem in detail, looking for the possible causes that generated this situation; to choose the most probable cause and thus correct the imbalance in order to make a decision with solid foundations (Cabeza et al., 2004).
Minztberg, Raisinghani and Theoret	This model is descriptive and represents how strategic decisions are made at a high level of management, but not how the process should be. For this "strategic" model it is important, in terms of the actions taken, the resources committed, or the precedents previously set. The Mitzberg model presents interruption cycles that allow a return to previous phases with the disadvantage that at each interruption there is a latent risk of not reaching a decision since changes in the organization affect the process (Lambarry et al., 2010).

Table 13.1 Continued.

Models	Description
Incrementalistic	It uses the technique called "decision-making by mutual adaptation," the latter being understood as the ability of human beings to coordinate with their peers without the need to share a common goal or objective and without the participation of intermediaries (Cabeza et al., 2004)
Vroom-Yetton	The model states that whoever wanted to be a leader should be able to quickly grasp the different situations, since this model relates leadership behavior and participation in decision-making (García, 2015). The leader's behavior must be adapted to the type of structure of the task.
Intuitive	It seeks a strategic vision, intuition is a matter of smell, of seeing what others do not see. The decision sciences suggest that, under certain conditions, intuition can facilitate decision-making in organizations (Michael & Pratt, 2007). It is important to better understand the conditions that promote the effective use of intuition to complement existing work and to identify when it is most likely to be used (Michael & Pratt, 2007).
Pragmatic	This model is based on experience; all decisions are based on learning, learning while finding solutions and each of these contributes assertively to the expected outcome.

Source: Own elaboration.

13.2.4 Elements involved in the managerial decision-making process

There are factors that affect the decision-maker, both individual (knowledge, values, attitudes, and intentions) and organizational (significant in other aspects and opportunity) (Jones, 1996). These factors turn out to be determinant and lead the decision-maker to take action according to the process he/she is going through, his/her individual traits, and the pressures of the environment.

13.2.4.1 Rationality in decision-making

There are constraints where the manager discovers acceptable solutions, understands management, and seeks satisfactory alternatives (Simon, 1987) asserts that rationality is bounded, and recognizes that people are free to choose and reason, because of their limited search, but, only within imposed constraints and in many scenarios. Decisions must be made with incomplete, scarce, or insufficient information (Simon, 1987). Therefore, rational behavior involves taking all possible alternatives; however, it can be difficult to think of alternatives when problems are very complex.

According to Bonome (2009), rationality is a process (or rather, a set of processes: choice, adaptation, problem-solving, etc.) that is analyzed through various scientific disciplines, while offering a philosophical conception of "rationality." The analysis of decision-making as a rational process is precisely the common thread of a wide range of knowledge (Social Sciences, Artificial Sciences, and Philosophy) (Bonome, 2009).

13.2.4.2 Uncertainty in decision-making

Daft (2007) states that the decision-making process must be made during constantly changing factors, unclear information, and conflicting points of view; it formally defines the process as identifying and solving problems. All decisions follow a common process and can be described by steps that apply to all circumstances; in most cases, the decisions made do not have information to ensure the outcome of the actions, which can be simple or complex. Thus, fuzzy decision-making many real-world decisions occur in an environment in which the consequences of possible actions are not precisely known (Baez et al. 2019; Blanco-Mesa et al., 2020, 2017). Now, new technologies and methods to deal with uncertainty, which allows capturing perception, reasoning, logic, and human semantics in simple methods to understand and use (Blanco-Mesa, 2020; Blanco-Mesa, 2020, 2019). Managers usually make decisions within a limited rationality because obtaining all the necessary information is difficult. Anticipate the consequences of their decisions and recognize all variants of behavior, so that they can rationally decide on them under turbulent conditions (Gigalová, 2017). On the other hand, uncertainty does not always stem from the absence of information. According to Vaiman et al. (2012), managers who have too much data are much more common compared to those who lack data.

13.2.4.3 Intuition in decision-making

Philosophers and psychologists have traditionally understood intuition as a mental process in which a belief or judgment is formed immediately, without any conscious awareness of a process of inference at work (Khatri & Alvin, 2000). Intuition is usually distinguished from reasoning, as it involves personal preferences, it is a hunch, a gut feeling, it is an immediate judgment, a judgment without any awareness of a reasoning process at work, and it is possible to describe it as intuitive (Resnik, 2017).

Emotionally intelligent decision-makers must exude confidence in their decision-making style (Hess et al., 2011). Intuitive decision-making is less structured and emphasizes perceptions, feelings, and judgments rather than facts and analysis. It is not only knowledge and experience that influence the intuitive decision-making process; both intuitive and rational decision-making are influenced by emotions (Gigalová, 2017).

Intuitive decision-making is inefficient because the strategy does not bring together all the components that can disrupt the decision and its outcomes. The main elements that characterize such a process are moral issues and moral agents: "a moral issue arises when an individual behavior may cause favorable or harmful consequences for others; a moral agent is an individual who recognizes the presence of a moral issue and acts according to his or her morality" (Zollo et al., 2017, p. 682).

13.2.4.4 Preparation for decision-making

In decision-making it is necessary to evaluate which elements interfere in the preparation of these decisions, although it is true that before making the decision there must be a training period in which the different alternatives must be evaluated for efficient decision-making, this stage takes more time since it will depend on the clarity regarding the factors to be included in the analysis: "Management can sometimes benefit and simply try to list alternative strategies instead of choosing among only the few strategies traditionally used" (Archer, 2014, p. 272).

The decision should be considered as the strategic choice in which managers should be involved (Rolland & Nicolas, 2004). Complex strategic decisions are important because they are more challenging and carry more risks and consequences for business performance, but they are not the only focus (Mckenzie et al., 2011). While a good manager makes balanced efforts to manage and support his employees, he sometimes consults them when making decisions, but these remain his sole responsibility (García, 2015).

13.2.4.5 Managerial skills

In the decision-making process, recognition of individual emotions is critical to determine not only the motivations behind decisions but also the impact of the decisions of others (Hess et al., 2011). The influence of personal factors is nowadays of main interest for many researchers who considered the decision itself as a voluntary action whose objective is the challenge in the face of problem-solving (Chaabouni & Yahia, 2014). Rather than proceeding simply as the linear unfolding of sequences of decomposed stages, decision-making processes are also driven by the emotion, imagination, and memories of the decision-maker (Sayegh et al., 2004). It has been noted that "decision-makers need experience in recognizing and responding appropriately to different contexts, and sensitivity to the way the problem presents itself and their own norms, habits and expectations" (Mckenzie et al., 2011, p. 410).

According to Fayol (1986), the traits that great leaders must have are: health and physical vigor, intelligence and intellectual vigor, moral qualities, reflective will, firmness, perseverance, activity, and energy. He also states that discipline consists essentially of obedience and is necessary for good performance and, therefore, the permanence of organizations in a changing and challenging environment. Likewise, the manager must be a strategist and evaluate the different alternatives. According to Archer (2014), the alternatives available in any decision problem are called "strategies." The number of strategies to choose from can vary from two to infinity and, depending on the individual's skills, abilities, knowledge, and experience, many of these are subject to the individual's skills, abilities, knowledge, and experience (García, 2015). Finally, the role of experience is crucial, as successful intuition-based decision-making is developed through personal experience (Provis, 2010). Similarly, ethics can focus on the development of expertise and accountability in decision-making and enhances the adoption of responsible approaches (Provis, 2010).

13.2.4.6 Business training

Business training can be defined as the union of knowledge, processes, and techniques of continuous improvement, management skills are part of business growth, they go hand in hand with years of experience, knowledge, and strategies. Although the Aristotelian moral virtues (prudence, justice, fortitude, and temperance) are the foundation for the exercise of management, the intellectual virtues (art, science, prudence, wisdom, and intellect), perhaps less well-known, also allow us to discover these observable and habitual behaviors called competencies (Serrano, 2017). Virtues are acquired operative habits that are developed through deliberate, effortful, and voluntary repetition of acts that strive to become better and better (Argandoña, 2010). This process of acquisition and growth of moral virtues takes place when the decision-maker strives to achieve what is good for himself and for others (Argandoña, 2011).

13.2.4.7 Business vision

Vision is the hallmark of management; it is much more a product of the mind called imagination (Mintzberg, 1990). It is important to create a common vision and to share common values, as the business vision provides the ability to discover threats and opportunities that may affect the company's competitiveness (Serrano, 2017). The integral vision of the person and the company makes the search for organizational excellence compatible with the full development of the person (Serrano, 2017). Also, managers should communicate their vision clearly, evaluate and monitor it on an ongoing basis, and allow stakeholders to actively participate in the process (Selart, 2010). Likewise, wisdom critically engages skills of judgment and choice, two qualities that underpin decision-making (Intezari & Pauleen, 2018). Thus, decision-makers need the self-confidence to admit that something is wrong and change direction (Mckenzie et al., 2011). For this reason, the decision-maker has an important role in the company's vision and the role it wants to play in the market.

13.3 Methodology

The research is developed under a qualitative approach, data collection is performed without numerical measurement to discover or refine, adjust and answer the research questions in the process of interpretation (Hernández et al., 2014). In this case, the main emphasis is to describe the investigation of the decision-making process in supplier companies in the construction sector. The research participants were chosen by convenience, applying the following inclusion criteria: 1) a company with a maximum of 200 employees, 2) a company dedicated to supplying goods to the construction sector, and 3) a company whose geographical location is the city of Tunja. The data collection instrument was a semi-structured interview consisting of 7 dimensions, managerial articulation, managerial competencies, organizational direction, organizational strategy, managerial challenges, decision-making, and organizational perspective (according to the categories of analysis), and 24 questions, which were tabulated, analyzed, and inferred. According to the qualitative approach, an information analysis strategy called content analysis is adopted, which consists of identifying common elements in the information collected, assigning categories, and drawing conclusions. In terms of Galeano (2015), content analysis "consists of a transformation of the text that is being subjected to analysis, governed by defined rules and procedures, and which must be justified by the researcher theoretically and methodologically through an adequate interpretation" (p. 126). This analysis is carried out by means of Atlas T.I. Software. After the consultation process and request for interviews with the managers of the companies, 6 of them were interviewed, which are listed in Table 13.2.

Table 13.2   Characteristics of research participants.

I	G	MAC	YME	NE	A	El
I1	Woman	Distribution of construction materials	16	28	44	Professional: Business Administrator
I2	Man	Distribution of electrical material and decoration	4	2	39	Civil Works Technician
I3	Man	Manufacture of metal-mechanical products for electrical installations	15	200	44	University
I4	Woman	Distribution of construction finishes	16	5	62	Professional: Public Administrator
I5	Man	Distribution of construction finishes	20	167	50	Bachelor
I6	Man	Construction of private housing	8	42	39	Professional: Business Administrator

Source: Own elaboration. I: Interviewed; G: Gender; MAC: Main activity of the company; YME: Years of management experience; NE: Number of employees; A: Age; El: Education level.

According to the theoretical analysis and literature review, seven categories of analysis of the elements that influence decision-making were established (see Table 13.3).

13.4 Results

The managerial decision-making process in construction supplier companies is influenced by different elements of managerial articulation, managerial competencies, organizational direction and strategy, the challenges faced, the way decisions are made, and the organization's perspective. This section examines these elements to understand their decision-making process.

13.4.1 Managerial coordination

The experiences, motivations, objectives, and characteristics of managers permeate the decision-making process; in this sense, this subsection analyzes the reasons that led them to become entrepreneurs, the relationship between their personal and business objectives, and the characteristics they consider necessary to exercise management (see Figure 13.1).

There are basically two types of motivations for managers in this sector to start their businesses: independence and employment generation, and the

Table 13.3 Categories of analysis of the research.

Categories	Description
Managerial Coordination (MC)	A manager experiences a variety of cognitive aspects, processes, and intuitive and emotional reactions that interact instantaneously during the decision process. In the midst of these dynamics, the manager can quickly make an effective decision (Sayegh, L., Anthony, W. P., & Perrewé 2004), if the manager does not understand the "raison d'être" of the company he will hardly be able to structure quality preference scales, which can lead to decide for action alternatives that adhere to his particular desires without rationally appropriating those of the organization (Arrendondo Trapero, F., & Vázquez Parra 2013) p.140.
Managerial Skills (MS)	The Aristotelian moral virtues (prudence, justice, fortitude, and temperance) are the foundation for the exercise of leadership, the intellectual virtues (art, science, prudence, wisdom, and intellect) also allow us to discover these observable and habitual behaviors called competencies (Serrano 2017) p. 209. Virtues are acquired operative habits that are developed through deliberate, effortful, and voluntary repetition of acts that strive to become better and better (Argandoña 2010).
Organizational Leadership (OL)	In organizations there must be coherence because when this does not exist, its processes do not flow normally, precisely Mintzberg points out that "an effective organization is one that achieves coherence among its components and that does not change one element without evaluating the consequences on the others," from this perspective, decision-making is a fundamental pillar for all organizations.
Organizational Strategy (OS)	The organization's strategy is very important for decision-makers, Ackert et al. (2010) state that it has been shown that more experienced decision-makers use a strategy-driven information search, while those with less experience are more likely to use a sequential search strategy.
Managerial Challenges (MC)	Organizations should embrace the idea that there is no shame in trying something new, even if the result is a failure (Brewis, 2017), since managers, due to their human condition, are imperfect and may or may not achieve success through their decisions. Decision-making by managers is composed of a set of variables such as management skills, knowledge, experience, and intuition among others.
Decision-Making (DM)	Fierro Celis (2014) states that "decision-making is the process by which managers respond to the opportunities and threats presented to them, analyzing options and making determinations, or decisions related to organizational goals and courses of action." In turn (Simon, 1987) argues that humans do not optimize their decisions because their cognitive capacity is limited and that decisions are often made under severe time and budget constraints, making it almost impossible to optimize them. Decision-making focuses on problem-solving in even the most predictable environments, decision-makers need both the experience to recognize and respond appropriately to different contexts, and sensitivity to the way problems are presented and their own norms, habits, and expectations (Mckenzie et al., 2011).

Table 13.3   Continued.

Categories	Description
Organizational Foresight (OF)	This is a component that goes hand in hand with the business, for (Mintzberg, 1990) vision is the hallmark of management, it is much more a product of the mind called imagination than the integral vision of the person and the company. It makes the pursuit of organizational excellence compatible with the full development of the person (Serrano, 2017). According to Selart Marcus (2010), The future should be clearly communicated, evaluated, and monitored on an ongoing basis, and stakeholders should be allowed to actively participate in the process. Stating the future of the business provides the ability to uncover threats and opportunities that may affect the company's competitiveness (Serrano, 2017).

Source: Own elaboration.

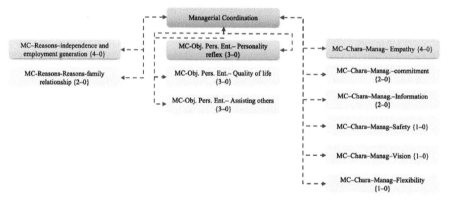

Figure 13.1   Elements of managerial articulation that permeate decision-making.
Source: Own elaboration.

continuation of the family legacy. The desire for independence is based on confidence in their own abilities, income limitations, and the vision of a better future, and the generation of employment is focused on providing opportunities for the inhabitants of the city of Tunja. The managers of these companies are the ones who have created these organizations, and management decision-making is done from the position of founders and managers of these companies. In some t companies, the managers have inherited the responsibility for the company they manage. In this sense, the decisions made at the managerial level assume positive or negative results for the family patrimony. Some managers mention that their personal objectives are focused on generating employment and economic development. In another case, personal objectives refer to the improvement of the quality of life and the company as the vehicle to achieve it. Managers' personality traits also have implications for decision-making; if the manager is diligent and creative, his or her decisions are aimed at ensuring that plans are executed and generating ideas to materialize them into innovations. Managers highlight several aspects that guide and are taken into account in decision-making, such as commitment, security, vision, flexibility to face changes and uncertainty (Daft, 2007), and information as a crucial factor for decision-making (Citroen, 2011).

13.4.2 Managerial skills

The competencies possessed by managers determine their ability to lead the organization and make decisions. This section analyzes managers' opinions regarding the training required to lead, the profiles valued in the sector and the role played by intuition in managerial skills (see Figure 13.2).

Technical, formal, and theoretical knowledge is fundamental for the management of a company. Academic training represents information and this information is an input for decision-making (Mintzberg, 1990). Some managers agree that the managerial profiles of the sector require a combination of academic training and experience and that the information necessary for decision-making does not only come from academic training, but also from experience (Ackert et al. 2010). Regarding the role of intuition in managerial decisions, some managers agree that presentiments and tacit knowledge about the direction of a decision are relevant in the management of companies. Elements of an intuitive model of decision-making are identified in these managers, where intuition is trusted when there is no complete information and some future conditions are foreseen, which generates agility in making a decision (Michael & Pratt, 2007; D. Resnik, 2017). However, some managers believe that it is unfeasible to be guided by intuition alone, as mistakes are bound to be made. These managers' opinions tend towards the bounded rationality model of decision-making, since they prefer to adopt positions and paths to follow according to the available information (Simon, 1987) and not leave everything to intuition.

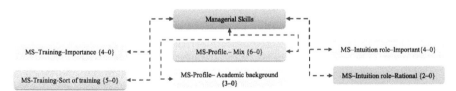

Figure 13.2 Elements of managerial skills that permeate decision-making.
Source: Own elaboration.

13.4.3 Organizational leadership

Organizational leadership involves the way in which the company is organized and the way in which the experience of employees is used to improve its processes (see Figure 13.3). The findings on these aspects and their relationship with the decision-making process are explained below.

Most managers indicated that their organizations have a hierarchical structure that integrates all processes, from the highest level, through the administrative area, to the commercial advisors and assistants. In these small companies, there is no robust organizational structure, in contrast to a medium-sized company that has a more complex structure, where committees are organized and are governed by technical standards. The medium-sized company has hierarchical levels according to its size and processes. In terms of the importance of the organization of the processes, the organization of the processes facilitates decision-making and allows the evaluation of the results, generating relevant and appropriate information to make decisions adjusted to the reality of the company and thus give continuity to the actions previously planned. The experience of the collaborators serves to improve the company's processes; managers show an open attitude to opinions and contributions that allow for better ways of doing things or new ideas. The continuous improvement of processes requires the reduction of limited information about what is happening in the company and in the environment, and this is often thanks to the contributions made by employees.

13.4.4 Organizational strategy

The business strategy reflects the decisions that have been made in the company to sustain itself over time, to increase or maintain the number of customers, and to face market eventualities (see Figure 13.4). These strategies are evaluated periodically, which also reflects the frequency with which the decisions made in the organization are evaluated.

Figure 13.3 Elements of organizational management that permeate decision-making.
Source: Own elaboration.

Figure 13.4 Elements of organizational strategy that permeate decision-making.
Source: Own elaboration.

In this category, managers agree that they have managed to sustain the company over time thanks to perseverance and patience to achieve results in the long term. In this case, perseverance, more than a strategy, is a personal value transferred to the corporate environment that guides the short- and long-term decisions of the managers of these SMEs, commenting that perseverance has largely allowed the success of these companies in the sector. The other sustainability strategies used have been framed in anticipation, good image, diversification, innovation, and business vision; these strategies have provided sustainability over time; therefore, decision-making is based on anticipating changes in the market, building and maintaining a good name, not competing with prices and diversifying and innovating in the product portfolio. With respect to strategies for increasing and maintaining customers, customer loyalty is emphasized through different perspectives. Customer loyalty guarantees greater efficiency and lower sales costs; this process is carried out through market segmentation, maintaining a close relationship, providing differentiating service experiences, and guaranteeing good customer service. In reference to good service, a strategy to increase and maintain customers lies in meeting their expectations and satisfying their needs in terms of time and quality. The above is a valuation framework that allows making decisions regarding the market and the way the organization markets itself; another important aspect to increase customers is to investigate market trends.

In this sense, there is no room for pragmatic decision-making models. Another strategy for customer growth is based on traditional media advertising and an incursion into social networks. However, most managers reported customer growth and maintenance strategies based on customer loyalty and good customer service, rather than strategies based on advertising and communication. Market dynamics demand flexibility and adaptation in decision-making in relation to the market; strategies should be implemented in the design and/or choice of products, in the portfolio, in the price, and in the management of sales seasonality and location strategies, thus ensuring variety for customers, generating satisfaction and loyalty of the company's target market.

The role of uncertainty in decision-making is evident here, so that factors in constant change and sometimes turbulent conditions must be considered (Citroen, 2011; Daft, 2007). The strategies and decisions implemented are evaluated monthly, that is, their effectiveness is verified in the short term, seeking to reduce and mitigate the risk assumed in decision-making. Some managers evaluate their strategies over longer periods of 2, 6, and 12 months. Thus, the evaluation provides opportunities to make new decisions based on the information gathered from the verification of the results of past decisions. This is the final stage of the rational model of decision-making and coincides with the verification that is done in the intuitive model and the learning that is achieved in the pragmatic model.

13.4.5 Managerial challenges

Challenges, limitations, and failures generate different lessons for SME management (see Figure 13.5). Decision-making takes place in difficult environments that, when overcome, have allowed companies to remain in the market.

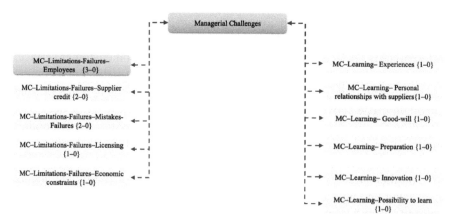

Figure 13.5   Elements of managerial challenges that permeate decision-making.
Source: Own elaboration.

SMEs have had to face the existing economic limitations to sustain the workload, which has led them to make decisions that allow them to comply with labor regulations and, in turn, ensure business growth. Also mentioned are the difficulties in finding qualified labor, in accordance with the functions developed in this industry and employment within the city. Linked to budgetary restrictions, we also find the supply of goods to the construction sector, since these imply large investments in inventory and warehouses that allow the storage of materials; hence, the main limitation is to have the economic resources to sustain the operation. Thus, one of the strategies used by SMEs is to obtain credit from suppliers to leverage the operation. In terms of mistakes and failures, the managers have made different mistakes that have led them to fail; however, it should be noted that most of them have managed to overcome these difficulties and have been able to surpass the break-even point in their companies, improving their decision-making over time, given the learning acquired from the mistakes made and the experience. The managers highlight different lessons learned in the field of management during their years of experience. The lessons learned to reflect good decisions made in the past related to building a good name, the need to have the capacity and experience to manage, innovate constantly, take advantage of opportunities, prepare to achieve goals, and maintain close relationships with suppliers.

13.4.6 Decision-making

This subsection analyzes who participates in decision-making, the distribution of power, pre-evaluation processes and scenarios, the use of indicators, and the difficult decisions made by management. Figure 13.6 shows the subcategories found for these elements.

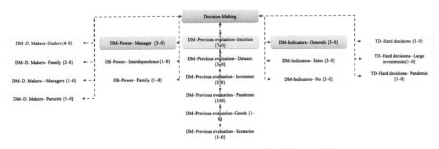

Figure 13.6 Elements involved in decision-making.
Source: Own elaboration.

Regarding the power of the people involved in decision-making, the role of the manager of the organizations is emphasized. The centralization of decision-making at the management and family level is evident. Particularly in the smaller companies the management functions are in the hands of their managers; however, one of the participating companies has 167 employees and, even so, the power of decision-making is in the hands of the founder, which implies that this process has not been fully delegated. In contrast, the manager of the largest company among the research participants indicated a more distributed power in decision-making, and it is evident that the company has a greater hierarchy in departments and a delegation of decision-making to each manager within his area, showing in this company the decentralization of the manager's power.

Regarding the way in which the decision is previously evaluated, most of the managers emphasize that intuition is relevant to determine the paths to take. The intuition used by the managers participating in the research is based on knowledge and information that they possess in a tacit, intangible, unconscious way and is based on previous experiences or observations of the environment. Decisions are evaluated prior to their execution by means of information, figures, data, and statistics. Figures reduce risk by knowing where the problem or opportunity exists. However, when this information is not at hand, intuition plays an important role in making decisions based on the manager's beliefs, experiences, and knowledge.

Forecasting through scenarios is what characterizes the evaluation made by managers to make decisions about the market in favor of the company's sustainability, growth, and competitiveness. The scenarios that are generally considered are those in which things could go worse, so that plans are made to minimize risks, preferring not to plan for overly optimistic scenarios. In the use of indicators to evaluate the decisions taken, two managers argue that they do not use this type of figure. Some managers state that they manage general performance indicators. Managers do not have established specific and exclusive indicators to evaluate decision-making; instead, they use financial, operational, and, above all, commercial indicators to verify the efficiency of decisions. Finally, the most difficult decisions that managers in this sector have had to make have occurred mainly when it has been necessary to dismiss employees. In this sense, labor decisions are difficult for managers because, in some of them, they go against the purposes for which the companies were founded: economic development and employment generation.

13.4.7 Organizational foresight

The future of the business as envisioned by the manager determines the way in which the purposes, opportunities for improvement, expansion, positioning, and succession are planned and defined in 20 years (see Figure 13.7). These elements are analyzed below.

Future purposes and the planning process are carried out mainly through the evaluation of how the company and the market are doing. Future planning and the decisions taken as a result are based on the periodic study of the market and the opportunities and threats that are visualized. This evaluation, as can be seen, depends on indicators and figures that can be obtained statistically; however, this information depends on the observation and reading that can be made of trends. In one of the medium-sized organizations, its manager indicates that planning is carried out in a decentralized manner, considering the opinion of the collaborators; this reflects the distribution of power in decision-making that exists in this organization, since each assistant manager is responsible for the goals, objectives, strategies, and budgets, and therefore, for evaluating the decisions made in each area of the company. In terms of opportunities for improvement, changes that may occur in the market and customer service stand out. Reading the market is one of the main activities of managers, especially if the activity is focused on trade and construction. The focus of improvements in this area is on improving customer service, having variety for the customer, and recognizing, anticipating, and innovating according to market needs. From the organizational perspective, managers recognize that internally there are different opportunities for improvement in customer service and internal processes, as well as the possibilities of organizing the company's processes through certification with international quality standards. The search for quality in processes and customer service

Figure 13.7 Elements of organizational foresight permeate decision-making.
Source: Own elaboration.

will frame management decision-making in the near future. Regarding the 20-year vision, the entrepreneurs show that their projections are in three areas: expansion, position, and succession. Entrepreneurs focus their actions on expanding by increasing the number of branches and warehouses throughout the national territory, which implies making long-term decisions that make possible the resources for such growth.

13.5 Discussion

The process and elements involved in decision-making permeate and influence the manager's decision-making and are fourfold: the information to which he/she has access, his/her personal characteristics, the strategic and value framework he/she possesses, and the organizational perspective he/she has envisioned for the company. In this section, the elements and processes found are explained and discussed and are summarized in Figure 13.8.

The prior evaluation carried out by the manager with this information is based on the use of intuition and reason to plan for difficult scenarios that may arise and decide whether the consequences can be assumed. The evaluation of the results of the decisions is based on the short-term review of financial, commercial, and operational indicators, which feeds back into the process providing new information that increases the manager's experience to make future decisions.

A main characteristic of the decision-making process shown in Figure 13.8 is that most of the managers of these companies have the responsibility and power to make decisions because they have ownership of the business and have not delegated this responsibility to their collaborators. In these SMEs, it has been found that decision-making tends to be concentrated in the manager or founder, which can lead to errors and delays in the processes (Gastón, 2017; Paz et al., 2020). However, these types of bottlenecks derived from the centralization of power were not found in this research, which can be explained by the small size of some companies and the quick response of managers. In medium-sized companies, these problems are not observed either, given that they have delegated a little more responsibility for decision-making in each area and have committees to make larger decisions.

The first group of elements related to decision-making is information. It highlights the influence of different sources of information such as constant feedback from employees, customers, and family involvement. Likewise, figures and statistical data and the manager's experiences, observations, and tacit knowledge play a very important role in decision-making. On the

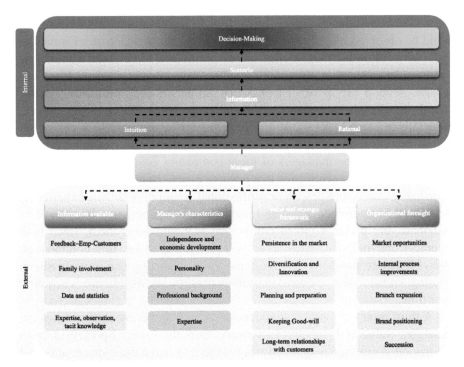

Figure 13.8 Elements involved in the managerial decision-making process in small businesses.
Source: Own elaboration.

other hand, some of the organizations are family organizations, as has been mentioned throughout the document, which is why the opinions of spouses and children are relevant when making decisions. Among the participating managers, it was observed that there are roles that are effectively defined and that decisions are made by family consensus, considering the opinions of all, and taking advantage of their strengths (rational, intuitive, numerical). This research shows that managers use information when they have access to it. However, they recognize that they do not always have the resources and time to access it, which is why there is limited rationality in their decisions (Simon, 1987; Gigalová, 2017). In this sense, the importance of intuition, experience, and knowledge in the decision-making process in these companies is ratified. Faced with the importance of experiences, observations, and tacit knowledge, it has been stated that intuition plays a fundamental role when previously evaluating the decision, some circumstances require relying on intuition when there is not enough time and information. In the results of this research, it could be observed that the use of intuition is not the absence of information, but it is based on tacit knowledge, observations, and experience acquired by the manager in his trajectory.

The second group of elements that influence decision-making corresponds to the characteristics of the manager (see Figure 13.8), which, especially in a family organization, create shared meanings in which his or her image, presence, and mental structure permeate the decision-making process (Gastón, 2017). The managers of these companies base their decisions and their interest on the search for independence, generating employment, their personality characteristics, their professional training, and their experience. Between the importance of professional training vs. experience, it is identified that managers prefer a mixed component that integrates them, since both technical and practical knowledge is equally important, this combination allows for more structured decision-making, considering that in professional training, knowledge is acquired in training centers, and experience is acquired over time.

A third group of elements influencing decision-making encompasses the managers' value and strategic framework. Here the value of perseverance in the market is emphasized, which has led them to make decisions to stay and adapt to changing circumstances. For them, it is also relevant to maintain a good name and make decisions thinking about doing things right to maintain their reputation. In terms of strategy, managers prefer to anticipate and prepare for market needs, product diversification, and innovation, in addition to knowing, building customer loyalty, and serving customers well to maintain long-term relationships with them; these elements are key and have a direct influence on the growth of companies and their permanence over time.

The fourth group of elements that influence decision-making is organizational foresight, that is, the long-term elements that managers consider relevant for the organization. In this regard, managers make decisions thinking primarily about market opportunities, internal process improvement opportunities, branch expansion, brand positioning, and the succession of the company to the next generation.

Once these elements are combined in management, it was observed that managerial decision-making in these organizations is carried out through a previous evaluation with scarce information, knowledge, experience, and a relevant role of intuition. Thus, managers are identified as having a combined use of a limited rationality model of decision-making, when they have access to information and it is possible to interpret it, and an intuitive model when this information is scarce. Through data and intuition, managers come up with scenarios of what might happen and the plans they must deal with them. The choice of scenarios corresponds to the decision-making process of the rational model and bounded rationality, in the sense of analyzing different options of outcomes prior to making the decision (Bonome, 2009; Uzonwanne, 2016); however, the final decision is made with the intuition of what can happen according to the available data and information. As can be seen in Figure 13.8, the decision-making process consists of four moments: consolidating information, performing a prior evaluation, making the decision, and performing outcome evaluation. Thus, the smaller the company, the simpler and less structured the decision-making process. In medium-sized companies, decision-making becomes more complex and requires delegating some decisions to area assistant managers for the organization's decision-making. Managers evaluate the results of decisions in the short term, mainly monthly, due to the seasonal nature of sales and the changing dynamics of the construction sector. To evaluate, they do not have established indicators for decision-making, but rely on financial, operational, and commercial indicators to verify the success or failure of the decisions made, and thus generate learning for future decisions. Finally, The main limitation is given by the size of the sample and the specificity of the case studies, which does not allow extrapolation of the results, but it does allow an approximation of what can occur in small companies in management decision-making.

13.6 Conclusions

According to the results, it is concluded that the decision-making carried out by the managers of the SMEs in this study is characterized by being centralized in the manager in the case of the smallest companies, and with a partial delegation to the assistant managers of the larger companies. Decisions in these companies are based mainly on feedback from employees, customers, and family. It is based on the consolidation of data, internal and external statistics, and the experiences, observations, and tacit knowledge of the manager.

Through the results, it is possible to identify the elements that intervene in the decision-making process, which are framed in four groups: available information, manager's characteristics, value, strategic framework, and organizational perspective. Likewise, it is established that, according to the size of the organization, the limitations of economic resources and access to information are the most relevant elements in the decision-making process.

Managers make the final decision using intuitive and reasoning processes, with the limited information available, and make a prior assessment through different scenarios.

Among the main findings, it was found that the valuation and strategic framework involved in decision-making is based on the importance for the manager to persevere in the market despite the circumstances and the importance of maintaining a good name and reputation. In terms of management strategies, managers value anticipating and preparing for market needs, prefer to diversify and innovate in the product portfolio and prioritize the maintenance of long-term relationships with customers. On the other hand, organizational foresight as an element that intervenes in decision-making, frames the search for opportunities, the options for improving internal processes, the long-term vision in the scalability of operations, the best positioning of the brand, and the succession of the business to the next generation.

In view of these findings, future work is recommended to investigate how the decision-making process is, and the elements that affect it, in large companies. In this way, it is possible to understand how decision-making varies at the corporate governance level and at the management level of these large structures. In turn, it is relevant to understand the role of risk management certification and implementation processes within the decision-making process.

Acknowledgments

This research was funded by Universidad Pedagogica y Tecnologica de Colombia, grant number SGI 3323, and Red Sistemas Inteligentes y Expertos Modelos Computacionales Iberoamericanos (SIEMCI), project number 522RT0130, in Programa Iberoamericano de Ciencia y Tecnología para el Desarrollo (CYTED).

References

Ackert, L. F., Iglesia, B. K., & Tkac, P. A. (2010). Un examen experimental de heurístico-based toma de decisiones en un entorno financiero. 135–149.

Ackert, L. F., Church, B. K., & Tkac, P. A. (2010). An experimental examination of heuristic-based decision making in a financial setting. Journal of Behavioral Finance, 11(3), 135–149. https://doi.org/10.1080/15427560.2010.507155.

Al-Tarawneh H. A. (2012). The main factors beyond decision making.Journal of Management Research, 4(1), 1–23.

Antunes, F., & Costa J. P. (2012). Integrating decision support and social networks.advances in Human-Computer Interaction, 2012, 1–10. 10.1155/2012/574276

Archer, S. (2014). The structure of management decision theory. The Academy of Management Journal, 7(4), 269–287.

Argandoña, A. (2011). La ética y la toma de decisiones en la empresa. Universia Business Review, 30, 22–31. https://doi.org/1698-5117

Argandoña, A. (2010). Las virtudes en una teoría de la acción humana. In Research paper (Vol. 3). https://doi.org/880

Arrendondo Trapero, F., \& Vázquez Parra, J. (2013). Un modelo de análisis racional para la toma de decisiones gerenciales, desde la perspectiva elsteriana. Cuadernos de Administración, 26(46), 135–158.

Baez-Palencia, D., Olazabal-Lugo, M., & Romero-Muñoz, J. (2019). Toma de decisiones empresariales a través de la media ordenada ponderada. Inquietud Empresarial, 19(2), 11–23. https://doi.org/10.19053/01211048. 9843

Beatrice Kovacs (1990). The decision-making process for library collections: case studies in four types of libraries. Greenwood Publishing Group. 208

Blanco-Mesa, F. (2020). La ciencia de la decisión. Rev. UIS Ingenieria 19, I–V.

Blanco-Mesa, F., León-Castro, E., & Acosta-Sandoval, A. (2020). Toma de decisiones estratégicas en entornos inciertos. Revista de Métodos Cuantitativos para la Economía y la Empresa 30, 79–96. https://doi.org/10.46661 /REVMETODOSCUANTECONEMPRESA.3845

Blanco-Mesa, F., & Merigó, J. M. (2020). Bonferroni distances and their application in group decision making. Cybernetics and Systems, 51(1), 27–58. https://doi.org/10.1080/01969722.2019.1660540

Blanco-Mesa, F., Rivera-Rubiano, J., Patiño-Hernandez, X., & Martinez-Montaña, M. (2019). The importance of enterprise risk management in large companies in colombia. Technological and Economic Development of Economy, 25(4). https://doi.org/10.3846/tede.2019.9380

Blanco-Mesa, F., Merigó, J. M., Gil-Lafuente, A. M. (2017). Fuzzy decision making: A bibliometric-based review. Journla of Intelligent Fuzzy Systems. 32, 2033–2050. https://doi.org/10.3233/JIFS-161640

Bonome, M. (2009). La racionalidad en la toma de decisiones: análisis de la teoría de la decisión de Herbert A. Simon.

Burke, R., & Demirag, I. (2019). Risk transfer and stakeholder relationships in Public Private Partnerships. Pages 28-43. doi.org/10.1016/j.accfor.2016.06.004.

Citroen, C. L. (2011). The role of information in strategic decision-making. International Journal of Information Management, 31(6), 493–501. https://doi.org/10.1016/j.ijinfomgt.2011.02.005

Chaabouni, A., & Yahia, I. Ben. (2014). Contribution of ERP to the decision-making process through knowledge management. Journal of Decision Systems, 23(3), 37–41. https://doi.org/10.1080/12460125.2014.886498

Cohen, Michael D., March, James G., \& Olsen, J. P. (2011). El bote de basura como modelo de elección organizacional. Gestión y Política Pública, 20(2), 247–290.

Daft, R. (2007). Teoría y diseño organizacional. In Teoría y diseño organizacional.

Dailey Robert. (1990). Comportamiento organizacional (Primera ed). Edinburgh Business School.

Fayol, H. (1986). Administracion industrial y general (3 ed.).

Fierro Celis, F. A. (2014). Errores comunes en la toma de decisiones estrategicas, un enfoque desde la racionalidad. Revista de Estudios Avanzados de Liderazgo, 1(3), 78–100.

García, J. C. (2014). Estrategias gerenciales para el proceso de toma de decisiones en la solución de conflictos laborales.

García-Solarte, M. (2015). Formulación de un modelo de liderazgo desde las teorías organizacionales. Entramado, 11(1), 60–79. https://doi.org/10.18041/entramado.2015v11n1.21111

Gigalová, V. (2017). Intuition and managerial decision-making 1. Human Affiairs, 27(3), 301–316. https://doi.org/10.1515/humaff-2017-0025

Gigante V. (2017). Racionalidad y razonabilidad una actualización de la toma de decisiones desde la economía del comportamiento, las neurociencias y la teoría evolutiva.

Harrison, E. F., & Francisco, S. (1996). A process perspective on strategic decision making environmental assessment. Management Decision, 34(1), 46–53.

Hernandez, R., Collado, C., & Baptista, P. (2014). Metodologia de la Investigacion (McGRAW-HILL (Ed.); 6th ed.).

Hess, J. D., Bacigalupo, A. C., Voyageur, U., & Uu, E. E. (2011). La mejora de las decisiones y los procesos de toma de decisiones a través de la aplicación de habilidades de inteligencia emocional, 49(5), 710–721. https://doi.org/10.1108/00251741111130805

Hess, J. D., & Bacigalupo, A. C. (2011). Enhancing decisions and decision-making processes through the application of emotional intelligence skills. Management Decision, 49(5), 710–721. https://doi.org/10.1108/00251741 111130805

Intezari, A., & Pauleen, D. J. (2017). La conceptualización de Gestión Wise toma de decisiones: un enfoque de la teoría fundamentada. 00(0).

Jones, T. M. (1996). Ethical decision making by individuals in organizations: an issue-contingent model. Academy of Management Review, 16(2), 366–395. https://doi.org/10.5465/amr.1991.4278958

Khatri, N., & Alvin, N. (2000). The role of intuition in strategic decision making. Human Relations, 53(1), 57–86. https://doi.org/10.1177/001872 6700531004

Lambarry, F., Rivas, L., & María, P. (2010). Modelos de decisión bajo una perspectiva de análisis de sus procesos. Universidad {\&} Empresa, 12(18), 146–173.

Mckenzie, J., Winkelen, C. Van, Grewal, S., Mckenzie, J., & Winkelen, C. Van. (2011). Developing organisational decision-making capability: a knowledge manager's guide. Journal of Knowledge Management, 15(3), 403–421. https://doi.org/10.1108/13673271111137402

Moody Paul E. (1983). Decision making: proven methods for better decisions (McGraw Hill Higher Education (ed.)).

Moody Paul E. (1991). Toma de decisiones gerenciales (McGraw Hill Higher Education (ed.)).

Michael, E., & Pratt, G. (2007). Exploring intuition and its role in managerial decision making. Academy of Management Review, 32(1), 33–54. https://doi.org/10.5465/amr.2007.23463682

Mintzberg, H. (1990). El trabajo del administrador Folklore y Realidad.

Mintzberg, H. (1889). Mintzbert y la Direccion (Diaz de Santos (Ed.)).

Provis, C. (2010). Virtuous decision making for business ethics. Journal of Business Ethics, 91, 3–16. https://doi.org/10.1007/s10551-010-0564-4

Pulgarín Molina, S. A., & Rivera R., H. A. (2012). Las herramientas estratégicas: un apoyo al proceso de toma de decisiones gerenciales. Criterio Libre, 10(1900–0642), 89–114. https://doi.org/10.18041/1900-0642/criteriolibre .16.1165

Riaz, M. N., & Riaz, M. A. (2014). En las organizaciones modernas toma de decisiones es considerada como la tarea total de un administrador (Singh, 2001). decisiones directivas afectan directamente a los resultados personales; subordina. 100-112, 24(2).

Riaz, M. N., Riaz, M. A., & Batool, N. (2014). Managerial decision-making styles as predictors of personal and organizational outcomes of in-service employees. Journal of Behavioural Sciences, 24(2), 100–116.

Rodríguez Cruz Yunier. (2018). Gestión de información y del conocimiento para la toma de decisiones organizacionales. Anales de Investigación, 11, 150–163.

Resnik, D. (2017). The role of intuition in risk/benefit decision-making in human subjects research. Accountability in Research, 24(1), 1–29. https://doi.org/10.1080/08989621.2016.1198978

Resnik, D. B. (2017). The Role of Intuition in Risk / Benefit Decision-Making in Human Subjects Research. Accountability in Research, 24(1), 1–29.

Rolland, & Nicolas. (2004). Knowledge management impacts on decision making process. Journal of Knowledge Management, 8(1), 20–31. https://doi.org/10.1108/13673270410523880

Rodríguez, Y., & Pinto, M. (2019). Evolución, particularidades y carácter informacional de la toma de decisiones organizacionales. Revista Cubana de Información en Ciencias de la Salud. Infomed.

Sajjad, H., & Francesca M. (2016). Unfolding critical events and strategic decisions: The role of spatial and temporal cognition. Management Decision, 54(7), 1813–1842

Sayegh, L., Anthony, W. P., & Perrewé, P. L. (2004). Managerial decision-making under crisis: The role of emotion in an intuitive decision process. Human Resource Management Review, 14(2), 179–199. https://doi.org/10.1016/j.hrmr.2004.05.002

Serrano, G. (2017). Competencias directivas y virtudes: un camino a la excelencia. Estudios Gerenciales, 33(143), 208–216. https://doi.org/10.1016/j.estger.2017.03.004

Selart Marcus. (2010). Una perspectiva de liderazgo en la toma de decisiones. https://doi.org/10.13140/RG.2.1.1471.1526

Stanovich, K. E., \& West, R. F. (2000). Individual differences in reasoning: Implications for the rationality debate? Behavioral and Brain Sciences, 23(5), 645–665. http://dx.doi.org/10.1017/CBO9780511808098.026

Simon, H. (1987). Making Management Decisions: the role of intuition and emotion. Academy of Management Perspectives, 1(1), 57–64. https://doi.org/10.5465/ame.1987.4275905

Uzonwanne, F. C. (2016). Rational model of decision making. global encyclopedia of public administration, Public Policy, and Governance, 1–6. https://doi.org/10.1007/978-3-319-31816-5_2474-1

Vaiman, V., Scullion, H., & Collings, D. (2012). Talent management decision making. Management Decision, 50(5), 925–941. https://doi.org/10.1108/00251741211227663

Zollo, L., Matteo, M., Cristiano, P., & Pellegrini, M. M. (2017). What sparks ethical decision making the interplay between moral intuition. Etical Bussines, 145, 681–700. https://doi.org/10.1007/s10551-016-3221-8

Zollo, L., Yoon, S., Rialti, R., & Ciappei, C. (2018). Ethical consumption and consumers' decision making: the role of moral intuition. Management Decision, 56(3), 692–710. https://doi.org/10.1108/MD-10-2016-0745

14

Analysis of Innovative Behavior in Long-term Microenterprises: A Perspective on Tunja Retail

Juliana Cortés Hernández[1], Fabio Blanco-Mesa[1], Ernesto León-Castro[2], and Héctor Adrian Castro-Páez[1]

[1]Universidad Pedagogica y Tecnologica de Colombia, Colombia
[2]Unidad Navojoa, Instituto Tecnologico de Sonora, Mexico

Abstract

The main objective is to analyze the innovative behavior in long-lived microenterprises with more than 5 years of existence in the retail trade of Tunja (Boyacá, Colombia). Frequency analysis is performed on the innovative behavior variable through the construction of relative position scales by quartiles. Likewise, the existence of a relationship between innovative behavior and time spent in the market was determined through the formulation of hypotheses. The findings show that innovative behavior has a low level. There is an intermediate scope of employee engagement and the generation and implementation of ideas, and less in leadership and the work environment. It is highlighted that innovative behavior presents a better level in those organizations in which light innovations are introduced, although there is no significant relationship between innovative behavior and time spent in the market. Finally, competent organizations and bodies have much to do to foster a pedagogy and culture about the importance of innovative behavior.

Keywords: Innovative behavior, long-lived microenterprises, retail companies

14.1 Introduction

In the competitive global marketplace, innovation is vital to a company's longevity. To this end, organizations are looking for new and alternative ways to motivate innovation (Cefis et al., 2020; Cefis & Marsili, 2006) in employees The development of innovations and good behavior toward this (Opoku et al., 2019), increases the probability of business survival since it is more feasible that these capabilities become a competitive advantage that prevents the closure of organizations (Confecamaras, 2019).

Becoming an innovative company is not easy; it is essential to have the right people and create an environment that encourages and promotes behaviors (Camps, 2015). One of the main factors that motivate innovation is represented in the exchange of knowledge among employees and the degree of perceived equity (Akram et al., 2020) However, this is determined by factors such as the intensity of knowledge and capital that differ according to the size of the business (Blanco-Mesa & Baier-Fuentes, 2017a).

According to Beltran and Pulido (2012), companies of not very large sizes have simple structures and fast communication channels, which allow them to quickly adapt to innovations. Thus, to generate this innovative dynamic, a previous phase is necessary that involves the modification or disposition of behaviors with the will to transform, called innovative behavior. This behavior is defined as the attitude of workers to establish new changes or related improvements to obtain benefits as the result of the main business activity in this sense, it must be important that companies create, among their processes, products, or organizational levels, some differentiator between competition that minimizes the probability of disappearing from the market (Guzman Pedraza, 2015).

Since this reality can be homogeneous for companies in the current environment, it is pertinent to investigate whether innovation and people's behavior have contributed to it. In this way, the focus of the study subjects is developed in the city of Tunja (Boyacá-Colombia). Trade within the service sector is the main activity that takes place in this city. Retail trade in non-specialized establishments with an assortment composed mainly of food, beverages or tobacco covers 21.8% of the most significant market share Also, the business fabric of the city is mainly made up of microenterprises with 98% where 62.9% of microenterprises are less than five years old, 36.5% are between 5 and 25 years old, and 0.6% are over 25 years old Thus, the motivation of the study derives from the representativeness of retail activity, the importance of innovation as a strategy for business survival and the theoretical gap in the study of innovative behavior in long-lived minority microenterprises in the region (Tunja Chamber of Commerce, 2019; Castro et al., 2019; Tunja Chamber of Commerce, 2019).

In this sense, the main objective is to analyze the innovative behavior in long-lived microenterprises, with more than 5 years in the retail trade of Tunja (Boyacá, Colombia). The methodological design was cross-sectional and non-experimental to analyze the identification of attitudes aimed at promoting innovative behaviors in long-lived micro-enterprises of commerce. Relative position scales by quartiles were constructed to perform frequency analysis of the innovative behavior variable and formulate hypotheses to determine the existence of a relationship between the innovative behavior and the time spent in the market. The results show that the study units have introduced slight innovations in the product, around the implementation of the home delivery service, the inclusion of information and communication technologies – ICT, the introduction of new sales services, the voucher redemption system, and the opening of a new service point. Likewise, innovative behavior has a low level. There is an intermediate level of employee engagement and the generation and implementation of ideas, and less in leadership and the work environment. It should be noted that the level of innovative behavior is higher in those organizations in which slight innovations were introduced. However, no significant relationship was found between innovative behavior and time to market. The study aims to contribute to knowledge in an analysis that makes the association of some variables and concepts in populations for which no evidence was found.

This document consists of five sections. The first addresses the literature review through two basic concepts, innovation, and innovative behavior. The second describes the methodological design of the research and conceptualizes the selection criteria for the population and the sample. The third presents the results of innovative behavioral traits and the relationship between innovative behavior and time spent in the market. Finally, the main conclusions and discussion of the findings are highlighted.

14.2 Theoretical Framework

The article starts from the main axis of innovation and its development through the study of non-intensive innovations, innovation in services, and innovative behavior. In this way, the innovation and services section include the definition and classifications of innovation, non-intensive innovations, innovation in the service sector, the definition of services, and dimensions of innovation in this sector. The next section deals with the definition and determinants of innovative behavior.

14.2.1 Innovation

Innovation is a term widely used and defined in different fields, it is essential for long-term development and success in organizations (Xing et al., 2020), It has been conceptualized and studied from various perspectives, especially the approach to innovative behavior from the exchange of knowledge, induced by motivation (Arsawan et al., 2020), in part also by the factors that determine the context at any given time. Recently, the Oslo Manual specified innovation as the placing on the market of a new or improved product or process, or a combination thereof, that differs significantly from the organization's previous products or processes and that has been put on the market available to potential users or put into use by the organization (OECD & EUROSTAT, 2018). Just as the concept of innovation has several definitions, the classification of innovation depends on the aspect, conception, approach, or perspective from which it is approached (Klosiewicz-Górecka, 2015).

Product innovation is the placing on the market of a new or improved good or service that differs significantly from the company's previous goods or services (OECD & EUROSTAT, 2018), refers to competitive business advantage, in some cases Technological that offers strengths from knowledge and management capacity (Lestari et al., 2020). Innovation organizations must be open, not just for that is working in R&D, promote from each of the functions of the employees, to promote novel ideas (Javed et al., 2019). Like this, the innovation involves the introduction or redefinition of the function of producing goods and services from an innovation strategy and transformational leadership (Hansen & Pihl-Thingvad, 2019), from the distribution, logistics, marketing, sales, and after-sales service functions. Innovations in products and processes are the most recurrent and towards which the other types of innovation focus. Thus, innovations in the market, organizational, incremental, radical, technological, or commercial, seek to improve processes and the final product, from which it is expected to obtain a greater benefit for the organization.

The concept of innovation and the types of innovation defined generally refer to changes and introductions involving broad levels of research and relatively differential changes. The traditional definition of innovation does not consider the optimization of resources, creativity, ingenuity, the appropriation of existing knowledge, or the addition of variants in products and services, as essential characteristics to solve consumer problems (Blanco-Mesa & Baier-Fuentes, 2017). However, the boundary between what is a change and what is not an innovation is subjective, because it is relative to the context and capabilities of each company. An improvement in an organization could represent a minor change for an innovation and development (R&D) intensive company but be a significant difference for a less R&D-intensive microenterprise (OECD & EUROSTAT, 2018). As a result, new perspectives on innovation emerge that include hidden features as a response to the traditional innovation model, which does not perceive or measure these changes in innovation (Blanco-Mesa & Baier-Fuentes, 2017).

In this sense, a concept of innovation-oriented toward non-intensive innovations is proposed. These provide the vision of effective and economical solutions to the problems and immediate needs of the environment, with differentiating added value and economic results for organizations. They carry out a bibliographic review in which through three types of non-intensive innovations (frugal, inverse, and (Blanco-Mesa & Baier-Fuentes, 2017) soft) they abstracted the generic aspects common in them and built a definition of light innovation. As a result, they conceive this innovation as a process that optimizes existing resources for the generation of differentiated and affordable products and services, based on creativity, the transfer, and dissemination of knowledge among different stakeholders; to create value through the solution of problems and social and organizational needs, aimed at specific and underserved markets.

Light innovation in the context of non-intensive innovations was not a type of innovation, but an area for types of innovation. It is pertinent to approach the scope of innovations from a light perspective in service microenterprises since due to their size and what this entails, it is not easy for them to implement innovations from the traditional perspective: large R&D investments.

Although there is currently an approach that recognizes the commonalities of innovation among different sectors of the economy, it is also stated that organizational culture is linked to innovative behavior, which affects employee performance (Rizki et al., 2019). Through innovation research, differences between the nature of manufacturing activities and services have highlighted the importance of developing innovative models for service companies. In this sense, the micro-retailers associated with the service sector studied here experience particular innovation dynamics that merit a specific analysis (Guzmán Pedraza et al., 2012; Miles, 2008).

14.2.2 Innovation in services

The diversity of service activities means that innovations in this type of organization and innovation processes take various forms. Only a small segment of service innovation fits the typical model in which innovation is organized and led by formal R&D and production engineering departments (Miles, 2008) in especially the industrial and manufacturing sector, found mainly patents for these, and trademarks for service companies (Taques et al., 2021), a situation that may favor more those that produce tangibles than those that offer services.

According to the service sector it has been perceived as not susceptible to innovations in the absence of a perception of tangibility and difficulties in measuring innovations. However, the observation of business practices has led to the conclusion that innovations can take place in all areas of the economy. Innovation in services is a process that (Klosiewicz-Górecka, 2015) consists more of the exchange of knowledge for the achievement of competitive advantages, which is structured in culture, relationships, and incentives (Oyemomi et al., 2019), especially from open innovation in ecosystems of technology transfer and knowledge exchange (Yun & Liu, 2019).

In general, the most important objectives of the introduction of innovations are the growth of sales revenue and the reduction of costs. In most cases, technologies created in the industrial sector are used and used creatively to establish innovative services (Klosiewicz-Górecka, 2015).

According to there are four main dimensions that describe the study of innovation in service: service concept, interaction with the customer, organizational or management system, and technological options. The first focuses on creating a new service in a particular market and generating a new value proposition. Many innovations involve intangible features and others involve new ways of solving organizational problems. The second reveals changes in the way customers participate in the design, production, and consumption of the service. The actions and resources provided by the client include their physical, mental, and emotional characteristics. The third considers the need for an organizational structure and an adequate management system that allows employees to perform new jobs and, consequently, to develop and offer innovative services. In addition, new services may require (Den Hertog, 2000; Li & Hsu, 2016a; Nardelli, 2017) different organizational forms, capabilities, and interpersonal skills and can design an organization and empower employees to leave room for innovations and unconventional solutions to practical problems. Therefore, the management system within service innovation is considered here as a basis for the study of innovative behaviors in microenterprises. The fourth highlights that ICTs are particularly important for services because they enable greater efficiency in information processing. Clearly, service innovation is possible without technological innovation. However, there are broad relationships between technology and service innovation, ranging from technology that plays an enabling role to supply-driven innovation or technology.

Innovation in each dimension involves particular sources of creativity and knowledge, which raises organizational and management problems. Many service innovations require some combination of these dimensions, an innovation that mainly involves one dimension can trigger the need for changes in other dimensions Thus, in the organizational context, innovative behavior frames any attitude oriented toward the establishment of changes, present in the phase prior to the development of innovations (Miles, 2008).

14.2.3 Innovative behavior

Innovative behavior is an important asset that enables an organization to succeed in a dynamic business environment (Guzmán Pedraza et al., 2012b; Yuan & Woodman, 2010a). Innovative behavior is the creation, introduction and intentional application of new ideas within a work role, group, or organization, to benefit any of them. Likewise, Guzmán argues that the attitude of the workers aims to establish changes that may be novel or related to improvements in the production process, both in the manufacturing and service industries to obtain a benefit in the internal structure of the organization, the business fabric or the results of the main activity. Studies on innovative behavior have been related to the work environment, the development of employees' skills in the generation and implementation of ideas, the influence of leadership, and the commitment of employees in the execution of their tasks (In this sense, taking as a starting point the bibliographic review and the comprehensive approach, it is considered pertinent to return to these four aspects as the main determinants of innovative behavior (Janssen, 2000; Guzman Pedraza, 2015)

14.2.4 Workspace

This is an aspect that allows obtaining detailed knowledge of the situation of the organization at a strategic and operational level Given its dynamic and influenceable character, in it, certain changes are generated that motivate innovative behaviors (Guzman Pedraza, 2015; Noefer et al., 2009). In general, a worker can be influenced to modify their behaviors through their internal and external relationships (Slåtten, 2011).

From an intrinsic position of the individual, emotions determine work environments, but they arise only until one evaluates or tries to understand what is seen or heard. Environmental assessment is a causal explanation of emotional processes. Emphasizing the feeling of joy stems from positive experiences or thoughts about the organizational environment in which you work. Therefore, it is reasonable to assume that joy helps a person to be more creative or innovative. Similarly, a person may also experience stress-related emotions because it is often difficult or impossible to meet all expectations. While some roles may lead an individual to perceive the task as a source of stress, it is also possible for the worker to perceive the role as an opportunity for visibility and career advancement, and even for fun (Al-hawari et al., 2019; Slåtten & Mehmetoglu, 2011a; Slåtten, 2011).

From the external position of the individual, the adequate provision of organizational resources is a manifestation of support for innovation. These resources include the provision of equipment, facilities, time, job security, development and training perspectives, open information policies, and work-life participation or balance. Another determining factor of the work environment is workgroups, where a workgroup provides cooperation and collaboration, the individual is more likely to see the organization as an innovation support system (Pundt et al., 2010; Scott & Bruce, 1994; Scott & Bruce, 1994).

Therefore, if the organization treats workers well and provides adequate rewards for performance and commitment, comfortable working conditions, or job equity, they correspond to the achievement of organizational objectives (Pundt et al., 2010; Janssen, 2000).

14.2.5 Generation and implementation of ideas

Innovative behavior is a process that begins with recognizing problems and generating ideas or solutions. This seeks the sponsorship of the idea and attempts to create a coalition of collaborators to build a prototype of innovation, which will be disseminated, produced in volume, institutionalized, or commercialized Employees can generate ideas by exploring opportunities, identifying performance gaps, or producing solutions, which are represented in new products, services, processes, or entry into new markets. Most ideas should be promoted, as they often don't match what's used in your workgroup or organization. Even if ideas have legitimacy, resistance to change tends to appear at this stage, as for most ideas it is uncertain whether their benefits will exceed the cost of developing and implementing them. In the implementation phase, employees can play a valuable role in demonstrating a strong personal commitment to an idea to persuade others of its value or invest effort in developing, testing, and marketing the idea (Scott & Bruce, 1994; De Jong & Den Hartog, 2007; De Jong & Den Hartog, 2007).

On the other hand, creativity is seen as an essential element of innovative behavior and stands out (Nederveen et al., 2010) in the first phase where problems are recognized and new or adopted ideas are generated, in response to a perceived need. Creativity is an intrinsic point of view of the individual that is linked to the interaction inherent in the work of contact with the client (De Jong & Den Hartog, 2007; Oldham & Cummings, 2014; Scott & Bruce, 1994; West, 2002; Yuan & Woodman, 2010). The participation of customer groups influences the generation as well as the implementation of ideas (Linde et al., 2021), specifically, customer participation in services can present opportunities that encourage employees to generate new ideas, which can be transformed into innovative behaviors. In addition, it can facilitate the implementation of ideas by participating in prototyping during deployment (Li & Hsu, 2016).

14.2.6 Leadership

Leadership focuses on the behaviors used to directly influence followers. There is consensus that managers are the support that companies give to employees, where they can sometimes act as leaders, to promote employee alignment and company goals through observation and communication.

Leadership is critical in the innovation process, as it requires participatory or collaborative leadership styles where creativity is promoted in the actors (Yukl et al., 2002; Guzmán Pedraza et al., 2012b; Nederveen et al., 2010; Pundt et al., 2010b; Scott & Bruce, 1994).

Transactional and transformational leadership approaches have gained popularity. The available research on the relationship between leader behavior and innovation has approached transactional and transformational leadership transactional leadership focuses on an exchange relationship in which the leader makes clear what he or she expects from followers. This leadership is based on reward, where it is clarified what the follower must do to be rewarded and what are the management components with which performance is monitored and corrective measures are taken when problems arise.

Transactional leadership can be perceived as controlling and demotivating, causing less innovative behavior Transformational leadership is characterized by the leader motivating followers to identify with the organization's goals and interests to go beyond expected levels of job performance Transformational leadership is style that transforms followers to rise above their self-interest by altering their morale, ideas, interests, and values, motivating them to perform better than initially expected (De Jong & Den Hartog, 2007; Nederveen et al., 2010; Slåtten & Mehmetoglu, 2015; Nederveen et al., 2010). In this sense, transformational leadership is assumed to foster creativity, as leaders here encourage followers to see problems in new ways and help them develop their potential by modifying their patterns to generate ideas (De Jong & Den Hartog, 2007).

14.2.7 Employee engagement

Engagement is like the strength of identification and participation of a person in an organization. This is characterized by three psychological factors: the desire to remain in the organization; the willingness to exert considerable effort and acceptance of their goals and values. The commitment of the worker is conceived as a positive, satisfactory, and work-like state of mind, which is characterized by vigor, dedication, and absorption. Vigor refers to the level of energy and mental resilience while working, the willingness to invest effort in the organization, and persistence in the face of difficulties. Dedication refers to a sense of enthusiasm, inspiration, pride, and challenge. Absorption captures the state of being focused and deeply absorbed at work (Porter et al., 1974; Slåtten & Mehmetoglu, 2011b; Schaufeli et al., 2002).

Likewise, commitment is a state of mind that is associated with the experience of positive emotions. The positive emotional state has two effects that can generate innovative behavior. First, people who experience a positive state of mind are more optimistic about opportunities at work, more sociable, and display helpful service-oriented behaviors. Second, positive emotions are associated with creativity. Therefore, an employee's positive emotional state helps them to be more creative and influences their innovative behavior (Slåtten & Mehmetoglu, 2011a).

Today, both the nature of work and the workforce change, where engaged employees can be a key to gaining a competitive advantage. This is especially true when it is shown that engagement produces effects on the levels of analysis of interest to management The findings show that employee engagement is closely related to innovative behavior For this (Macey & Schneider, 2008;

Oyemomi et al., 2019) reason, it is necessary to make organizational investments in social capital to promote influences on the engagement of service employees, your job performance and organizational behavior (O'Cass et al., 2013; Slåtten et al., 2019).

14.3 Methodology

The methodology used for this research is shown below. First, the case study is described, followed by the method and instruments used.

14.3.1 Case study

The study is conducted in retail micro-businesses that had the characteristic of being long-lived. Therefore, the terms microenterprise, retail, and business longevity are defined. Companies have been classified according to the number of employees, sales volume, the volume of income, and, in some cases, the economic sector where they are located About the economic activity of the retail trade, is defined as the purchase and sale without transformation, of goods or products, intended for consumption or personal or domestic use (final consumer). For its part, business longevity is generally considered as the ability of an organization to maintain its continuity and adapt to changes in its operating environment In this sense, for any company to be maintained, it must be continuous, stable, and durable. Business longevity is an aspect that takes time to ensure that the organization constitutes a trajectory in the market Time is a vital feature of longevity, but there is no single criterion that specifies when, over time, an organization is considered long-lived. According to this trip, it is due to the presence of more than 25 years in the market (González Alvarado, 2005; DANE, 2019; Rivera, 2012; Napolitano et al., 2015; Galadanchi & Bakar, 2018; Collins & Porras, 1994).

Based on the above, to determine the unit of study, the specification of the business activity, the formal registration with the chamber of commerce, and the time spent in the market have been taken into account. In this sense, the population is defined from the database acquired through the Tunja Chamber of Commerce, which reported 79 retail microenterprises in non-specialized establishments with an assortment composed mainly of food, beverages, or tobacco; With more than 25 years of permanence in the market (counted to December 31, 2019) and active registration in the Chamber of Commerce. When developing the fieldwork, a response rate of 37.9% (30 companies) is obtained, which is identified as a weakness of the study. This degree of response is associated with the lack of interest of managers to participate in the study. Likewise, a significant difficulty arose due to the health emergency declared by the coronavirus disease (COVID-19) pandemic, which prolonged the implementation stage and led to further skewing the interest in participation.

14.3.2 Methods

The methodological design is cross-sectional and non-experimental to analyze the identification of attitudes aimed at promoting innovative behaviors in long-lived micro-enterprises of commerce. For data collection, a pre-designed questionnaire is used. This has a rigorous validation performed during the research under the parameters outlined by the grounded theory that is based on constant comparison, development, and characterization of categories and systematic coding (Guzman Pedraza, 2015; Robrecht, 1995).

Under this instrument, adjustments are made according to the needs of the study and application in the Colombian context. The pre-adjustment process involved the validation and determination of the reliability of the tool. Validation is carried out through the review of an expert academic in innovation and entrepreneurship, and the determination of reliability through a pilot test carried out in 10 analysis units domiciled in the municipality of Chiquinquirá (Boyacá). To do this, the method of divided halves based on the Spearman-Brown coefficient is used, which is adjusted when the measurement scale of the variable is ordinal The resulting coefficient is 0.87, which indicated the existence of a high correlation between the items of the instrument and high reliability of the questionnaire to be applied in the population segment (Hernández et al., 2014; Hernández et al., 2014).

With the information collected, through the scores obtained, the frequencies are analyzed, determining relative position scales by quartiles, for the characterization of the level of the variable and the determinants. Table 14.1 shows the equivalence of the quartile with the level of interpretation for the analysis of the results, according to the ranges of scores calculated for the variable and the determinants. In this way, it is understood that the presentation of results in quartile 1 reveals a low level of the attitudinal scale; quartile 2 an acceptable level; quartile 3 a mean level, and quartile 4 a high level of the scale of measurement of innovative behavior.

However, to determine the relationship between innovative behavior and time spent in the market for long-lived micro-enterprises, the processing of data depends on the statistics calculated on the distribution of sampling. In

Table 14.1 Equivalence of the quartile and level of interpretation of the results.

	Equivalences			
Quartile (Q)	1	2	3	4
Level of interpretation of the quartile	Low	Acceptable	Middle	High

Source: Own elaboration.

this sense, considering that the sample consisted of 30 observations, it is appropriate to apply the Shapiro–Wilk (W) statistic to determine the distribution of the sample. To this end, the following hypotheses were proposed (Rial & Varela, 2008):

H0: The population sample comes from a normal distribution.

H1: The population sample does not come from a normal distribution

In this case, the assumed significance (α) was 0.05 with a confidence level of 95%. Thus, if W is accepted $>$ p H0; and if W $<$ p H0 is rejected and H1 is accepted. Thus, the W statistic is 0.82 and the p-value is 0.93. Therefore, H0 is rejected and H1 is accepted. It is then concluded with 95% confidence that the sample does not come from a normal distribution. Considering that the sample does not come from a normal distribution and that the level of measurement of the variable is ordinal, non-parametric analyses are performed to determine the relationship between the variables. The systematization and analysis of the information were carried out to give rise to the statistical package (SPSS) version 24 (Hernández et al., 2014b).

14.4 Results

The results are presented in two sections; the former provides introduced light innovations and innovative levels of behavior; the second shows the analysis of the relationship between innovative behavior and longevity of the organizations under study.

14.4.1 Introduction to light innovations

Reportedly, 53.3% of long-term microenterprises introduced innovations in the service and 46.7% did not. Regarding the reasons why innovations are not introduced, 57.2% argued that the main reason is not to have considered this possibility, 21.4% affirm that, although they have the idea, no support is managed to carry out innovation processes and an equal proportion (21.4%)

affirmed that they are developing innovations around the implementation of improvements in ICT.

Organizations that introduced innovations reported different initiatives. The simultaneous implementation of the face-to-face service and the inclusion of ICT are the most frequent (37.5%). The introduction of new services (25.0%) such as the sale of retail items, greengrocers, and fresh meats. Then, with 12.5%, the home service, ICT, and the bond exchange system were implemented. Then, also frequently (6.3%) are located, the inclusion of home service; ICT; the parallel introduction of households, ICTs, and the opening of a new point of care; and a case like the previous one, but to which they add the system to redeem bonds.

14.4.2 Innovative behavior

From the scores obtained, the relative position tables are constructed by quartiles for the analysis of frequencies of innovative behavior and their determinants, as shown in Figure 14.1. Compared to the variable 40.0% of managers consider the management system for the promotion of innovative behaviors; 26.7% average; 23.3% high and 10.0% acceptable. As described, the management system is somewhat regular, since the categories are low and acceptable (50.0%) equal to medium and high (50.0%), and the highest frequency is in a low category. Below is a description of the characteristics of each of the determinants of innovative behavior.

14.4.3 Scope of work

The scope of work for the promotion of innovative behaviors is not so propitious, the relationship between the low level (40.0%) acceptable (16.7%) versus the medium (23.3%) high (20.0%) (see Figure 14.1). Thus, employees adhere little and gradually to organizational change seeking to maintain open communication between them, positively valuing ingenuity, and providing support in the application of new ideas. For its part, management does not always promote a favorable work area. They do not have mechanisms to evaluate suggestions or follow up on ideas that lead to improvements in service delivery. Employees also have no perception of improving their job position, since the size and structure of organizations do not facilitate it.

An additional fact is that 96.7% of organizations mention not having implemented a reward system to motivate innovation; the remaining 3.3% implemented additional salary bonuses due to the volume of sales, but not as an incentive to innovation in the organization. It is clear that the policies and management of organizations have not formally and strategically consolidated an enabling environment for innovation in services.

14.4.4 Generation and implementation of ideas

There is an equivalence in the performance of the determinant between the low categories (40.0%) acceptable (10.0%) and the middle (40.0%) high (10.0%) (see Figure 14.1). The results show that, in some organizations, suggesting ideas to improve or implement a service is part of the duties of the job. In this sense, workers informally comment on the desirability of generating and implementing ideas, but do not elaborate on a rigorous feasibility analysis. This could be because these organizations do not have a formal policy of innovation and linking workers with basic training, usually secondary. However, managers argue that workers are given to improve their performance and persuade the team to implement ideas, generated from perceived needs.

This confirms the claim regarding organizational change, as employees facing the implementation of changes are 43.3% passive, 46.7% active, and 10.0% indifferent. This reality allows us to say that, while workers are creative and proactive, they are a bit resistant to change; perhaps because innovation is not a central axis of organizations or because there is an aversion to real participation in innovation processes.

14.4.5 Leadership

Leadership reflects a higher level (40.0%) acceptable (20.0%), compared to the average level (16.7%) high (23.3%) (see Figure 14.1). In this sense, supervisors in long-term microenterprises are mostly agents who respect creative work, but who do not consider the opinions of workers when making decisions. However, they know the needs of their team, provide a willingness to collaborate in problem-solving and express satisfaction with the work of their collaborators.

One aspect to keep in mind is that the administrators involved in the resolution of the questionnaire are the same leaders or supervisors referred to in this section. This fact could generate some bias that would lead to self-valuing leadership at this level; as well as the possibility that the participants had sought to be impartial and in fact reflected in the results, demonstrates the reality of leadership that encourages, even slightly, innovative behaviors in organizations.

14.4.6 Employee engagement

Employee engagement is mostly low (43.3%), then average (33.3%), then high (16.7%), and to a lesser extent acceptable (6.7%) (see Figure 14.1). This determinant finds a balance since the low and acceptable versus the medium and high categories represent equally 50.0% of the sample. However, the highest proportion is at the low level.

This shows that commitment is only intermediate, because, in some way, they manifest work with dedication, have autonomy and independence for the development of their duties, are creative in the fulfillment of their tasks, and have a team that positively influences the performance of their roles; but they are not personally and emotionally involved in the work, nor is an investment in employee training encouraged.

14.4.7 Innovative behavior concerning the introduction of innovations

To complement the above analysis, a comparison is made of the extent of the media determinants of innovative behavior between micro-enterprises with the introduction of innovations and micro-enterprises without innovations. It is important to mention that being a population with a non-normal sample distribution, the results of the median and not of the mean were considered since atypical scores and score jumps in the mean could lead to inconsistent interpretations (Hernández et al., 2014).

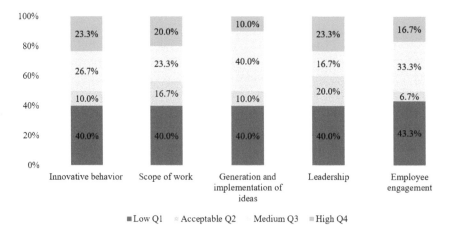

Figure 14.1   Proportion of scores for innovative behavior and its determinants.
Source: Own elaboration.

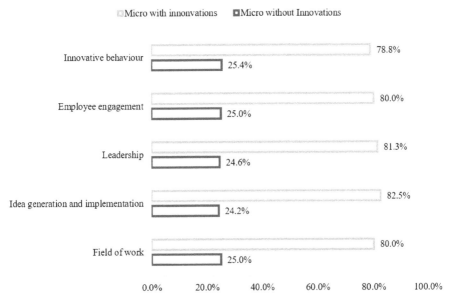

Figure 14.2 Comparison of innovative behavior in microenterprises with innovations and without innovations.

Source: Own elaboration.

Figure 14.2 shows the determinants and in the variable of innovative behavior, the scope of the medians of microenterprises with innovations becomes, in all cases, twice as high as if there is no introduction of innovations. The results suggest that innovative behavior is positively related to the introduction of innovations, although no causal link is found.

14.4.8 Relationship between innovative behavior and time spent in the market

A company's age is an indicator that captures a company's overall cumulative experience over time. Older companies have generally accumulated more knowledge than younger companies about how to implement change. Learning over time can affect both the ability to innovate and the outcomes of innovation (Huergo & Jaumandreu, 2004; OECD & EUROSTAT, 2018).

Based on the above, the motivation arises for the statistical determination of the relationship between innovative behavior and time spent in the market. First, the application of Pearson's non-parametric chi-square test (X^2) is performed, since the sample comes from a non-normal distribution,

Table 14.2 Categories of measurement of innovative behavior and time to market.

Variables	Categories			
Innovative behavior	Low	Acceptable	Middle	High
Time on the market (years)	Between 26 and 30	Between 31 and 35	Between 36 and 40	Between 41 and 45

Source: Own elaboration.

Table 14.3 Chi-square proof of the relationship between innovative behavior and time spent in the market.

	Value	Mexico City	Asymptotic (bilateral) sig.
Pearson square chi	156. 917a	156	0.464
Reason for plausibility	88.110	156	1.000
Linear to linear association	0.270	1	0.603
Number of valid cases	30		

Source: SPSS Database.

the variables under study are categorical and the level of measurement of the variables is ordinal Table 14.2 details the categories of measurement of innovative behavior and time spent in the market, with which the X^2 statistic is established (Hernández et al., 2014).

To determine the relationship between the variables, the following hypotheses are previously proposed:

H0: The innovative behavior of long-term retail microenterprises in the city of Tunja is not related to their time stay in the market.

H1: The innovative behavior of long-term retail micro-enterprises in the city of Tunja is related to their time in the market.

For the calculation of the X^2 statistic, a significance level of 0.05 is assumed with a confidence level of 95%. Therefore, as a rule of decision, if yes $p > a$, H0 is accepted; and if $p < a$, H0 is rejected and H1 is accepted. In that case, after performing the X^2 test, Table 14.3 shows the asymptotic value p or sig. (0.464) is greater than the significance level (0.05). As a result, with 95% confidence, it is accepted that the innovative behavior of long-term retail microenterprises in Tunja city is not significantly related to the time they spend in the market.

However, the X^2 statistic determines whether a relationship exists, but not the degree of relationship. Thus, it is decided to apply the Spearman correlation coefficient (rs), as an additional analysis to confirm the result obtained and establish the degree of the relationship. The rs statistic, like

Table 14.4 Spearman's proof of the relationship between innovative behavior and time spent in the market.

		Correlations	Time to market	Innovative behavior
Rho de Spearman	Time to market	Correlation coefficient	1.00	−0.059
		Sig. (bilateral)	.	0.755
		N	30	30
	Innovative behavior	Correlation coefficient	−0.059	1.00
		Sig. (bilateral)	0.755	
		N	30	30

Source: SPSS Database.

X^2, is recommended to be applied when the sample comes from a non-normal distribution, the variables under study are categorical and the level of measurement of the variables is ordinal (Hernández et al., 2014).

Table 14.4 shows that the correlation coefficient rs (−0.059) reveals a low inverse relationship (between 0 and −0.20); that is, the longer in the market, the lower the level of innovative behaviors. However, the relationship is not significant (the *p*-value or bilateral follow-up is greater than (a)). It is confirmed that there is no significant relationship between time spent in the market and innovative behaviors. Consequently, it can be said that the permanence in the market of long-term microenterprises is related to other factors, without the existence of innovative behaviors.

However, it is expected that the result of the relationship between innovative behavior and longevity will be deductive as determinants considering analyzing each of them. Table 14.5 shows the results of the application of the X^2 and rs tests. As for the correlation coefficient rs, the following is found. The scope of work, the generation and implementation of ideas, and leadership have a low inverse relationship, that is, the greater the longevity, the lower the conditions of the work environment, generation, and implementation of ideas and leadership. In the case of employee engagement, the relationship is direct, but still low, denoting that the greater the longevity, the greater the employees' commitment to developing innovative behaviors.

However, these results are not statistically significant, since the asymptotic or bilateral sig. of each determinant is greater than the significance level (*a*) of 0.05 in X^2 as in rs. Therefore, the scope of work, the generation,

Table 14.5 X^2 and p(rho) tests of the relationship between the determinants of innovative behavior and time spent in the market.

Variable	X^2		rs	
	X^2 value	Asymptotic (bilateral) sig.	Correlation coefficient	Sig. (bilateral)
Scope of work	104.000	0.482	−0.077	0.688
Generation and implementation of ideas	126.917	0.250	−0.205	0.277
Leadership	110.250	0.319	−0.042	0.827
Employee Engagement	85.331	0.648	0.002	0.991

Source: Own elaboration from the SPSS database.

and implementation of ideas, leadership, and employee engagement are not significantly related to time spent in the market.

The above results provide empirical evidence of the absence of a meaningful relationship between innovative behavior and organizational longevity.

14.5 Discussion

This research shows that the innovations developed and introduced correspond to the introduction of new vent services, the inclusion of ICT, the home service, the voucher exchange system, and the opening of new points of attention, the most frequent being the provision of the home service and the inclusion of ICT, based on the use of data phones. The innovations found in the study are recurrent among microenterprises, suggesting, as it points out, that there are external agents to the organizations that promoted the development and distribution of knowledge for the promotion and dissemination of certain types of light innovations in the sector (Blanco-Mesa & Baier-Fuentes, 2017).

In this sense, it is worth mentioning that in Colombia innovation is becoming increasingly important as a strategy to combat the vertiginous changes suffered by retail sales (Rodriguez, 2019) Buying habits have been constantly changing forcing merchants and entrepreneurs to anticipate and adapt the way they will take products to consumers (America Retail, 2019).

Innovative behavior shows a barely moderate performance in the microenterprises studied. In them, employees often gradually adhere to organizational change, maintaining communication, positively rating ingenuity, and providing support in the application of new ideas. state that when a working group provides these degrees of cooperation and collaboration, individuals are more likely to see the organization as a support system for innovation. However, the management of organizations does not always promote a favorable area of work for the promotion of innovative behaviors. This could have been a key factor that has not promoted better performance because when workers perceive those efforts are not sufficiently rewarded, they tend to restrict their behavior (Scott & Bruce, 1994; Janssen, 2000).

In this regard, the role of supervisors is fundamental. Supervisors of long-lived microenterprises are agents who generally respect creative work and support the ideas of their collaborators, but their opinion is not usually considered when making decisions. The leadership exercised by the managers of the studio occasionally suppresses the creativity of the employee, since it is not given enough prominence to give free rein to the generation and implementation of ideas. Therefore, leadership is critical in the innovation process, requiring styles that promote creativity in workers (De Jong & Den Hartog, 2007b; Scott & Bruce, 1994b).

Another notable finding is in relation to the valuable knowledge of staff and the type of innovations introduced as highlights around ICT, indicating that technology is important for the long-term micro-enterprises under study. According to him, the implementation of technologies has led to the configuration of a varied range of services. Based on the benefits offered by technology, a reseller or entrepreneur provides the opportunity for customers to make purchases, service payments, and/or cash withdrawals in a single moment Therefore, the reality of long-term retail microenterprises located in Tunja does not differ from the global reality. The use and use of ICT and the services provided through the implementation of data phones are common in the tertiary sector of the economy (S. Castro, 2017; America Retail, 2019).

On the other hand, we sought theoretical and practical evidence on the relationship between business survival and the development of innovative behaviors to determine the degree of statistical relationship between the variables. This revealed a low inverse relationship, where the longer the time in the market, the lower the level of innovative behavior. Likewise, the work environment such as the generation and implementation of ideas and leadership was found to have a low inverse relationship, and employee engagement had a direct but equally low relationship. Since the results were not statistically significant, the findings indicate that the business uptime of long-lived microenterprises in the Tunja market is not significantly related to the innovative behavior found in them.

Similarly, microenterprises introduced light innovations in service, presented innovative behaviors (few) and workers (employees and managers) showed some willingness towards innovation, which indicates that a strategic projection of these organizations must be configured. Although this lack can be due to many factors, the main cause is the lack of owners (supervisors) who are academically trained to manage companies and shape a culture of innovation through the promotion of innovative behaviors. Although professional or higher education is not a certainty of a promising vision of the organization, it is assured that it will be a measure of managers' management skills that can shape a more strategic perspective on them (OECD & EUROSTAT, 2018).

This change will be promoted through a process guided by public policymakers, such as chambers of commerce, governance, mayors, and other competent entities since it is from them that actions and decisions will be directed to guide the business fabric of the region. These entities will have to design more robust strategies, not only to promote spaces for training and training in innovation but to ensure that the target population appropriates and takes advantage of this knowledge to see in the promotion of those behaviors, the relevance of organizations that constantly think through innovation. It can be done through alliances with institutions and education and research centers, the implementation of workshops, personalized talks, seminars, and workshops, among others.

Hence, the limitations of this research motivate a study in a larger population, to confront the results of the variables described, since the sample is not representative. Subsequently, with the implementation of measures or policies against innovation and innovative behavior, an exploratory study could emerge to determine the confirmation or attraction of the findings found here. See notes that the course of this research takes place right in the transition from relatively normal economic dynamics to the pace of change that the economy experienced with the coronavirus disease (COVID-19) pandemic. This event involved changes in consumption patterns, communication of value to customers, the opening of new lines of business, and the permanent redefinition of services supported by digital initiatives that allow digital transformation and electronic commerce. It is likely that these new dynamics which retail microenterprises have had to undergo will be analyzed, in the short, medium, and long term. Indeed, innovation can take on a key role by increasing the use of ICTs and reducing staffing but to recognize and strengthening the potential for continuous improvement. For this reason, conducting a post-pandemic study would surely bring interesting findings.

14.6 Conclusions

Through the review of the literature, it is evident that innovative behavior is a field of study derived from innovation, developed more frequently after 2007. This research is intended to contribute to the study of innovative behavior from innovation in service, based on a slight scope of innovation in long-term microenterprises retail in Tunja. The following are some relevant aspects that determined the development of the research based on the objectives set and the results found.

Innovative behavior underperforms, especially in the field of work and leadership in microenterprises. While the generation and implementation of ideas and employee engagement had a higher level of measurement, employee attitudes in these ways still need to be strengthened. This will be done to the extent that innovation is part of the culture of organizations, by promoting innovation through systems of reward and recognition of creative work.

Under the test of hypotheses and correlation coefficients, empirical evidence is provided on the absence of a significant relationship between innovative behavior and organizational longevity. However, these results could be due to the absence of a sufficiently representative sample of the population studied. This suggests conducting a study with a significantly larger population. Hence, there is much to work on internally in organizations and the same to project from competent entities, to promote a pedagogy and culture on innovation in services and innovative behavior.

The development of the study is limited methodologically and practically, due to the size of the population and even more so due to the lack of participation of the managers associated with it. This suggests conducting a study with a slightly larger population, perhaps in the department, since the proportion and characteristics of the business fabric are similar to those of the city of Tunja. Another factor that affected the research but was not planned at the beginning of the study is the expansion of coronavirus disease (COVID-19) and its impact on the execution of fieldwork. Although the aspects discussed here had no effect on the arrival of the pandemic (compilation of facts prior to it), there is an impact on the expected interest of participation of the population. Today's pandemic motivates and will continue to motivate new changes in the economy, which promise the development of studies for the redefinitions generated by this health contingency, of social and economic order.

Future lines of research may revolve around determining the degree of influence between innovative behavior and time spent in the market for long-term microenterprises. In the analysis of the relationship between the dimensions of innovation in service and the determinants of innovative behavior or specific analysis to explain why the levels found in the dimensions and/or determinants studied.

Acknowledgments

This research was funded by Universidad Pedagogica y Tecnologica de Colombia, grant number SGI 3323, and Red Sistemas Inteligentes y Expertos Modelos Computacionales Iberoamericanos (SIEMCI), project number 522RT0130, in Programa Iberoamericano de Ciencia y Tecnología para el Desarrollo (CYTED).

References

Akram, T., Lei, S., Haider, M. J., & Hussain, S. T. (2020). The impact of organizational justice on employee innovative work behavior: Mediating role of knowledge sharing. *Journal of Innovation and Knowledge*, 5(2), 117–129. https://doi.org/10.1016/j.jik.2019.10.001

Al-hawari, M., Bani-melhem, S., & Shamsudin, F. (2019). Determinants of frontline employee service innovative behavior: the moderating role of co-worker socializing and service climate. Management Research Review, 42(9), 1076–1094. https://doi.org/https://doi.org/10.1108/MRR-07-2 018-0266

America Retail. (2019a). 10 technological innovations for the retail sector.

Arsawan, I. W. E., Rajiani, I., Wirga, I. W., & Suryantini, N. P. S. (2020). Harnessing knowledge sharing practice to enhance innovative work behavior: The paradox of social exchange theory. Polish Journal of Management Studies, 21(2), 60–73. https://doi.org/10.17512/pjms.2020.21.2.05

Beltrán, A., & Pulido, B. (2012). Innovation: strategy that contributes to ensuring growth and development in micro, small and medium enterprises in Colombia. Special, 1(19), 104–113.

Blanco-Mesa, F., & Baier-Fuentes, H. (2017a). Towards a Comprehensive View of Light Innovation: Conceptual Analysis of Non-Intensive Innovations. Cuadernos Del CIMBAGE, 2(19), 79–103.

Tunja Chamber of Commerce. (2019a). Business fabric of Tunja.

Camps, X. (2015). How and why to create an innovation strategy.

Castro, H., Sáenz, H., Suárez, L., Sánchez, J., & Suárez, H. (2019). Municipal profiles Jurisdiction of the Chamber of Commerce of Tunja.

Castro, S. (2017). The service sector: are we on the right track?

Cefis, E., Bartoloni, E., & Bonati, M. (2020). Show me how to live: firms' financial conditions and innovation during the crisis. Structural Change and Economic Dynamics, 52, 63–81. https://doi.org/https://doi.org/10.1016/j.strueco.2019.10.001

Cefis, E., & Marsili, O. (2006). Survivor: the role of innovation in firms' survival. Research Policy, 35(5), 626–641. https://doi.org/https://doi.org/10.1016/j.respol.2006.02.006

Collins, J. C., & Porras, J. I. (1994). Built to last: successful habits of visionary companies (1st ed.). HarperBusiness.

Confecamaras. (2019). Determinants of business survival in Colombia.

DANE. (2019). Monthly Retail Trade Sample -MMCM-. National Administrative Department of Statistics.

De Jong, J. P. J., & Den Hartog, D. N. (2007a). How leaders influence employees' innovative behaviour. European Journal of Innovation Management, 10(1), 41–64. https://doi.org/https://doi.org/10.1108/14601060710720546

Den Hertog, P. (2000). Knowledge-intensive business services as co-producers of innovation. International Journal of Innovation Management, 4(4), 491–528.

Galadanchi, H. A., & Bakar, L. (2018). A study of factors that support longevity of business enterprises. Journal of Business and Management, 20(1), 53–59. https://doi.org/https://doi.org/10.9790/487X-2001025359

González Alvarado, T. (2005). Problems in the definition of microenterprise. Revista Venezolana de Gerencia, 10(31), 408–423.

Guzman Pedraza, C. (2015a). Innovative behaviour and commitment of employees in companies in the service sector: the case of a family SME in Spain. Universitat en Administració i Direcció d'Empresas.

Guzmán Pedraza, C., Bravo, E. R., Oliveira, H., & Blanco-Mesa, F. (2012a). Innovation in Service Firms: Perspective From Innovative Behavior. 9th International Conference on Intellectual Capital, Knowledge Management & Organisational Learning, 104–112.

Hansen, J. A., & Pihl-Thingvad, S. (2019). Managing employee innovative behaviour through transformational and transactional leadership styles. Public Management Review, 21(6), 918–944. https://doi.org/10.1080/14719037.2018.1544272

Hernández, R., Fernández, C., & Lucio, P. (2014a). Research methodology (6th ed.). Mc Graw Hill.

Huergo, E., & Jaumandreu, J. (2004). Firms' age, process innovation and productivity growth. International Journal of Industrial Organization, 22(4), 541–559. https://doi.org/10.1016/j.ijindorg.2003.12.002

Janssen, O. (2000a). Job demands, perceptions of effort – reward fairness and innovative work behaviour. Journal of Occupational and Organizational Psychology, 73(1), 287–302. https://doi.org/https://doi.org/10.1348/09 6317900167038

Javed, B., Abdullah, I., Zaffar, M. A., Haque, A. U., & Rubab, U. (2019). Inclusive leadership and innovative work behavior: The role of psychological empowerment. Journal of Management and Organization, 25(4), 554–571. https://doi.org/10.1017/jmo.2018.50

Klosiewicz-Górecka, U. (2015a). Innovativeness of service sector enterprises: innovation objectives and types. Handel Wewnętrzny, 5, 176–187.

Lestari, S. D., Leon, F. M., Widyastuti, S., Brabo, N. A., & Putra, A. H. P. K. (2020). Antecedents and consequences of innovation and business strategy on performance and competitive advantage of SMEs. Journal of Asian Finance, Economics and Business, 7(6), 365–378. https://doi.org/10 .13106/JAFEB.2020.VOL7.NO6.365

Li, M., & Hsu, C. (2016a). Customer participation in services and its effect on employee innovative behavior. Journal of Hospitality Marketing & Management, 26(2), 164–185. https://doi.org/https://doi.org/10.1080/ 19368623.2016.1215946

Linde, L., Sjödin, D., Parida, V., & Wincent, J. (2021). Dynamic capabilities for ecosystem orchestration A capability-based framework for smart city innovation initiatives. Technological Forecasting and Social Change, 166. https://doi.org/10.1016/j.techfore.2021.120614

Macey, W., & Schneider, B. (2008). The meaning of employee engagement. Industrial and Organizational Psychology, 1(1), 3–30. https://doi.org/https: //doi.org/10.1111/j.1754-9434.2007.0002.x

Miles, I. (2008a). Patterns of innovation in service industries. IBM Systems Journal, 47(1), 115–128.

Napolitano, M., Marino, V., & Ojala, J. (2015). In search of an integrated framework of business longevity. Business History, 57(7), 955–969. https: //doi.org/https://doi.org/10.1080/00076791.2014.993613

Nardelli, G. (2017). Innovation dialectics: an extended process perspective on innovation in services. Service Industries Journal, 37(1), 31–56. https: //doi.org/10.1080/02642069.2017.1289513

Nederveen, A., Knippenberg, D., Schippers, M., & Stam, D. (2010). Transformational and transactional leadership and innovative behavior: The moderating role of psychological empowerment. Journal of Organizational Behavior, 31(4), 609–623. https://doi.org/https://doi.org/10.1002/job.650

Noefer, K., Stegmaier, R., Molter, B., & Sonntag, K. (2009). A great many things to do and not a minute to spare: can feedback from supervisors moderate the relationship between skill variety, time pressure, and employees' innovative behavior ? Creativity Research Journal, 21(4), 384–393. https://doi.org/https://doi.org/10.1080/10400410903297964

O'Cass, A., Song, M., & Yuan, L. (2013). Anatomy of service innovation: introduction to the special issue. Journal of Business Research, 66(8), 1060–1062. https://doi.org/10.1016/j.jbusres.2012.03.002

OECD, & EUROSTAT. (2018a). Oslo Manual 2018: guidelines for collecting, reporting and using data on innovation (4th ed.). OECD.

Oldham, G., & Cummings, A. (2014). Employee creativity: personal and contextual fectors at work. Academy of Management Journal, 39(3), 607–634. https://doi.org/https://doi.org/10.5465/256657

Opoku, M., Choi, S., & Kang, S. (2019). Servant leadership and innovative behaviour: an empirical analysis of Ghana's manufacturing sector. Sustainability, 11(22), 1–18. https://doi.org/https://doi.org/10.3390/su1122262 73

Oyemomi, O., Liu, S., Neaga, I., Chen, H., & Nakpodia, F. (2019). How cultural impact on knowledge sharing contributes to organizational performance: Using the fsQCA approach. Journal of Business Research, 94(August 2017), 313–319. https://doi.org/10.1016/j.jbusres.2018.02.027

Porter, L. W., Steers, R. M., Mowday, R. T., & Boulian, P. V. (1974). Organizational commitment, job satisfaction, and turnover among psychiatric technicians. Journal of Applied Psychology, 59(5), 603–609. https://doi.org/10.1037/h0037335

Pundt, A., Martins, E., & Nerdinger, F. (2010a). Innovative behavior and reciprocal exchange between employees and organizations. Zeitschrift Für Personalforschung (ZfP), 24(2), 173–193. https://doi.org/https://doi.org/10.1177/239700221002400205

Rial, A., & Varela, J. (2008). Practical statistics for research in health sciences (First). Netbiblo.

Rivera, H. (2012). Business durability: concept, studies, findings. Administration Notebooks, 28(47), 105–115.

Rizki, M., Parashakti, R. D., & Saragih, L. (2019). The effect of transformational leadership and organizational culture towards employees' innovative behaviour and performance. International Journal of Economics and Business Administration, 7(1), 227–239. https://doi.org/10.35808/ijeba/2 08

Robrecht, L. C. (1995). Grounded Theory: Evolving Methods. Qualitative Health Research, 5(2), 169–177. https://doi.org/10.1177/10497323950050 0203

Rodriguez, G. (2019). The resilience of supermarkets. In The Republic (p. 1).

Schaufeli, W. B., Salanova, M., González-Roma, V., & Bakker, A. B. (2002). The measurement of engagement and burnout: a two sample confirmatory factor analytic approach. Journal of Happiness Studies, 3, 71–92. https://doi.org/https://doi.org/10.1023/A:1015630930326

Scott, S., & Bruce, R. (1994a). Determinants of innovative behavior: a path model of individual innovation in the workplace. Academy of Management Journal, 37(3), 580–607. https://doi.org/https://doi.org/10.2307/256701

Slåtten, T. (2011a). Antecedents and effects of employees' feelings of joy on employees' innovative behaviour. International Journal of Quality and Service Sciences, 3(1), 93–109. https://doi.org/https://doi.org/10.1108/17 566691111115108

Slåtten, T., Lien, G., Lupina, E., & Gravingen, K. A. (2019). Promoting an internal market-oriented culture (IMOC) in healthcare services. Journal of Service Science Research, 11(2), 157–182. https://doi.org/10.1007/s12927 -019-0008-3

Slåtten, T., & Mehmetoglu, M. (2011a). Antecedents and effects of engaged frontline employees: a study from the hospitality industry. Managing Service Quality: An International Journal, 21(1), 88–107. https://doi.org/https://doi.org/10.1108/09604521111100261

Slåtten, T., & Mehmetoglu, M. (2011c). What are the drivers for innovative behavior in frontline jobs? a study of the hospitality industry in Norway. Journal of Human Resources in Hospitality and Tourism, 10(3), 254–272. https://doi.org/https://doi.org/10.1080/15332845.2011.555732

Slåtten, T., & Mehmetoglu, M. (2015). The effects of transformational leadership and perceived creativity on innovation behavior in the hospitality industry. Journal of Human Resources in Hospitality and Tourism, 14(2), 195–219. https://doi.org/https://doi.org/10.1080/15332845.2014.955557

Taques, F. H., López, M. G., Basso, L. F., & Areal, N. (2021). Indicators used to measure service innovation and manufacturing innovation. Journal of Innovation and Knowledge, 6(1), 11–26. https://doi.org/10.1016/j.jik.2019 .12.001

West, M. (2002). Sparkling fountains or stagnant ponds: an integrative model of creativity and innovation implementation in work groups. Applied Psychology, 51(3), 355–387. https://doi.org/https://doi.org/10.1111/1464-059 7.00951

Xing, Y., Liu, Y., Boojihawon, D. K., & Tarba, S. (2020). Entrepreneurial team and strategic agility: A conceptual framework and research agenda. Human Resource Management Review, 30(1), 100696. https://doi.org/10 .1016/j.hrmr.2019.100696

Yuan, F., & Woodman, R. W. (2010a). Innovative behavior in the workplace: the role of performance and image outcome expectations. Academy of Management Journal, 53(2), 323–342.

Yukl, G., Gordon, A., & Taber, T. (2002). A hierarchical taxonomy of leadership behavior: Integrating a half century of behavior research. Journal of Leadership & Organizational Studies, 9(1), 15–32. https://doi.org/10.117 7/107179190200900102

Yun, J. H. J., & Liu, Z. (2019). Micro- and macro-dynamics of open innovation with a Quadruple-Helix model. Sustainability (Switzerland), 11(12), 1–17. https://doi.org/10.3390/SU11123301

Index

About the Editors

Ernesto Leon-Castro is a research professor in Instituto Tecnologico de Sonora, Unidad Navojoa (Mexico). He is a Doctor in Administrative Sciences from the Universidad de Occidente (Mexico). He is part of the National System of Researchers (SNI) Level 1. His research areas include information aggregation operators, decision making, innovation, finance, fuzzy logic, and other related topics. He has more than 30 publications in different journals indexed in the Web of Science/Scopus and has participated in various international conferences. He is part of the Ibero-American Network for Competitiveness, Innovation and Development (REDCID) and is a member of the research group Business Studies in Uncertain Environments. He has directed more than 10 theses as director/co-director and has taught at different universities in Mexico, Colombia, and Chile.

Manoj Sahni is a dedicated and experienced Mathematics teacher and researcher with more than 18 years of experience and is currently serving as an Associate Professor and Head in the Department of Mathematics, School of Technology, Pandit Deendayal Energy University, Gandhinagar, Gujarat, India. He has an excellent academic background with M.Sc. degree (mathematics with specialization in Computer Applications) from Dayalbagh Educational Institute (Deemed University), Agra, M. Phil. from I.I.T. Roorkee, and the Ph.D. degree in mathematics from Jaypee Institute of Information Technology (Deemed University), Noida, India. He has published more than 70 research papers in peer-reviewed Journals (SCI/SCIE/ESCI/Scopus), Conference Proceedings (Scopus Indexed), and book chapters (Scopus Indexed) with reputed publishers like Springer, Elsevier, etc. He also serves as an Advisory Board Member, Technical Committee Member, and Reviewer for many international journals of repute and conferences. He has organized 1st, 2nd, and 3rd International Conferences on Mathematical Modeling, Computational Intelligence Techniques, and Renewable Energy (MMCITRE). He participated in the scientific committee of several international conferences and associations and also delivered many expert talks at the national and international levels. In addition, he is a member of many international professional societies, including the American Mathematical Society (AMS), Society for Industrial and Applied Mathematics (SIAM), IEEE, Mathematical Association of America (MAA), Forum for Interdisciplinary Mathematics (FIM), Indian Mathematical Society (IMS), IAENG, and many more.

Fabio Raul Blanco Mesa is an International Doctor in Business from the Department of Economics and Business Organization of the University of Barcelona. He has a Master's degree in business, finance, and insurance research and a Master's degree in sports business management from the University of Barcelona and a Sports Administrator degree from the Francisco José de Caldas District University. He has experience in research activities in the international field, management of research, and teaching groups. With several publications of scientific articles in international journals, book chapters, and conference proceedings, such as: *Knowledge Based Systems, Journal Computational Optimization in Economics and Finance, Innovation in Service Firms: Perspective from Innovative Behavior, Soft Computing in Management and Business Economics, Technological and Economic Development of Economy, Advance in Intelligence Systems and Computing, Soft Computing in Management and Business Economics, Journal of Intelligent in Fuzzy Systems, Kybernetes, etc.* He is also involved in the development of revision, control, and verification tasks for different international journals. He has interest in issues related to decision making, competitiveness, interest groups, entrepreneurship, regional development, strategic analysis, diffuse systems, and aggregation operators applied to management, uncertainty, and bibliometrics.

Victor Alfaro Garcia is an International Doctor in Business with specialization in models for the treatment of uncertainty in decision making. He is an author in refereed journals, books, and book chapters, as well as leading speaker at national and international conferences. He is the Deputy Coordinator of the Ibero-American Network for Competitiveness Innovation and Development REDCID, a program attached to the Ibero-American Program of Science and Technology for Development CYTED. His national and international professional experience include: Financial Consultant (Management Solutions - Mexico and Peru), Project Coordinator (Prosegur, Spain), and Technology and Development Consultant (TTR – Group, Germany).

José M. Merigó (Highly Cited Researcher in computer science) is a Full Professor with the School of Systems, Management and Leadership at the Faculty of Engineering and Information Technology at the University of

Technology Sydney and Part-Time Full Professor at the Department of Management Control and Information Systems at the School of Economics and Business at the University of Chile. Previously, he was a Senior Research Fellow with the Manchester Business School, University of Manchester (UK) and an Assistant Professor with the Department of Business Administration at the University of Barcelona (Spain). He holds the master's and Ph.D. degrees in business administration from the University of Barcelona. He also holds B.Sc. and M.Sc. degrees from Lund University (Sweden). He has published more than 400 articles in journals, books, and conference proceedings, including journals such as *Information Sciences, European Journal of Operational Research, IEEE Transactions on Fuzzy Systems, Expert Systems with Applications, International Journal of Intelligent Systems, Applied Soft Computing, Computers & Industrial Engineering, and Knowledge-Based Systems.* He has also published several books with Springer and with World Scientific. He is on the editorial board of several journals including *Applied Soft Computing, Technological and Economic Development of Economy, Journal of Intelligent & Fuzzy Systems, International Journal of Fuzzy Systems, Kybernetes, and Economic Computation and Economic Cybernetics Studies and Research.* He has also been a guest editor for several international journals, member of the scientific committee of several conferences, and a reviewer in a wide range of international journals. Recently, Thomson & Reuters (Clarivate Analytics) has distinguished him as a Highly Cited Researcher in Computer Science (2015-2017). He is currently interested in decision making, aggregation operators, computational intelligence, bibliometrics and applications in business and economics.